INSIGHTS INTO THE
BHAGAVAD GITA

Insights
into
THE BHAGAVAD GITA

Vimala Thakar

MOTILAL BANARSIDASS PUBLISHERS
PRIVATE LIMITED • DELHI

First Edition: Delhi, 2005

© MOTILAL BANARSIDASS PUBLISHERS PRIVATE LIMITED
All Rights Reserved.

ISBN: 81-208-2675-2

MOTILAL BANARSIDASS

41 U.A. Bungalow Road, Jawahar Nagar, Delhi 110 007
8 Mahalaxmi Chamber, 22 Bhulabhai Desai Road, Mumbai 400 026
120 Royapettah High Road, Mylapore, Chennai 600 004
236, 9th Main III Block, Jayanagar, Bangalore 560 011
Sanas Plaza, 1302 Baji Rao Road, Pune 411 002
8 Camac Street, Kolkata 700 017
Ashok Rajpath, Patna 800 004
Chowk, Varanasi 221 001

Printed in India
BY JAINENDRA PRAKASH JAIN AT SHRI JAINENDRA PRESS,
A-45 NARAINA, PHASE-I, NEW DELHI 110 028
AND PUBLISHED BY NARENDRA PRAKASH JAIN FOR
MOTILAL BANARSIDASS PUBLISHERS PRIVATE LIMITED,
BUNGALOW ROAD, DELHI 110 007

CONTENTS

EDITOR'S NOTE

Vimalaji gave a series of inspired talks on the *Bhagavad Gita* to a group of Italian yoga teachers, in three separate seminars, during 1992 and 1993, covering the first twelve chapters. Some of these talks were printed in our magazine *Contact*. We now present the complete text of all these talks.

Could it be that Vimalaji only commented on the first twelve chapters of the *Gita*, because, as she put it: 'in the twelfth chapter, we have come to the essence of the *Gita*. From the thirteenth chapter onwards will begin the metaphysical part, the theoretical philosophical part. But from the second chapter to the twelfth, we have the scope to understand, learn, study and get transmuted or transformed.'

I have divided the book into the twelve chapters. They do not, in most cases, correspond to Vimalaji's daily talks. I have indicated, where necessary, the end of one day's talk and the beginning of the next day, by a line of dots, to show, why in some cases there seems to be an interruption in the flow of the theme, sometimes in order to clarify a point made earlier, or for bringing to our attention some more universal insights.

Anita Sterner
Editor

INTRODUCTION

The whole world is passing through a great turmoil. Living in this turbulent world, a handful of us feel concerned about discovering the nature of ultimate reality and learning to live in the awareness of that reality, while dealing with appearances of names and forms, qualities, their interactions etc.

We will be embarking upon a study course, which would require sustained seriousness, integrity of enquiry and an openness of mind, which will enable us to listen. It is quite a job to listen, not just to hear the words, but to listen to the throbbing of Life, the throbbing of the meaning contained in the words. It is only when the throb of Life is felt in the words that are spoken, that a dialogue takes place between the speaker and the listener.

With your cooperation, one would like to introduce the foundation, background, structure and essence of the message of the *Gita*, as regards to our daily living. We shall be going step-by-step, diving deep into the secrets of the *Bhagavad Gita*.

I wonder if you are aware that the ancient sages, living in the oriental hemisphere of the planet, were deeply interested in the mystery of Life. They were tremendously interested in the act of living, their relationship to innumerable expressions of Life surrounding them, their relationship to the inner drama taking place in their bodies, on the biological and psychological level, as well as in the states of waking, dreaming and deep sleep. They were fascinated by Life itself.

One does not know, at the end of the twentieth century, what with the advances of science and technology, the network of trade and commerce, the means of transport and communication, what with all this, if the interest in Life is sustained. It is very difficult for the twentieth century human beings to feel fascinated by the Cosmic

Life, to have an interest in learning to relate their movement of living to the mystery of Life by which they are surrounded.

And yet, we will spend the coming weeks with the ancient sages and what they have to say about Life, about appearances, about reality, how to discriminate between them and how to live with them. There is nothing in Life that can be discarded. There is nothing to be rejected, nothing to be acquired. There is everything to be seen, understood, related to, and everything to enjoy in the movement of living.

Out of this concern for the discovery of reality, emerged the Vedas and then came the Upanishads. The Vedas seem to be explorations of bliss that result as a direct perception of reality, not in an abstract way, but as a direct perception of reality at the sensual level. So the Vedas, as far as the speaker is concerned, are verbal exclamations. It is an ecstatic poetry, it is not systematized thought.

The Upanishads, on the other hand, are verbalized dialogues between teacher and student, a beautiful way of transmitting the awareness of reality, the perception, through words, of reality into the consciousness and, perhaps, into the whole being of a student. The Upanishads are not conveying information; they are not giving knowledge about reality. Knowledge is systematized thought. They are dialogues between the teacher and the student. Only that much is expressed and revealed, which is related to the enquiry. It is not a narration, it is not an assertion. The teacher responds to the requirements of the student.

After the Upanishads, which were about five hundred in number, of which one hundred and eight are still available in various countries of the world, there emerged the Six Systems of Indian Philosophy. From exclamations to verbal transmission, and from verbal transmission we come to systematisation of knowledge, in the Six Systems of philosophy.

After them came the *Bhagavad Gita.*

BACKGROUND

The teacher and the student are not sitting in some quiet place, on the bank of some river, or in the depth of some forest, or in a mountain cave, as was the case in the Upanishads. The dialogue takes place on the battleground of Life, which is the place for religion to be lived, for spirituality to breathe. Spirituality cannot breathe in the deep-freeze of abstraction. It cannot breathe in isolation from Life.

The *Bhagavad Gita* is a dialogue between two individuals, Arjuna and Krishna, taking place some five thousand years ago, in Dharmakshetra Kurukshetra. The message of the *Gita* being universal, it is however not necessary to relate it to the physical location of Kurukshetra, a place in India.

'*Kshetra*' means region. '*Kuru*' is derived from the root *kr*, to do; to act. So, 'Kurukshetra' can be interpreted as 'the field of action'. And the word '*dharma*' in the *Dharmakshetra* stands for Religion with a capital R; or spirituality. Not the formal structured, organised religions that exist in various parts of the globe.

The dialogue takes place on the battleground of relationships, their interactions, the dejections, frustrations, ambitions for power, ambition perhaps for property, for land. The setting of the dialogue is actual life.

The truth, the absolute truth about reality, has to be revealed in the context of an individual's life and the challenges that the individual has to face. It is not a discourse. We are going to visit Krishna and Arjuna right there, on the battlefield and listen to their dialogue. That is the *Bhagavad Gita*.

'*Gita*' means song. It is that which is sung. It is the Song of Life, that has taken place between Krishna and Arjuna, on the battlefield of Life. Look at the setting, then at the tenderness of the song. It is not a philosophy; it is a song of Life, sung by two friends together. Enquiry is also a singing, not only of that which is explained, but also of that which is enquired into.

The word 'Bhagavan' (in the *Bhagavad Gita*) is used for the personalized form of reality, individuated expression of reality. A person who transcends the inbuilt limitations of I-consciousness, and grows into the maturity of Cosmic consciousness, is called Bhagavan. We are dealing with the Sanskrit language, not with any mythology. The *Bhagavad Gita* is not the property of the Hindus; it is not there to teach Hinduism, it has a universal message.

Reality is neither eastern nor western, nor southern, nor northern; it is the essence of universal Life, of Cosmic Life. And the *Gita* shows the path for getting united with that essence, getting united with the beingness of Life. Not of getting united with Krishna, the son of Vasudeva, not of getting united with an individuated expression in human form. But getting united with the undivided wholeness of Life, the essence of Life, which remains unmanifest behind the glorious variety of the manifest, behind the dance of birth and growth, decay and death, emergence and submergence, the dance of the manifest and the unmanifest.

Krishna, as the history goes, was capable of expressing through words and actions, through deeds, through the language of his being, by his very presence, the qualities of reality. A person who revealed beauty in the physical form, revealed the ecstasy of truth in his actions and the sacredness of love and compassion, that was Krishna. Thousand names have been attributed to that person.

And Arjuna, as a relative, a brother of Krishna, humanly speaking, is the enquirer. The word 'Arjuna' is derived from the word *arj*, which in Sanskrit means the elegance of innocence and simplicity. Arjuna, as an enquirer, has that beautiful capacity of being simple, straightforward, no pretensions, no images about himself; he is straightforward, simple, innocent.

Arjuna represents the qualities of enquiry and Krishna represents the personification of the ecstasy of understanding, may I use the word the divinity of understanding. Can we disinfect the word divinity from all the overtones and undertones of formal religions, and use it as a scientific term to indicate that which has not been touched by human thought or hand.

If it has been possible for me to clarify these points, let us proceed to another aspect of the ancient oriental wisdom. The purpose of Life is to grow into the maturity of the state of *yoga*. The word '*yoga*' is derived from the Sanskrit root *yukta*, 'to connect'; 'to unite'. It has a nuance of reunion of that which was separated by an illusion. That, which was separated because of the glamour of appearances and the lack of the capacity to discriminate appearances from reality. When separation ends and reunion takes place, that is the real meaning of the word '*yoga*'.

When you ask me, what would you say about Hatha Yoga, Jnana Yoga, Karma Yoga, Bhakti Yoga, they are outer paths for growing into the essence of the inner yoga. The outer paths and outer systems, by their very nature, are bound to be limited. The inner is the undivided whole. The outer, on the physical, verbal, and psychological level, gets limited by outwardness. So, whether it is Sankhya Yoga, Karma Yoga, Jnana Yoga, Bhakti Yoga, all those paths are meant to enable a person to arrive at the inner essence of *yoga*, reunion with reality, with absolute truth.

The purpose of the *Gita*, the epitome of Vedic philosophy, is to enable a person to get acquainted with the outer and appreciate the inner, use the outer paths and systems for the sake of the inner. The purpose of the *Gita* is to create the awareness of the necessity of growing into the state of *yoga*, the state of consciousness of *yoga*.

The *Bhagavad Gita* has eighteen chapters. In this structure, the first chapter gives us the background, the situation that created dejection and frustration in the mind of Arjuna. So from the universal message we come now to the framework in which this message has been incorporated as it were.

As the history goes, there was a king, called Dhrtarashtra, who had a brother called Pandu. Dhrtarashtra had many sons called the Kauravas. And Pandu's sons were called the Pandavas. Pandu died and the throne went to his brother, Dhrtarashtra, who was blind.

There was a quarrel. The sons of King Dhrtarashtra did not allow their cousins, the Pandavas, to have their share of the kingdom. Much was done, many ways were experimented, to explain to the king that the kingdom belonged fifty/fifty to the Pandavas and the Kauravas. But Dhrtarashtra's eldest son, who was very obstinate, very ambitious, very jealous, would not part with the land.

In the end, after fourteen years of different efforts having been made and because of the failure of all those efforts, Krishna went to negotiate: 'don't give half the portion; give five villages to the five brothers. No? One village. No.' Not even an inch of land.

So, it was Arjuna, as the leader of the Pandavas, who took the decision that there was nothing else left, but to fight against the injustice. 'It is an injustice. We are rightfully entitled to have half the kingdom, we were prepared to have five villages, one village, but no. So let us fight.'

Arjuna goes to Krishna asking: 'Will you please help me?' and Krishna offers himself to stand by Arjuna. The son of Dhrtarashtra also goes to Krishna for help, and to him he says: 'I can give you my army'.

CHAPTER I

THE DESPONDENCY OF ARJUNA

And so they find themselves on the battleground. The armies are facing one another. Suddenly, Arjuna realizes that those with whom he is going to fight are his relations, his uncles, nephews, teachers who had taught him archery, the sciences and art of war, who had taught him the Vedas, the Upanishads.

He had known all that before, when he took the decision to fight, but knowledge is one thing and encounter, physical, sensual encounter with the facts, is quite another. Knowledge has an abstraction about it. So yes, he had to fight against them, he had to fight the injustice, etc. But when he was standing there, face-to-face, he got dejected:

'What is the use of fighting, they will be killed, the army which is fighting for us will be killed. What to do with the bloodstained victory? Let me not fight.'

He had taken the decision to fight, brought his army there, everything had been done, but suddenly he intellectualizes and says: 'Krishna I won't fight, I can't fight. My body is trembling, my intellect does not work.'

Doesn't this happen to us? We enquire what is reality, what is meditation, what is the known, the unknown, and there is an urge to transcend the known, to be with the unknown. And then you come to the frontiers of the known and are in intimate contact with the unknown. There is a tremor because one does not know what the contact with the unknown will do to one's being, what it will do to the way of living that one has been used to. So one gets frightened. Isn't that what happens to us? We are frightened when we are in silence, there is nowhere to go, nothing to do.

No investment is possible into the unknown. Investment into the known is possible, not into the unknown. You cannot anticipate the reaction of the unknown, you cannot anticipate and calculate the movement of the unknown and try to prepare yourself to meet that movement or face that movement. That is why the unknown frightens us.

We enquire about the Cosmic reality and get frightened.

'What will the Cosmic reality do to me? I am shaping my life, I am controlling, I am directing. If the ego gets completely liquidated, if the I-consciousness goes completely into abeyance, what will happen?' No calculations, no bargaining, no anticipation. And the person, who has spent years and years in verbal enquiry, gets dejected, depressed, or frustrated when there is an encounter with the emptiness of silence, with the emptiness of meditation, when there is a realization that one would get reduced to nothingness and nobody-ness.

Something of that kind must have happened to Arjuna. It was a direct encounter with death. The battleground represents death. Until that moment the idea of dying, for fighting the injustice, was a romantic one. The Kauravas have done evil things, so they must be killed. An idea. But when it came to actual killing, killing your uncle, your grandfather, your nephew, even the memory that they had done injustice goes into the background. 'Oh yes, they did it because they were foolish, they were stupid, but we understand the truth, why should we kill them? Are we going to add another folly to their folly, are we going to add stupidity to their stupidity?'

You know, in the first chapter, Arjuna gives quite a sermon to Krishna. He explains the disadvantages of war and what happens after a war, how society gets contaminated, how all culture disappears, the wailing of the widows, the screams of the orphans. It is quite a description that he gives.

It is Arjuna Vishada Yoga that is the name of the first chapter. Vishada is the culmination of dejection into a sense of frustration. So Arjuna turns to Krishna who says:

'Didn't you know all this before? You have known all this before. You are a warrior, you have fought many wars. Supposing you do not fight against these people, what will you do? Will you go to some forest, live in some isolation? You have been brought up and taught the science and art of fighting, you are a Kshatriya (one belonging to the warrior caste), you have been trained for this. Wherever you go, all your conditionings of resisting the injustice and evil will be there. Why are you trying to escape from your responsibility now? Now you are getting tortured by an inward cowardice? Do you want to escape from your responsibility?' That is the question Krishna asks Arjuna.

So Arjuna says: 'please instruct me, what is my *dharma* here? If not to fight is an escape, if turning away is an escape, what do I do now?'

The dejection and frustration has converted itself into an enquiry. When we get dejected and depressed, we also try to find a network of escapes. We want to do something and we fail. That failure creates dejection. We love someone, and that someone turns away from us and we get depressed. We see callousness around us and we become cynical.

You see, that dejection, that depression, that frustration, if it leads to escape, cynicism and isolation, it removes us from the field of action. Is it not our experience in daily life? Somebody hurts us and we get dejected and living gets suspended completely, for hours together. We sit down in an easy chair, or lie down on some bed and play with the memory of how we were hurt. We suspend the movement of living. We may suspend it for hours, for days, weeks.

The Vedas, the Upanishads, the Indian philosophy says: 'that which turns you away from Life and living is a sin.' There is no other sin in Life but to turn away from Life. When you try to escape from the responsibility of living, of facing challenges, of meeting them, then you are committing a crime against Life; you are committing a sin against Life.

So Krishna says: 'we are not going to turn away. We will question what is death, what is Life, what is killing, what is religion. We will question. Turning away is no solution. Escape is no solution.'

In the general introduction to the *Gita* we looked into the characteristics of the ancient oriental people, for whom religiosity was love of Life, for whom spirituality was the act of living. Nothing could divert the attention of the sages and seers from Life and living. So we started from there, and the poetic exclamations of perception in the form of the Vedas. Then the dialogues of the Upanishads. Then the systematized knowledge about reality in the Six Systems of Philosophy.

The Vedas and the Upanishads do not give you knowledge. It is not systematized thought; it is just a verbal transmission. You know, verbal transmission is quite different from giving information. The Six Systems of philosophy are systematized knowledge about reality. They do not deal with the perception of reality. They do not have that ecstatic characteristic or directness, the beauty of the poetry of the *Chandogya Upanishad* or the *Isha Upanishad*, or the *Mandukya Upanishad*. And after the Six Systems, you come to the essence of all that, in the *Gita*. So the eighteen chapters of the *Gita* are the essence of all the Upanishads and the Vedas.

The *Gita* is the revelation of Brahma-Vidya, of the highest reality, and it is also an elucidation of the science of *yoga*. It will tell you about the absolute reality, but not in abstraction, always in relation to daily living, in the movement of relationships.

The Bhagavad Gita is a beautiful song that we will be studying together. It is the revelation of *yoga*. It tells you about reality and it indicates the path to get re-united with that reality. And the path is *yoga*. Not the exclusive partial compartmental path of Karma Yoga, Bhakti Yoga etc., these outer paths or systems, though necessary, are limited and the sum of them all also will be limited. The essence is undivided wholeness, and unless there is awareness of that undivided wholeness, what you do with the outer systems and the excellences that you cultivate in practising them, will still leave something missing. The *Gita* helps us to provide the missing clue.

The first chapter gives us the background of dejection and frustration of Arjuna, which will get converted into a positive constructive enquiry. Krishna uses the dejection as a motivation for the study of *yoga*, not allowing the dejection and frustration to lead to an escape, to lead to isolation, but using all that agony and pain.

You know there is tremendous dynamic potential in sorrow, in pain, in agony, if one does not allow the ego to use the pain and agony for gratifying itself. We will see what Krishna does with the pain and agony of dejection, how he tackles the potential energy in sorrow, for a creative enquiry.

Vedic literature is an ocean, a verbalized ocean of perceptions of truth, may I say perceptions of reality. On the one hand the Vedas would tell you what existed before creation. They do not talk only about the genesis; they talk about that which existed before creation:

'There was neither the real nor the unreal then. There was neither death or dying, life or living. There was neither the light of day nor the darkness of night. Only That existed, That in its undivided wholeness, in its absoluteness, existed.'

What was That? The Vedic sages called it Brahman. It is a very interesting word. Derivatively, it means that which is ever dynamic, that which ever recreates itself, that which is self-creative and self-sustained. It becomes many and in spite of becoming many, it retains its oneness. It retains its undivided wholeness in spite of manifesting the splendour of manyness out of its own substance.

On the one hand the Vedas give horizons, which have no limitations, and on the other, they probe into the mystery of creation. How out of emptiness, space exploded, how out of space, sound was born and fire out of sound and water out of fire and the earth out of water. It gives you the whole process of genesis or creation. It tells you about the uni-cellular system becoming the multi-cellular system, about the mineral kingdom, the vegetable kingdom, the emergence of birds, creatures, animals, human species. About sound getting converted into words and words developing into languages. They talk about music, sex, the science of genetics, about economy, education, astronomy and so on. That is why I called it an ocean.

But I am not here to elaborate about the expanse and depth of the Vedas.

The genius of the Indian people consisted in developing the Six Systems of Philosophy out of all this. And the *Gita* is the sum and substance of the whole Vedic literature. It has only seven hundred verses, divided into eighteen chapters, in the framework of a dialogue between a teacher and a student who were most intimate friends. This crest jewel of the Vedic literature has been and is still very popular with people in every country of the world.

The main concern of the Indians was liberation: unconditional inner freedom. Commentators have interpreted the seven hundred verses, to expound their ideology. For example, Sri Shankara says that Brahman, the supreme intelligence, the existential essence, is real and everything else is illusory. Brahman is absolute and everything else is relative, or *maya*, conditioned by time and space. According to him the message of the *Gita* is a message of renunciation. 'Know thyself to be that absolute reality.' 'Thou art That.' 'Renounce the illusory, the forms, that which is limited and get tuned into the absolute reality of Life.' Out of these teachings of Sri Shankara came the cult of *sannyasa*, renunciation, which you will find in India. We have to remember this, for as we proceed with our study and take up chapter after chapter, the word renunciation, *sannyasa*, will come in.

According to another commentator, the message of the *Gita* is action, Karma Yoga. Gandhi, who studied the scriptures of different religions while in South Africa, wrote, on his return to India, a commentary on the *Gita* called the yoga of non-attachment. According to him the message is: 'Do everything, but remain non-attached.'

Shankara says do everything, but within you there should be the grandeur of renunciation, a stronger word than non-attachment.

Gandhi was followed by Vinoba, another intellectual giant, with whom I worked for ten years collecting land for the poor, walking the length and breadth of this country. He was a scholar. But his first love was the Vedas. He would get up at 2.30 in the morning and start singing the Vedas, the *mantras*, the hymns. I can hear them even now. According to him, the teachings of the *Gita* are: 'Realize your own nature, Brahma-Vidya, know and realize you are Brahman and then, with the awareness of your own nature, plunge into the battle of relationships, or Brahma-Vidya Yoga.'

CHAPTER II

YOGA OF KNOWLEDGE OF REALITY

We are going to look at the second chapter this morning, which to my mind gives the essence and summary of the whole *Gita*. If anyone were to study only the second chapter, they would still get the essence of the teaching, they would get the message. Now, where does the dialogue begin, in the second chapter? It is a marvellously complex and fascinating chapter.

Imagine the incredible situation of two armies on the battleground, confronting each other, thousands on both sides. And, in between the armies, a huge chariot with seven or eight horses and two warriors in it, one standing, the other sitting. Krishna is the chariot driver; he is standing and holding the reins of the horses and behind him Arjuna, the friend, the student, the ever-tortured one, with doubts and indecision. That is the scene, if you can imagine it with me? It is the historical description.

In fact our own relationships are battlegrounds. To live is to be related, multifarious relationships. You have to be related to nature, to the planet, the earth, the skies, the rivers, the oceans, the forests. You have to be related to the creatures, the birds, to the plant world, to fellow human beings around you, you know. You have to be related to those whom you call your own. Life is relationships, and the act of living implies the act of being related.

How to be related without losing your balance, without losing the inner integrity? Every imbalance is an impurity. There is no other impurity in life, but to lose the spontaneous equipoise inside you. The equipoise of consciousness is virtue.

Yoga is inner spontaneous equipoise in consciousness as well as outer balance in the sensual behaviour, involving your brain, which is also a sense organ, maybe a subtle one, a complex one, with millions of cells in it, implicating the whole neurological system and so on. So yoga is spontaneous inner equipoise and outer balance, which relationships require.

We get disturbed and upset, we lose the sensual balance and the inner equipoise, the majestic peace, the tranquillity, the glorious state of relaxation, we lose it every other moment. Something happens which hurts and we are swept off our balance. We feel that the ego is attacked and we are disturbed. Getting disturbed, upset, distracted, getting tense, getting worried, you know the variety of imbalances we go through. We are Arjunas.

And when we get overwhelmed by that imbalance, we want to turn away from the act of living, as Arjuna wanted to turn away from fighting, from the battle, knowing fully well what this battle meant. He was a warrior, he had prepared for it. He had requested Krishna to come and help him, he had invited all his friends to join him and then, when he came face to face with the facts, he wanted some excuse to turn away. Doesn't that happen to us?

So how to retain the inner equipoise and the outer sensual balance and move through relationships, that is the crux of the whole philosophical problem. How to be aware of the absolute and remain in the limited, how to be aware of the timeless eternity and deal with time, with the moment, the hours, the days, the centuries. How to be aware of the time-free isness of Life and move through past, present and future. How to be aware of the real and live with the unreal. That is the question Krishna is going to take up in the second chapter. But look at the way he takes it up:

'Arjuna, you are grieving over that which does not deserve to be grieved over. You are giving me a talk about the ills of battle, the ills of violence, of conflicts. You say that you are not going to get anything out of a victory. You are telling me about all this, like a scholar. Look my dear; one who understands the nature of Life does not grieve over the things that you are grieving over, saying that you are not going to fight.

On the one hand you say to me that I should teach you. You say I am your teacher, come and teach me. You are turning to the inward intelligence in you, for solutions to your embarrassment and what is the pre-condition? You say: 'I am not going to fight. Tell me what to do. But I won't fight. Don't ask me to fight. Tell me anything else to do, but not that.'

How can there be an enquiry with pre-conditions? Can an enquiry be conditioned? Can there be a way of learning and discovering the truth, without upsetting my present way of living? Can learning, can enquiry; can discovery be launched upon with certain reservations and inhibitions?

Is not a conviction of an ideology, an inhibition? Can inhibited reason discover anything at all? Theory, ideology, idealism, bring up norms and criteria, these are all cerebral reservations, all that paraphernalia of norms, criteria, theories, value structures, God knows what. Are they not? Do you see the contradiction? This is not only the contradiction of Arjuna five thousand years ago; it is the contradiction in each one of us.

We are here as enquirers of the meaning of Life. That is we are confronted with the question of how to live, what is this mystery of relationships, how do we relate while retaining inner freedom, how do we share Life with others and so on. When Arjuna repeats the request, Krishna says:

'My dear friend, first throw away this petty weakness of your heart, throw away the inhibitions that you have gathered in your heart. Stand up. This weakness, the decision: 'I won't do this', is inhibiting you from finding out the truth of the situation. We shall look at the truth, but first let there be an openness.'

You know, an openness of consciousness, which has no reservations or inhibitions, is called humility. One who wants to learn should be careful that there is no arrogance of knowledge inside, such as: 'I know this, and on the basis of this knowledge, tell me what you have to tell next, so that I will add that to this, convert what you say into another piece of knowledge and add it to the memory. And then I'll go and live.'

As long as we want our actions to be based on knowledge, as long as we want our relationships to be conducted on the basis of that sterile past, which is knowledge, the known, learning and discovery and growth cannot take place, leave aside transformation, which is a dimensional change.

So Krishna says: 'are you willing to renounce, to throw away the weakness of inhibitions? You have been talking about many theories; you have been depicting the ills of battles and war. They may be true, but can you brush them aside, if you want to listen to me?' A very significant question.

When thousands would gather around Krishnamurti in Saanen, India or California, he would say: 'Sir, do you know what it is to listen?' And people would get disturbed by this question. 'Listening is total action, so can you listen to me?' he would ask. And in the beginning I used to be perplexed. Why is he asking this? And then one discovered that people really do not listen, they hear the words, they compare the words, they want to know, not listen. Listening leads to learning, hearing leads to knowledge, to information.

In the last verses of the first chapter Arjuna says: 'my limbs are trembling, my mouth has gone dry, I cannot even hold my bow and arrow, I am feeling giddy.'

The last five or six verses are a description of what happens to you and me, perhaps every day, when we are faced with challenges. Our intelligence sees the way out, but our hearts are not willing to follow the path suggested by the intelligence. We get divided within, we get fragmented within. Arjuna, on the battlefield, was completely imbalanced. Not exactly a nervous breakdown, but bordering on it. All the symptoms of inner imbalance were there.

As soon as there is an inner imbalance, it gets reflected on the physical organs. You cannot hide the inner imbalances, the tensions, the worries; you cannot cover them up by theories. You may conceal them from the world, you can't conceal them from Life. You know Life is intelligence. The energy of intelligence permeates everything. Life itself is divinity. Intelligence is that divinity, unqualified, unmodified, uninhibited, unpolluted by theories and dogmas and ideologies. That pure crystal clear intelligence is the Krishna within you, within me, within the universe. We turn to it when we get perplexed, but when it shows clearly what is to be done, in razor-like sharp words, we become nervous and back out.

Now Krishna says: 'leave all that, and let us see what is the way out.' In a psychological crisis what can be done? Now the crucial portion of the second chapter begins.

It is not something unusual that Krishna talks about. In the west, Socrates had said: 'Know thyself.' And do you remember Browning: 'The light of truth is within you.' It does not arise from anywhere outside. The inmost centre of your being is the light, is fullness. The prince of human beings, Jesus of Nazareth, also said: 'Know thyself', know the essence of your being, you are light. And Krishna is asking Arjuna to do the same, to look at the essence of Life within and around. 'You are perplexed and embarrassed because I think you have forgotten the nature of reality within you and around you. You are confusing something.'

Taking Arjuna by the hand, Krishna is now going to show the path of knowing the reality, of understanding the reality. The word 'knowing', 'jnanam', is used. This first portion of the second chapter deals with Sankhya Yoga, the path of knowledge, the path of reason. Please do not confuse it with the Sankhya philosophy, which is something very different. The Sankhya philosophy, in the *Sankhya Karikas*, is a system of philosophy based on enumeration, where *sankhya* means to measure, to calculate, to enumerate.

Here, the word *sankhya* has another meaning, which is reason. In the first part of the second chapter of the *Gita*, Krishna is using the word *sankhya* to mean *jnanam*, the Path of Reason, the path of Jnana Yoga, the reunion with reality through reason, through knowledge.

And the second part of the chapter deals with Karma Yoga, the Path of Action. The chapter is divided into these two portions.

Now what does reason and rationality say about the nature of Life? What does it say about the real and the unreal? What is the real?

What can we call real? That which does not get destroyed, that is real. Forms can be destroyed, they can be modified, they can be qualified, they can be destroyed. Can space be destroyed? Space is the expanse of emptiness. Emptiness cannot be destroyed, space, the skies, *akasha* cannot be destroyed. *Akasha*, space, emptiness, permeating all Life, is real.

Forms, though they are necessary, though they are useful, though without them we cannot live, are unreal. Unreal is not false. Forms can be touched, seen, you can use them. Forms are limited; they come into existence at a moment in time, so they are time-bound. They require some space, they are space-bound. That, which has a form, has an appearance. So everything that appears is unreal, that is to say it is not absolutely real. Please pay attention to these two terms, real and unreal, used in Indian philosophy.

The unmanifest is real, they say, because it cannot be destroyed. It must have been there even before the human species visited the planet and it shall be there after the human race, in its stupidity, destroys itself. That which ever has been, that which ever shall be, that which cannot be changed by human hand or thought, is called the absolute real.

And that which can be qualified, modified, changed in quality, shape, colours, forms, is called unreal. Let us not interpret the word unreal as an illusion. It is not false. It is relative. There are relative truths and there are absolute truths. This is the Path of Reason, this is the Path of Sankhya. A person, who uses reason to analyse, is called a Sankhya Yogi.

Krishna says: 'Arjuna, the forms that have a beginning, have an end.' Whether the form of a human creature or a non-human creature, a tree or a mountain, a river or a lake, or even perhaps the planet, the solar systems and so on, that which has a beginning in time, that which has a location in space, that which emerges as a form, merges back into the formless. That which emerged from the unmanifest and appears to be manifest, appears to be real, because it can be touched by the sense organs. It is only real in a relative sense. Today it is there; tomorrow it may not be there.

A volcano erupts and villages are destroyed. There is an earthquake and thousands die. The beauty of Life is its unpredictability. Human calculations cannot take in their grasp the whole dance of Life. That which is there at this moment, a building, a human being, a form, may not be there the next moment. Unpredictability defies logic.

Here, it is sufficient to say, that Krishna makes Arjuna aware that the real essence of Life is the intelligence, which moves in the space of emptiness. It is Life. We are expressions of that Life. And that Life cannot be killed. Arjuna says: 'how can I kill my nephews, my relatives?' Krishna says: 'Arjuna, you cannot kill the Life in them. The forms of Bhishma or Drona, their minds, their bodies, their brains have been supporting the injustice, they have been supporting the evil, and the battle implies fighting against that evil. But you cannot kill Life. Life has no death.'

Krishna is answering what Arjuna said in the first chapter. 'Do you think that you and me and they, whom you call the Kauravas, have not existed before? When you call a fruit a fruit, you are not referring to the skin of the fruit. The skin preserves the essence. In the same way Life necessarily does not mean the form, the shape, the qualities attributed to the form, attached to the form. When you say Life and living, you are referring to that essence. Arjuna, that essence cannot be killed. You have not created it, nor have I. That is indestructible.'

Arjuna is asking whether to fight or not to fight, while Krishna is taking him to the understanding of self-knowledge, understanding of the nature of reality. He points out that Life, as the absolute reality, is indestructible.

'Don't grieve. You are grieving for that which does not deserve your grief'.

The Bhismas, the Dronas, the Kauravas, what they have done to the Pandavas and others, being drunk with power and arrogance blinding them, is to violate the law of justice, violate the law of human dignity. You have to fight against that domination and injustice and chaos. *Dharma* means order, *adharma* means disorder.

They have created disorder in the whole kingdom. You are fighting against the disorder. You can't fight against abstractions. You are fighting against them, who are the instruments of disorder.'

Birth and death are related to emergence and merging back of forms, names, qualities and substances. And Life is something which ever has been, without beginning and without end. That is what we mean by the word immortal, that is what we perhaps mean by the word eternity, infinity. Krishna is pointing out to Arjuna the essence of Life.

We have been here before, in some other form, some other name. There is this endless emergence of forms and substances, the dance of their interactions, beautifully described by Frithj of Capra in his books, by David Bohm in his implicate and explicate order of evolution. Truth is the same, whether the *Gita* talks about it, or a physicist talks about it. The language differs, according to the time in which the truth is verbalized; it does not become less sacred because a Sheldrake or a Capra, or a David Bohm or someone else points it out. It does not become more sacred because it is expressed in the Indian language. Life itself is sacred and one who verbalizes the perception of that truth, that perception is something sacred.

Verses eleven to thirty-one, of the second chapter, elaborate the path of reason, the path of Jnana Yoga, also called Sankhya Yoga. It is only from the thirty-second verse of the second chapter, that we will turn to the yoga of action, or Karma Yoga.

It is a mind-boggling thing even to understand verbally that, encased in this tiny little body, is the eternal truth, encased in this network of the nervous system, the chemical system, this body of flesh and bones, tissues, muscles, is the supreme intelligence flowing through it. And we are that. 'All is Brahman', says Shankara Acharya. 'Aham Brahmasmi', I am that Brahman. 'Tat Tvam Asi', you are That. 'Sarvam Khalidam Brahman', the essence is one and the same in you or me. In the all-ness in the manyness is the oneness of Life.

Arjuna says: 'if That is real, why should I act at all? Why don't I enjoy the intoxication of even the feel that I am the universal?'

That is a very intoxicating thing. As an idea it is intoxicating. As a reality it is marvellously relaxing, rejuvenating. Arjuna asks Krishna: 'if you say that they have ever been and we have ever been, and Life never dies, and nothing can be killed, why should I fight? Why shouldn't I turn away, be a mendicant, beg my food somewhere?' That question will be answered from verse thirty-two onwards. Now we are diving into the depth of the *Gita*.

I would like to clarify one point. We have mentioned that there are Six Systems of Indian Philosophy, one of which is Sankhya. It is a dualistic philosophy, expounding that there are two principles as the essence of creation. One is matter called Prakriti, and the other is Purusha, the energy of intelligence. These two energies are at the core of existence, they run parallel, they exist in every expression. It is a dualistic approach.

When, in the second chapter of the *Gita*, Krishna refers to Sankhya as a part of yoga, he is not referring to Sankhya as the dualistic philosophy. If at all it could be given a name, the exposition of Krishna would be called monism. In other words, at the core of existence is the energy of supreme intelligence, and the whole creation is a manifestation of that energy. Creation in essence does not differ qualitatively from the source of its manifestation.

If intelligence is the source of creation, it is also the substance of creation. There is nothing like matter. What we call matter, are transitory forms emerging out of the ocean of intelligence, due to the profundity and the vertical/horizontal simultaneous movement of that energy of intelligence. Krishna calls *sat/chit/ananda*, absolute existence/consciousness/bliss, the source of creation. Many words are used to denote the energy of intelligence. It is called Atman, Paramatman. It is not a personalized god, not an individuated expression, but a non-divisible, non-individuated, non-personalized principle of intelligence permeating the whole Cosmos.

The innumerable forms, which you call material objects, are manifestations of intelligence. They are clothed in time and space, they are clothed in the appearance of a form, but their substance, their essence is the same intelligence. In them the intelligence is encased or embodied in a particular form. The unmanifest permeates everything, therefore it has no form. So Sankhya Yoga, as indicated by Krishna in the second chapter, is a monistic approach to reality.

In the same way, the yoga that Krishna is going to expound, is different from Patanjali Yoga, in which *ahimsa*, non-violence, is a requirement of the student of yoga. The *Gita* is not concerned with the question of violence or non-violence; it is not propounding Patanjali Yoga. It is propounding something different, the fundamentals of which are applicable to each path, whether Patanjali Yoga, Sankhya Yoga, Karma Yoga, Bhakti Yoga, or any other yoga and which they will have to learn and understand.

In the second chapter we are dealing with those fundamentals. What are they? That what you call Cosmos is only a dance of energies. Can you describe the energy, call it Atman, Paramatman, Chaitanya, give it any name? All names gathered together will fall short of pointing out the wholeness of that energy. Each name will perhaps illuminate one aspect of that energy. But that undivided non-fragmentary wholeness of Life, the isness of that energy, defies verbal description and definition.

So there is the unmanifest, the *avyakta*, which is formless because it is all-permeating intelligence. It is unwinding itself, expressing itself through the innumerable variety of forms, colours, shapes, sizes, which are the result of the interaction of that energy, because of its movement, which is simultaneously horizontal and vertical, which could be symbolised by a cross.

Now, the expressions, the forms located in space, emerging in a moment in time, are qualified and modified in their existence. They emerge and merge back, that is what is called the dance of Life. Emerging is called birth, and merging back is called death or dying.

All forms, whether they are clothed in flesh and blood, or in the form of water, of a tree, a mountain, all forms are perishable by their very nature of getting clothed into space and time, clothed into particularity, clothed into specification or individuation. They are transitory.

The *Gita* is trying to convey to us, through the dialogue between Krishna and Arjuna, that we are born in the midst of forms, in the form of a human body. We cannot run away and need not run away from the world of appearances or forms. We have to live here; we have to relate to them. And what is the test of relationship? The test of relationship is that we do not lose our inner freedom.

The unmanifest beingness of Life, the unmanifest wholeness of Life, does not get fragmented, though it is manifesting all the time through all the eons and ages and centuries in innumerable forms, it does not get fragmented.

In the same way, while we relate to nature, to fellow non-human beings and fellow human beings, let us be watchful that no fragmentation takes place within us, that we do not get deprived of our inner freedom of wholeness, due to the movement of relationships. I hope you do appreciate this, how to remain whole in the midst of various relationships. There will be relationships on the biological level, on the psychological level, as a member of society, as a member of global totality, and so on. The beauty of human life is the opportunity to relate on many levels and in many fields at the same time, like an orchestra.

The unmanifest wholeness, the isness of Life, expresses its splendour and glory and wealth in every expression, be it a tiny blade of grass, its deep green colour, its tenderness and freshness. The wholeness of Life smiles at us through the blade of grass, through the flow of water, through the rain drops, through the frightening lightning, the depth of the ocean, the expanse of space; we are embraced by that wholeness of Life, that isness of Life.

We are surrounded by the dance of relationships, female, male, man, wife, husband, father, mother, sister, brother, educationalist, industrialist, politician, you know so many responsibilities that one has to go through, in order to be related to Life as it is. And we create misery because we are ignorant about the secret of getting related without losing freedom, without losing our wholeness. We get involved, we get attached, we become infatuated, we sow the seeds of misery in our life. That is what the *Gita* is trying to point out to Arjuna.

I cannot go into the physical history of the Kauravas and the Pandavas, how they were brought up, their clashes and conflicts with one another, the vanity of Bhima, the weaknesses of the eldest brother Yudhisthira, the pride of Arjuna, the arrogance of Draupadi, their wife, how these also contributed towards the war or a confrontation situation, along with the lust for money and power of the Kauravas. They would do anything; go to any length, to retain the money and the power, the kingdom, the land. They would sacrifice everything, every relation. They won't mind rivers of blood, through which they will have to wade to retain the kingdom.

The *Gita*, which is a part of the *Mahabharata*, is meant to indicate to the human race their weaknesses and excellences, and their interaction. So the situation of confrontation was created by the Pandavas and the Kauravas together.

There is good and evil in society, but it is extremely rare to come across goodness not contaminated by any aspect of evil altogether. And it is equally rare to come across evil, which does not contain some aspect or seed or potential of goodness in it. That is the beauty of life. Unmixed good or unmixed evil is extremely rare to come across. It is only a person who discovers and has a direct encounter with the unconditioned reality at the centre of his or her being, who can grow into a state of consciousness and a style of living which transcends the duality of good and evil, of violence and non-violence. Suffice it to say that the *Gita* is not treating the issue of violence or non-violence. It neither preaches violence, nor does it teach non-violence. It helps us to learn that Life is for living.

And I am coming to the next question: what is the Cosmic purpose? Is it only fighting evil or injustice and defending the good? Is that purpose sufficient to explain the existence of Life? What is a purpose, my friends? What is a purpose? What is a motivation? What is a goal? What is an aim? Are not they the requirements of the human mind? Why should Life require any purpose for its existence or movement? Does a smile require a purpose? What purpose has a smile, the emergence of a smile, the flowering of a smile, the beauty of a smile?

The purpose-free expressions are the real essence and sacredness of Life. Has beauty any purpose? And does not beauty move us in our life? Why should the sunshine help the sun in its purpose, beyond shining? Is not the radiation of light in the being of the sun its nature? The sun can't help it, can it?

Self-expression does not require any purpose, any motivation, any goal, any aim away and independent of its own content. The content of Life is intelligence, and the nature of intelligence is unwinding, uncovering itself, expressing itself. Life is fulfilled through its expressions, and by its expressions. It does not express itself far from them; it is its very nature, as the nature of water is to flow.

The spontaneity of the ever-expressing isness of Life baffles the human brain, because the human brain is conditioned to find out the purpose, the aim, then direct its activities in that direction, and then attain it, arrive, achieve.

The human brain is conditioned. It built up laws and criteria. That is why it constructed logic, the law of causation, the science of ethics and morality. These are the psychological requirements of human beings. The human mind cannot function without a motivation. If there is no other motivation, then it can convert the instinct for self-preservation into a motivation, then build a philosophy around that instinct of survival, rationalize it, theorize it, decorate it.

What I am trying to say is that Life is purpose-free, and the expressions of Life, the one manifesting as many, the one turning itself endlessly into the many and yet remaining whole, is as glorious as the unmanifest. That is why we call it infinite, this dance of expressions, the manifest, the multifarious, the emergence and merging back, without moving anything.

The transitoriness, the emergence, flowering, blossoming and radiating its content for a moment, an hour, a day, a week, a year, they are your calculations. You measure them because a human brain cannot relate without measurements. It measures human life as hundred years, fifty years, the life of flowers into weeks, that of trees into centuries, and so on.

I am sorry to disappoint you; there is no purpose for the existence of Life. It is a spontaneous existence, and we are it. The essence of our being is that reality.

Don't you express yourself, when you are visited by love, without any purpose or motivation, without wanting to gain anything in return? It is that reality which is creating a compulsive urge to express itself through the tenderness of love, through the grandeur of compassion, an urge for selfless friendship. Do you see how man gropes for fields of expression without motivation, and glorifies mother's love for the child, that of the beloved and the lover, the love between friends, the love of sages for humanity, the compassion of sages and yogis for humanity?

Man has always glorified innocence, has glorified beauty, not purposes, not calculations, which are the requirements, the motivations, the circumferences that we have built around ourselves. We have used them, as we build houses around ourselves for security and safety and use them. But have you seen a house without a space?

So purpose is a limitation, which cannot reach the intelligence. All purposes, aims, ideas, ideologies are in the dimension of the psychophysical structure. And Life is structure-free. It has no structure at all. Truth is not structured, reality is not structured, it has no pattern, no structure. So what is the Cosmic purpose? No purpose.

In the same way, we the human beings, born in society, encased in forms, are limited, not only by external limitations, but we are limited within also, by physical and psychological inheritance. They are limitations, because inheritance stimulates various trends, traits, peculiarities, characteristics, idiosyncrasies, which have a momentum, the momentum of biological impulses.

Living in society and being educated by that society, we require languages and again our brain gets conditioned by that. Philosophy, political science, economics, culture, all these are limitations. The best of the brain with the brilliance of intellect can use all these, and we have to learn to use them, so that they do not disturb the harmony.

There seems to be a music of harmony floating in the Cosmos, in the ether as it were, whether it is in the earth or the oceans, in the water, in the principle of fire, or the principle of sound, or the principle of the emptiness of space, they seem to cooperate with one another, in a majestic harmonious way. They retain their individuality and cooperate with one another. Their cooperation results in the emergence of a harmonious and orderly Cosmos for us.

Can we realize the oneness, the freedom, the spontaneity, the non-fragmented indivisible nature of the essence of our being? says the *Gita*. And on the sensual level, on the verbal level, on the psychological level, can we function in such a way, that we do not disturb the harmony, rather enrich the harmony existing in the Cosmos? Unfortunately we have not learned this.

In spite of the *Gita*, the Upanishads, the Vedas, the *Bible*, the *Koran Sharif*, the Teachings in the synagogues, we have yet to learn that secret of harmony, of cooperation, eliminating the necessity of confrontation, eliminating the habit of domination, of dependency, which is the beginning of exploitation, eliminating the lust for money, power, sex. Are they necessary ingredients for relationships?

Lust creates an imbalance, lust creates an emotional involvement, it leads to attachment, whether to sex, money, power, or knowledge, it is immaterial to what you are attached. The state of attachment is the source of all imbalances, please do see this. That is what the *Gita* wants us to see and learn. Krishna is trying to point out to Arjuna that his uncles, brothers, teachers etc., which he knew as belonging to him, just as he belonged to them, are all expressions of one and the same reality.

'You did not know that, and therefore there was this drama of enmity, of hatred, of confrontation, that you have created for yourself. Now don't run away. You have built up this action yourself, you cannot escape from it, you have to take it to its logical conclusion.

If you run away from the battleground and go to the mountains to live somewhere as a hermit, even then your characteristics as a warrior, your tendencies as a fighting person, will not leave you, even there. They will build up situations, even in a cave or an ashram, where confrontation will become necessary.

So know that you are neither the creator, nor the destroyer. Know that all forms are transitory, all relationships man-made. Know also that Life cannot be destroyed, it is indestructible.

Discharge your responsibility as a person who conquers himself to fight, by inviting the armies and declaring the war. You have your commitments. And commitments, voluntarily taken, are your responsibility. How can you run away from them? Learn to live without getting committed. Be committed to Life only, committed to the truth that you understand only. But now you have to discharge the responsibility that you have invited on yourself, that you have inflicted upon yourself.'

Then comes Arjuna's question: 'how can I do this?' And Krishna's answer: 'by action born out of a state of *samadhi*, by action born out of the state of meditation.'

We are coming to the last portion of the second chapter. Arjuna asks Krishna: 'you have used the word *samadhi*, you said one who is rooted in *samadhi*, one whose consciousness has the dimension of *samadhi*. You are telling me that action born out of the state of *samadhi*, out of meditation, will be free from enmity, hatred, bitterness. What is that *samadhi*? How does a person in *samadhi* sit, stand, move, talk? How does he move in relationships?'

The last twenty verses of the second chapter deal with the dimension of *samadhi*. Krishna must have been waiting for that question: How does a person live in this mad world, after having known the reality, being aware of reality, being rooted in *samadhi*? There are so many responsibilities, so many roles to play, so many ups and downs, the dance of pleasure and pain, honours and humiliations, sorrows and joys of life. How does one retain the state of *samadhi*, and let actions flow, let relationships flow out of that?

The innocence, humility, and the real urge to learn are expressed by Arjuna. And Krishna catches it. Gone is the rigid attitude of: 'I will not fight, I will not do that!' That language has disappeared by the end of the second chapter.

'I am surrendering my ego to you, Krishna. Will you please tell me how the movement of relationships takes place in the dimension of meditation?'

As a student of *yoga*, you may start with Mantra Yoga, with Hatha Yoga, Tantra Yoga, but the point of culmination of growth is *samadhi*. That is when a person has the strength to ignore the compulsive urges created by the demands of the mind.

But how to be aware of those demands? In order to be aware, you must look at them. If you close your eyes, then you will not see them. If you try to wish them away, if you try to cover them up, if you try to suppress them, deny their very existence, then you will get bogged down, you will get stuck up with them. So when the demands on the mind come up, look at them, be aware of them, and yet have the strength, the vitality to ignore their momentum.

When you look at the fact, may be a very powerful fact, when you look at it without giving in, without trying to change it, you are ignoring the momentum, though you are cognisant of the fact. You require quite a strength in your nervous system to resist the compulsive urge and momentum on the biological and psychological level, to contain them, you know.

How do you restrain the horses when you drive a chariot? And there are five or six horses to the chariot in which Arjuna was sitting. You have the reins. What do you do with the reins attached to a horse? You restrain the movement of the horses with them. Now, the compulsive urges brought about by the senses are referred to here as the horses, and the human body is the chariot. The intelligence is the driver Krishna, and the ego is Arjuna.

First the ego, the self, has to learn to restrain, to have the austerity and the vitality to resist the momentum. Not reject. And how do you resist, how do you ignore? Just be with the compulsive urges. You require patience to look at them and say: 'yes, I know you are there.' You are looking at them, your awareness will not allow the demands of the mind to overtake you, to overwhelm you, to overpower you, to pollute your response, your behaviour.

'O Arjuna, when you are satisfied with the isness of your life, the beingness of your life, the fact that you are living, that you are capable of moving, that you are capable of seeing, hearing, responding, your isness decorated by so many faculties, when you are satisfied in your beingness and the capacity to uncover or express that beingness, then the restraint takes place, then the power and the strength to ignore the momentum takes place. And that moment, when you are contained in your being and the bodily impulses are neither destroyed nor fought against, neither suppressed nor resisted, you are there and you are there with them in that being together, then the dimension of meditation wakes up in you.'

Now comes the elaboration of the state of meditation and how it is expressed in the midst of relationships. That is the topic of the last twenty verses of the second chapter.

The dimension of samadhi is the culmination of meditation. When the state of meditation does not remain restricted to the consciousness, but percolates through the psycho-physical structure, down to the sensual level, when the indivisibility, non-fragmentation, the freedom and wholeness of the state of meditation flows through the senses in the movement of relationship, when the waters of meditation flow freely through the biological, the verbal and the psychological, when it is lived every moment, then that person is said to be living in the dimension of samadhi.

When meditation becomes a normal dimension of consciousness and the energy of supreme intelligence is released through every action, then you say that the person is living in samadhi. It is the culmination of meditation.

Otherwise, people can be in the state of meditation when they are alone, living in solitude, far away from the turmoil of relationships, but at the very first touch of the interaction with people, the touch of pleasure or pain, the touch of success or failure, humiliation or honour, the state of meditation withers away and it gets replaced by the ego-centred state of misery and suffering.

When the demands of the mind are seen, understood and ignored, when there is a sense of fulfilment in being alive and expressing the aliveness through words, deeds, gestures and so on, then Krishna says that the individual is living in samadhi.

Being clothed in a biological structure, encased in flesh and blood, one cannot avoid the game of duality. Pain and pleasure, as sensations in the realm of duality, are bound to be there. Krishna says to Arjuna: 'when pain causes hurt or a sense of suffering, a person living in meditation cognises the pain, the physical pain, the psychological hurt. It is felt, and yet no sense of misery or no continued suffering is generated out of that pain or hurt. O Arjuna, he is living in *samadhi*, who goes through the sensations of pain and pleasure without generating a sense of like or dislike, preference or prejudice, distraction or excitement out of them.'

The word '*dukha*' stands for pain, physical as well as psychological. An undistracted mind, one whose mind and body remains in the dignity of inner poise when visited by pain or pleasure, whose mind does not have a sense of craving or yearning for the repetition of the experience of pleasure, in short, those who move through the corridors of pain, agony, pleasure, etc., without loosing their inner poise, without loosing the dignity of their freedom, without getting damaged as regards the inner peace, consider them to be living in samadhi.

If they so live, what will be the natural consequence? 'Arjuna, those who thus live without generating likes, dislikes, preferences, prejudices, covetousness or a sense of contempt for pain, they will find that they are free from the fear of the world, they are free from the fear of Life.' Fear is a fertile soil for many imbalances and impurities. Krishna says that in the dimension of samadhi there is fearlessness, because there is neither an inclination towards pleasure, nor a disinclination towards pain.

Pain and pleasure are part of the game of living; they are part of Life, from whom none can escape. They are to be faced; they have to be gone through without any crystallization of inclination for the one, or disinclination for the other. It is the inclination that develops into likes, and the likes develop into attachment, which develops into infatuation and obsession, and so on. And if you have disinclination, it can develop into a sense of contempt, a sense of indifference, then a mild hatred, and a desire to reject or avoid it. Krishna says nothing can be avoided, in the realm of the material world, on the physical level; this duality of pain and pleasure cannot be avoided.

As a psychologist **par** excellence, Krishna analyses the movement of the human mind and says the human mind and body are condensed human past. The demands of the mind are the demands of the condensed human past in you. And that past wants to pounce upon the present and mould it in such a way, that it gets rendered into memory. The past moves acquisitively towards the present, pounces upon the present, as if it were a pray, and becomes quiet or subsides only after converting the vibrating, throbbing, living present into a dead past. We are dealing with the sum and substance of the Vedas and the Upanishads. The *Gita* gives the essence of the Vedic culture, of the Vedic philosophy.

It is not a rejection of the mind, but it is the perception of the nature of the mind that creates this special attitude towards the past, this intelligent relationship with the past, which is embodied in our body, our brain etc. Such a person then is free of fear, free of violence, because free of attachment and detachment.

How is this arrived at? That is Arjuna's question. And the next verse is a beautiful explanation. 'When a person gathers unto himself or herself the outgoing movement of the senses, as a tortoise gathers the movement of its legs towards itself, when the movement is not needed.' The outgoing activity of the senses is gathered when it is not relevant. When it is relevant, the senses are allowed to reach out to the outer world, the eyes are allowed to register shade, colour, size, quality. The capacity to smell, to hear, to touch, the capacity to speak, all these outgoing activities are necessary for the physical sustenance, for feeding the body, for clothing the body, for sheltering the body, for communicating with one another.

The outgoing activities, the outgoing movement of the senses, are taken recourse to when relevant, and when they are not relevant they are gathered unto themselves. You may be living surrounded by beautiful objects, tasty foods, glamorous clothes etc., but the mind does not register any reaction towards them, because they are not necessary for the sustenance of Life.

When the sense organs do not rush towards their relevant objects, except when necessary for physical sustenance, when they go into natural spontaneous non-action, they are not suppressed, you do not dry them out in the name of penance, you do not affect the sensitivity of the senses and sense organs. Keeping everything intact, the sense of discrimination is there. Then the pain or pleasure, the dance of duality cannot do you any harm. A person living in the dimension of meditation preserves the inner solitude, though surrounded by the world.

But why should we not take an easier path, by moving away from the world? If we have to live the life of a celibate, why should we not move away, women from men, men from women, why shouldn't we isolate ourselves from the objects, so that the sense organs have no occasion for outgoing activities? Human beings like to escape from challenges. To remain with the challenges and live in the austerity of alertness and awareness is something they don't like.

So, Arjuna asks: 'why not take an easy path, Krishna? Why don't I move away from all this, and live somewhere alone, where there is no question of restricting the movement, containing the

movement, no question of educating the senses to move only at
relevant moments, and going into non-action when it is not relevant?
All this is too difficult, Krishna, why don't I move away?'

And Krishna tells Arjuna that it is not by moving away from the
world of objects, by starving the senses, drying the tenderness of
sensitivity in them, that one will renounce objects. The starved
physical and psychological structure cannot become the conveyor
of reality. Reality, which is love, which is the tenderness of
compassion, reality which is beauty, which is sacredness or holiness,
reality which is wholeness, cannot express itself when one starves
one's senses.

By making the body fast, keeping a vow of silence, removing yourself
from the company of men and women, by depriving the senses of
the impact of their presence, by depriving them of the opportunity
of facing the challenge, you are creating a kind of atrophy in your
sense organs. Outwardly, you may be called a holy person, a celibate
who does not look at a woman, a person who eats only once a day,
and so on. Deprivation and starvation can create an outward
appearance of renunciation. But the soul of renunciation would not
be there, because inwardly the mind would be craving for all that.

As a hungry person thinks of food, so a biologically, sexually,
psychologically hungry person becomes greedy. Do not think that
the path of deprivation is the path of *yoga*, or the path of isolation is
the path of spirituality.

While educating yourself in Hatha Yoga, Mantra Yoga, Raja Yoga,
Tantra Yoga, taking up a specific path, you may have to remove
yourself into solitude for some limited time, but that cannot be a
way of living. You may do it for education. But living implies the
stream of relationships and the flow of freedom and wholeness in
the interaction involved in relationships.

The mind which takes tremendous interest in pleasure from food,
sex, clothes, from the innumerable variety, that interest lurking in
the mind, that inclination of rushing towards objects will be wiped

out completely only when the ultimate nature of reality is perceived directly, through awareness.

You perceive the invisible; you perceive the unmanifest through the sensitivity of awareness, where words cannot reach, where the mind cannot reach. It is only the subtle energy of awareness and intelligence that can put you into intimate encounter with the truth of Life.

The inclination contained in the biological and psychological structure subsides unconditionally, or goes into non-action irreversibly, only after realizing the nature of reality. 'Therefore, Arjuna, whether you fight or do not fight, please first understand what Life is.' And Krishna goes on describing poetically, in very romantic terms, yet in the lucid language of the *Bhagavad Gita*, the marvellous dimension of *samadhi*.

The condensed substance of the whole *Gita* is contained in the second chapter. It is an extremely important chapter, dealing in a nutshell with the elaborated teaching that spreads through the next sixteen chapters. We have been told, very vividly, that Life is the one and the many together; Life is the unmanifest and the manifest together, unity and diversity together. The diversity, the manyness, the manifest, has relative reality, because it is bound by time and space. Its emergence has a beginning in time, and its duration has an end in time. The ancient wise people called it transitory.

Everything that has a beginning and an end, everything whose form, shape, size, colour and qualities are conditioned by the laws of physical nature, governed by the law of causation, is called maya, that is to say not absolutely real. It is not *maya* in the sense of false, or in the sense of an illusion. If you attribute permanence to the transitory, then it becomes *maya*, unreal.

You take care of the fruit and the tree that grows the fruit, you handle them with care and gentleness, not for the skin of the fruit, but for the essence, which you assimilate in your body. In the same way Krishna is teaching Arjuna the art and science of handling the diversity with care, concern and gentleness, and relate to the oneness, the unity contained in it. The diversity contains the unity.

As a garland of flowers contains the thread, which is concealed from your eyes, you see the flowers; you wear the garland, not for the sake of the thread, but for enjoying the flowers. Yet the garland would not be there, but for the thread onto which all the flowers are gathered, which keeps all the flowers together.

The togetherness of the diversity of Life, the harmony running as a thread in the multiplicity of expressions, on the physical and material level, contains the essence that is Life, contains the supreme intelligence as a thread. The energy of intelligence runs, like a thread in the garland, in the whole Cosmos.

Figuratively, the *Gita* says the Lord is wearing the garland of the Cosmos. They were very poetic people; their sensitivity was not blunted by what you call science and technology. The tenderness of sensitivity, which perceived the Cosmos through their eyes, resulted in poetic expression.

Now, the thread of oneness running through the manyness, the undercurrent of unity keeping the diversity together in an orderly way, in a harmonious way, is the essence of Life. Living is to be related to both, related to the unity, the oneness, the wholeness, the unmanifest, and also getting related to the manyness, the diversity, the variety of colours, flavours, shapes, sizes, tastes, etc.

The splendour, the glory, the divinity of Life, makes its abode both in the unmanifest and the manifest equally. That is the message of the *Gita*. And living is being related to these two aspects of Life simultaneously. On the sensual and psychological level you relate to the many, the diversity, and on the level of awareness, the level of intelligence, you are related to the one, to the wholeness, the undividedness, the unity.

You know, being related means being capable of responding. A response is a relationship. Please do see this. When the *Gita* and the Upanishads use the term being related, they are using the term scientifically. Your eyes are open and if you do not perceive the beauty around you, you are not related to it. The beauty is perceived because there is the faculty of sight, which enables you to see.

When that beauty is perceived and that perception is appropriated by the ego, which says: 'I have seen it', then the relationship is snapped completely. It is the nature of response that it can be bondage, or a gateway to liberation, to transformation. Respond we have, there is no Life in isolation. The question is how do we respond? As soon as the response is appropriated by the ego, the I-consciousness, the self, disaster begins.

Because there was sight, perception took place. You were born with it, you did not cultivate it, you did not acquire it. Because there was the power of audition, the sound was heard. But the I, the ego says: 'I have heard it', 'I have seen it', and with such appropriation of the event of interaction, appropriation of a spontaneous response, interaction between the faculty of perception or audition and the objects around you, the event gets converted into an experience.

The I says: 'I have had an experience of seeing the beauty of the dawn', or 'I have had an experience listening to ecstatic music'. The sacred holy interaction and the joy of communion radiating through that interaction, is captured into verbalization. Every verbalization is an abstraction of reality. The I-consciousness, the ego, appropriates the event of interaction, calls it its own experience and feels gratified. The idea that 'I have had an experience', the verbalization, the abstraction, that very gratification gives pleasure. Pleasure is a reaction, manipulated by the ego, out of the interaction between the senses and their faculties, that are spontaneous, and the objects, which also exist spontaneously. We have not created Life, we have not built up the Cosmos, it is not a totality built up by the human race. It is love, the compassion of Life, that takes the form of the Cosmos.

When it is verbalized and a sense of gratification is sucked out of it, that gratification is called pleasure. And then the I says unto itself, 'when shall I have that again? Next hour, next day, next month?' It begins to covet, to crave, to yearn for the repetition.

Experiences can be repeated by manipulation, but joy can never be repeated. And, therefore, in every repetition of pleasure there is a diminishing quality, like the diminishing utility in economics. The gratification diminishes with every repetition and the ego craves for still more and more, it wants to change the objects of interaction, the individuals of interaction.

If the spontaneous interaction between the senses and their faculties and the Life that exists around you, is allowed to remain at the level of joy and if the flavour of that joy is allowed to flow through your nervous system, then there is relaxation and there is happiness. But with every verbalization and abstraction, thought comes into existence. Verbalization is the source of thought.

This introduction was necessary, to understand the following verse, which contains the whole psychology of *yoga* in a very compact manner.

A person thinks about objects, because it had verbalized about the event that had taken place. When you verbalize an event, you create an abstraction, which is an idea. You suck pleasure out of that ideation and you want its repetition.

Human beings, on whom is conferred the benediction of a variety of senses and sense faculties, of the beautiful neurological system, the immensely complex organ called brain, billions and billions of cells, the chemical system, etc. etc., came upon, stumbled upon the art of converting sound into words. But instead of using words for communication, they were used for abstraction. Thought is an abstraction, thought composed of words has no factual content.

A human being goes through interaction with various objects, through various sense organs. If the joy of the interaction gives you a sense of fulfilment, you do not verbalize, you do not indulge in abstractions, you do not create and carve an idea out of it and you do not want to repeat it. Remember, in the state of *samadhi* there is a sense of fulfilment in being alive; there is a sense of fulfilment in the feel of Life in you.

When you breathe in and out, you can feel fulfilled. When you open your eyes and look at the innumerable expressions of Life, there can be a sense of fulfilment, without wanting them to become your own. You hear music and there can be a sense of fulfilment. A sense of fulfilment can be a response; it can be a relationship with Life around you.

An appropriation of the effect of interaction by the ego, converting it into its own property, which is memory, is another kind of response.

The first response could lead to liberation, enlightenment, transformation, because there is communion with the real, the oneness. Joy is the perfume of communion with the real with the help of the unreal, which is a vehicle as it were. We must be very grateful to the so-called unreal material world. Energy makes the essence of matter. But if matter did not embody the energy, would there be any fun in living at all?

But the necessity of pleasure is unlimited, because of greed. I think about the object, inwardly I am keeping company with the object, the idea of the object, the name, the memory of pleasure. And this continuity of thinking about objects, maybe material objects, maybe a woman, a man, maybe music, it can be anything and everything, that thinking leads to attachment.

It is not the outer object that attracts you and leads to attachment. It is your thinking about the object that stimulates attachment. You may turn away from the world and go to the mountains, live in a cave, but if your mind goes on thinking about a man or a woman, about food, about beautiful things in the world, about praise and flattery, the pleasure of having money in your name, the power of domination over others, if you go on thinking about the world while sitting in a cave, there will be the same quality of attachment.

You may starve your sense organs, you may deprive them of the opportunity of interaction with the outer world, but the attachment can be equally in the mind of a hermit or a recluse, as it can be in the mind of a person living in the world, because it is thought that creates attachment.

Please, do see the subtlety of the understanding of psychology by the author of the *Gita*, who has condensed the Vedic literature into seven hundred verses, in a poetical way, in the form of a dialogue.

So, thought is the source of attachment and not the presence of the objects around us. When there is this inner attachment, due to the repetition of thinking about objects and imagining the pleasure, the idea of pleasure, then covetousness, infatuation, lust, begin to move stealthily in your heart. The attachment leads to the awakening, the concealed awakening, the hidden awakening of infatuation.

The word *kama*, desire, can be translated in many ways, it has many nuances. It is a very important Sanskrit word, used in the Upanishads, the Vedas, the Six Systems of Philosophy, along with the *Gita*.

When they write about the Cosmo-genesis, they say the divinity has the desire (*kama*) to manifest its oneness in the form of manyness, to manifest the splendour of its unity, its wholeness into manyness. So, the word *kama* can represent desire. It can also mean a decision, *sankalpa*, another word for *kama*.

A very beautiful point warrants communication here. Desire is the flame of vitality contained in Life. Desire is very sacred, it is not a sin, it is not a crime, it is not a disaster by itself. But look what we do with that sacred flame of vitality, that flame of passion, having tremendous dynamism, tremendous explosive potential in it.

When this desire, this vitality is related to the urge of learning for the sake of discovering the nature of reality, that very vitality, its depth, its intensity, its velocity, becomes a blessing. Desire is the primary principle of energy and vitality contained in intelligence.

But when that flame of vitality is directed towards transitory objects, towards the procurement of those objects for the sake of pleasure, it becomes the cause of imbalances. Because that vitality can never be satisfied, if it is geared to the unreal, the transitory, the momentary. It can never be satisfied, when we direct it, due to attachment, due to thought and thinking, towards objects: food, clothing, furniture, houses, gadgets, fame, name, money, man, woman, towards sensual, sexual, psychological pleasures.

We can't escape pleasure; every occurrence of joy will leave behind it the lingering sensation of pleasure. You don't have to crave for it. But when we direct, due to attachment, all our energy and intelligence towards objects and want to obtain them, own them, possess them, then the misery begins.

If you really get that for which you have created a want in your being, you become dependent on it, you loose your inner freedom. Your attachment, which was concealed at a non-verbal level, becomes a physical thing. If you get it, there is attachment, obsession, loss of freedom. And if you don't get it, when the attachment is thwarted, then there is disappointment, frustration, anger.

Before the flame of desire creates wants for material objects, if it gets directed towards the essence, the reality, the divine, then the responses to the material world, to the transitory world, may not become unhealthy, in the sense that it may not generate any imbalance.

But due to attachment, the moment a desire is thwarted, it results in a state of obsession (which is a complete loss of inner wholeness, of inner freedom) or anger. You say: 'I wanted this, but I could not get it' and you begin to compare: 'he got it', 'she got it'. You sow so many seeds of misery; you inflict so much suffering on yourself.

In the *Patanjal Yoga* there is this verse: 'the ending of psychological suffering is liberation, kaivalyam, nirvanam, it is transformation.' In the midst of relationships you learn the art and science of responding and relating without generating any suffering and misery for yourself and others.

What does anger do? It begins to bite you from within; it affects the whole psychophysical structure. It produces not only tension, but it makes your inside sour, as it were. And anger leads to confusion. You are hypnotized by confusion. You begin to believe that you are really confused. It is thwarted attachment getting converted into a state of sourness, which is anger, which generates confusion. You don't know any more what is fact and what is belief, what is a want and what is a natural need. You become confused and you feel that wants, stimulated by attachment, are the real needs.

You know what a need is? The physical needs necessary for survival, so that the marvellous movement of breathing in and out, the divine faculties embodied in the human form, can function smoothly, harmoniously.

Anger generates confusion, which disables you. You lose your capacity to discriminate between a fact and a fiction, a fact and a belief, an idea and reality. A fact and a concept get confused. That affects the memory. The memory gets mutilated. A confused person begins very speedily to believe that his opinions, his evaluations, were facts, his wants were natural.

Memory gets mutilated, the sense of time disappears, a person is lost. And the specific faculty of Homo sapiens, the power of discriminating the truth from the false, cannot work any more. And, therefore, a person gets completely lost.

See what thought does, what an addiction to thinking, an addiction to verbalization does? Thought may be a very powerful and useful instrument, but if that instrument becomes the owner and dominates the consciousness, wants to possess the whole consciousness, this is what can happen.

'Therefore, Arjuna, you have to learn to respond.' Yoga is the art of responding, of getting related to the real and the unreal simultaneously, in the midst of the so-called unreal, in the midst of the manifest, in the midst of the many, the diversity, in which you are placed by Life. Care for them, handle them gently, respect them for encasing the unmanifest reality, but never mistake them for the eternal, for the immortal, never mistake them for the substance, the existential essence of Life.

Move in the world of names, forms, shapes, objects, the world of energies, innumerable energies expressing themselves through innumerable objects. You know, Life is a dance of energies. You can be a witness, a perceiver, an enjoyer of the glory of their interaction. Water has one kind of energy, earth another, the sun has one kind of energy, the stars have quite a different soothing energy, fire another kind of energy.

Perception is the beginning of response. Recognition of the fact is the next step to a response. And then relating to that, which has been perceived, recognized and understood, according to the needs of survival, of decent aesthetic healthy survival. Health is holiness. So, perception, recognition, understanding.

And now we come to the point of sensual interaction. Relationship, when the word relatedness or relationship is used by the *Gita*, includes all these aspects. It is a multi-dimensional thing. Now we turn to the next verse.

'Walk into this forest of the material world of objects, enter it, walk into it, but beware that any interaction generates either attachment or detachment.'

Indians have created a cult of detachment, as disastrous as the cult of attachment and indulgence. Detachment deprives you of freedom and wholeness, as much as attachment does.

'Your consciousness and your senses have to be educated in such a way, Arjuna, so that they can move through the jungle of this manifest world of objects and interact with them, without generating any like or dislike, preference or prejudice, attachment or detachment.'

When you thus relate to the objects around you, as for the needs of physical survival and aesthetic joy, then that interaction between your faculties, your senses, including mind, brain, everything, (how would you perceive without the help of the brain, how would you discriminate the darkness from light if you did not use the brain, the intellect), when that interaction on the sensual and psycho-physical level is without the dichotomy and duality of preference and prejudice, attachment or revulsion, then that interaction will result in prasad, that is a blessing or benediction of relaxation and happiness. Joy always relaxes, doesn't it? It does not create a tension, like pleasure.

Krishna sums up: 'do not run away from the world, O Arjuna. Fulfil your commitments, discharge your responsibilities, with the awareness of the real, and the necessity to respond to the unreal.

The body you are wearing (the flesh, the bones, the muscles, the tissues, the nerves, the arteries) is also a part of that transitory world. It is here today, tomorrow it will become a useless instrument for Life to move in. You will give up the ghost, you will lay down the body. It is equally perishable as these others are. That does not deserve your grieve, Arjuna. That which is real can never perish and that which is unreal cannot be converted into eternity or infinity, though you may increase the longevity of its duration.'

We are coming to the concluding passage of this theme. It is a beautiful treatment of psychology. That is why I am taking so much time to dwell on it.

'When in the midst of the movement of relationships, the consciousness remains whole and retains its freedom, when it remains relaxed and retains a sense of fulfilment of being what it is, then, in that sense of fulfilment, O Arjuna, is the ending of all manner of psychological suffering and misery.'

Religion is ending of psychological suffering and misery. Physical pain or sickness may not be totally eliminated, but psychological suffering can be ended. Religiosity is the ending of that self inflicted misery generated by thought and knowledge. That is why it is said that meditation is the ending of knowledge, the ending of the movement of thought.

'The by-product, O Arjuna, of relaxation and happiness, is the ending of all misery and suffering.' The by-product of this relaxation and happiness is the ending of all manner of misery and suffering.

Say that, as an actor, you play the role of Desdemona or Othello, knowing jolly well that you are not Desdemona or Othello. But for three hours there is no duality between the two. You play the role, you do justice to that role. You don't say halfway: 'I am not Othello or Desdemona, I have just come here to act and play the role'. That would take away all the charm of the play.

You play the role of a husband, a wife, a mother, a son, a leader, a teacher, a student, you play the role, doing full justice to it, dedicating all your energies to playing that role, while inside you are aware that the essence of your being is neither the perishable form, nor the stream of thought contained in the consciousness.

The essence of your being is beyond the region of words, thoughts and ideas. The essence of your being is unnameable, immeasurable, indescribable; it is Life itself. Divinity is the essence of your being, not an idea. This is pointed out logically, step by step, scientifically.

We have dealt with five or six verses, which I always call the condensed psychology of *yoga*. The treatment of psychology is throughout the second chapter, but this is a condensation. If somebody asks you what is the psychology of *yoga*, say: it is to enable one to retain the wholeness, the freedom, the sense of indivisibility of one's being, while moving through the drama of relationships, which is our responsibility, because we are born of society, in society and we live in society. We are coming to the end of the second chapter, which, in a way, constitutes the whole message of the *Gita*.

We will have to look back once again to the very beginning of the chapter before we depart from it.

The *Gita* brings to us the message of the science of non-duality. The content of existence is non-dual, say the Vedas, the Upanishads and also the *Gita*. Due to the limitations and inbuilt conditionings of the human organism, our perception of the reality is dual; it takes place on two levels.

That which is tangible and visible, which yields to knowledge and verbalization, is termed by us the manifest. That which cannot be perceived by the senses, which cannot be captured in the framework of thought and thinking, which defies every effort of verbalization because of its wholeness, because of its interrelatedness, we term the unmanifest. The world has a form and Life is formless.

Now, the unmanifest, the invisible, unnameable, immeasurable, being whole, is empty. The unmanifest could be described as the space of emptiness. It may appear to us as having the shape of an egg, which we call the Cosmos. Even the word Cosmos reflects upon our limitations and conditionings behind perception.

The unmanifest is space, it is emptiness, because it is whole. It is non-divisible, non-fragmentable, it is an organic wholeness. Please, let us note this characteristic of the unmanifest, because in the womb of this unmanifest emptiness or space is contained the innumerable variety of the manifest. In the womb of emptiness is contained, concealed, conceived, the manifest. There is no dichotomy between the two.

A child, born of you is as whole as you are; it is another human being like you, having all the creative energies intact. Your child is not a part of you, it is born of you and yet it is another whole being. It is not a part of you like a wheel of a car. In the same way a mountain, a tree, is not part of the unmanifest, they are born of the emptiness of the unmanifest. Every expression in the manifest world of forms, shapes, colours, flavours, sizes etc., every expression is as whole as the unmanifest space is whole.

Every expression that you call manifest, when it emerges out of the emptiness of the unmanifest, brings with it the breath of the unmanifest. So the wholeness of the unmanifest permeates every expression of the manifest, and the manifest is contained in the unmanifest. Do you see the non-duality?

Non-duality or advaita is not a theory, it is not a dogma, it is a statement of fact. The reality of Life is non-dual. When the unmanifest contains the manifest, when the manifest is permeated by the unmanifest, how can you call them two? They are complete by themselves, on their own, in their own right. A drop of water is not a part of the ocean; the quality of water-ness is contained in the drop, as it is contained in the ocean. So, Cosmic Life is not a totality of parts, it is not something assembled by the human genius and integrated into a totality. It is a spontaneous isness.

It is due to its spontaneity that we call it divinity. It is not structured by human thought, human knowledge has not created Life and therefore we call it divine, divinity. Life is holy whether you call it the manifest or the unmanifest. The *Gita*, the messenger of Brahma-Vidya, of the ultimate reality, tells us about this essence of Life. Let us proceed. How did even the idea of duality creep in? Where does it come from? A very interesting question and a very interesting fact.

The creativity in the human organism invented the art of converting sound into a word. The art and science of verbalization is a contribution of the human genius. This verbalization developed into the process of naming, for the sake of recognizing and identifying. Naming and identifying became a medium for relating to the outer world.

Verbalization became a channel for communicating what was happening within the body: communication of the inner, naming and identifying of the outer, both necessary for living together as a society, as a group. Both purposes were served by this invention of language, of verbalization. Thus far no harm done.

But by virtue of naming and identifying, the consciousness got cluttered with names, with words, with associations of ideas and emotions attached to the words, and instead of remaining an instrument helpful for communication, the process of putting words together, the process of developing ideas out of those gathered words, that is to say the process of thinking became an instrument of response.

Duality begins when thought is the instrument of perception and thinking is the instrument of response. When they become the authority for perception and response, that is to say relationship, then they create by their very movement duality. Verbalization as a blessing, and verbalization as a curse, because we did not know how to use it. We don't know how to use science and technology, do we?

Let us proceed to the second fundamental point of the second chapter of the *Gita*. The message is: 'remain in the state of non-duality, remain in the state of silence at the moment of perception, of audition, at the moment of relationship through the senses to the outer world.'

We are avoiding the word meditation at present. Tentatively let us use the word silence. Silence is the non-dual state. You remember what we saw yesterday, that when you think of an object, you go on ruminating about the pleasure the sensual contact had given you in the moment of intercourse with the outer world, interaction with the outer world. The idea of pleasure, the idea of repetition goes on fermenting in the nervous and chemical system.

Did not the *Gita* tell us that a human being, with the help of thought and thinking, creates the complications of attachment? The outer objects are not the cause of attachment. It is the habit of moving constantly, psychically, with the help of the thinking process that creates attachment. And we have seen how attachment distorts perception and response.

In order to remain in the state of non-duality, in order to remain merged in the supreme Cosmic intelligence, as a drop of water remains merged in the ocean, it is necessary to educate ourselves not to be harassed and tortured by the thought process.

Let thinking, let thought, let knowledge be a healthy factor in the consciousness, to be used if and when necessary. But let perception be the result of direct communion between the intelligence contained in you and the intelligence contained in the outer world, which you call the manifest material world.

Matter is energy. Even the words 'material world' are out of date now. Matter is nothing but energy, solidified energy, and Life is nothing but a dance of innumerable energies interacting among themselves. I wonder if you are aware of the fundamental revolution that is taking place in the science of physics. So it seems necessary to retain the state of non-duality.

A tree is beautiful; it lives the essence of non-duality. Mountains are non-dual and so are rivers and oceans and so on. This habit of instigating duality, due to the thought process, has to be transcended. That is the purpose of yoga. It has to culminate into the emergence of a state of consciousness, where there is no authority of thinking, of thought, of knowledge. They remain helping factors, but they are not the active agents. And they have no authority whatsoever on your perceptions and responses. This is the psychology we have seen yesterday.

Now, if you have been with me on this verbal voyage of exploration, let us proceed further. When one remains in the non-dual state or the state of silence, then all knowledge contained in your nervous system, in your chemical system, in drops of your blood, in the marrow of your bones, is intact but not active, intact but not regulating, controlling or directing your perceptions, not colouring them, not inhibiting them. They, knowledge and experience, are the content of your being, because they are the product of the past, the total human past.

There is no denying the existence of knowledge and experience and the conditioning, so no denial, no rejection, no fight against them. The only thing is that we do not accept their authority as the source of perception, as the controller of responses and relationships.

Therefore, absolutely new relationships. The science of *yoga* induces a new relationship with the manifest, with the unmanifest, with the sensual, with knowledge, with verbalization, you know, as if you are born anew, as if you are reborn within yourself.

If the state of non-duality, that is silence and emptiness, becomes the fact of your life, a psychophysical fact of your life, then, as we have seen yesterday, there is the benediction of unconditional relaxation. The whole biological organism becomes unconditionally relaxed.

This word relaxation is not a psychological attribute, it is a word that can denote and indicate the state of the biological organism. It is necessary to note this, because I am going to take you with me to perceive the biology of perception and the chemistry of cognition.

We are living in the era of science and spirituality has to be understood in the context of a scientific approach. Not a dogmatic approach, worshipping theories and ideologies, or the formal structures of religions. The word is never the thing, whether it is the words of the Vedas, or the *Bible* or the *Koran*.

Now, when the movement of thinking, the movement of knowledge, the movement of the past, does not go on within you all the twenty four hours, does not affect the rhythm of breathing, does not affect the flow of the blood circulation, does not create pressure on any of the organs in the body, and the marvellous state of relaxation is there, then only, Krishna tells Arjuna, will you be able to perceive.

The biology of perception requires a steadiness in the nervous system. As long as the thinking process is going on, as long as the movement of knowledge is going on within you, the nervous system will be pressurized, will be tortured by the associations, the preferences, the prejudices, the evaluations, the value structures, by a variety of pressures on the nervous system. Don't think that knowledge is harmless. It is quite a precarious thing, if one does not know how to use it. It could be a poison.

A steady nervous system and a pressure-free chemical system of your body is required for contacting the reality outside of you, through your senses, for the perception to take place as a communion between the fact outside and the awareness inside. A steady nervous system is absolutely necessary.

Otherwise you will perceive only a part of the fact, a fragment of the fact. If there are tensions, pressures, maybe the very act of perception will get distorted. Mutilated perceptions, distorted perceptions are our mental sicknesses, of which we are not aware. And the spirituality of the twenty-first century is going to purge the psyche, disinfect the psyche, of all such distortions and mutilations. There is going to be a holistic approach to spirituality. Please do see this.

Meditation is a holistic state of your being, a holistic way of living and therefore we cannot afford, even for a fragment of a moment, to indulge in distorted perceptions and twisted responses. They are the source of all violence, of all conflicts in human relationships.

The science of *yoga* is a science of purification. You purify your biological organism and the psychophysical structure through Astanga Yoga (spiritual discipline). Then the growth culminates into the dimension of *samadhi*. The science of yoga cannot be limited to the practice of spiritual discipline or a little practice of concentration. It is a path of inner revolution. And if it does not culminate into that inner revolution, converting you from a fragmentary divided human being into the wholeness of your being, then all achievements and attainments in the practices becomes futile.

Without the fusion into the supreme energy of intelligence, which is the perfume of wholeness, life is really drudgery. You drag the days and push the nights, pressurizing yourself to move through so-called relationships. Life and living do not become ecstasy; there is no vitality, no passion, no freshness, no creativity. One is just repeating and projecting patterns. One would like one's friends to live first-hand, living the bliss that is the birthright of a human being. It is not an achievement of a few privileged individuals. It is the consummation of human growth.

The biology of cognition, the biology of perception, requires that the nervous system is steady, like the flame of a candle kept in a corner, not exposed to the vagaries of the wind. The *Gita* uses the words *yukta* and *ayukta*, joined and not joined. One who is not joined to the manifest, as the unmanifest is joined to the manifest, through proper perception and response, his brain is incapable of being steady, he is *ayukta*. He is not joined to the manifest, neither to the unmanifest through awareness.

Awareness is not a bridge joining the two banks of a river; it is like the positive and negative wires joined together, radiating light. The negative of the individual consciousness and the positive of the Cosmic consciousness blended together, that is meditation.

The brain is not steady, and therefore cannot become an instrument of perception. And now, take one more step with me. The emotional aspect, the chemical aspect of one's being, also cannot function properly when the nervous system is not steady, when the brain is not steady. Then the chemical system of one's being, which expresses itself in the form of emotions, wishes, desires etc., also cannot function properly.

The steadiness of the nervous system and the relaxed chemical system, expressing themselves through the act of perception, establish a correct relationship with the outer material world.

If the brain is not steady, if the nervous system is not free of tension and the chemical system is not free of pressures, then this triple unsteadiness results in chronic unsteadiness of the mind. It knows no peace. Peace is the perfume of steadiness. Happiness is contained in peace.

The mind remaining restless all the time, is this not the fact of our daily living? Minds are restless, brains are unsteady, nervous systems are tense. And chemically, either we are shrinking within ourselves through fear, or we become aggressive due to fear. Do you see the abnormality of our daily living? And yet we feel we are normal human beings.

We don't know how to live. We think we only have to solve the problems with our brain, with our knowledge, with our ideologies, with our capacity to inventing high technology and so on, thus we will solve, resolve the human problem. The human problem, the seeds of all human problems are within us, in the triple unsteadiness, the triple restlessness.

If that restlessness is the factual content of our lives, what are spiritual disciplines, *asanas* and *pranayamas* going to do? How are they going to result in transformation, into a state of meditation or *samadhi*? Do you see the point? So the biology of cognition and the chemistry of perception, joined together, will have to be taken care of. The purification has to take place at that level.

The human race has failed on the level of relationships, individually, in families, in organisations, in nations, internationally, and so on. The misery and suffering is due to the failure of unveiling the mystery of relationship, the dynamics of human relationships.

You know, meditation will give you a new dynamics of human relationships, dynamics of harmony, of cooperation, of peace, of sharing Life. We are not learning *yoga* for the petty little achievements of occult powers, and heaven knows what. We are studying the *Gita* or the Upanishads on behalf of the whole human race. We are doing it because of our concern for the misery of our lives and the misery and suffering of the human race. Suffering has to be ended. If psychological suffering can be ended, we can take care of the physical injustices, exploitations, and so on.

Each verse in the second chapter is so pregnant with meaning, containing the whole message of the *Gita*. What is the way out of this triple restlessness or unsteadiness? That is the question lingering in Arjuna's mind. Krishna sees that question written on Arjuna's face, and immediately proceeds.

'The senses have to be educated in the art and science of restraint.' We are coming to a very interesting word: restraint. It is not control. Control is from outside. The mind controlling the senses, the patterns of discipline controlling and regulating the sense organs, in the name of ethics and morality. Restraint is neither discipline nor control.

When the senses are educated, through yoga, to relate to their respective objects, to receive and assimilate what the objects have to give, for the sake of physical survival and existence, not for indulging in unnecessary, unwarranted contact with material objects, educated when to touch the outer object, or word indicating that object, and when not to touch it, then the senses develop restraint. You see, this is an issue of education. Sense organs have to be educated, then the senses develop restraint. The power of restraint is a by-product of sensual education.

Krishna says to Arjuna that if the sense organs are not thus educated, if the senses are not filled with this power of restraint, as a consequence of that education, then it is futile to hope to be able to control your sense organs in the name of discipline, ethics, religion or spirituality. As a sailing ship is led astray by strong winds, in the same way the ship of your mind will be led astray, when the sense organs get tickled by the impressions of the material world.

Controlling, disciplining, suppressing, will not be of any use, only the inner sense of restraint will help. When you try to discipline yourself by giving a pattern, you are using a kind of force. Education is through persuasion, not through coercion. Coercion or even a subtle force does not work with the human organism. It is an electro-magnetic sensitive organism, the more you try to pressurize it, the more it shall revolt. Developing aesthetically a sense of restraint is the way out, not discipline, not pressure, not violence.

Superstitions and beliefs lead to chaos in personal life. Reason, rationality and logic create an inner order. In the same way, educated senses and sense organs develop a restraint to relate where it is necessary and warranted, to relate properly, with accuracy, with precision and otherwise to remain spontaneously in a state of abeyance, of non-action.

Stillness and movement get mingled together. You do not have to take a vow or a pledge of silence or stillness. Action and non-action, silence and speech, stillness and movement, mingle together in a beautiful wholeness and get expressed when relationships require them.

'Triple restlessness will disappear, Arjuna, with proper education of the biological structure.' The dialogue between Sri Krishna and Arjuna is for the sake of clarifying the mystery of Brahma-Vidya, of being aware of the highest truth, and *yoga*, on how to relate to that truth. It is a vertical journey.

If this point is clear, let us proceed to another point, to a very significant verse, interpreted in so many ways, by so many commentators, with whom I beg to differ, whether it be Shankaracharya, Vivekananda, Vinoba or any other. I can share with you only my understanding, not wasting our time elaborating upon theories and experiences of other people. We are here to share Life. The verse is:

'That which is night for all human beings, is day for the *yogi*, and that which is day for all the people, is night for the *yogi*.'

That is the literal translation of the verse. It is a code language. In the whole Vedic literature, ignorance is called darkness; the period of ignorance is referred to as night. The emergence of understanding is called the dawn, and the permeation of understanding at all levels of your being is called day.

All human beings live in darkness, that is to say in ignorance of the nature of the self, the nature of the ego, the mechanism of their mind. They live through it, night and day, and yet they never take the trouble of understanding what is that I, the I-ness. People would go to that sage of South India, Sri Ramana, and say: 'I want to understand.' And the sage would smile and ask only one question: 'What is that I, find out, then come to me.'

The ignorance of the nature of the self is called the dark night. A person who has studied yoga and has arrived at the dimension of inner restraint of the sense organs, of speech, of the functioning of knowledge, the functioning of the brain, of every aspect of the being, has the elasticity of a spontaneous sense of restraint, which does not smell of any outer compulsion, of any rigidity. You know, anything that creates rigidity in life takes you far far away from the path of meditation and spirituality, anything that induces structures and patterns and their authority takes you far away from the path of spirituality. Elasticity, pliability, spontaneity, vitality, unstructured content of the inner being; that is the grandeur of Life. That is Life.

A student of *yoga*, a person who has developed that inner sense of restraint, who has discovered the nature of the ego, that person is no more in darkness about the anatomy of the I-consciousness, the mechanism of thought and its movement, the chemistry of emotion. He has discovered all these aspects of the I-consciousness, he is aware of their clandestine or overt movement and therefore, when the I-consciousness moves in any direction whatsoever, for any purpose or motivation whatsoever, the student of *yoga*, the enquirer, does not take cognisance of those movements. There is no cognition of all the manipulations of the I-consciousness, and therefore there is no response to the vagaries, the whims, the manipulations of the I-consciousness.

People, who live in the darkness of ignorance about the nature of the ego, get harassed by it, tortured by it. But one, who has seen through it, is not affected by that. What happens to his consciousness if there is no cognisance of the manipulations of the I-consciousness, of the divisions and fragmentations that the ego contrives and brings about? What is the content of that consciousness? It is in the state of non-duality, in the state of magnificent silence. It is in the state of emptiness, and therefore tuned into the supreme intelligence permeating the Cosmos.

Human beings whose minds are unsteady, whose brains and nervous systems are unsteady, get affected by the velocity of the past, by trends and inclinations, because of physical or psychological inheritance, because of cultivated habits, theories, ideas, ideologies, they get affected by one or the other, thus distorting their perceptions and twisting their responses. But one who has cultivated the art and science of inner restraint, of a peaceful nervous and chemical system and a steady brain, is awake in darkness and relaxed in turmoil.

I wonder if some of you were exposed, some time or other in your life, to the talks of J. Krishnamurti. He used to ask his audience: 'Sir, are you awake?' Not the being awake as one of the three states of being awake, dreaming or sleeping that we refer to generally. He was a teacher expounding the truth he had understood.

So, when he asked: 'are you awake?', the meaning behind the question was: is there a cognisance of the movement of the ego, are you aware of the duality, the fragmentation that the I-consciousness brings about, are you aware of the limitations of knowledge?

Here, the *Gita* has used the code words: the state of awakening and the state of deep slumber. Slumber and the state of awakening, these two, are very significant words used in this verse, typical words of Vedic spirituality. What more happens to a person who has cultivated this inner aesthetical sense of restraint and who is aware of all the manipulations of the ego? What more happens to him?

And Krishna says to Arjuna: 'have you ever watched the ocean? All the rivers pour their waters into it, but the ocean does not flood the earth.' It remains in its own majestic existence, within the limits of the shore, with indescribable depth and expanse. It is self-contained in itself. Nothing is detracted from its fullness, if the rivers do not pour their waters into it, and nothing is added by the pouring of the waters of the rivers. It is a self-contained being.

Just as the ocean does not grab the water of the rivers, does not deny them, in the same way the senses and the sense organs of a student of yoga do not get affected by the innumerable impressions thrown towards him by the material world.

Now, just a minute, when we see an object, what happens to us? Does it not create a desire to acquire it, to own it, to possess it? The impression of an object, received by the sense organs, results in the awakening of a desire to own, to possess, to relate to it, to derive some pleasure from it. But in the life of a person who has developed inner restraint and feels fulfilled by being alive, the sensual contact with the objects does not result in the awakening of a desire, or of any acquisitive tendency whatsoever.

See the difference. In us it stimulates the acquisitive desire, if not owning or possessing the object, at least acquiring some pleasure from it. But in the life of a *yogi*, the sensations, the vibrations, come towards the body and go back, because there is no one to receive them, no ego or I-consciousness to receive them, to cling to them, wanting to derive some pleasure from them. There is a sense of fulfilment in being alive.

To be alive is a benediction. To be vibrating with the creative energy of intelligence is fulfilment. You know, to be alive is its own fulfilment. To be able to relate to the world through perception and cognition, to relate to it through responses if and when necessary and to relate to the unmanifest essence through awareness, all this is so greatly fulfilling. Such a person feels wholeness. Fulfilment enriches the sense of wholeness within you.

We are coming to the last portion of the second chapter. A *yogi* is always fulfilled in being alive. The sense of being alive, the vibrations of the vitality, of intelligence within, confers upon him such an ecstasy, that he does not move towards the outer world with a begging bowl for seeking pleasure.

And when you do not seek pleasure, there is peace within. It is only a pleasure-mongering mind that creates the fear of pain and stimulates restlessness. Peace is the nature of relaxation, is it not?

So the life of a *yogi* is like a self-contained, self-fulfilled ocean. I hope you are not amused by the analogy that an ocean is as much a being as you and I. The earth is a being vibrating with intelligence, vibrating with Life; the whole planet is a being. In fact there are no 'things', there are only beings, our fellow human beings and fellow non-human beings. I don't know from where the idea of loneliness came to the stupid human mind. Where is there scope for being lonely?

When you are in the midst of the ecstasy of Life, such a state could be called the culmination of yoga. 'Arjuna, this is the ultimate absolute state.' You have touched the absolute, you are merged in Brahman, you are merged in the absolute reality, though you are living in a conditioned, limited human form and organism. This is the culmination of meditation, this is called the state of *samadhi*, of Brahman Nirvana, you may call it the state of satori if you like, use any word.

From this, the culmination of human growth, the consummation of human growth, there is no turning back. There is no relapse into a consciousness haunted and harassed by the centre of the me, compelling you to perceive the world divided into subject and object.

This morning we have seen the essence of Life, non-duality as the essence of reality. We have seen the movement of thought artificially creating the illusion of duality, distortions taking place due to that hallucination of duality. We have seen the necessity of educating the sense organs, that is when to reach out towards the outer and when not to move.

Thus ends the second chapter, referring to the culmination of yoga into the dimension of *samadhi*, which is enriched with the sense of fulfilment. It is the blending of a dual relationship with the unmanifest through awareness and with the manifest through restraint. Energy of restraint and energy of awareness for the outer and the inner. I wanted to do justice to the second chapter.

We had looked at the first chapter, looking at the setting of the dialogue and some historical background of the two persons Krishna and Arjuna and then we focussed all our time and energy on the second chapter.

Next week, if Life so wills, we shall take up the third and the fourth chapter of the *Gita*.

CHAPTER III

YOGA OF ACTION

It is extremely difficult to explain the meaning of certain special words used in the *Gita*, to those who are not acquainted with the Vedic language. Simple literal translation might not help us to grasp the essence of the communication.

The word *yajna*, which is going to accompany us throughout the *Gita*, has been used in the *Rig Veda*, the first and most ancient of the four Vedas, in a metaphysical sense. It says the body of the supreme Purusha, the cause of all creation, was torn to pieces by himself and scattered in all directions in space. And that is how the Cosmos was created.

'Purusha' is a code word implying the supreme energy of intelligence, which is also called Atman, Paramatman, Samvit, Chaitanya, half a dozen terms are used by the same Veda to convey different nuances and aspects of being or beingness. So the explosion of the body of Purusha created the innumerable universes.

'It is my flesh and blood that has been scattered in all the quarters, in all the directions. This is my supreme *yajna*,' says Purusha.

For the twentieth century intellectual human being, the meaning of the word *yajna* would be the pouring of the contents of one's own being into every movement, at every moment. That is the metaphysical meaning of the word *yajna*.

If you share your knowledge with all those who do not have the opportunity to acquire that knowledge, then you are conducting a very sacred and holy action, a *yajna*. Those who have money share the money, those who have knowledge share knowledge. Through devotion and dedication, through service to the Cosmos, to fellow beings, you are also conducting a *yajna*.

We have to learn that it is the responsibility of the human race to share in this Cosmic *yajna*, to join the supreme intelligence, by pouring our wholeness into every action that we go through. Living becomes a constant *yajna*, it becomes the conducting of a *yajna*, a sacred action, a holy movement. It is the act of living that confers holiness on you,

Now, what is the meaning of the word *dharma*? The quality of the act of living, the texture, the fibre, the pouring of the wholeness of your being, doing everything that you have to do with a sense of responsibility, is the meaning of the word *dharma*. *Dharma* is your special unique characteristic. *Dharma* is that action that joins you with the divine. You know, like *yajna*, *dharma* is also a code word.

The *Gita* comes after the Six Systems of Philosophy, after the Upanishads and the Vedas. So the terms used in the Vedas and the Upanishads are taken up by the *Gita*. Those who really want to study the essence of the communications of the *Gita* will have to have some general information about the background.

The word *maya* for example is derived from the root to measure. Maya is measure. What is called *maya*, is the diversity that you see sensually in the manifest world around you. The diversity is the measure of the inexhaustible potential of the unity of Life.

Life is inexhaustible. That is why, through millions and billions of years, the unmanifest has been pouring its infinite, inexhaustible, immeasurable potential into diversity; scores of solar systems, planets and stars, and who knows, other planets and stars that the human race has not yet been able to see. Whenever the Vedas or the Upanishads want to indicate the bewildering puzzling diversity, the innumerableness of expressions, it uses the word '*maya*'.

Not to get obsessed by the variety, but to relate to the material objects, for the sake of decent aesthetical physical survival and sustenance. Not for the attraction or infatuation of the objects themselves, not for the sake of gratifying the desires that diversity stimulates in your consciousness, but because the relationship between the sense organs and their respective objects is the only way to sustain life. The union of the sense organs with the objects gives the joy of the concealed unity. Joy is the experience of the concealed unity of Life. Pleasure is the consequence of the gratification of the acquisitive tendency of the mind. It has nothing to do with joy, or bliss.

Brahma-Vidya, discriminative wisdom, teaches us to enjoy Life. Not to be a pleasure-mongering race, afraid of pain and obsessed with pleasure. This obsession with pleasure, this obsession with fear of losing pleasure, which is called insecurity, and the fear of disagreeable sensations, which is called pain, isolates us from the mainstream of Life.

The same word *maya* is used, in another place, to indicate the infinite power, the supreme intelligence, figuratively personified in the form of Krishna. Not literally but figuratively, poetically. Krishna is looked upon as personified supreme intelligence.

That supreme intelligence is, as it were, talking to Arjuna and telling him: 'look, if you think that you can conquer nature, which is the manifestation of my inexhaustible powers, the inexhaustible potential of my being, if you think that you are going to conquer the content of my being, you are mistaken. All your physical might and psychological tricks will not be able to penetrate the depth of my beingness, the expanse of my being.'

There the word *maya* is used to indicate the power, the potential, the existential essence of the supreme being, which was figuratively called 'my blood and flesh, my body' in the *Rig Veda*.

I can take you as deep as you are willing to dive. The word *maya*, in the Six Systems of Indian Philosophy, is used as a code word to indicate that which is only relatively real, that is to say that which is ever changing. We are born in the Cosmos, where everything around us is in a flux of constant change. Nothing is static, nothing, whether the cycle of seasons, or the cycle of birth, growth, decay and death. The Cosmos is changing its form, its expression of characteristics, its specific qualities, practically every moment. The ever-changing world is real for a moment, is not there the next moment, like the tender flower called shipali, whose life lasts but a few minutes. There are flowers whose blossoming is their decaying, whose birth is a signal of death. So this relatively real and ever changing world is called *maya*.

People translate *maya* into English as illusion. It is an illusion if you look at the ever-changing world as absolutely real. If you understand its temporalness, its mortalness, its ever-changing nature, then you call it relatively real.

This word has been popularised by Shankaracharya, the first exponent of Vedanta. People have translated one of his basic sayings: '*Brahma satyam, jagat maya*', as the eternal beingness is the real, the world (*jagat*) is unreal (*maya*). The word *jagat* is derived from the root which indicates motion, that which is constantly moving. So that which is ever moving is unreal.

That is why Gautama, the Buddha, called it: 'That which lasts only for a moment.' If you get emotionally involved in that, then you generate attachment, which is *dukham* (pain). You are inflicting pain onto yourself by getting emotionally involved in things, which cannot last, by their very nature. They are fleeting. They are changing. You get attracted by one form, one quality, one aspect of it, one characteristic of it, and you want to cling to it. You cannot cling to things that are ever changing. The path of Nirvana is the path of realization in which the world you are living in is a fleeting world of ever changing qualities.

Do you see now that words used in the *Gita* have different shades of meaning, taking it for granted that the reader is acquainted with the terminology of the Vedas, the Upanishads, the Six Systems of Indian Philosophy etc. I do not want to take you into all that, and therefore I was referring to the words in such a way, that you would get the essence of the chapters. The message of the *Gita* is that the consummation of human growth is the state of *yoga*.

A number of times Arjuna is told: 'grow into the state of *yoga*.'

Act in life, in the movement of relationships, without the fever of preferences and prejudices, without creating the psychic clutter of pleasurable and painful memories, of likes and dislikes. They would clutter your consciousness, not allowing the supreme intelligence to flow through your nervous system, flow through your senses, going down to your sense organs, expressing its beauty, elegance, and majesty. This was a clarification of the words *maya* and *yajna*.

Before we proceed, let us look at the word *karma*, the law of *karma*, which is taken up by the Hindu religion as one of its four pillars. But the *Gita* does not belong to the Hindus alone; it is a clarion call of the eternal truth, capable of universal application and implementation, irrespective of country, race or community. Otherwise, we would not take it up here.

We are concerned with the fate of the human race, to which we belong. We are concerned that the human race corrects its ways of living, purifies its ways of living, so that the chronic imbalance of violence, which has spread into the human psyche as a cancerous growth, would be wiped out completely.

The destiny of the human race is to share the harmony of the Cosmic nature. The destiny of the human race is to grow into the maturity of expressing, through its movements and relationships, the elegance of love and the majesty of compassion. This would create a human society worth the name.

We have come to the word *karma*. It is derived from the root to do, to act. *Karma*, that which is acted upon, that which is done. That is one aspect of the meaning of the word *karma*.

Karma is figuratively used to denote your inheritance, your physical structure, your psychological conditioning. They are your *karma*, that is to say, they are the past actions not only of your parents but of your forefathers. So, as a human being, it is your karma to be born in a conditioned human frame.

You can go on analysing the conditioning as the conditioning of your father's side, your mother's side, of the community in which you live, conditioning imposed by the socio-economic structures, racial conditioning, collective unconscious, and so on. You may analyse it for the pleasure of the intellect and the satisfaction of the science of logic that we have created, for gratifying the law of causation that we have created as the foundation of logic, or for the sake of other human creations.

To satisfy all that the *Gita* says: 'your physical structure and your psychological conditioning are your *karma*, your destiny, your fate. In other words, it is your inheritance which you cannot escape.'

There has been a period of twenty-five to thirty years in this century, when a cult had come about wanting to reject the physical and psychological inheritance, reject and escape from all that the human race had given one, such as the sophisticated cultured intellect. 'Run away from it, follow your whims, your urges, your trends.' A kind of reversal in evolution, going back to the animal level. 'Don't think, don't analyse, do what you feel in the name of freedom, whether sexual freedom, sensual freedom, or freedom from religious structures. Reject and try to escape.'

An illusion was created, as if one can reject one's own body, its limitations, its conditioning. What is wrong with conditioning? They call conditioning in India (*samskara*), the essence of culture. It is taming wildness, bringing it under the yoke of reason and rationality. That is culture that is conditioning.

But the behavioural psychology made the word conditioning rather unpopular. If you wanted to condemn something, you would say it is your conditioning. Please let us not use any term in a derogatory sense. When we open our mouth and use words, we should be grateful for those who formulated languages, who coined words. They must have struggled hard to pour meaning into them by the fibre of their relationship and made those words living for us. We are living because others have sacrificed their lives for us. Physically, psychologically, intellectually, they must have toiled, struggled, worked hard, exercised their creative energy to create these words for us, create literature, philosophy, music, fine arts.

Spirituality does not require rejecting anything at all, because it has no interest in acquiring anything. It is interested in perception, understanding, and expressing the understanding through one's movements in Life. That is all there is to what you call spirituality, transformation, meditation. It is a new dimension.

The law of *karma*, to which we are going to refer, is a very comprehensive term, used in different nuances and shades, in different places. Your friend Vimala has spent her childhood and youth studying all this. Before she completed her university education, she had worked hard by herself, studying not less than eighteen commentaries on the *Gita*. And because the reading was for learning and not for acquiring or collecting pieces of knowledge, it has not left any scars behind.

We have seen that you cannot escape the responsibility of action. You cannot escape physically your inheritance, your destiny, your *karma*, your *prarabdha*, that which has already been set into motion. You are interlocked with the universe; you are inter-related with every other being, which is an expression of the Life and blood of the supreme Purusha, the supreme intelligence.

You are related to that ever-sacrificing supreme intelligence, which is pouring itself into innumerable universes, which we call the emergence of universes. Scientists tell us that we don't know exactly how many universes exist, how many solar systems exist, we have come so far across twenty-four solar systems, but there may be many more.

Every human being is like a solar system, related, as the solar systems are related, to the Cosmic supreme intelligence. We, the so-called individuals, the human beings, originate from that supreme intelligence and are interlocked with it. So the urge to express ourselves into our actions, the urge to manifest our essence, is there as our life-breath, as it is the life-breath of the supreme. Do you see our organic relationship?

Physically, psychologically, metaphysically, *karma* is a *yajna* that you have to go through. And those who indulge in sensual pleasures and forget the responsibility of conducting *yajna*, that is to say doing action in order to share, they suffer. They have lived in vain.

The *Gita* uses the word to steal. You steal something from the universe when you do not give anything back. Those who acquire, own and possess only for their self-centred pleasures, they are thieves, they commit a sin against Life. They have lived in vain, says the *Gita*, because the sensual pleasures entangle their consciousness in such a way, that they forget who they are, what they are, and they loose the zest, the passion, the energy, the vitality of being a living cell of the Cosmic intelligence, of the supreme intelligence.

The humaneness of a human being, the inexhaustible potential of creativity contained in a human being, is fulfilled, not so much through acquiring as through sharing, not so much through preserving the talents but through manifesting them for the well-being of all.

As the intelligence keeps the universes together, making it possible for the diversity to move in the wheel of Life harmoniously, so human beings, through their *karma*, through their actions, have to keep the cycle of social life going, the wheel of life, the wheel of *dharma*, a term used in Buddhist and Jain religious literature, the wheel of action going. Whenever they want to denote wholeness, they use the term wheel.

As we share the fullness with the Cosmic Life, let our actions be a *yajna*, sharing with others the best, manifesting our inner fullness, wholeness, creativity, etc. Let no movement be out of inattentiveness, half-heartedness, distraction, irresponsibility. Let no movement be casual, lightly gone through. Do you see how attentiveness, alertness, is necessary, so that action does not become activity?

Activity is always fragmented, partial. A desire comes up, it creates an inner compulsion. You are dragged into a movement. It is not the expression of your whole being, it is only a part, a fragment. How is action to be gone through? How does an action become the expression of our wholeness and fullness? The third chapter gives us a clue.

'Be awake, be alert, be conscious of what you are doing and why you are doing it.' *Dharma* or *yajna* is an action that is gone through with full consciousness. You can't say, after having talked for ten minutes: 'I did not mean this.' Why did you say it, if you did not mean it? Why did you not act accurately? You see, attention, accuracy, precision, is the *yogic* way of living.

Those who are seeking pleasure all the time, or are afraid of the unknown part of life, seeking so-called security through some structure or pattern or some exclusive framework, they get isolated, they turn away from the ever open all-inclusive intelligence and awareness. And in that isolated exclusive corner of the psyche, the manoeuvring, the manipulating of activities, of words and deeds, takes place. Life does not become a *yajna* then, there is something clandestine about it, the need to hide, to conceal, accompanied by the need to pretend. A double life.

The *Gita* tells us to be awake. Let your consciousness be rooted in the awareness of the unity of Life, in order that your movement in relationship, your movement of action, does not degenerate into fragmentary exclusive isolated activity, dictated by fleeting wishes, desires, or compulsive attractions. Let your psychological conditioning be rooted in the awareness of the divinity of intelligence. You are sharing that intelligence.

When consciousness is united with the awareness of divinity, with the awareness of the unity of Life, the imperishableness of the Cosmic Life, then consciousness residing in your cerebral organ, contained in your nervous system, becomes steady. Otherwise the consciousness is always restless. That restlessness reaches the senses and makes the sense organs restless. Then your days and nights become chains of reactions. So beware, beware: not activity but action. Not fragmentary but holistic expression is your *dharma*, is your responsibility, because you are born in a human frame.

Now, will you please accompany me to look at the psychological aspects of *karma*. We have seen in the second chapter the psychology of Sankhya Yoga, the understanding of the supreme truth. Now we will see the psychology of *karma* and Karma Yoga.

Only people who loved Life and who loved living could penetrate into the secrets of Life so vividly, experience them, live them, and be able to verbalize about them. They must have been marvellous people.

In this third chapter there are a number of verses, which tell us that every movement that we go through in our biological organism and psychological structure, in the state of being awake, is conditioned. It is conditioned in the biological organism by the laws of nature, and in the psychological structure by the human past, by civilization, culture. You see the difference in the conditioning.

We have to live in the biological organism, along with the psychological structure, and yet learn, through the art of *yoga*, to transcend the conditionings of both and remain united with the unconditioned. Living and expressing through the conditioned, the limited, the fleeting, the ever changing and remaining rooted in the imperishable, the immeasurable, the unnameable. Using the biological and psychological organism and structure as a vehicle, while remaining rooted in the essence of divinity.

That is why this chapter tells you that the Atman, the imperishable Life content, cannot be destroyed by a sword, cannot be burnt by flames, cannot be drowned in the ocean, and so on. It is all a figurative language. It is a very interesting way of putting across truth through poetry. 'This Atman cannot be cut into pieces, cannot be burnt, cannot be drowned. It is imperishable, it is indestructible. Like the emptiness of space which is the essence of fullness, it cannot be destroyed, O Arjuna,' says Krishna.

The biological organism is the vehicle through which we are going to express. Everything that we do is going to mould, shape, qualify, modify our inner senses and also affect the quality of consciousness. The relation between action and mind, knowledge, memory, intellect, brain, everything that is gone through in the waking hours, affects the quality of the brain, the nervous system, the sensory system, the glands, the muscles, the tissues, you know what you call 'me'.

Whether you act out of habit or because you have accepted some patterns, or because you are compelled by society, whatever you do, everything which is taken in by the senses is called a diet: the way you stand, sit, use your voice, eat, the quality of food that you eat, the way you drink and what you drink, the way you talk and what you talk about. Receiving sound is also a diet. The way you listen is a diet, receiving thoughts is also a diet.

It is not only food that you take, that constitutes your inner being. Everything which is taken in by all the senses, that which is contained, retained, all that is diet. It is the substance of your being. It is constituted not only of liquids and solids that you take, but by what is seen by the eyes, taking in by impressions. This is your *karma*.

When you look at things or human beings with hatred, with anger, with lust, with appreciation, with unfriendliness, with indifference, with attachment, the way you look is the way you are taking in impressions. Because it is attachment that reaches the object and brings back the sensation. This is diet. What you look at, what you listen to, what you touch, what touches you, is diet. We are talking about *yoga*.

The science of *yoga* is only the foundation. The culmination is the dimensional transformation into *samadhi*. A healthy, symmetrical, beautiful body, polished speech, that is the beginning. The science of yoga is the science of dimensional transformation in the content of consciousness, in the content of the human organism, and the dynamics of human relationships. You know, that is the beauty of *yoga*.

The socio-economic conditioning and the traditions of the times, in which the pieces of literature are written, in fact, language itself, is a reflection of the culture and the way of living of a people.

The Vedas communicate the perceptions of reality of the seers and sages of nearly pre-historical times. They are clothed in pure poetry. It seems to me that the nature of reality creates a poet the moment the perception takes place. The nature of reality is poetic, there is rhythm and music in the vibrations of reality, so that without wanting to be a poet, the person gets converted into one and the communications get garbed into poetry.

The Upanishads, which come after the Vedas, have the garb of a dialogue between teacher and student. The perceived reality is conditioned somewhat to the needs and requirements of the student. Thus various aspects of reality are treated in special ways in different Upanishads.

The *Ishavasya Upanishad* gives a communication about reality in one way, and the *Chandogya* gives the communication about the eternal truth in quite another way. The *Katha*, the *Mundaka*, the *Brhadaranyaka Upanishad*, each gives different expressions of the eternal truth, each in the form of a dialogue.

The six Systems of Philosophy, Sankhya, Yoga, Nyaya, Vaisheshika, Vedanta, etc., are in the form of treatises, of essays. They are serious systematized literature. And then you come to the epics, like the *Ramayana*, and the *Mahabharata*. In the *Ramayana* you come across the exposition of the eternal truth, not only through the life of Rama and his spouse Sita, but through practically all the characters depicted in the epic. The same is true of the *Mahabharata*. Clothed in poetical form, it expresses the complexity of human psychology, of human relationships, generating tensions, conflicts and contradictions, due to the complications, leading to violence, hatred, anger, bitterness, greed, etc.

In the *Ramayana*, you will find the character of Rama, the hero, emphasizing certain aspects of truth and reality relevant to the times in which he lived. Thus, the personality of Krishna, representing the eternal truth, speaks in a different way from that of Rama,

When you study such epics as *Ramayana*, *Mahabharata* and *Gita*, which is a part of *Mahabharata*, one has to be aware of two different factors. One is the setting of the dialogue, the setting of the whole drama of human relationships, conditioned by the historical times in which the characters are depicted. And the other is the communication of the perception of reality, the absolute values of Life, communicated through the characters in the drama. So that the temporary or transitory and the eternal get blended together.

Here in the *Gita*, in the dialogues between Krishna and Arjuna, Krishna expounds the science of *yoga* and how it is rooted in Brahma-Vidya, that is in the awareness of the highest truth. The science of *yoga* implies the science of conjoining the unmanifest to the manifest, the science of joining the awareness of the nature of reality to every movement of your life. So action gets rooted in the discriminating wisdom about the real and the unreal.

The science of *yoga* starts with an acquaintance of the body and mind, the brain, acquaintance with its mechanism and way of functioning, the inter-relatedness of all the sense organs, the senses, the energies contained in those senses, and their way of functioning.

The science of *yoga* also teaches how to purify the sense organs, so that the energies contained in them can flow harmoniously and smoothly, without any damage or mutilation. It teaches the way to purify the psychophysical structure, containing the conditionings of the past. It helps us to learn to be conscious of the psychophysical structure and to be aware of that which is beyond, behind, beneath the psychophysical structure. It looks upon education as the only way of purification.

It is a science of non-violence with the body, with the brain, with speech, with the movement of relationship. Education is the path of non-violence, of eliminating the impurities, imbalances and distortions, healing the damage, letting the essential creative energy manifest itself through our being.

Because we are beginning chapter three, one felt it necessary to sum up what we have gone through. In this chapter, the very first verse with which Krishna begins is very significant. He talks about the two different faiths, faith in Sankhya Yoga, in the path of discrimination and knowledge, and faith in Karma Yoga, in the path of action. 'Persons like me have been talking about this since ancient times. Since ancient times I have communicated about these two separate paths.'

When he uses the term 'me' or 'I' he is not referring to the son of Vasudeva or to Krishna, the person who lived for hundred and ten years and died. The terms 'me' and 'I' are used here for all the seers.

These two paths have existed because, psychologically speaking, humanity has these two separate characteristics dominating them.

Reason, rationality dominates among some, which merely makes a person introvert, inward looking. Here, inward means inside the form, making him probe deeper rather than handling the surface. If they look at matter, they go inward to find out what kind of energy is contained in it. If they encounter the energy, they begin to question where the energy comes from. If they encounter emptiness, out of which the energy explodes, they still question. Their questioning goes on.

Psychologically speaking, especially in the western world, they are called introverts. They think, analyse, and get a sense of fulfilment. They feel that they have lived when they have understood intellectually. They do not care for the nature of their relationships, it does not bother them whether they represent or reflect their understanding. Their actual life and relationships follow the social norms and criteria. But inwardly, because they have worked hard in analysing, in discovering, they intellectually understand the truth. This path of reason leading to knowledge, creates an illusion of fulfilment. And yet this path of reason and knowledge, this path of Sankhya, is incomplete, is one-sided, because one does not live by brain alone.

Living implies the movement of your whole being. Your sense organs, your body, the faculties, the energies, their interactions, your speech, your gesticulations, your actions, your reactions, your responses, all that together is called living. Not only the cerebral movement of the most sophisticated type. So Krishna says the introvert aspect of psychology is incomplete, though such persons may acquire and possess erudition, scholarship, and may be called philosophers, thinkers, and so on.

The other predominant characteristic is that of the extrovert. They are attracted to the outer forms, to shapes, colours, flavours, beauty. Variety attracts them and they move from object to object, from activity to activity. They must be doing something all the time, with the outer or inner world, objectively or subjectively. They must express themselves through some activity.

'This incessant activity, which is looked upon as action, Arjuna, is not real action.' Activity out of the inner compulsion of impulses, ideas, theories, ideologies, or activity, born out of inner compulsion of inherited trends, is not action. Action is that holistic movement which is rooted in understanding. They are unlike those who talk about *Karma Yoga*. They must be busy with doing something. They must meet people, talk, react, be reacted upon, otherwise they feel empty.

The first category feels empty unless they read books or discuss, or talk about theories or ideologies, about their opinions and understanding. No necessity of action for them. Both these paths are incomplete and one-sided.

Life is fulfilled by the understanding of reality and its awareness, as much as it is fulfilled in every movement, at every moment, on the biological, psychological, verbal and trans-verbal level of living. Why did Krishna feel it necessary to talk about this duality and their incompleteness? Because he knew what Arjuna's next question would be:

'Krishna, you talk about Sankhya and Yoga, about knowledge and about action. I am perplexed. Please tell me what to do.'

And Krishna, being a real friend, is not at all interested in dictating the answer, in dictating the solution. He is not going to tell Arjuna whether to fight or not. He is going to explain to his dearest friend what is action, what is understanding, what is mind, what is brain, leaving him completely free to act. Because action is the expression of the content of your being.

Your words are the flowers on the creeper of your consciousness, they are your expression. Words which are borrowed, experiences that are manipulated, theories and ideologies that are appropriated from the past, patterns which are imitated from society, all these constitute a second-hand life, a mechanical life.

Arjuna pleads with Krishna, saying: 'I have surrendered myself unto you, please tell me what to do', and Krishna answers: 'Don't surrender your understanding, don't surrender your life.'

We are diving deep into the spirit of the *Gita*, which gives us the essence of the Vedas. And the Vedas stand for unconditional psychic freedom, they cannot stand the touch of bondage at any level, in any manner whatsoever.

It is this crux of unconditional freedom that makes us uncomfortable. We want the religious scriptures to give us something to cling to emotionally, to accept without exerting our brain, without exerting our discrimination. My friends, the *Gita* defies all this.

It seems to me that the *Gita* is related to the complexity of Life. The inter-locked nature of the manifest with the unmanifest cannot be separated. The very existence of the manifest and the unmanifest depend upon each other. The manifest declares the unmanifest as its essence, and the unmanifest declares that the variety of the manifest world, the diversity, is contained in emptiness. The one declares the existence of the other. Diversity decorates the unity, and unity breathes into every expression of diversity.

When Arjuna asks what to do, Krishna answers: 'there are two paths, one of knowledge, and one of action. Both are incomplete, it is necessary to join them.'

Be conscious of the material, the conditioned, the limited. Learn to use the material, the physical, the biological in an aesthetical way. Learn to use all the energies contained in matter, in your body and in the body of the Cosmos around you. And be aware that the emptiness of space is the ocean out of which the bubbles of the material objects come forth and merge back.

Awareness of the eternal and consciousness of the transitory.

Awareness of the universal and consciousness of the particular, with which one has to deal. Living includes relationship with the particular rooted in the awareness of the universal.

Let us proceed. Krishna says: 'Arjuna, it is impossible to live or exist without action. Even if you want to run away from action, please see with me that you can't.' Breathing in and out is action. Drinking a glass of water is action. Thinking a thought is action. When you consume a morsel of food, it is action. You digest it, it is action. So how can one run away from action? One can't.

You may physically isolate yourself from the rest of the world, but even in that isolation, you cannot run away from your body. You are not going to drop the body. So living in the physical body means being related to the physical world, the earth, water, fire, air, space. Life is action, to live is to act.

The question is whether you act haphazardly, crudely, un-aesthetically, or you act properly, with an aesthetical restraint and orderliness, which is beauty. Whether you act scientifically, that is to say without any imbalance, or you go on moving, collecting impurities with every movement, gathering the dust of reactions in every relationship.

Physically it is impossible even to exist without the movement of action. Life is inter-relatedness, which is divinity. We are interlocked with the universe, we are inter-related to the Cosmos. And does not inter-relationship indicate constant interaction?

Nature acts upon you, and you act upon nature. Heat acts upon you, and you act upon the heat. There is a heavy snowfall in the Himalayan range and you get icy cold winds at Abu, seven hundred kilometres away, because the earth is one. Separation is an illusion. Unity is a fact. 'Unity which is inter-relatedness being a fact, Arjuna, you have to act.'

Let us see what is meant by separation being an illusion. Take the example of what you call a river. We are going to look at a fact, at the truth contained in it, and at the reality behind that truth. Fact at the physical level, truth at the psychological level, and reality at the trans-psychological level. The three levels in which we live simultaneously. We are a multi-dimensional race, we are not one-dimensional creatures.

Now, we have all seen rivers. Is a river real? According to the *Gita*, the Vedic literature, and the Upanishads, river is not real, it is unreal. 'Oh, but we see the river.' What do you see? You see a curvature in the earth and water flowing through that curvature. And you see the two banks of the river. Are they two?

The fact optically observed by you may be true and yet not real. The curvature is real. But though there is a curvature, there are not two banks. It is the same earth, it is one. But your eyes see the two banks. The fact can be an optical illusion: your eyes see two banks. The sense of two-ness that the eyes see, and the enumerative cognition to which we are used, makes us say that there are two banks of the river and only one curvature.

We see the river flowing. No, you see water flowing in and through the curvature. All right, then river is an idea, but water is real. No. Water is H_2O. Enquirers of truth, enquirers of the meaning of Life, have to probe and dig and question everything.

So the person says hydrogen and oxygen, together H_2O, is real. Water is the by-product. It is relatively real. You see the result is a fact, which is an optical structure. River is a concept grafted upon a percept. Please do see, it is something beautiful that we are working on together, because purification of perception is the source of transformation. If perception is corrected, the rest takes place by itself. We do not have to move a finger.

River is a concept, which has brought about the usage of 'I see a river'. The curvature is the truth. The fact of two banks is a concept that the human mind has created and the brain has accepted; I stand on this bank and you stand on the other bank, this and the other. The otherness is an optical illusion, but it is felt as a fact. Because human perception is conditioned by the authority of this duality, which is a psychological construct. Without it, human civilization and culture might not have been possible. The grafting of the conceptual level on the perceptual is the source of all civilization and culture. It is something beautiful.

So river is an idea, the two-ness of the banks is an idea. The water flowing has factual content, but the reality is hydrogen and oxygen. Are they absolutely real? No. There is a vibratory friction in the emptiness of space and out of that friction the by-product is oxygen and hydrogen, or carbon dioxide. They are also relatively real. You see fact at the physical level, truth at the psychological level and reality at the trans-psychological level.

An enquirer is he who is not tired of questioning, who probes till the absolute is reached and no further questioning is possible. Not because of my likes and dislikes, not because of my preferences or prejudices, but by the very nature of Life, further questioning is not possible.

In the *Chandogya Upanishad*, a great woman called Gargi goes to the gathering of King Janaka, where the sage Yajnavalkya is expounding the truth. She asks: 'Please tell us, Yajnavalkya, what upholds the skies, what upholds the emptiness of space?' And Yajnavalkya answers: 'That which cannot be verbalized, the emptiness of the skies is upheld by that where mind cannot reach and words cannot penetrate. You may call it the absolute reality, Atman, Brahman. O Gargi. Brahman, the unverbalized, unknowable and therefore indescribable reality holds space. And space holds diversity together.' You see, the Upanishads are the cows, which Krishna is milking for Arjuna, that is the *Gita*.

Krishna says: 'You being inter-related with the Cosmic Life, you cannot escape action. You cannot escape the movement of being related with Life. So why not act? Why deny karma? Is it because you think you have understood the reality and therefore you have no responsibility?'

Responsibility is responding. And responding constitutes relationship. That is how human beings live together. It is the capacity to respond that constitutes relationship that expresses togetherness, that expresses the inter-relatedness of Life and therefore living is to be related. Life is relationship.

Krishna takes Arjuna to another level. 'You have seen that physically you cannot exist without action. Now see with me, morally.'

The sun pours its being, which is light, through its rays. Therefore we live. Water flows and we drink its liquidity, its coolness, its energy of quenching thirst, and therefore we live. The earth gives bountifully and therefore we live. If they were not to pour the content of their being, (the word *yajna*, sacrifice, is used here as the pouring of their being), Life would not be possible.

Pour the content of your being into everything that you do. Every expression is a pouring of the content of your being. Whether you look at a person, or talk to a person; your glance is pouring your being into sight. Words also are a pouring of the content of your being, as the sun pours the content of its being, and the moon, the earth give their bountifulness. It is all *yajna*.

Life without *yajna* is not possible. The earth, space, the sun, the moon, water, trees, they are all conducting *yajnas*. Why should you, in this human form, not conduct a *yajna* in the movement of relationship, by pouring the wholeness of your being into it? Don't keep some aspects of your being for yourself. Don't conceal, don't hide, don't be greedy about preserving the essence of your being.

'They who try to save it, loose it, and they who loose it for my sake, gain it'. Do you remember these words of Jesus of Nazareth, the Son of Man, the divine in human form? Divine is not superior to humanness. Divine is through the human form. When the fullness of Life gets expressed, you call it divinity. The existence of divinity can be felt, it is a sacrifice, it is a sharing, it is a poem, as Vimala would call it.

How can you live without sharing? You go on receiving from the universe and you don't give back to it. Don't you see what the human race has done with this planet, sucking up the resources, misusing them, abusing them, using them roughly and selfishly, not bothering even about its own progeny? What kind of oceans are we handing over to our children, what about the mountains, what about the virginity of the skies, of space? In our greed, lust and hate, fooling about with high technology and robots, etc., we have polluted the planet. If we had learned the art of yajna, if living for us had been sharing, then the planet would not be in the plight it is today.

'So Arjuna, look, morally you are receiving the bounty from the wholeness of Life. Do you mean to say that you would run away and not give anything back? You won't share? That would be a sin against Life.' The path of action means the path of responsible responses and restrained relationships. You cannot run away from that. Rooted in Jnana Yoga and Sankhya Yoga, knowledge and awareness of the highest reality, your destiny is Karma Yoga. You have to act.

The *Isha Upanishad* says: 'doing *karma*, you will be living here, on this planet, a century.' Action, *karma*, never creates bondage. It is lust for the fruit, for the consequences of action which you plan, calculate and bargain for before you begin the action, that binds you, that limits you, that conditions you, not action by itself.

In this third chapter Krishna says: 'look, what have I to gain or acquire in this world? Throughout the whole universe, Arjuna, there is no need for me to come here as the driver of your chariot, to help you, or to help the Kauravas. It is not my responsibility. I am not going to gain anything out of your war, whether you or the Kauravas are victorious.

I have been acting because action is a *yajna*. Living is participating in the Cosmic *yajna* that is going on, it is the dance of sharing that is going on. As the energies share bountifully their own content, human beings also have to share with one another, share with the trees, the earth, the mountains, the rivers, the birds, the animals. They are all co-beings sharing the planet with us.

So morally, Arjuna, act you must. The only thing is that each action of yours should unite you to the otherness of reality. That is Karma Yoga. Action must be the medium to keep you united, conjoined to the awareness of the real.'

What will that do? The awareness of reality, vibrating in every movement of yours, will enable you to deal with the material, the conditioned, the transitory, the temporal, the mortal, without getting unnecessarily emotionally involved in it. It is the emotional involvement, which leads to attachment. You handle things respectfully, with care, concern, affection, you use them with a sense of gratefulness, but you don't get emotionally involved, you don't create a dependency between them and you.

The path of action, the movement of relationship is a *yajna*, which the human race cannot avoid, even if it wants to. Living is being related and relationship is awareness of that and responding to the needs of that relatedness. It can exist along with inner freedom and the wholeness of your being.

Brahma-Vidya, awareness of the supreme reality, teaches you to remain whole, and Karma Yoga teaches you to express the wholeness at the biological, verbal and psychological level.

Today our relationships stink of inner fragmentation and dependency, of the desire to dominate. They don't reflect our wholeness, that which we are essentially. The *Gita* is going to teach Arjuna to grow into the state of *yoga*, of inner spontaneous equipoise, to retain and express that. 'Retain the wholeness and freedom in action. Determine to respond to the needs of your role in life. Wake up, my friend, and shake off all weakness or cowardice that has come up in your heart.'

So far we have looked at the first nineteen or twenty verses of chapter three. The message of the *Gita* is to share in the process of constant sharing, which is *yajna*, with the awareness of our inter-relatedness, which is the unity of Life.

The message of the *Gita* is to live with the mortal, the temporal, the transitory, the material, because we ourselves are encased in a human form, which has a beginning and an end. The beginning and the end are to be respected, the process of growth and decay is to be respected and through all this, we conduct the *yajna* of sharing. Life is fulfilled in pouring the content of our being, because to live is to be fulfilled. There is no fulfilment apart from the movement of Life and living. So the *Gita* is teaching us the *yoga* of Life, the *yoga* of living.

The action as activity leaves impressions on your biological organism and on your psychological structure. If you go through movements and relationships hurriedly, if you go through activities thoughtlessly, recklessly, carelessly, then scars of those half-lived activities will be there, scratches on the inner being, scratches of both pleasure and pain. Half-lived activities, half-done jobs, will leave un-verbalized dissatisfaction. It can leave un-verbalized tension behind, because you had not gone through them completely.

It is only when you live thoroughly, at every moment, fully pouring your whole being into it, that pouring of your being becomes an act of self-expression, an act of dying. Nothing gets converted as a residue, called memory, because you have lived so fully. The pouring, the doing of *yajna*, the expression of the wholeness of your being, was so fulfilling, that you did not want anything back from it. You lived, you did, you died, so that the next moment you are reborn.

We are coming to the law of *karma* and the law of reincarnation. Unfortunate words which have been used rather wildly, doing great injustice to them.

If you would like to live, be awake and alert and do not indulge in fragmentary activities, which will become the source of psychological misery. Inattentive fragmentary incomplete hasty activities will become the seeds of further suffering. Learn to do *karma*, learn to live every moment and move through every movement with wholeness. Let every movement be a sacrifice, a *yajna*, a pouring, a sharing, so that no imprints will be left behind.

The eyes of a *yogi* are open and the sight sees objects, but a *yogi* does not look at them and therefore nothing is registered in the brain as memory. The *yogi* moves through action, perhaps throughout the day, surrounded by a variety of friends, on which the person has to act and yet every action, every movement, every relationship, is a breath of wholeness. And therefore nothing is registered inside as likes, dislikes, preferences, prejudices, which are the result of fragmentary living, the result of imbalanced living, the result of impurity of inattention, of cruelty or callousness.

Spirituality is the science of living. I am not throwing around words lightly. It is something holy, something serious and fascinating. If inside there are no scars, scratches, tensions, conflicts generated by unscientific fragmentary movements, then the state of consciousness is the state of something very clean. Emptiness is very clean, isn't it?

You go to the mountaintop, you breathe in the air and you feel it is pure. Space has made it pure or rather made it retain its purity. When you live wholly, from moment to moment, expressing the fullness of your life, that very act of expression becomes the act of rebirth. It becomes the act of dying and the act of getting reborn.

If the activities are manipulated by thought, ideas, ideologies, you calculate according to your ideology, you want to bargain according to your ambition, then your movements are not the expressions of the content of your being, but are the content of conditionings.

If the action, the *karma*, is rooted in thought, then there is endless suffering and endless misery, because people around you are also conditioned by the thought structure. They also bargain, calculate, manipulate. They struggle and, in the name of relationship, there is a constant battle of self-centred defensive movements. Our life is a battleground, where self-centred defensive movements are trying to drag the other person towards itself and defend itself against others.

You know what happens in families, in organisations, at social, national, and international levels, both individually and collectively. What we call relationships is drudgery. You drag yourself through them, because they are isolated, defensive, fragmentary, self-centred, movements. Please do see.

To move out of this dimension of isolated defensive movement and open up, that is the essence of religion. Religiosity is to be rooted in the wholeness of Life, so that living does not become a spiritless dry business of dragging, pushing, pulling, but you are whole, you are vital, passionate, never stale. I have elaborated a little on this, because the chapter makes a very interesting point, namely that a *karma-yogi* moves through Life without getting wearied, without getting tired, without getting bored.

Karma Yoga or the path of action is not a path of mechanistic repetitive movements born of patterns of behaviour, of psychological structures, of ideologies. The path of action is not the path of slavery, being dragged or whipped into motion. If thoughts and mind whip you into motion, then it is not *karma*, it is not the *yoga* of action any more.

The Yoga of Action is the path of freedom, as Sankhya Yoga is the path of freedom. Unless there is inner freedom, how can there be harmony amongst us, how can there be an urge for spontaneous causeless cooperation with one another? Unconditional inner freedom is the most urgent requirement of the human race.

In order to have a healthy consciousness, it is necessary to move in Life remaining awake, alert and responsible. You do not get wearied and you do not tire others by your behaviour. That person is alive whose presence, whose actions, do not cause any exhaustion, weariness and boredom to others, and who does not get bored or weary or exhausted after going through actions or movements.

'That is my devotee, very dear to me, who lives in human society as the fish live in water They do not get frightened by the powerful waves in the water. As the fish live in water without fear, drink the water, are sustained by it, and by the air contained in the water, so are my devotees who understand me and live in meditation. They live in the ocean of supreme intelligence, rooted there, and move intelligently in the world. Hence Arjuna, if you want to live, be a *yogi*.'

A last point. Your action, gone through out of inner fullness and wholeness, becomes virtual meditation. *Karma*, action, becomes *dhyana*, meditation. You do not have to sit down and spend hours in meditation. The movement of Life and living is a dynamic meditation.

If your action is not an activity, if it is not fragmented, if it is not manipulated, if it is not dictated, if it is a spontaneous response of the fullness of your being, to the fullness outside of you, then the path of discriminative wisdom, Sankhya Yoga, the Path of Action, Karma Yoga and the path of meditation, Dhyana Yoga, all three mingle into one. If these points are clear, come with me to the battleground, where Krishna and Arjuna are standing.

Why has Arjuna to begin this war and fight? Because it is the *karma* the Pandavas had built up systematically, along with the Kauravas, not only because they were born in a warrior caste.

The identification with the caste system, affecting the psychological structure of Indians, is a reality. How did they create the caste system, is an issue quite independent of the message of the *Gita*. Because, in the *Gita*, Krishna says: 'based on the characteristics and the nature of the action, the division in psychological structures came about.' He does not talk about caste. He only talks about various trends in human psychology. Some love knowledge, study and learning, and they dedicate their lives to the study of knowledge. I would call Einstein a Brahmin, because he had dedicated his life and energy in the pursuit of science.

That Arjuna had to fight had nothing to do with the caste system, which came about in India. Krishna tells Arjuna to fight, not because he was born a warrior, but because his whole psychological structure and biological organism was trained for fighting. His psychological reactions were of a fighter, of a warrior. And what had happened between the Pandavas and the Kauravas had brought them to the point of war. After the failure of the peace negotiations, there was no choice left to the Pandavas, who were committed to resist the injustices and the cruelty of their cousins the Kauravas. There was no choice left to Arjuna but to fight.

So Krishna says to Arjuna: 'you are going to fight, not because you hate them, not because you are going to punish them, but because you had built up your *karma* in such a way, that it is your responsibility now to respond according to what was done to you and for what you have been trained. All the efforts through negotiations for peace having failed, you have no choice. If you fight because you hate Duryodhana, who has insulted and humiliated you, if you fight out of that hatred or anger or resentfulness, then it will not be *karma*, it will not be sharing in the universal sacrifice.'

You come across people who spend their life in social service. If behind the social service there is the idea of charity: 'people are suffering, so I must do something', it is the ego, the I-consciousness, dominated by a kind of concealed clandestine self-righteousness, by a superiority complex, which wants to give. Please do see this. So if that social service, that Karma Yoga, is contaminated by un-verbalized clandestine ego instinct and impulse, then the person may go on serving the society for sixty, eighty years, it will not be the life of a *karma yogi*.

It is not a physical biological activity which makes you a *karma yogi*. A person who wants to earn money to become rich, he may work hard for twenty hours a day, he may forego his meals, forego the pleasure of the company of his family, he may forego so many things for the sake of becoming rich, yet he is not a *karma yogi*.

In Karma Yoga there is no possibility for the process of becoming. The possibility is for expressing your being. It is a display of beingness, rather than engagement in the process of becoming.

So if people say: 'we have been working for forty years,' OK, you have done good work, but that does not become Karma Yoga. Some may spend their lives with books, discussing their knowledge, displaying their intellectual collection. That does not mean that it is Sankhya Yoga.

It is only the awareness of the imperishable indestructible all-pervasive all-permeating intelligence, the awareness of the unity of that intelligence with the diversity, that is the manifest world, and an attitude of respect and sanctity towards both the unmanifest and the manifest equally, whatever you do, that becomes *yoga*. Then, whatever is done, is done out of love. You know what love is? Ever sensitive alertness of intelligence is love. Love is a perfume. So whatever is done out of love cannot harm, does not harm. It doesn't harm you, it doesn't harm others.

CHAPTER IV

YOGA OF RENUNCIATION OF ACTION THROUGH KNOWLEDGE

It seems necessary to refer to aspects of symbolism, incorporated in the Vedic culture and referred to in the *Gita* by Krishna himself. Symbolism constitutes a significant aspect of culture, because people at large find it difficult without it, to have a sustained awareness of the fundamental principles of religion, or the fundamental aspects of reality. Along with the verbalized description, decorated by concepts and ideas, human society developed a variety of symbols, which have been kept alive through formal structured ceremonies called rituals.

We have seen the metaphysical and philosophical aspect of *yajna*, which refers to the act of pouring the fullness of your being in every movement of Life. *Yajna*, as a traditional formal religious ceremony among the Hindus, came about to educate the people and get them into the spirit behind the symbols.

As a formal religious ritual, *yajna* implies offering. It has a traditional beautiful form also. *Yajnas* were born in the agricultural civilization, when production was plentiful. So those who wanted to conduct a *yajna* would collect sandalwood, rosewood, wood that had a natural scent and they would take a handful of rice, which historically might have been the staple food of the Aryans and represents nourishment; a handful of sesame seeds which contains oil and represents love or affection and they would have clarified butter or ghee, representing light and the warmth of Life. They would collect such things as offerings.

A person would collect all these things, make a fire, sit down by it, along with his wife. The *yajna* was never done by a man alone. The couple represented a wholeness, the sharers of creative energy, sharers of Life. So they would sit there and they would offer a few grains of rice into the fire and say: 'though I have produced it, it does not belong to me. But for the principle of Life and fire I could not have produced the grains in the field. So I am offering them back to the Cosmos, I am offering them back to the principle of fire, to the principle of Life.'

Different *mantras* would accompany these symbolical actions of offering rice, ghee, sesame seeds, sandal wood, into the fire, saying: 'I offer this for the welfare of the Cosmos, I offer it for the well-being of all living beings.' Beautiful mantras. Most of the Ayurveda refers to a variety of *yajnas*, giving details about their methodology, technique, and so on.

Remembering all that, Krishna says to Arjuna: 'Just as those who perform *yajnas*, giving offerings to the principle of fire, which is the principle of purification, which represents the sun or the principle of light in the Cosmos, so also every human being has to perform a *yajna* in his own body.' And how is that *yajna* performed? By offering the gross to the subtle, and offering the subtle to the still more subtle.

Very briefly, at the outside of your body are the sense organs, the eyes, the ears, the nose, the hands, the palate, etc. These sense organs have been trained through centuries to react to their respective objects. So sight contained in the eye immediately gets in touch with the objects around it, and discriminates the light, size, shape, weight etc. It is an involuntary activity by the sight contained in the eyes. So is the involuntary organic activity of audition contained in the ears, as is the faculty of smelling in the nose, and the faculty of feeling the touch in the seven layers of your skin.

These sense organs contain energies and they have been trained to react. It is not within your control to hear or not to hear sounds. When you are awake, audition takes place, impressions get recorded in the inner system and the psychological structure decides what to do with them. You cannot avoid the contact of the sense organs with the outer objects in the Cosmos.

Now, the conditioning or the patterns of reactions in which the sense organs have been trained, should be offered as an offering to the mind or to the psychological structure, which has knowledge, which also has discriminative wisdom, if it has cultivated it.

The patterns of reaction are sorted out and analysed by the discriminative wisdom contained in the mind, so that the sense organs do not drag you and the biological impulses do not push and pull you. In other words, those reactions, those patterns, are offered as an offering to the thought structure.

Thought by itself cannot take a decision, because it can be attached to a tradition, it can be afraid, it can be inhibited by ambition. So the value judgement passed by the thought structure should be offered, as an offering, to the intelligence, which is still a more subtle energy than intellect or thought.

Gross are the sense organs. Subtle is the mind, more subtle than the mind or the thought structure is intelligence. But beyond the energy of intelligence encased in a human body, is the Cosmic intelligence, which is all pervading, all permeating, non-individuated, non-divided and therefore more powerful, more free than the intelligence embodied or encased in the human body.

'When you decide what kind of action you want to go through, O Arjuna, through meditation, through *yoga*, let your intelligence be tuned into the Cosmic intelligence, let your intellect be subservient to your intelligence and let the sense organs be subservient to the brain.' It is a beautiful description.

Krishna says to Arjuna: 'you, who are the progeny of King Bharata, due to whose name India is called Bharata, please learn this art of performing a constant *yajna* in your body, so that the action on the physical, the verbal, and the psychological level is purified by exposure to the intelligence, by the exposure to the Cosmic supreme intelligence. Such purified action would not constitute any bondage.

Look at me. What have I to gain out of the war between you and the Kauravas? I do not want to gain anything. I stand by truth, I support the course of justice, and I help those who stand up for truth, justice and freedom. Look at me, I have nothing to acquire, I am self-contained, and yet I act.

No action of mine has ever become a bondage for me. Why don't you learn from me, Arjuna, this art and science of purified action; action washed clean and correlated to the perspective of the whole Life? It does not become a fragment of your life, but becomes the expression of your holistic perspective, your holistic awareness and the urge to manifest that awareness and wholeness in the movement of relationship.'

Now let us proceed to the fourth chapter. Let us turn to a very interesting opening by Lord Krishna. At the beginning of the third chapter he had pointed out the two distinct characteristics, the temperamental leanings among human beings, some being introvert, and some extrovert, some being attracted to the path of knowledge, and some infatuated by the path of action.

He then proceeded to point out that these two paths are partial and fragmented and how the two paths of knowledge and action had to be conjoined, so that every action is rooted in the understanding of the real and the unreal.

Now here, at the beginning of chapter four, Krishna says: 'whatever I am pointing out to you, O Arjuna, does not belong to me as a personal truth. I am not giving you some new idea or a new experience, as a property of mine. I am re-stating the eternal truth to you. This truth has been stated by ancient seers and sages.'

A very interesting expression, which might confuse non-Indians. He refers to the ancient sages and seers as 'I' and 'me'. 'I have told this imperishable *yoga*, the eternal truth, to them (and he mentions the names of Indian kings of pre-historical times), and now I am telling it to you.' It is a code language. In the spiritual realm of Indian life, of oriental life, when a person transcends the circumference of personality, when a person transcends the I-consciousness, the ego-consciousness, he gets converted into a seer, a sage and belongs to the race of seers and sages. Those who perceive the eternal truth constitute a race by themselves.

Buddha also refers to the Buddhas that had been before him. In the same way Krishna refers to bygone sages and seers as 'I', ' I have told this...' Once you see the truth, you do not remain an individual born of such and such a person. You ascend to the race of seers and sages and belong there. So figuratively he identifies himself and says: 'I have told this imperishable *yoga*, the eternal truth, long long ago, in so many ages, in so many centuries. It has been told by me many times.'

When truth is verbalized by a seer, it is impersonal. Not that the truth belongs to him or her. He or she is only the conveyor, the communicator, the perceiver. Truth is always impersonal. Krishna is pointing out, in the first three verses, this characteristic of eternal truth as being impersonal, communicated by different individuals at different times in different ways. That is the beauty of human life.

But here, in India, the Hindus have interpreted this chapter, perhaps the whole of the *Gita*, as if Lord Krishna was the sole incarnation of total divinity. He was the perfect superhuman being and therefore they had to create him into an idol, install him into a temple, worship him, chanting and dancing in his name. You know, people like to organize truth and build dogmas and sects around it. But truth, by its very nature, is impersonal.

So Krishna narrates, in a very amusing way, the names of the kings who have been exposed to the truth. But now, in the time of the Mahabharata, that pristine *dharma*, the essence of human life, has been clouded over by the dust of ambitions, lust, desires, greed, hatred, violence. And whenever the real essence of eternal truth is thus covered up by the dust of human emotions, by conflicts, tensions and violence, the unmanifest bursts forth into a human form and conveys the same eternal truth once more. The divinity bursts forth, as it were, in response to the agony and pain of the human race, which by its stupidity has put itself under a heavy stress and strain of untruth, cruelty, violence, hatred and so on.

Whenever the stress on the human psyche becomes unbearable and the agony of it tortures the human race, there appears a teacher, who points out the eternal impersonal imperishable truth and points out how to correlate the truth to the respective conditions of that time. Krishna is trying to correlate the eternal truth, for the sake of Arjuna and through Arjuna, for all human beings living in that century. He is teaching through Arjuna, how to correlate to their problems, their challenges.

The responsibility of every teacher is only to correlate the eternal truth to the time-bound challenges of the age in which the teacher appears. So, sometimes devotion is emphasized, sometimes knowledge is emphasized, sometimes the formal structure of rituals is emphasized, sometimes meditation is emphasized. And due to a variety of emphases, an illusion is created as if the emphasized point is a path by itself.

The emphasis is due to the needs of the time. Buddha and Shankara had to emphasize the rejection of formal ritualism and traditions, because the people living in this land were so enamoured of the glamour of religious ceremonies and rituals, that they had forgotten the very purpose for which the symbolic ritual had to be gone through.

Buddha never mentions the word god. He only mentions the necessity of analysing that which is, finding out how there is nothing permanent. Therefore one should not get attached to the ever-changing impermanent drama of the material world.

He talks about Nirvana. A mind that has renounced all attachment to the transitory is in a state of Nirvana. A mind that has renounced all belief in theories and ideas imposed upon the divinity, converting the divinity into god, was emphasized by Buddha. And Shankara also emphasized renunciation, *sannyasa*, because the hollow empty ritualism and formalism had covered up the understanding of the fundamentals.

So please do see with me why Krishna says: 'what I am telling you, Arjuna, is not my idea, it is an ancient truth.' Truth shall always remain ancient and eternal, though conveyed and communicated in different ways, in different centuries, by different embodiments of divinity.

Arjuna had his share of stupidity in not understanding the spirit behind the words of Krishna. He says: 'Krishna, you were born fifty or sixty years ago, how could you be there when those ancient kings were born? They were born thousand and thousand of years ago.' He was measuring time by human calculation. He did not understand the figurative, poetical language of Krishna, when he says; 'I get embodied in a human form, whenever the human psyche is under stress.' He thought Krishna was referring to himself as the son of Devaki and Vasudeva, the particular personality.

The box in which you keep jewellery is not the jewellery. In the same way, the embodiment in human form, which contains perception, awareness and vibrations of the eternal truth, is not limited by the human form. A seer appears to be a person, but has impersonal content, because the centre of the I, the me, has disappeared completely. It is wiped out as an agent of perception or response. It lies defunct, as it were, in some anteroom of the human psychology. It has no role to play, except provide words, provide references to memory, whenever necessary.

So we have to learn from this chapter and this communication that the incarnation, that is to say the individuation of wholeness and fullness bursting forth in times of crisis, when religion is forgotten and the riot of anarchical desires and chaotic thoughts torture and harass men, is an event, a global event. Please do see.

The emergence of a teacher is a global event. It is the response of the divine to the needs of the human race. The human race cannot say: 'now is the crisis, therefore we will create a teacher, we will carve out a teacher out of someone.' It is a mysterious aspect of Life. Just as the emergence of universes out of the emptiness and fullness of space has no logic behind it, no cause, no purpose, the descent of the supreme into a human form among human beings is a Cosmic event, defying all human effort.

These verses of the fourth chapter, from the third to the ninth, have been a ray of hope to the people living in India. In fact, they have been like a double-edged sword. They have done some good by providing hope to the downtrodden, the underdog, the exploited ones, in that some day, in some way, from somewhere, a saviour would come.

But it has also done immense harm to the human psyche in these parts of the globe, because the hope of tomorrow became an inhibition, disabling the human psyche. They lost the urge to respond to the injustices and exploitations of the moment. With bend backs and bowed heads, they went through the humiliating exploitation of the power-hungry and money-hungry kings, rulers, priests and what not.

This might help you to understand the Indian psyche, even in present times. It is not non-violence that holds them back from resisting the cruelty of domination, the deprivation of their fundamental freedoms, their civil liberties, economic exploitation, the humiliation of the caste system, and the ideas of status and gradation attached to it. You see a mentally disabled race occupying the country, because of the misinterpretation of verses like these. Religious books can become poison, unless they are understood and interpreted correctly.

When the human mind gets entangled in symbolism, in rituals, in concepts and in verses like these, where Krishna says: 'I will come century after century, O Arjuna, for the protection of the good people and for the destruction of the evil-minded, for the exposition of religion, I will come down to the earth, and save them', one trembles even to utter these words. Unless one is acquainted with the mystery of Life and the impersonality into which a seer, a sage, a yogi, gets transformed, such verses can become sources of psychological slavery.

Your friend has been born and brought up in this country, you can see the sorrow and agony she goes through and has gone through, when she had to be a witness to all this in the name of religion. 'We don't have to do anything, the saviour shall come, the redeemer shall come.' Loss of self-confidence, loss of self-respect, loss of a sense of responsibility and the atrophy of the creative energy, all that in the name of religion and spirituality. Can you imagine?

When eternal truths are attached as an appendage to personalities, when such truths are claimed as properties of certain individuals, then the harm begins. You arrest the growth and you strangle the potentiality of the human race.

In the fourth chapter, Krishna is using figurative poetic terminology, verse after verse, which is the way among the race of seers, those who are transformed into supra-mental consciousness, who live in the dimension of meditation, of dimensional transformation.

What I am trying to share with you, is the Cosmic law of responding to the needs of the manifested world. The unmanifest responds to the needs of the manifest. As long as the manifest indulges in its unscientific, unhealthy ways and does not realize that the misery, the sorrow, the pain, the agony, is due to their own actions and their own thoughts, their own conflicts and contradictions, there is no response from the unmanifest, as it were.

But when, in the human race, sections of people scattered over the planet begin to realize that something is amiss, that somewhere we have taken a wrong turn as a race and that it has to be corrected, and they feel they cannot correct this by themselves, they require some help, they begin to enquire, they begin to seek, they begin to question, they begin to revolt.

When the human psyche is in such a turmoil and is on the point of exploding, like an earthquake, a psychic quake as it were, then the response comes in the form of some human being expounding the eternal truth again, the imperishable *yoga*, the path of light, the path of clarity, the path of sanity. And the turmoil subsides. That is how the cycle of Life moves on.

Human beings, being what they are, there is this darkness of ignorance about their own nature, ignorance of the self, Atman. There is no self-knowledge; there is ignorance about the nature of reality. And in this darkness of ignorance, crimes get committed, follies get made, mistakes occur. In order to dispel the ignorance comes the Teacher. It seems to be a principle of Life itself. Like the laws of nature, causation in psychology, this compassion in the trans-psychological world seems to be the principle, for lack of a better word.

Arjuna had felt the pain, the agony of the whole drama of violence that the Kauravas and Pandavas had structured together. While he was busy preparing for war, he had not realized what disaster they were bringing on themselves, what dance of destruction they were going to indulge in. But after all the preparations were met and he was physically encountering the agencies of destruction in the form of human beings facing each other as the armies of the Kauravas and the Pandavas, then suddenly he was shaken, not only by dejection and depression, but by sorrow, by agony.

'Is this the fate of the human race, this violence, this destruction? Why have we done it, what is it in our hearts that has dragged us to do this?' It is only when Arjuna's agony, pain, anguish, burst out and he begins to question, that Krishna responds. Till then Krishna had been a witness who knew everything, who understood everything. Divinity is not assertive, it responds, it never asserts.

If Krishna had told the whole *Gita* not on the battleground of Kurukshetra, but in the palace of the Pandavas, I wonder if Arjuna would have listened at all. For he was busy preparing for war, as we are busy in the industry of war, in trade and commerce, in destruction. What are weapons for otherwise? The economy of countries depends on the industrial production of arms and ammunitions, seeking markets for them in unfortunate countries, which are torn by inner strife and conflict.

So please do see that the state of agony, of pain, of utter dejection and frustration, has also a dynamic power in itself. When sorrow is felt, it has a sharpness. It does not allow you to breathe, it makes you restless. There is a dynamic power contained in sorrow, which comes about through personal suffering, pain and agony. Joy is different from pleasure. Sorrow is a different dimension, qualitatively different, from ego-centred, self-centred suffering or pain.

When it encompasses the destiny of the whole human race, sorrow gives one a holistic perspective. When you sit by the dead body of your beloved, your mother, father, husband, son, friend, whatever, it begins with a sense of personal loss, and it develops into sorrow for the whole human race. 'Is this the end of human life?' You run around, you earn money and you do everything for fame, name, property, and this is the end one day? Sorrow lifts you up from the dimension of self-centred suffering and pain, self-centred hurt, to global human consciousness of pain and hurt of all, along with you. So the dimension of sorrow has its own dynamic power, strength.

It is necessary to look at two important points communicated by Krishna to Arjuna. What is called action is very complex, the complexity of the nature of action or *karma* borders nearly on the verge of mystery. The nature and functioning of *karma* is mysteriously complex.

'You will have to learn, Arjuna, to perceive the non-action contained in action and action contained in non-action. Wise people call that person responsible and knowledgeable, who is capable of seeing action in non-action, and non-action in action.'

It should not be very difficult to understand the connotation of the words action and non-action, if we turn to daily living, to the movement in our personal living. Who is acting or what is action when we act out of habits cultivated since childhood? Is there a movement at the level of intelligence, at the subtle most inmost depth, at the deepest chore of our being? Is there any movement there? Perhaps none.

Because, while repeating a pattern of behaviour, a mode of conduct since childhood, which might have been absorbed or assimilated unconsciously, unintentionally, but which has become a part of our life in that repetitive, mechanistic movement of the brain and the sense organs, the chore of our being is not touched. And therefore movements, which are repetitive and mechanistic in nature, which are a continuity of the past, have no spiritual quality at all.

One may go to a temple, a mosque, a church, sing hymns, chant *mantras*, go to holy places, do all sorts of things because it is a tradition sanctioned by society, accepted on belief or accepted on some authority; this is a movement of the past, of the known, a movement of society, of the forefathers. It is not your action. And therefore, going to a temple five times a day has no virtue in it, no sacredness, it is as good as non-action, because it is not you, who voluntarily rooted in your understanding, is doing something.

It is only your personal movement or action, born out of your perception or understanding, that can have the quality of spirituality or virtue. If lives are spent in repetition, in projection of the past, in the continuity of tradition, allowing our bodies and brains to be used by religious, social, economic, political authority, for the continuation of certain patterns or structures, then Krishna says: 'there is non-action, though physically and outwardly you may appear to be very active. It is the past that is acting through you, not you.'

So please, do see the mysterious complexity of *karma* or action. It is only when the subtle most inmost chore of your being, which is intelligence, moves, exercises itself through the brain and the sense organs, that the action becomes your action.

Now take another example, somewhat different. You are sitting in a chair, or lying on a bed and people think you are not moving, so you are not doing anything. But inwardly you are busy with your reactions, memories, wishes, inclinations, anxieties. You are either brooding or you are torn by anxieties, worries, or you are re-collecting experiences of pleasure or pain. Inwardly, the psychological structure is moving though outwardly the body is motionless, motion free. People might think you are relaxing, but you are jolly well busy, moving furiously with memories of the past or ideas of the future.

'This outward apparent non-action does not result in relaxation, Arjuna. It also has no virtue.'

As the outward incessant activity, repetitive and mechanistic in nature, has no value, this apparent non-action or apparent relaxation also has no value whatsoever. Apparently a non-action, but inwardly very active. Or apparently active and inwardly motionless.

'So Arjuna, you have to be very observant to discriminate what is action and what is non-action. It is the voluntary action born out of your understanding that can have a spiritual quality. A person going through such actions, such *karmas*, can be called a *karma yogi*.'

You remember how Krishna had warned Arjuna, in the beginning of chapter three, not to follow the partial compartmental path of knowledge (*Sankhya*), nor the partial compartmental path of outward action (*karma*). He has been emphasizing the need of action or *karma* to be rooted in, born of the deepest chore of one's being. Unless the movement in relationship is rooted in intelligence, it will not join you to the Cosmic intelligence.

Karma has to be *yoga*, that is the *yoga* of action. *Yoga*, the state of *yoga*, the state of equanimity, of equipoise, that is of inner poise and sensual balance, results only when movements on the physical, verbal and psychological level, on the mental level, are rooted in the exercise of intelligence which is available to each one of us.

It is the tender soft voice of intelligence in every human heart, which whispers time and again when one goes astray and very softly points out what is false and what is true. We are so busy listening to the trumpets of desires, of impulses, of ambitions, so that either we neglect the soft tender voice of inner intelligence, or we ignore it if we happen to hear it.

Krishna is asking Arjuna to learn to listen to the inner voice of intelligence and see that every movement is in harmony with the suggestions of the inner voice. The inner voice is not aggressive. It is not even assertive. It makes its presence known to us, noticeable to us, giving hints, intimations of its existence, and leaves us completely free either to listen to it and act upon it, or ignore it and go our way.

I am putting this very briefly. About eleven verses have been spent by Sri Krishna to explain the mysteriously complex nature of *karma*, describing the quality of religiosity, of spirituality, or otherwise. A very interesting portion.

Arjuna listens to Krishna and says: 'look here my friend, how do I
learn to listen to the inner voice, how do I learn to discriminate the
whisperings of ego, of vanity, pride, the whisperings of the I-
consciousness from the tender compassionate whispering of the
inner intelligence? I don't know how to discriminate between the
two. I always hear the dictates of the ego, the compulsive
motivations. So how can I discriminate?' A fascinating question.

Now we come to a point, which we have to take into consideration.
We are here studying the *Gita*, not listening to Vimala. We are
listening to the message of the *Gita* conveyed as objectively as
possible by a friend.

Sri Krishna points out the necessity of living in the company of a
person who has gone through dimensional transformation, in whose
Life, out of the ashes of personality, has emerged the impersonal
content of imperishable truth. So the physical body remains the
same, but the inner contents have changed.

It is only the transcendence of the centre of the I, the dismantling
of the whole structure that the I-consciousness has built up, the
dismantling of the thought structure, the transcendence of the centre,
which results in a state of *samadhi*, in a state of *yoga*. You remember
the last twenty verses in the second chapter giving a description of
the dimension of *samadhi*. Krishna comes back to it in every chapter
in a new way. So he says:

'Look, Arjuna, you cannot learn that refined discrimination. It
requires the cultivation of sensitivity that does not come by
knowledge. There are always seers and sages in the world. You
will have to look for one and live near the person, observe how
that person moves in Life, how that person conducts himself in the
movement of relationships, in the travail of daily life. Because the
transcendence of the I-consciousness, the dismantling of the thought
structure has activated in such a seer, such a yogi, a radically
different quality of sensitivity, of perceptive sensitivity. It is the
perceptive sensitivity or Cosmic intelligence that vibrates through
the flesh and blood of that person. Watch that person, how he acts,
how he responds, observe and study him, because there is non-
action of the ego and action of the intelligence.

There is indulgence in activity when the senses drag the mind and the mind pushes the brain into stupid imbalances of jealousy, anger, bitterness, callousness, or cruelty. All that is absent in the life of a yogi. There it is only the flow of intelligence. Like water flowing through the curvature, which you call river, the Cosmic intelligence, the supreme intelligence, flows through the body, the brain, the senses, the sense organs.

In other words, Krishna points out the necessity of a *guru* or a master with whom the student lives and studies Life. It is the observation, the interaction with such a person, the intimacy of presence that activates our inner sensitivity and enables us to discriminate between the dictates of the ego and the whispers of the intelligence, the dictates of the *ahamkara* and the whispers of the Atman.

About six or seven verses in the fourth chapter are spent in describing the inevitability, the necessity of living in the company of a master, living as a pupil, as a student. The relationship between an enlightened one and the enquirer can at best be of a teacher and a pupil. Not a relationship of emotional involvement, of belonging, of having claims on each other. Not that worldly business. It is something holy, something sacred, because it pertains to the discovery of the truth and meaning of Life.

'So Arjuna, when by such company, through observation and interaction, your outer ear and outer eyes can listen and perceive the action which is not at all contaminated by the thought structure or the I-consciousness, then perhaps your inner ear will be able to listen to the soft voice of the teacher or master within your heart.'

It is a fascinating thesis the *Gita* gives of the necessity in the outer, the material, the physical life, of a *guru*, as a guiding light to enable the pupil to listen to the inner *guru*. The outer master functions as a bridge, as it were, because there is a gap created by the thought structure between the intelligence and the senses and sense organs. And the master says: 'come on, I bend my back, walk on me, see what I do, listen to what I say, observe how I live, and get to the real *guru*, the inner *guru*, the Atman, the intelligence, Life, the master par excellence, the supreme master.'

You hear a different thesis today, when there is talk of life-long psychological relationships, of dogmas, sects, and claims of owning and possessing the *guru*, owning and possessing the students, the pupils.

It is very important to decode the words of the *Gita*, which are condensed Vedas, and get at its essence. So, the necessity of a master, yes. Is it a permanent necessity? No. It is a necessity, in a phase of enquiry, to activate the sensitivity, not to provide verbal knowledge, but to activate the sensitivity. It is the transmission of energy that takes place in the informal, intimate, interaction between a teacher and a student. Education cannot have a formal structure. Education is the transmission of wisdom; it is the activation of inner intelligence, leaving the pupil utterly free to find out his or her path of Life.

People might ask you: 'doesn't the fourth chapter talk about the necessity of a *guru*?' Yes, it does. But it points out the nature of that necessity and the limitations of the phase in which it is needed.

When you are studying, you don't remain in one grade all your life. You study for a year and then you cross over to another. So why glorify the need for a *guru*? Why not take it easy and see a *guru* as a necessity in the ascendance from matter to energy, from energy to emptiness and from emptiness to intelligence. One may need help and one takes it. But building a dogma around it, resulting in a permanent incapacity or disablement of the psychological structure in the human psyche, is really misinterpreting the Upanishads or the *Gita*.

Life is a mystery. A mystery implies something, which cannot be analysed by the human brain, which cannot be captured in the framework of human thought, to which the law of causation and the concept of time cannot be applied. That which is self-generated, self-sustained and self-destructive is called a mystery. The ancient wise people, living in these parts of the globe, used the term divine and divinity for conveying the implications of mystery. To the question: 'why is there creation?' the Upanishads, the Vedas and the *Gita* would say: 'it is there, because it is there.'

The question 'why' is a wrong question, because it relates to a mind, to subjectivity, to a purpose, to a motivation, an aim, a goal. The human brain cannot find out why there is creation or why was creation brought about by a big bang, or why there was a soundless explosion of silence into millions of universes? Whatever analysis, exploration, experimentation with electronics, high technology, or whatever else might be used, the self-generated spontaneous existence of the Cosmos will remain an un-analysable mystery. So they say Life is divine. Life is divinity as well as mysterious at the same time.

Ask any scientist at the end of the 20th century about the relation between a particle of matter and the quantum of energy contained in it, ask them if they can calculate, describe or define it, and they say it is inexplicable. The relation of the smallest particle of matter and the quantum of energy contained in that particle defies both logic and arithmetic. Ask them why should matter contain energy at all? Energy is qualitatively different from the characteristics of matter in which it makes its abode. Where do these two qualitatively different ingredients of Life, matter and energy, meet? How is the one contained in the other? Ask the scientist, and they'll just say it is so.

What is the logic behind the interaction of the dance of innumerable energies taking place in the temple of silence, in the cathedral of Cosmic space? And how does the solidification of energies, constituting matter, take place? Life is a mystery. And this is being said not because one is a religious person, but because the scientific study of Life as it is, obliges us to say that it is divine, that it is a mystery.

Up till now it has been beyond the reach of natural sciences, physics, chemistry, biology, etc. to analyse the nature of the inter-relationship between energies and the beings that inhabit the planet. So the second characteristic of divinity or mystery is the organic inter-relatedness. All the expressions of Life in the Cosmos are inter-related, interlocked. Their sustenance depends upon one another; they contribute to the richness of one another.

This is not an interdependence between different parts of a machine, it is not an inter-connectedness of logical premises, it is not something imposed by the human brain on the existential essence. The organic inter-relatedness is the expression of divinity, the expression of mystery.

This clarification was necessary to understand what Krishna implies, when saying: 'my birth and actions, my life, both are full of mystery, full of divinity, because there is no cause outside of me, independent of me, that makes me act. There is no goal, no aim, which prompts my actions.' Individuation of Cosmic intelligence into the form of a human being is a global event, a Cosmic event, defying human logic and language. We are proceeding today where we had left off yesterday.

When it comes to the physical birth of Krishna, the Hindus have interpreted it to be the result of Immaculate Conception, just as Christians will talk about the birth of Jesus, the Christ. This is how a sense of divinity, a sense of mystery, is being explained in human terms. It is however a futile effort to explain the inexplicable, to know the unknowable. Krishna refers to the manifestation of his life as a part of the mysterious inter-related Cosmic events. He says: I am a part of the Cosmic event, of Cosmic Life.

I would request the students of the *Gita* to free themselves from the traditional interpretation of this verse, the claims that Krishna, or Christ, were born of virginity. To give a mythological garb to this deep spiritual truth, is a pathetic effort of the human race to gratify its collective ego: that it knows and that it can explain.

So Krishna says to Arjuna: 'the way Life manifests and the way Life functions, if it is not contaminated by human purposes and motivations, is divine, is mysterious.'

Those who understand the principle of Life, understand the way it functions spontaneously, causelessly, innocently. Innocence is divine, isn't it? What we call the Cosmos has a beingness, but it is not a person. When the term Cosmic being or Cosmic intelligence is used, people say: 'Ah, if there is intelligence, there must be a mind.' They forget that intelligence has nothing whatsoever to do with the thought structure or what you call mind. It is an energy born of the space of meditation, an energy activated in the space of silence, a causeless activation, a direction free movement permeating the whole body.

If the energy of intelligence can get activated in your own body causelessly, spontaneously and can function entirely free of the thought structure and its mechanism, why can't we see that in the Cosmic beingness, the all-permeating Cosmic intelligence can operate in exactly the same way?

If the energy of love, of tenderness, of compassion defy your logic, calculations and bargaining and transport you in a non-subjective ego free action and relationship, why can't we understand the energy of love and compassion operating in the Cosmic beingness with the same beauty of innocence, which is divinity.

So, Krishna says to Arjuna: 'those who understand the principle of Life, understand that Life has a beingness.' Not a person. A person or a personality is something cultivated, related to the context of life, to the nature of society in which the individual lives. It is something put together. It can be developed, it can be cultivated, it can be damaged. A being need not necessarily be a person. That which is all permeating is obviously impersonal, is it not?

'So you being organically related, O Arjuna, to this mysterious beingness of Life, the Cosmic beingness of Life, why not learn to act out of spontaneity?'

Now let us proceed with Krishna and look at the word 'spontaneously', which is again a code word from the terminology of spirituality, which is the science of Life. Every word is so pregnant with indications, denotations, connotations, expressing various shades of the wholeness of Life.

That which is spontaneous is uncovering, unwinding, revealing its contents. The unmanifest is constantly revealing its contents through the manifest. Creation has no other logic behind it but this mysterious spontaneity, which is fulfilled by expressing itself, manifesting itself, uncovering itself; the implicate becoming the explicate to use the terms of modern physics.

David Bohm has written a great deal about the implicate and the explicate order. Frithjof Capra talks about the *Tao of Physics* and the Cosmic dance of energies and David talks about the implicate manifesting itself in the explicate, and the explicate going back through involution to the implicate and so on. It is very interesting how physics and metaphysics go together. And physics seems to be on the verge of becoming metaphysics.

The beingness of Cosmic Life manifests, reveals or expresses its own contents. There is no reward for it; there are no fruits for it. The beingness is fulfilled through the revelation, through the manifestation. Krishna says: 'I am an organic expression of that Cosmic principle of Life. Though I am in human form, I am an organic expression of the wholeness and the principle operating in that wholeness.'

This way of looking at it throws quite a different light upon the issue of incarnation. If this point is sufficiently clear, let us proceed to the next point that Krishna is making at nearly the centre of the fourth chapter. He says: 'Life is self-fulfilled, it is fulfilled in being what it is.'

In the human body there is that organic expression of Cosmic Life, which is called 'Atman'. 'Atman' is an interesting term used by the Sanskrit language. The root means to eat, to devour, to consume, to assimilate. That which assimilates everything is Atman, and that which radiates the essence of what it has assimilated is also Atman. A fascinating word. Atman, Paramatman, that which is all-permeating, all-pervading, omnipotent, omniscient, omnipresent, consuming everything that is existing in the Cosmos and expressing it back again. So Atman, for which they use the term 'self' also, some use the term soul, is not an entity. The way of the *Gita* is to give the word first, explain it, and then proceed further.

'Arjuna, I say unto you that you need not worry about the fruits or the rewards resulting from your actions. The Atman does not need any reward, the Atman, the energy, the intelligence encased in your body, embodied in you, does not require any fruit, any reward. It can neither be punished nor rewarded. Nothing can be added unto it, because it is self-contained, holistic by its very nature.'

A drop of water is holistic, having the quality of quenching thirst, as a bucket full of water has. The quality is the same.

So: 'don't be under an illusion that I am asking you to act, not to run away from action or *karma*, because if you do not act, the Atman will be deprived. Or if you act, something will be added to the Atman. Please do not be under that illusion. Being an individuation of the Cosmic beingness, there is an urge concealed in every human heart to express itself. So let your actions, let your *karma* be rooted in the urge of self-revelation, self-expression, self-manifestation, so that the worry, the anxiety about the fruits that you might get out of specific actions, would not be there.'

Now, here let me discriminate two things. You go to school and you get an education. You have to study, you have to pass exams. Krishna is surely not saying: 'do not work hard, don't care whether you pass or fail your exams.' You have to earn your livelihood in a commercialized industrialized society, where work is valued in terms of money, where your life is weighed in the scale of money. It is a social responsibility. The compulsions of material life make you take up a job, as it was a compulsion for Arjuna to fight, being a warrior.

Action is something that you do voluntarily, not because of some compulsion from outside. You have to respond to the compulsions as a member of society. That you may. Calculations, organization, planning, you have to go through it as for the context of your life, whether you are living in an agricultural civilization, an industrial civilization, or a cybernetic civilization. The *Gita* is not talking about that social aspect of life. The *Gita* is talking about human relationships and the voluntary actions that you go through.

If you behave kindly to someone and your mind expects acknowledgement from the person about your kindness, then you are expecting a reward, an agreeable fruit of that kindness. If you give something in charity to the poor and then want recognition of that charity from society, then it is a voluntary action attached to the idea of a fruit. You want something in return, you are selling your kindness, you are selling your charity. You don't want to purchase anything from it, but you would like to purchase acknowledgement, recognition, praise, respectability, fame. We are talking about such rewards and such fruits.

If you have had affection, concern, care for people and they turn away, not only that, but they do some harm to you and the mind says: 'Oh, I did so much good and look what has been done to me!' Then, Krishna says you did not know how to live. If you were kind with the concealed motivation of gaining acknowledgement as the fruit of your kindness, then you did not know how to live.

It is a question of human relationship that is taken up. Let your actions be rooted in the urge for self-expression, which is a characteristic of intelligence, which is a characteristic of Cosmic beingness constantly manifesting itself.

Let us be with Krishna and look from another angle at the same fact. He says: 'Life is a mystery and inter-relatedness is the content of that mystery.' And because there is this inter-relatedness, living involves interaction, interaction between the earth and the sun, the sun and the oceans, the oceans and the moon, the trees and the rain. Inter-relatedness results in a marvellous drama of interaction of energies among all the expressions of Life.

When your eyes see beauty, the sight is fulfilled by the action of seeing, and the existence of beauty is fulfilled by being seen. It is an interaction. But when the mind says: 'it is so beautiful, I must have it,' then we have gone beyond the play of inter-relatedness and the play of interaction, because I want something exclusively for myself.

I need a house, I need clothes, I need food, I need other means for a decent aesthetic life. But when, in human relationships, we create the idea of exclusive claims, ownership and possession, then it is called attachment. In chapter two it said: 'those who keep on thinking about objects, attachment for the objects creeps up in their minds.'

Here Krishna is talking about the responsibility to respond and interact with nature, because inter-relationship requires interaction. You till the land, you plough the fields, you sow the seeds; beautiful interaction between the earth and mankind. You stand under the open sky, space is fulfilled by your presence and you feel fulfilled by the touch of the emptiness of space, which rejuvenates you. Water is fulfilled when you bathe and the whole biological organism is fulfilled by the sensation of freshness, of refreshment. Interaction is for the event of that communion.

Action is for re-uniting you through the interaction to the roots of Life, to the source of Life, to Brahman, the ultimate reality.

The mundane, the worldly, the physical consequences would be there and you would go through them, because you are living in society, you are living with people. Interaction with nature is a responsibility of being organically related to the Cosmos. And interaction with human beings and human structures is a social responsibility. The laws and regulations and principles of relationships on the socio-economic-political level are not discussed here. This is a spiritual treatise, giving us the source of inner happiness and peace.

'When you feel that you have acted choicelessly when you were interacting with nature or with human beings, you have poured your being into that action then, Arjuna, that karma unites you with Brahman, it unites you with me.' He uses the term me for the impersonal Cosmic beingness.

It is a dialogue between friends. Krishna says: 'you are my beloved, you are my friend, I am sharing the secret principle of Life with you. You see it personified in me, but it is the principle of Cosmic Life, of whole Life. Understand that, so that suffering and misery come to an end. Never again will you get dejected by the travail of daily life, the result of duality through which you live.'

For an action to be non-subjective is quite a challenge to modern western psychology. Please do see this. The *yogic* psychology is a challenge to European and American psychology. Action without motivation is not talked about, or acknowledged or appreciated in western psychology. Freud interpreted the movement of a one-day old child through the principle of libido, a sex-centred interpretation of human life. While Marx and Engels gave us the material interpretation of human history.

The *Gita*, the Upanishads, the Vedas, talk about the possibility of growing into a dimension of spontaneity where, in human relationships, motivation-free action is possible, *karma* as a self-fulfilled movement is possible.

There is a world of difference between the two psychologies. Even modern Indians will find it extremely difficult to grasp this mystery of innocence, the mystery of the urge of spontaneity, the urge for love and compassion in every human heart. Arjuna is being led towards that.

Karma does not add any richness to the Atman, nor is it going to detract anything from the Atman. Those who learn to act thus, in the dimension of spontaneity in human relationships, are called sages or seers by the people. Love is the perfume of that spontaneity; compassion is the expression of that spontaneity.

'Such a dimension of spontaneity becomes possible, Arjuna, when you understand that what you call yourself, the physical frame, the psychological structure, is the abode of Cosmic beingness.' In each heart resides Cosmic beingness. In the heart of every human being resides that all-permeating principle of Life. If it had not been so, innocence, spontaneity, love and compassion would be impossible for human beings.

The students of *yoga* must be acquainted with the term *samadhi*. This term has been popularized by the study of Hatha Yoga, Tantra Yoga, Mantra Yoga and Bhakti Yoga in various countries of the world. This morning we have to get acquainted with the communication of Sri Krishna about the word *samadhi*.

In Hatha Yoga, a state of neuro-chemical stillness can be stimulated in the body, through manipulation of the energy of *prana*, the vital energy, through *pranayama*. And such manipulated, cultivated, stable stillness, sustained passivity, is called *samadhi*. The duration of such *samadhi* depends upon the motivation for which one enters into it. So *samadhi* with great effort, systematically gone through, manipulated *samadhi*, is possible.

In Tantra Yoga you manipulate the sex energy. And through the manipulation of the sex energy, making it travel through the various *chakras* or significant nerve centres, you can stimulate the same state of stable stillness and sustained passivity. This *samadhi* is called *savikalpa samadhi*, *sabija samadhi*, into which one can enter and out of which one can move as per one's intention.

In Mantra Yoga you use the sound energy, manipulate its vibrations in such a way that you can hypnotize your sense organs and bring the body into a state of manipulated intoxication, manipulated ecstasy, and remain in that state of manipulated sustained ecstasy, which is called *bhava samadhi*.

In Jnana Yoga, the Yoga through the verbalized knowledge about the nature of reality, it is possible to renounce all cerebral activity, and therefore all chemical disturbance in the body. And through such renunciation one can enter what is called *nirvikalpa samadhi*. These words are specially addressed to the students of *yoga*, the word *samadhi* has been used technically in different senses, in different branches of *yoga*.

Krishna communicates to Arjuna *Brahma-karma-samadhi*. It is a very significant term that we are being introduced to this morning. *Brahma-karma-samadhi* does not need any manipulation of the neuro-chemical energy, does not require any sublimation of biological impulses, does not require any renunciation of cerebral movement or of sensual activity. It is a state that can come about effortlessly, naturally, that is to say, spontaneously, if *Brahma-agni* is kindled within the heart.

We are coming to the second term, a very significant term used by Krishna: *Brahma-agni*. It is the first chapter in which this fascinating significant term, the awareness of Brahman as fire (*agni*) kindled in your consciousness, the awareness of the nature of reality, the awareness of the non-dual substance of reality, is mentioned.

That awareness is called a fire, which is kindled in the consciousness that is conditioned, that is limited.

It is in the abode of consciousness, in the house of consciousness, in the house of the thought structure that the fire of awareness is kindled. That awareness and the light of that awareness permeate the nervous system, the chemical system, it pervades the whole metabolical system, it vibrates through your senses and sense organs. Therefore, when you move into any relationship or any action, it is the awareness of Brahman, or Brahman itself who is moving.

And this movement of the sensual, the physical, the psychological, this action, this *karma*, is an offering by the individual to the Cosmos. So figuratively Krishna says; 'Brahman is conducting a *yajna*, Brahman is making oblations in the fire of awareness.' And such an action, on the sensual and psychological level, is vibrating with the awareness of Brahman. So the action is Brahman, the actor is Brahman, and that which is offered is also Brahman.

Therefore, the movement of such *karma*, of such action, results in a natural spontaneous dimension of samadhi, into which you do not have to enter by effort, into which you do not have to enter through manipulation, but you grow into that, you live in that. You remember in the *Chandogya Upanishad* it said: 'One who understands the nature of Brahman verily gets converted into a living, mobile Brahman itself.'

These are not only figurative poetic terms, they are a narration of experiences gone through by the ancient wise people, called enlightened ones, called seers and sages. So that is *Brahma-karma-samadhi* or *Brahma-nirvana*. *Nirvana* is not related to the physical death of the body. The term *nirvana* refers to the dimensional transformation to the mutation in the psyche.

So *samadhi* through action, dimensional transformation through the movement of relationship, through the movement of action, is the message Sri Krishna is giving his friend, sharing the secret of Life and living, sharing the secret of the yoga of living, with his dear friend Arjuna.

Now, what has to take place in order to kindle such a *Brahma-agni*, the fire, the flame of Brahman in your consciousness? This is described in a number of verses, which we are going to cover this morning.

A person, realizing that she is organically related to the absolute Cosmic divinity, not a part of that divinity, but a holistic emanation of that divinity, that Brahman, that supreme intelligence, such a person feels absolutely contented, fulfilled, happy in being alive. To be alive is a benediction. The grace of the divine is upon us when we are given an opportunity to realize the organic relationship with the absolute Cosmic divinity, and that in a human form with multi-dimensional energies of consciousness.

One who feels already fulfilled in being alive and being granted an opportunity to manifest the aliveness through all manner of movement, is *nitya-trupta*, ever contented in being alive. The movements, the *karmas*, the actions, are not going to add anything to his being and therefore the world does not become something to which he has to cling, to get involved in, to get attached to. He does not have psychologically the need to cling to the objects around him for feeling alive.

You know the stuff of our daily lives; you feel alive when you think, when you go on spinning thoughts within you, weaving ideas, wishes, desires, jealousies, comparisons, evaluations of your actions as success or failure, measuring the reactions and responses of others about the thoughts that you have been spinning. This is the stuff of our lives. Every relationship is a counter at which we bargain, we seek something from the world.

And Krishna says: 'Life is not for seeking happiness, or peace, or love, they are not things that the world can give you.' You may live in a palace, roll in worldly riches, literally surrounded by dozens of people and yet you may be inwardly lonely. You may be wealthy and yet be dissatisfied, you may be a successful person in worldly terms and yet you may be absolutely bitter, cynical and discontented within you.

It is the state of your consciousness, it is the state of your mind, which determines the quality of your life. If the mind is restless, discontented, unsteady, unstable, then all the successes and riches of the world will not be able to confer happiness on you or cause the emergence of peace in your heart.

The emphasis, in all the chapters, is upon the state of consciousness, which gets reflected in action. A person has first to get acquainted with his body, with his mind, how they function and what is behind and beyond the mind, the brain, what is beyond the forms of matter around. First explore, investigate, perceive and understand, and after understanding: grow into a state of nitya-trupta, ever contented in being alive.

You know the gratefulness one feels for being alive, the thankfulness to the divine that day after day you are allowed to leave your bed as a living being, all energies intact, and the Cosmos around you to interact and human beings around you to discover the nature of the inner state of your being. What more can Life give unto us? All this is a benediction.

Therefore the world is not the support, the world does not make him feel alive, he feels alive by himself. The feel of being alive vibrates in the heart causelessly, motionlessly. The feeling is there. Nobody has to tell you how to feel alive. And it is that spontaneous feel of Life which is the proof of supreme intelligence, which is self-generated and self-sustained. No philosophies, no scriptures, no teachings are necessary for us to have that feel of Life within us, pulsating within us.

If you are sensitive, then you feel the movement of that vital energy, *prana*, going out of and entering your body, the movement of the ingoing and outgoing energy. It is not that somebody has filled your lungs with oxygen. You are born with that energy of receiving the Cosmic *prana* and also throwing out the carbon dioxide, which gets generated through friction within the body.

Self-contented and self-reliant. You understand the term self-reliance now. Self-reliance is not ego-centredness, it is not psychological isolation. There is much more to the words self-reliance, self-confidence, self-contentedness. They refer to the feel of Life and not to that centre, the I-consciousness, or the ever-manipulated ego.

With such a state of consciousness, when one moves into action, when one is not seeking anything from that action, be it peace or love, not seeking any psychological gain, then that *karma* does not contaminate or pollute you in any way. Don't be afraid that by doing *karma* you will be tainted or contaminated or polluted. No manner of pollution or contamination will enter your heart, if the actions are gone through with the foundation of the awareness of your nature and therefore self-contentedness and self-reliance.

You may question the fear that *karma* will pollute you, that you will be contaminated by the impulses. The state of self-reliance and self-contentedness is all right, but what about the senses and the sense organs that get attracted by the outer objects, by the world around? To that Krishna's reply is: 'kindle the fire of restraint at the sensual level.'

Education is the answer. Education leading to understanding. Understanding kindling the fire of awareness. And awareness purifying your whole being. So Krishna is gradually leading Arjuna, in the fifth and sixth chapter, towards the study of Hatha Yoga. 'You have to educate your sense organs, you have to educate the sense energies, purify them through education, so that they behave with a natural restraint.'

The senses receive the impressions of the material objects around them, when they need nutrition, sustenance. When there is appetite, then there is a need of food or diet and the senses are willing and ready and eager to receive the food or diet. When they have received the food and the digestive organs are satisfied with the intake of food, then the receptivity towards food closes for a few hours.

Such a person may be surrounded by a variety of food items, the mind does not even take cognizance of those objects because it is not necessary. Please do see, education to be receptive and open for the sake of sustenance. Survival in a decent aesthetic reasonable way is something that has to be taken aboard by a religious enquirer.

The senses and the sense organs are thus educated to be receptive, to register and recall when the need for sustenance is there and to close the receptivity when satisfied, so that surrounding objects are incapable of printing any impressions on your neuro-chemical system. The eyes are open and yet nothing is registered and recorded, unless it is necessary to look at a person and relate through glances or through verbal communication. The ears are open, the sound energy and sound vibrations reach the auditory instrument of the body and the sounds go back. Nothing is registered, nothing is recorded and therefore there is no reaction.

You know, we are talking of the science of restraint at the sensual level. When the sense organs are thus educated, then the self-contentedness and self-reliance receive cooperation of the restrained sense organs and therefore the solitude, the inner solitude of such a person moving through actions, moving along with people, is not at all disturbed or upset. It is invincible.

Now let us proceed to another important verse. We are talking about a dimension of *samadhi* without manipulation, without effort, without sublimation, something marvellous. This message of the *Gita* is a contribution to human culture. It indicates the potentiality contained in a human being, to grow from simple consciousness and self-consciousness, to an awareness without a centre. *Samadhi* is not a theory; it is something very much alive.

In order to indicate the state of mind, which can conduct this *Brahma-karma-yajna*, the *yajna* in which your *karma* is offered to the awareness of Brahman, of reality, for this the mind, the cerebral organ has to be educated. We have dealt with the sensual education, for kindling the fire of restraint on that level.

Now let us see how to kindle a fire of orderliness and austerity of movement, of action. A person who is free from the hope of tomorrow, hope for the next hour, his whole being is focussed on acting in the present, which is the substance of eternity, which is the manifestation of infinity. During such action, such movement, there is no diversion due to hope of future, due to the idea of getting something for tomorrow out of that movement.

Our movements in relationship, our glances, our smiles, our words, are all investments for securing the stability of relationships for tomorrow. Please do see this. All our human relationships, what we do with one another, how we guarantee that the person will remain with me tomorrow, so that he or she has still the same attitude towards me, the same approach towards me; in fact those movements are not offered to Brahman. They are not offerings or oblations into the fire of awareness. They are all investments towards the future, like your bank balance.

You try to please the person at the cost of truth. You tell a half-truth, you indulge in a lie, a falsehood, an exaggeration, an understatement, overstatement, somehow concealing the fact. Don't we do that? We initiate pleasure for the person with whom we are dealing, for a moment, for an hour, for a day, for a month, for life. It is the procurement of his or her pleasure that we manipulate. Is it not manipulation of energies, sexual energies, vital energies or *prana*, is it not sublimation or manipulation there? We are manipulating during action. We manipulate words, facial expressions, the tone, the accent, we pretend. Pretension is a manipulation called hypocrisy.

Supposing we are concerned with the rightness of our words or actions. That is to say I am aware that what I am doing is done choicelessly, as per my understanding. I cannot do otherwise. Then you act towards others, you speak towards others in the simplicity and elegance of that understanding. Not harshly, not to flatter. No pretensions and no concealments.

Fearless simplicity flows through your glances, words, deeds, responses. Do you see? As long as one is concerned with the next moment, next hour or the next day in human relationships, to secure the steadiness of the relationship, the stability of the relationship, in order to give a continuity to the relationship, being afraid of loosing something, then the action becomes unholy. It is not an offering to the Cosmic Life. Don't our relationships stink of all such manipulations, contamination, or pollution?

Krishna says: 'hope is not the regulating factor. Hope is related to the future, which is non-existent. Being totally focused on the present, hope or expectation is not there.' The movement in relationship is free of psychological expectation. Please let us not confuse it with social necessities, where planning, organization, calculation, is very much necessary. We are talking about human relationships, which are the major part of our life.

One whose heart is free of expectation from the future, because he is dwelling in the present, dealing with eternity condensed in the present, he is free of the entanglement of expectation and therefore never comes across disappointment or frustration. All frustration blossoms in the shade of expectation. A heart free of expectation is a heart full of love. What is love? Freedom from expectation obviously activates the energy of love. So when you say free from hope and expectation, you are in other ways indicating the energy of love.

It is expectation, which does not allow your heart to remain controlled or restrained. The passions, the wishes, the ambitions, take your consciousness astray from the path of simple straightforward action. The crookedness of manipulation begins. 'Arjuna, when the heart is free of the entanglement of expectation, then it is restrained.' Your heart is won over by this, it becomes self-regulated, it does not enter into any excess. Depression is one kind of excess, excitement is another kind of excess. So, without any excess.

Excess is imbalance. So one lives without any excess, without any imbalance, free of the illusion of duality, free from jealousy, never comparing what one is doing with what others are doing, not wanting to evaluate oneself in terms of the life of other people, not desiring to become anyone else than what one is. It is comparison that creates the illusion of duality; the desire to compare, the desire to become something different from what we are. Comparison leads to self-manipulation, does it not?

Krishna says: 'Please do not be afraid that *karma*, action, will bind you. The bondage is not in the *karma*, the bondage is in the heart. Comparison leading to jealousy, creating the tension of duality, entangling you in the network of expectations, that is the path of bondage, Arjuna, not action done outwardly.'

Psychologically speaking there is the fire of non-duality kindled in the heart, which keeps the psychological behaviour free from bondage, as there is a fire of restraint on the sensual level.

When you live in society, you live with people of various natures, conditionings, various idiosyncrasies. It is a jungle of temperamental varieties. Every dawn may bring you across people with patterns of reactions you are unacquainted with. To live is to deal with the unknown on the physical and the psychological level. These are marvellous challenges of Life, so that you do not get stuck in self-complacency and become stale. Life keeps you alert, on your toes, as it were.

The third point that has to be gone through is the fire of alertness at the cerebral level. The cerebral level is a figurative way of saying the level of the nervous and chemical system, the brain being the monitor of the whole. This whole structure of knowledge can be sluggish, can lack promptness, accuracy, due to expectations, due to lack of education in self-restraint.

'Arjuna, when at the sensual level there is the fire of restraint, and there is the fire of austerity or non-attachment, non-expectation at the psychological level, then the brain is kindled with alertness, with a flame of alertness, which is a quality of sensitivity.'

Not even for a moment is there the darkness of inattention, passivity, sluggishness, indifference, callousness. If you really feel that to be alive is a benediction, how can one ever be indifferent to a moment, indifferent to anything? How can one ignore, reject, or run away from any challenge of Life? You cannot suspend living, can you?

But we suspend the movement of living in the name of ideologies, in the name of renunciation, in the name of spirituality, and heaven only knows what other pretensions we have to escape from the challenge of living, the challenge to be alert, attentive.

Through the flame of awareness, the known is orderly, the brain, which has been refined by the human race, is alert. When that flame is burning, then whatever action takes place, the action itself kindles the fire of Brahman, the fire of supreme intelligence. It is kept alive through your actions, through your being, through your relationships. This is the real fire sacrifice (*agnihotra*).

The formal religious ceremony of the fire sacrifice, mentioned in the Vedas and becoming popular in the west, has a religious significance. But metaphysically speaking, speaking philosophically, the real meaning of *agnihotra* is that your whole body is the vessel in which you are going to kindle the fire. Every breath that you take in is an oblation to the inner Cosmos and when you breathe out, it is an oblation to the outer Cosmos. They say the fire should never die.

At the sensual level, when the attraction of objects wants to drag down the senses and sense organs and those impulses are exposed to the fire of restraint, they are consumed by that fire. Out of the ashes of those impulses there is purification. This is a figurative language. We must listen to the voice of the Vedas not literally, but take the spirit of it.

Those of you, who have heard about the fire sacrifice, may have heard that plants that absorb those ashes of the *agnihotra* grow faster. I was in Poland and they were talking about *agnihotra*, in England they talked about it, and when I was in Chile and Argentina, they said how those ashes have tremendous potential. Be that as it may.

Here we are referring to impulses getting converted into potential ashes, which become the manure for psychological austerity. Ashes are always associated with austerity. Ascetics in the Himalayas put ashes on their forehead, they cover their body with ashes.

The human race drags down to the gross level communications about subtle events. The touch of reason has helped us to get beyond superstitions, but has dried up to some extent the poetic sensitivity of the human heart. The more we live with machines and gadgets, the less sensitive we grow. So let us not translate these verses literally.

The potential energy of the impulses is not destroyed by offering them to austerity, but gets converted into something else, just as the known offered to the unknown becomes a potential energy of a different kind. Knowledge becomes an energy, when it is offered to understanding. The potential of understanding increases a hundredfold when it is offered to the fire of awareness. This is a language of sacrifice, of oblations, of offerings, and the offering, when it is apparently converted into ashes, is really being converted into a subtle energy.

That seems to be the contention of Krishna. So through *Brahma-agni*, offering to the supreme intelligence, the awareness of non-duality burning bright in the heart, prevents the stimulation of the illusion of duality and all the tensions of fear and insecurity arising out of it.

We are now going to deal with the flame that is kindled through *pranayama*, as an offering to the Cosmos. Krishna is saying that the whole Life is an offering. The interaction has to be gone through, not for seeking anything, but for offering what we have, thus uncovering, unwinding, revealing, manifesting, expressing. Expression is an offering.

You see the sense of sanctity attached to the act of living? And we think living is a bondage, we think relationships create bondages and *karma* or action contaminates one, and that the purity of the heart is lost. We have so many illusions.

Here Krishna says: 'The whole Life is an offering and every breath is an offering, every word is an offering.' They have no words in Sanskrit for discourse, speech or talk. Whenever you open your mouth, be aware that you are going to conduct an offering. Be careful that your words do not attack the emptiness of space harshly, through the intonation, the pitch, the volume.

Thus we have seen that the offering to Brahman, to the supreme intelligence, the oblation of the awareness of Brahman conducted by the person who is a part of Brahman, the dimension of *samadhi* in which these *karmas* are gone through, unites that person with

Brahman. And therefore you live virtually in *Brahma-karma-samadhi*, in the dimension of *samadhi* .

Let us now look at three terms before proceeding. One is the term *jnana*. One comes across this word right from the first chapter to the last. In most of the translations the word *jnana* has been translated as knowledge. But it seems to me that the meaning remains incomplete. In English, for example, knowledge can be verbal, intellectual, theoretical, or academic and it is also used for understanding, which is qualitatively different from knowing.

Interestingly enough the word *jnana* implies knowing and understanding blended into one. So Jnana Yoga cannot be called a *yoga* of knowledge unless you qualify the term knowledge by the term understanding.

Words contain their meaning, as fruit or vegetables contain the substance within their skin. You have to peel the fruit or the vegetable in order to receive and assimilate the essence of the fruit or the vegetable. In the same way you have to peel the words, peel them of their traditional associations, their sectarian and dogmatic interpretation, take them back to their source, their root, look at their history and development, so that one can touch the original meaning for which the word was intended, formed, coined. Whenever we translate the word *jnana* by the word knowledge, do please include psychologically understanding along with knowing. In Sanskrit there is only one root for knowing and understanding.

The second term is *karma*, which is translated by the word action. It is easy to discriminate action from activity. But we have also to probe a little deeper and see that any movement, which is the result of inner division, compartmentalization or fragmentation, is not called *karma* in the Vedic literature. That which flows from the wholeness, the fullness of the being, is called *karma*. If it is born of inner division, conflicts or fragmentations, it is called *kriya* (activity) and not *karma*.

So the word karma should be translated into English as action, qualified as action, when flowing from wholeness or fullness.

Actions of a schizophrenic person suffering from a crystallized split resulting in perverse activities, those actions cannot be called *karma*. Such a person may be active twenty-four hours a day and yet no movement of the inner perversion or inner split can be called *karma* or action. These are technical terms. We are dealing with the science of Life and living, so one has to be careful if one really wants to study the *Gita*.

The third term is *shastra*, translated by the word science. You must have come across Yoga Shastra, Tantra Shastra. The word implies organized and systematized elucidation of fundamental principles. That is one part of the meaning of the word *shastra*. And the second part is guidelines for the implementation of those principles in daily living. Both together make *shastra*. In English you would say natural and applied sciences. You discriminate between theory and practice. Here, they are blended together, not only combined but blended together, so as to make a whole.

We have to educate ourselves, educate our senses in order to kindle the fire of natural spontaneous restraint; not a compulsory discipline from outside, but an awakening of an inner sense of restraint. The magnificence of that inner natural sense of restraint is indescribable. All the disciplines, all the patterns of behaviour collected together do not have that elegance and beauty. They have rigidity by their very nature. Restraint, like intelligence or love, cannot be structured. It has its own movement in its freedom.

In order to educate the senses in kindling the flame of restraint, the student of *yoga* has to get acquainted with Ayurveda and Hatha Yoga. This Vedic approach is a holistic approach. Even if you want to study classical music, the study of Ayurveda and Yoga Shastra becomes necessary. You have to have an acquaintance with the intricate field of energies that is the body, the interaction of these energies and the art of harmonizing those energies is Ayurveda.

Ayurveda tells you what kind of food to eat, in which season and at what hour of the day. It tells you what are the nutritional values of liquids, solids, fruit, etc. in detail. In order to educate the senses in the art of restraint and kindle the fire within you, it is necessary to get acquainted with the physical structure, the biological structure, its mechanism, its requirements, diet, etc. Diet is purified by the simplicity of austerity.

The energy of understanding, the energy of awareness, released by that event of understanding, is so subtle, its velocity or momentum is so different from the momentum of thought energy, that unless the biological organism is thus purified, it will not be able to hold that energy, to contain it, leave aside express it or manifest it.

It is quite possible that the neuro-chemical system, not educated, not having the strength, the vitality and purity, may break down under the impact of the depth, intensity, and momentum of that energy of awareness, that Cosmic energy of intelligence.

Many feel that by reading books or listening to talks they understand verbally and transformation will take place. Many feel that when one understands the truth and one turns away from action, one becomes a renunciate and that is that. It is not that easy. You may turn your back on outer expressions of activity and be furiously active inside, mentally, through thoughts, feelings, emotions, reactions, memories, etc.

So the *Gita*, like the Upanishads and the Vedas, emphasizes that, in order that your system can hold the subtle flame of awareness, you have to educate the senses. The science of Ayurveda and the science of Hatha Yoga will help you to purify the senses. Purity is vitality. Then the nervous system becomes like steel, bends but does not break.

At the sensual level restraint can be grown into, with the help of Hatha Yoga and Ayurveda. At the level of speech one can grow into the dimension of spontaneous restraint by studying the sound energy, *nada shakti*, which is the source of speech: how sound travels in the body, the stages of its development and its conversion into a word, etc.

In the *sadhana* chapter of Patanjali Yoga Sutras, speech is analysed, sound is analysed and the significance of silence is expounded very skilfully. The study of silence purifies the quality of speech, which flows out of that source of silence, and an aesthetical restraint comes about in the communications, in the verbalizations of that person.

Let us go further. The flame of restraint at the thought level can be kindled by the study of mind and its movement. One has to study what is *vritti*; that which begins to vibrate like a ripple in the heart, then becomes a wave, then becomes a circle, going round and round, that is called *vritti*, till you give it an outlet of expression. Observe and study the mind, its mechanism, the movement of thought, emotion, sentiment, every movement of the thought structure.

Go to its source, and when you thus penetrate the I-consciousness, the ego, the contrived centre of the consciousness and discover that it has no substance as a fact, but only substance as an idea, as a concept, then all attachment to that centre, attachment to every manipulation of that centre, disappears.

Krishna elaborates this process of educating the sensual, the verbal and the psychological structures into a new mode of operation, a new dynamics of behaviour, so that every movement of the physical, the verbal and the psychological becomes an offering purified through restraint, an offering to the Cosmic intelligence, to nature around you, an offering to Brahman.

Briefly, we have talked about the secret of *yajna*, of sacrifice, of oblation and the necessity of taking help of the *shastras*. People are mistaken, if they think that the occurrence of the activation of supreme intelligence can take place without educating and equipping the psychophysical structure. *Jnana* (knowledge and understanding) and *karma* (action) have to go together.

How can action take place, if the instrument in which the action has to take place, is not equipped to receive that energy, to contain that energy, to let it flow through itself? There are people who say you just follow the *shastras*, the formal structures. The *shastras* give the guidelines and people build up dogmas around the guidelines and make crystallized patterns of 'must and must not': 'this is sin and this is virtue'. The *shastras* don't talk of virtue or sin.

We see the necessity of equipping the whole structure, not succumbing to dogmas or rigidity and also not succumbing to abstractions given by thought and intellect, but blending the understanding with the action. Then your life itself becomes a *yajna*. Life is a *yajna* and whatever you do is an offering, an oblation, and you are fulfilled by the opportunity you get, of offering. It is a great privilege to be allowed to offer your contribution to the Cosmos.

How to be aware that living is a *yajna*, how to be aware of its sacredness, of the sanctity of Life and living? Krishna says: 'turn to the movement of breath, the vital *prana*.' The Cosmic *prana*, the vital energy is entering you with every breath. It moves in your body and goes back to the Cosmos. The *prana* entering your body through breath is birth and the exhaling of breath is death. Like an artist, Krishna is describing the mystery of Life, of living and dying blended into one act of *yajna*. It is not only the actions not leaving a scratch of memory behind, he is taking us still deeper, to an inner deeper dimension.

Now, what do you do when you focus your energies? Krishna says: 'you are capable of breathing, not because you want to breathe, but it is the movement of Life. The whole Cosmos is breathing.'

The Cosmos has a beingness. There is a movement of that energy inside the wholeness of the Cosmos. You are within the Cosmos, but you are individuated. So you inhale the Cosmic energy. When you inhale the energy, don't say unto yourself: 'I am inhaling in order to become healthy'. Treat that breath as an offering to the inner being. When you exhale, treat that breath as a humble offering to the Cosmic Life.

After all, purity comes about by the change in attitude, by the qualitative change in perspective, in approach. If the oxygen contained in your breath purifies your blood, your consciousness of the sanctity of Life will purify the breathing movement itself. 'Cleansing through oxygen and purity through awareness, Arjuna, that verily is the highest kind of *yajna*.'

When the breath is taken in, retaining the breath is called the offering. You are offering it to your whole body. How the breath, the energy, travels through various organs is quite a fascinating drama that goes on in our body. And when you breathe out and you exhale the breath, hold it there. You are offering your outgoing breath to the Cosmos. And when breathing in, you are offering it to the divinity within you.

Whether you breathe in or out, if there is awareness of the fundamental principle of Cosmic unity, the fundamental principle that Life is one, inter-related, organically inter-locked, then breathing in and out, which goes on for twenty four hours, can be the highest kind of *yajna*. It can be conducted all the time. Not like actions, Karma Yajna, which is limited by space and time. Here is a *yajna*, which goes on with you, living and performing the *yajna* go on together.

If breathing is a sacred *yajna*, a worship of the divine, what is the student supposed to do? The rhythm that is going on in breathing should not be disturbed. It should be allowed to flow smoothly, unobstructed, undamaged. You will say who is going to damage it? How can anyone else damage or hurt it? No one else but we can do it. Mind you, there is not a single point given by Vimala, she is just a translator of the *Gita*. Krishna refers to the diet, to physical behaviour, mental behaviour, verbal behaviour, making it a beautiful complex whole. That is *Gita*.

Krishna points out that if you are not careful about diet, if there is no sense of restraint, if you have not educated yourself in restraint, if you are not careful about the intake by your senses, then the inner structure will be overloaded, either with impressions of sound, overloaded with thoughts, impressions of words or pictures, or overloaded with food which the body does not need, introducing a foreign element in your body, because it is not relevant to the sustenance of the physical health. If that is so and the digestive organs are exploited, if you tortured them, then the rhythm of the breathing system is hampered and the sacrifice gets obstructed.

If you have not educated yourself in the art of restraint as far as verbalization goes, then talking can pressurize the breathing rhythm, which is a very delicate thing. It is the subtle most part of your being. Sex energy, breathing energy, the energy of sight, the energy of audition, these are energies conferred by nature, conferred by the divinity of Life, and they are very tender, they are very subtle.

If one is thoughtless, reckless, and overloads the body with impressions, solid or liquid, and pressurizes the body to digest them with stimulants, etc., then the breathing system gets hampered and the *yajna*, the sacrifice, cannot be performed. One has to be very careful.

Therefore, the fire of restraint has to be kindled, so that every movement on the sensual, the verbal, the psychological is an offering to the flame of restraint. Don't think you are doing it for your sake. You are not, Life is. You may be the owner of the house, but the one who dwells in that house is the divine Life. The divinity of Life is the owner of the Cosmos, if you have to use the term at all. That is one way the rhythm of breathing can be obstructed and damaged. So be careful.

If you suffer from ignorance about the nature of reality, if you have not wiped out the ignorance through investigation, exploration of the nature of ultimate reality, then the sin of ignorance takes its toll, as far as your mind is concerned. Then it creates fear, it plays with the idea of security, it imagines the future and worries about it. If there is fear, the breathing rhythm gets disturbed and gets sluggish. If there is anger, breathing becomes quick and instead of five or six breaths you take ten or twelve. So the energy is consumed too fast, affecting the longevity of life. Please do see in what depth and detail the *Gita*, the Upanishads and the Vedas go.

When people perform *yajna*, they fast, they observe celibacy, they wear certain clothes, they clean the place, they chant *mantras*. A sense of purity is created. They charge the atmosphere, they charge themselves with the attitude of sanctity, of holiness, etc. A sense of purity is created in the atmosphere.

Krishna says: 'Let not the rhythm of breathing be affected by the onslaught of anger, fear, worry, anxiety, tension.' When there are neurological tensions, the breathing is not normal. When you shrink within your heart due to fear of imaginary things, or even objectively of factual things, the rhythm gets affected. So: 'conservation of vital energy through rhythmic breathing is the highest type of *yajna*, Arjuna.'

The whole third chapter was on Karma Yoga, the *yoga* of action. The second chapter was on Jnana Yoga, the *yoga* of knowledge. But here Krishna has combined Jnana Yoga with Karma Yoga, and Hatha Yoga (the science of physical exercises and breathing) with Raja Yoga (being one pointed on the ultimate reality). The dialogue between Krishna and Arjuna is an exposition of the highest reality, leading to the formation of the Science of Yoga.

Do you appreciate what we have heard about the flame of awareness in the intelligence, the flame of austerity in the thought structure, the flame of restraint at the sensual level, and the flame of rhythmic movement and conservation of energy at the level of *pranayama*? In Sanskrit it is a beautiful verse, expressing how the inhaling and exhaling breath wait upon each other. The ingoing breath waits upon the outgoing breath that is inside, offers itself to that, the outgoing breath waits upon the breath that is eager to come in, and serves it as an offering.

One is really fascinated by the description of *pranayama* as the highest *yajna*, the highest worship of the divine and the responsibility for the conservation of that vital energy by maintaining the rhythm and not allowing the vagaries of the mind to disturb it, or the irresponsible habits of diet to damage it in any way. You see the life of a *yogi*?

'Inner equipoise is the essence of *yoga*,' says Krishna at one place and then at another place he says: 'Move in the battleground of relationships without generating the fever of attachment or the bitterness of detachment. Let them not enter your heart and affect your senses, Arjuna, while you are in the battleground of relationships.'

The inner and outer are always kept together. They are not allowed to be separated. Life is not allowed to be fragmented. *Yoga* is a holistic way of living. *Hatha, mantra, tantra, jnana, karma*, they are different aspects of *yoga*. They may be treated as different branches, but the whole of *yoga* blends the inner and outer together, because in Life, in reality, there is neither the inner nor the outer, there is neither one nor multiplicity. Life just is.

For communication sake you may say unity decorates itself with diversity, the oneness manifests itself as manyness and multiplicity. But Life is beyond enumeration, beyond verbalization. That is why we started by saying: Life is a mystery, it is divinity. It is self-generated, self-sustained.

In our own body we can witness the dance of the divine. A student of *yoga*, by himself, arrives at the realization of reality, if he observes the breathing system, the miracle of food getting digested and converted into tissues, muscles, plasma; the uni-cellular system developing itself into a multi-cellular system and the dance of innumerable energies functioning harmoniously in your body, which is condensed Cosmos. Then one understands why there is an inner bowing down to the all-permeating divinity. It becomes very clear.

We have come to the point now where *karma*, action, culminates into understanding and understanding flows through the senses in the form of action. They complete one circle of Life. As breathing is a circular movement, in the same way investigation, exploration, understanding flowing through the senses, educated and purified senses, leads to awareness. It is the dance of Life. Capra calls it the dance of Shiva.

If we remember what was said about *jnana*, which is knowing and understanding together, we will be able to explore the meaning or the secret of the last seven verses of the fourth chapter. In the *Isha Upanishad* the term *vidya* and *avidya* had been used. *Vidya* is knowledge about the knowable. The knowable about yourself, your body, your brain, your mind, and also about the Cosmos around you. *Avidya* is ignorance about the knowable.

In the first part of the *Chandogya Upanishad*, the teacher asks his student to collect a seed from the banyan tree and bring it to him. He then says: 'are you aware as to when the seed is sown, the gigantic banyan tree will come about? Now break this seed open to find out whether the tree is concealed in it.' The student breaks open the seed and says: 'Sir I can't see anything inside it.' The teacher says: 'do you realise that your seeing is not the criteria of existence? You cannot see the tree concealed in the seed and yet when you sow the seed the tree comes about. In the same way, out of the nothingness of emptiness the whole universe explodes.' That was the way of teaching of the ancient seers. Thus, the pupil came to know the secret of creation and understand the mystery behind it.

Krishna says to Arjuna: 'when you once understand the principle of Life, the mystery behind its spontaneous beingness, the mystery of so many universes manifesting out of the emptiness of space, then you will never lapse into a state of *moha*, confusion.'

What is confusion? Absence of clarity. When there is absence of clarity, then you get embarrassed. Embarrassment leads to indecision and indecision stimulates a state of suspense, which is paralysing your energies, which is a negativity. And then you begin to suffer. Confusion brings along with it a trail of suffering and misery.

Krishna is trying to communicate that all confusion is due to ignorance about the knowable aspects of Life. It is quite irresponsible to remain ignorant about the things that can be known. You can never know the unknowable, but vast parts of Life are knowable. The human race today is confused or embarrassed or immersed in a variety of negativities, because modern civilization keeps human beings ignorant about so many things. Specialization has converted ordinary human beings, like you and me, into ignorant passive consumers.

Something goes wrong with your health and you take a patent medicine or you go to the doctor. Something goes wrong with the mind, and you go to a psychologist. Technology, automation and so on, have made people unable even to cope with such things as financial matters. They find an accountant who will sort things out for them. A human being does not know much about the body, the mind, the brain, about health, diet. Everything is organized, standardized, regimented.

In ancient days it was the responsibility of those born in human form to know the knowable. And ignorance about the knowable was a sin against Life. The second verse, which we will look at now, deals with the word 'sin'. I'll try to correlate the two. Do you remember, in the *Yoga Sutra*, the five-fold suffering and misery was described by Patanjali and he began by *avidya*, ignorance about the nature of the self, leading to wrong identification. Then emergence of preferences and prejudices, due to wrong identification and emotional compulsions, due to those preferences and prejudices. Patanjali says that everyone suffers from this five-fold psychological misery. And it begins with *avidya*, ignorance.

So, whether it is Patanjali in the *Yoga Sutra* or the Upanishads or the *Gita*, the message is very clear: it is the responsibility of a human being possessing a brain, a neuro-chemical system, intelligence, it is his responsibility to know the knowable aspects of Life. Socrates used to say self-knowing is virtue. And the wisdom of the East says: self-ignorance is sin.

Sin is something that results from the ignorance of the knowable. Crime is something you commit intentionally against the laws of society. A mistake or a folly is something, which happens due to inattention or distraction of the mind. We have to discriminate between a mistake or a folly, and a crime or sin. Sin is always against Life. It is against the essence of Life, the divinity of Life.

If the meaning of the word 'sin' is clear, let us see what Krishna is saying: 'Arjuna, in the human world there is nothing as holy, as sacred, as *jnana*, knowing and understanding.' Knowing and understanding are called holy, sacred, pure, because they wash off ignorance, which is darkness.

Identification with the ego is called *avidya*, ignorance; it is a wrong identification. Instead of identifying with the wholeness of Life, you are identifying with a tiny expression of that wholeness, you are reducing yourself to a tiny separate entity. While you are yourself wholeness, fullness, divine, you are imagining yourself to be limited, to be in bondage.

Nothing purifies Life like the waters of understanding, because they remove the basic ignorance of identifying oneself with the ego, which is just a contrivance to be used for collective living. We identify with the ego, instead of realizing our nature of organic relationship with the wholeness of Life. A ray of the sun is as much light as the sun itself. In the same way an expression of divinity in the human form is as much divine as the Cosmos. That is the message of the *Gita*.

It is not verbal, organized, systematized information, which is called pure or holy, it is knowing and understanding together. Peel the words, receive the meaning, assimilate it, so that the flame of awareness is kindled in your heart. That is *jnana*.

Shankaracharya has commented upon this verse, that people get fascinated by the outward form of action, the structure of religious ceremonies, the mechanism of rituals. Performing those sacred sacrifices, using plenty of money and all the ingredients prescribed for it by the scriptures, inviting Brahmins, chanting *mantras*, etc., they get fascinated by the physical expression of it all. They don't bother to understand the inner meaning, the meaning of the symbolism behind the concept, which is grafted upon perception. Nor do they bother to know why this symbolism came into existence. So Shankaracharya says: 'You may perform hundred sacrifices, but if you do not understand their meaning, you may be born a hundred times, and yet you will be far away from liberation.'

Do not allow actions to get reduced to mechanistic, repetitive activities of the body, of speech, of mind, but probe deeper behind the ritual, the form, the structure, understand the meaning. It is the meaning that will liberate you. It is the understanding of the meaning that kindles the flame of awareness, not only the performance.

Performance can be an aid, a helping factor, but it is not the essence. This whole philosophy of Advaita Vedanta, expounded by Shankara, based on the *Brahma Sutra*, based on the *Gita*, on the Upanishads, centres round this basic principle of knowing and understanding. Ignorance is darkness and it cannot be dispelled by the repetitive mechanistic performances only. It is a peripheral approach.

Ignorance, the idea of a separate entity, can be dispelled only when you make an effort to know and understand the meaning of the knowable. It is the understanding of the known that reveals the nature of the unknown. It is the understanding of the knowable which uncovers for you the secret of the unknowable. The unknowable is to be felt. It is perceived only through sensitivity and sensitivity is a feel, which you experience with the wholeness of your being.

A sentiment or an emotion is a ripple in the psychological structure, a ripple caused in the senses. But the feel is something which is vertical and horizontal at the same time, which vibrates in the whole of your being, permeating it, pervading it. It cannot be destroyed. Once it is there, it is there. So the presence of the unknowable, the immeasurable, the unnameable, can be felt by the sensitivity, which is kindled by the understanding of the known. That's it.

So, one cannot afford to ignore the known and the knowable. The pilgrimage begins with the known and culminates into the secret cave of the unknowable. First knowing and understanding dispel *moha*, confusion. It creates clarity, because it washes off wrong identifications. It washes off ignorance: all the wrong identifications, all the unscientific identifications due to the illusion of separateness, the illusion of independence.

Everything is interlocked, interrelated, so physically, psychologically, cerebrally there is no independence. Independence exists beyond the brain. On the physical and psychological level, personalities are possible. Individuality is beyond the brain. It is a trans-psychological event.

'When the confusion is cleared, when ignorance and unscientific identification are washed off, then, Arjuna, you will be liberated from the inauspicious aspects of Life. Having known and understood this, you will be liberated from the clutches of inauspiciousness.'

Ashuba is translated by many a commentator, including Max Müller, as 'evil'. But the Vedas, the Upanishads and the *Gita* do not recognize the independent existence of evil or that of a devil. *Shuba* and *ashuba* should be translated as auspicious and inauspicious. What is 'auspicious'? That which by its presence and interaction contributes to the welfare of all. *Ashuba* is that which causes harm, damages the natural movement of well-being or welfare around you, in objects or in individuals. Commentators have translated them by good and evil.

The Vedas proclaim non-duality (*advaita*) as the essence of Life. Obviously they will never recognize a separation of good from evil, or the independent autonomous existence and functioning of evil or the devil.

Liberation is always from the inauspicious, from attachment and identification with limitedness. Liberation or enlightenment is not something positive to be acquired, obtained, appropriated. You dispel ignorance and the light of understanding is there, not because you have created the light, but because you have taken the trouble of dispelling ignorance. It is a negative approach.

Spirituality, like science, has a negative approach, not the assertive dogmatic approach of: 'there is a god and therefore you must believe in him.' That is not spirituality. Negatively eliminating, pointing out the limitedness of the conditioning, pointing out the existence of the unlimited, that is all spirituality does. Pointing out the inbuilt limitations of knowledge, it refers to the existence of that which is not accessible to knowledge and knowing. Assertiveness is unknown to the language of spirituality. There is tentativeness of approach, pliability, elasticity in attitude, and humility arising out of the direct encounter with the vastness, the infinity of Life.

It takes a Newton to say: 'Whatever I have known is like a pebble on the shore of knowledge.' Humility, elasticity, tenderness arises when the presence of the wholeness is felt, when the mystery of interrelatedness is felt. The presence of that mystery in which we are dwelling, of which we are a part, generates what you call humility. Not a compartmental humility, that is to say humility in relation to certain individuals and not to others. That which is compartmental is untrue. Truth by its very nature is holistic, all-pervading.

Krishna says to Arjuna: 'you will be liberated from the clutches of inauspiciousness.' What is inauspicious? Wrong identification and the preferences, prejudices, likes, and dislikes that result from those identifications. If there is no identification, or in modern language, if there is no image of yourself that you carry around and try to project in different ways, in different fields, if there is no image, would there be any attachment, would there be any identification, would there be any preference or prejudice?

It is the image that generates a like or a dislike, because the image creates its own norms, criteria, and wants to pass value judgements upon every person that it comes across. When there is no image, no criteria or norm carried in the briefcase of memory, you don't judge others.

'Do not judge others, let me be judged.' That also was a way of saying it, but who bothers to probe into the secret behind those beautiful words of the Prince of mankind? It is as good as a *mantra*, the handsome words have the perfume of the authenticity of Life behind them. They are not borrowed from books, but learned from the book of Life, digested.

'Inauspiciousness results from wrong identification and wrong identification is the result of ignorance. So it is the ignorance of the knowable that causes all manner of bondages in life, Arjuna. Therefore you must know and understand. When the sun rises and there is light, darkness is dispelled from every corner of the earth, which is in contact with the movement of the sun. In the same way, when understanding dawns upon the heart, then ignorance is wiped out completely, not partially. The understanding of the principle of Life, the mystery of interrelatedness in Life will wipe out completely the roots of ignorance in your consciousness. It was ignorance that was inauspicious and you are going to be liberated completely from the clutches of that ignorance.

And when the wiping out of the roots of ignorance through knowing and understanding happens, Arjuna, you will see that you have arrived at peace, an invincible peace, which will not be disturbed by any happening of pain or pleasure, of honour or humiliation in your life. Success or failure will not disturb your peace. Peace will be a dimension.

At this time you are in a state of confusion, Arjuna, which is embarrassing you and paralysing your actions. Because you have forgotten the known, what you have done, what the Kauravas have done, how everything between you in the last fourteen years, has been: preparing for war. You have been preparing for it with your actions, with your reactions. In so many ways you have contributed towards the preparation for war.

And now, on the battlefield, when you stand here, you want to take upon yourself the role of a self-righteous person, saying: 'the Kauravas are stupid to want to fight. I know it is bad, we should not fight, it will cause bloodshed, it will cause this and that. So Krishna, I am not going to fight.' You want to pretend to be a self-righteous superior person to them. But you have been preparing for war, Arjuna, you have forgotten the known, you have forgotten what you have contributed. So now you say: I cannot hold my bow, my body is trembling, I do not want to fight. I wont fight.'

Krishna is taking him to task. 'All your descriptions of war as inauspicious, cruel, and the bloodshed in war, did you not know all this the last fourteen years, when you were contributing towards the preparations? Now you get into the attitude of helplessness, self-pity, self-righteousness. That will not do.

You are forgetting the known, what you have done, what you have thought, felt. Every movement of yours is action, whether you think a thought, whether you utter a word or you go through a deed, they are all actions, every movement is action. When you were acting in the darkness of inattention, of attachment, of wrong identification, of preferences and prejudices, you were contributing to the state of restlessness, the triple restlessness that we have seen. All that was inauspicious, Arjuna.

Free yourself from the clutches of all that, recollect that you have been preparing for war, and stand up and fight like a man. Put yourself in the state of *yoga*, face the consequences of what you have done, clandestinely, openly, overtly, inwardly, through wishing, through imagining, through thinking, through talking. Face the situation that you have created for yourself in life, Arjuna, face it like a man.'

The Gita's message tells us not to run away from Life, not to escape into any sophisticated network, because that is sin. Life is for living and living is a movement of relationships. So when Krishna comes to the last words in the *Gita*, he says: 'clearing asunder the roots of ignorance, get up, O Arjuna, awake, arise, lift yourself up in the state of *yoga*, put yourself in a state of union with divinity.'

What does: 'Awake, arise and unite yourself with divinity, through the awareness of its presence' imply? Remember the unity of Life. Multiplicity is the outer form, the manyness is the garb. Within the manyness, within the diversity, the unity, the oneness, is the essence, because everything is interrelated.

The state of *yoga* is to be united with divinity through awareness. Self-realization or the realization of divinity does not imply that you become god or divinity or the Cosmos. You are condensed Cosmos, your tiny human form is a miniature Cosmos, a field of innumerable energies. Harmonize them, get acquainted with them, and don't obstruct their functioning by introducing a centre of 'me', which begins to manipulate these energies, manoeuvring them. Let them flow, Arjuna.

Action or *karma* is the destiny of human beings, because of three reasons. The human organism is a product of time, it is a product of civilization and it is the net result of human conditioning. Conditioning means conditioned energies. The human body and the human brain contain conditioned energies. The movement of those conditioned energies has been set into motion. That which has been set into motion previously, is called *prarabdha karma*.

Isha Upanishad: 'There is no other path for mankind but to act.' There are energies which have been conditioned, set into motion already, in the form of human bodies, let them function. You are not going to be the agent, though you are the doer. The agent is those conditioned energies. See to it that they operate harmoniously, not in conflict, not with tension.

Action is necessary, because the very human form, including the brain, is full of energies given to it by civilization and culture, which are going to create their own compulsion. Is there an energy that does not create a compulsion? Can energy ever be idle? Turn to physics: energy can never be idle. So it creates its own compulsion. Innumerable energies contained in your body will create their own compulsion. When?

As soon as your senses come into contact with the outer world. When sight comes into contact with light, it sees. Seeing does not depend upon your volition. Hearing does not depend upon your volition. Sound is heard, form is seen, things are touched, because there is the energy of touch in the skin. Please do see. So what you call action is really the spontaneous interaction between the energies contained in you and the energies contained in the Cosmos. They are interacting. Why do you come in between and say: 'I do this.' You may appear to be the doer, but the agent is the whole human history of which you are a part.

Along with the conditioning, there is that potential of intelligence in the human form. Behind, beneath, between the dance of energies is concealed the intelligence. That intelligence demonstrates itself in the rhythm of the breathing system, which again does not depend upon your volition. So intelligence has been conferred upon us, that all-pervading principle of intelligence lives in the abode of every human heart. Let us say that it lives in non-human hearts also. We can add to the *Gita* and create our *Gita* for the twenty-first century. The last word in spirituality has not yet been said.

The human race is waiting for dimensional transformation. And through the human beings who have gone through that holistic transformation, a new race and a new dynamics of human relationships manifests, because there is intelligence, which creates the urge for love, for sharing, for compassion, for truthfulness, for friendliness. These are all non-rational urges. That intelligence will create its own compulsion to know, to act. And therefore act you must.

And furthermore, the Cosmic energies existing outside of you, will pull you into the orbit of interrelationship and interaction and make you act. So: 'there is no question of you wanting to act or not wanting to act, Arjuna. This is your destiny, the way you have to live, in order to remain united with divinity; through acting and moving in relationship. You are not obliging anyone by doing *karma*, it is the cycle of Life. If you create a bondage out of that movement, then it is your responsibility, your fault.'

A tree lives happily, contributing flowers or fruit; it grows, decays and dies. It manifests its potential, it contributes its potential to the Cosmos. Human beings can do the same: manifest their potential, contribute through their actions, which are deeds, words, thoughts, breath. Breath is also an action.

Get established in that state of *yoga*, where sacrifice through breathing is going on smoothly, where ignorance and wrong identification are wiped out completely. Therefore, the roots of inauspiciousness are also cut off. Face the challenges that you have created for yourself.

Why did Krishna say: 'get established in the understanding.' To get established, rooted in the understanding implies, my dear friends, equipping the senses to cope with the intensity and depth and the velocity of understanding, in order to equip the sensual, the verbal and the psychological structures of the organism and mould their energies. When that is done, then you are established in your understanding.

People may arrive at understanding, but they don't get rooted in the understanding. It remains as an abstraction, as an idea, as a piece of knowledge in their brain and, therefore, it does not cause any qualitative holistic change in their life. They become better human beings, no doubt. But here the *Gita* is talking about enlightenment or liberation. *Yoga* is liberation from impurities, liberation from imbalances.

Life has very strange ways. A few Italian Hatha Yoga teachers wanted to study these ancient texts. Now this study has spread to other countries. If you take up such a study, go into it as deeply as possible, as extensively as possible. So, let us thank the Hatha Yoga teachers for creating the opportunity for this interaction.

I had to focus all my energy five thousand years back and be with that fellow, to feel what he was trying to communicate. You know, quite a job. We are also thankful to others who have joined as observers.

CHAPTER V

YOGA OF RENUNCIATION

The *Gita* was written 5000 years ago. It is the combined product of the Upanishads, the Six Systems of Indian Philosophy and also the essence of the Vedas. The ancient land of India and the people who lived there, were concerned primarily with understanding the nature of the Cosmos and the modalities of Cosmic energies. They were also interested and concerned about knowledge (*vidya*) about the macrocosm or Brahman and knowledge about the microcosm or Atman.

Macrocosm or Brahman is the non-differentiated and non-differentiable organic wholeness of Life. And microcosm is the individuated particularized expression of that wholeness. So they were interested both in Atma-Vidya and Brahma-Vidya. Having understood the nature and mechanism of both, they were interested in applying that knowledge to their living. That is how the science of *yoga* came about.

Rooted in the knowledge of Atman and Brahman, they developed a science of handling the energies contained in the microcosm or the individuated expression, and utilized them in such a way, which would be harmonious with the functioning of the Cosmic energies.

So, *yoga* is a science which helps you to remain grounded in the understanding of the Cosmic Life, while equipped to handle the energies contained in your psychophysical structure and thus live harmoniously with both, united at one end with the microcosm and at the other with the macrocosm.

That was the science of *yoga*, which is the foundation of all the systems of Indian philosophy, such as Sankhya, Yoga, Nyaya,

Vaisheshika etc. The Yoga Shastra of the *Gita* is based upon Brahma-Vidya. That background should be very much alive in your consciousness, if you wish to understand the dialogue that takes place between Krishna and Arjuna.

In that dialogue we are confronted with two individuals, living in two different dimensions of consciousness. When you live in a different dimension, you have a different perspective of Life and also a different attitude towards Life, as well as a different approach in meeting the challenges from moment to moment. You will appreciate this difficulty between Krishna and Arjuna. After having listened to Krishna in the first four chapters, Arjuna asks a question, which he had already asked in the second chapter and which was referred to in the third chapter. He asks:

'You praise both *karma sannyasa*, non-action, and Karma Yoga, *yoga* through action. Please tell me precisely which is the better of the two?'

Karma sannyasa, *yoga* of non-action, is also called *Sankhya*. It means that *karma sannyasa* is based on knowledge derived from the invisible, unnameable, immeasurable wholeness of reality. So, *sankhya* and *sannyasa* mean the same thing. Sometimes Krishna uses *sankhya*, sometimes *sannyasa*, a code language in the science of spirituality. Arjuna asks which is the better of the two: the path of non-action, which is known as renunciation (*sannyasa*), also called the path of knowledge (*Sankhya*), or the path of action, which is known as the path of Karma Yoga?

From the very first chapter, Arjuna seems to want not only a value judgement but a decision from Krishna, so that he can follow it. But Krishna is bent upon not giving any particular value judgement or decision to Arjuna. Krishna wants Arjuna to take his own decisions in the freedom of his understanding. That seems to be the tussle between Krishna and Arjuna and perhaps we will be witnessing this tussle between the two throughout the remaining chapters of the *Gita*. Arjuna will keep on raising the same question, from different angles and Krishna will reply from different angles, without giving any judgement of his own.

Now, the confusion in the mind of Arjuna seems to be due to ignorance, which persists about the implications of the term *sannyasa*. Renunciation or *sannyasa* or non-action does not refer to any psychophysical activity. It is a state of consciousness. It could at best be called an attitude, but it does not refer to any physical activity. You cannot say: 'I have renounced.' It is not an act of the ego. It is not an effort of the will. But when there is no attachment, no desire and no hate in the consciousness, then your every breath has the perfume of inner renunciation.

Arjuna must have seen, as you have probably seen, people called *sannyasins*, who wear ochre robes, who have given up their homes and property, who have turned away from their family, changed their names etc. That is not what *sannyasa* means either in the *Gita* or in the Upanishads.

The path of non-action, the path of *karma sannyasa*, implies being and living without attachment or aversion (*raga* or *dvesha*), as referred to in the seventh verse in this chapter:

'Such a person lives and moves with the movement of relationships, without any desire and without any hatred.' When there is no attachment, no repulsion, no hatred, then your consciousness is in a state of renunciation. Taking a meal, bathing the body, sleeping the body, clothing the body, are actions in the eyes of the people, but in essence they are the movement of inner non-action.

We are dealing with the essence of the Vedas and the Upanishads. You have to be very alert and sensitive to establish a rapport with Krishna and his words. So, when Arjuna asks him which is better, the reply given by Vasudeva (a name of Krishna), in the first seven or eight verses, is: 'the path of non-action is difficult for those who have not mastered the secret of *yoga*.'

Here, he is referring to the secret of the eightfold aspect of Raja Yoga, that is *yama, niyama, asana, pranayama, pratyahara, dharana, dhyana* and *samadhi*, for equipping your psycho-physical organism with the necessary purity, necessary sterling vitality, etc. The path of non-action for one, who has not equipped his psychophysical organism with this eightfold aspect of *yoga*, is very difficult.

But if you take the path of action, having mastered or even without having mastered this eightfold aspect of *yoga*, it will be easier for you to grow into the dimension of non-attachment or renunciation or *sannyasa*. There is no superior or inferior path. But it is easier to purify your organism through the eightfold aspect of *yoga*, while at the same time discharging your responsibilities and commitments in society.

Krishna says: 'there is no superior or inferior path. These two paths can go together. While discharging your responsibilities and purifying your organism simultaneously, the state of renunciation flowers from within. However, the path of action is preferable.'

Krishna does not say superior, higher or lower. It has a kind of uniqueness, which helps ordinary people to remain in society, in their family, discharging their responsibilities, fulfilling their commitments, and simultaneously educating themselves in purification.

After all, Raja Yoga is the science of purification. You learn to eliminate all the toxins, all the imbalances, impurities, from your body and brain, equipping them to be precise and accurate like the edge of a razor. You make your whole organism very piercing, so that there is accuracy in receiving impressions and precision in their retention. And in their reproduction also there is the same sharp, penetrating precision. Then your biological and psychological organism, this magnificent electro-magnetic apparatus, moves through Life with glory and majesty, with the grandeur of precision and accuracy.

In the second verse, Krishna says there is no difference between the actual worth of the two paths. The choice is not to be made on so-called merit. They are the same. One refers to the attitude, the other to the psychophysical organism in which you are living.

What will happen if a person masters this eightfold aspect (self-control, control of the vital energy or *pranayama*, *asana*, here state of mind control, truthfulness, non-stealing, continence, abstention from greed in thought, word and deed, etc.)?

Krishna says: 'When you are equipped with the secret of *yoga*, when you equip your body with the eightfold aspect of *yoga*, your mind gets purified.' Then, whenever the brain/mind complex gets into motion, its expression, its action is pure; there is restraint.' When the brain and mind move in action, not in reaction, but when there is a need to act, that act is pure. Then every cerebral, every psychological movement, when warranted, is pure.

Everything fed into the brain and into the neuro-chemical system is called in the Vedas and the Upanishads *samskaras*, conditionings, tendencies. There are many conditionings fed into the mind: into the whole cerebral neuro-chemical structure, the nervous system, the chemical system, the innumerable brain cells, the blood stream, the breath stream, etc.

First, there is action, you are acting. Secondly, the reference is to the conquest of your reactions. All the *samskaras* are called reactions. Everything that is fed into the brain and into the neuro-chemical system is called in the Vedas and the Upanishads *samskaras*, conditionings, a word used by modern psychologists.

In *yoga* there is no conquest, there is restraint. The movement of conditioning becomes spontaneously restrained when a person has mastered the eightfold *yoga*. Its spontaneous movement is pure and the movement of conditioning contained in it, is restrained.

You see the propriety of using two words: first purifying and then restraint. We must appreciate the particular connotation contained in these two words, even though the word *atman* is used in both the words. In ancient days, the days of the *Mahabharata*, of the *Gita*, people used to refer to one another as *atman*. They would ask: How do you do, *atman*?

The word *atman* here refers to the body, the mind, the brain, and then if you go deeper, that which holds the body and the mind together. Atman is a very pregnant word. Sometimes it will be used in reference to the physical body, sometimes to the mind, sometimes to the conditionings and sometimes to that ultimate reality, the ground of existence. We are dealing with the ancient Sanskrit language.

So first the whole cerebral instrument is purified. Then the conditionings are restrained. Then the senses and the sense organs are trained through the eightfold aspect of *yoga*. Krishna talks about training, restraining, purifying the gross biological structure, to arrive at the state of *yoga yukta* (being established in *yoga*).

When you have trained the senses through *yama* and *niyama*, through proper diet, through all the eightfold *yoga*, they behave themselves; they do not enter into excesses. The trained sense organs, the restrained conditionings, the purified cerebral instrument, all this is the cumulative effect in a state of *yoga yukta*.

'Arjuna, if you equip yourself with such training; with restraint, purification, etc., then it does not matter whether you follow the path of action or the path of non-action, as they are called by society'. Non-action is the state of consciousness when thoughts do not move unless thinking is warranted, when conditionings do not move unless their movement is needed. There is silence, call it renunciation, call it non-action, call it motionlessness.

Karma sannyasa is a dimension of consciousness. And Karma Yoga is the way of handling the psychophysical organism, which is loaded with conditionings of millions of years, which cannot be thrown away, which cannot be ignored, which cannot be wished away, which cannot be explained away. You have to live with that.

To utilize the energies contained in the conditionings, you remove first the chaos in those conditionings, the incompatible in the conditionings. Thus, you create a non-chaotic non-anarchic crowd of thoughts, experiences and knowledge. That is you grow into a beautiful organic harmonious wholeness in your conditionings. You don't integrate them with the needle and thread of some philosophy, ideology or theory, but through training, restraining and purification you create the kind of lovely wholeness in the conditionings. So, whenever they move, they move in a built-in spontaneity of restraint. No need to suppress, repress, control, or compel.

All the energies of the conditionings have to be channelled and used. Right now, while we are sitting here, we are channelling our energies, our conditionings, so that the dialogue takes place within you and me. If we do not understand the same language, if your memory does not bring up the same meaning at the same time, while listening to the words, there cannot be a dialogue. The language I am using is purely from memory, but what I am saying is not from memory. I have to use the psychophysical instrument as well as the energies, but what I am saying is not from memory.

You give a diet to the body; you are nourishing the biological structure. While seeing with the eyes, or listening to words, you are using energy. The harmonious use of the energies at the microcosmic level may enrich the existing harmonious energies in the macrocosm. Do you see the union between the microcosm and the macrocosm, the union between *Atma-vidya*, and *Brahma-vidya*, through the science of *yoga*?

The point that is touched upon by Vasudeva is a fascinating one. First, he refers to the physics of consciousness, when he talks about *Atma-vidya/Brahma-vidya*, now he is going to take up the science of matter and energy. Spirituality is both: the physics of consciousness and the science of matter and energy.

So, he says to Arjuna that the harmonizing of the microcosmic and the macrocosmic energies is going to be elucidated, is going to be elaborated upon and explained. In three verses Vasudeva puts this across beautifully. He says:

'As there is energy in the Cosmos around you, there is energy in the senses, in the sense organs, called *indriyas*, which you think you possess and are going to control. The energies in your body and brain and the energies functioning outside of you are interrelated. They attract one another, they invite one another.'

When in the organism there is a sensation and you say: 'I am hungry,' you are not the creator of the appetite. It is the interrelationship of all the organs in the body that create the beautiful state of appetite and your whole body is permeated by that energy of appetite.

The energy of thirst gets attracted towards water; the energy in thirst and the energy in water are cosmically interrelated. You feel the sensation of thirst and you reach out towards water. You drink a glass of water. It is the thirst that has drunk the glass of water. Your hand, your throat, your mouth, are just instruments but the emergence of the upsurge of thirst, upsurge of appetite, and the consuming of diet are Cosmic movements.

The senses move towards their respective objects when they are trained to move as for their needs and not as for the conditionings artificially imposed upon them. The science of *yoga* teaches you to discriminate between the natural appetite and the artificially imagined illusory appetite, that the modern civilization imposes upon you.

The organism has a rhythm of appetite, of thirst. There is an urge to move. There is an urge to sleep. These movements of the sensory organs take place without your volition. Those energies are built-in your system. Energies exist outside of you in the Cosmos. Their interrelationship brings about the movement of eating, drinking, sleeping, responding to sex-impulse, sex-instinct. You are not the doer. You are not the creator of those energies.

The whole Cosmos is a field for the dance of innumerable energies and so your body, the microcosm, is also a field of innumerable energies, which interact, interplay. You impose the idea upon yourself that 'I have slept', 'I have taken a meal.' But it is a movement going on in spite of and irrespective of your volition, it is bound to happen. When you take a meal or you work for earning your livelihood, you believe it to be the path of *karma* and you believe yourself to be the doer. But it is the Cosmic movement and the Cosmic energies that are the doer.

Watch a plant when you water it or provide it with some manure, or when it gets good air and sunshine. If one has the sensitivity, one can notice the smile, the shine on the leaves. Their colour, the shade changes because it has had its meal. In the same way, your body has a sense of gratification when it has been properly fed, properly slept. It is not you who are doing all this; it is you that cause this, but not doing this.

The sun when it rises causes movement in the world. People, who were sleeping, get up when the day breaks and sunrise takes place. They start moving. The sun does not ask you to move. The sun does not move you. And yet the existence of the sun causes the urge to move in the whole world. Waking, sleeping, eating, drinking, talking, taking, giving; people believe they are doing all these things. But it is *prakriti*, it is matter, the fountain of energy that is functioning. Beautiful verses, verses eight and nine. Why attribute these psychophysical movements to your volition and believe you are the doer, the actor?

Once you understand this, then you have become a *sannyasin*. You allow those movements to take place and by training, restraining and purifying you have created a harmony there. In the undifferentiated organic wholeness there is a built-in spontaneous harmony.

But when the wholeness gets individuated, particularized, then that spontaneous Cosmic balance is disturbed in the very process of individuation and particularization. It gets limited by space and time. It gets limited by form. The energies get solidified and we call it matter. In the individuated expression of the human body it gets limited, it gets conditioned, it gets added to. That is the conditioning of the human race. So there are many imbalances, there are many disharmonies. Those have to be corrected.

The science of *yoga* helps you to correct the imbalances, to eliminate the impurities that have come about in the process of individuation, of particularization, a kind of isolation that has come about through the sense of separateness. The identification with that exclusive individuated microcosmic identity, itself creates impurities. So there is a forgetfulness, ignorance (avidya), about the essence of wholeness of our own nature. And there is identification with the limited, the conditioned, the individuated, creating an illusion of separateness. And the travail of human life begins.

But through the science of *yoga*, when you go through training, restraining, purifying and harmonizing, that forgetfulness disappears. You become aware of being an organic expression of the wholeness of Life, an expression of Brahman. You become aware of your real nature, Atman, of reality. Though it gets clothed in an individuated form, it is there. The science of *yoga* teaches one to remain united through awareness, remain united through harmonization of the energies, at one end in our body and at the other end with the Cosmos.

Let us look at verse ten again in depth, before we proceed to verse eleven. 'Planting the *karma*, the actions, into Brahman.' How can you plant your *karma*, actions, your movements, in Brahman, which is indivisible non-fragmentable, the organic wholeness of Life?

The ground of existence, the supreme reality, the undifferentiated, non-individuated organic wholeness of Life is called Brahman by the Vedas and the Upanishads. So you plant every movement of yours, which is action, *karma*, in the awareness of Brahman.

We have seen that the microcosm, the individual consciousness, and the macrocosm, the Cosmic consciousness, can be united through the energy of awareness. That is the whole theme of the science of *yoga*; to be united with the wholeness of Life through perception of it, understanding of it and awareness of it. In every breath of yours, in every movement of yours, in every relationship of yours, is the theme of the science of *yoga*. That is planting all your *karmas*, all your actions, in the awareness of the ultimate reality.

And what was the content of that awareness? We were told by Vasudeva that the energies in the senses, in the sense organs and the energies contained in nature outside of us, were interrelated. There is a constant interplay going on between the innumerable energies operating in the Cosmos and the limited conditioned energies contained in the human body. Whether we call it animate or inanimate, Life is a field of innumerable energies and the dance of those energies, of which we are also a part, goes on in Life.

When the senses are attracted towards the energies in nature and there is a movement either of reception or of response, you are not the doer, the actor. It is the nature of Life that the interaction goes on. You are the field in which the interplay goes on, in which the interaction happens, occurs.

Let us proceed from that point. You plant your movements, your relationships, your actions, in the awareness of that organic wholeness. You plant it in Brahman means: in the reality of the existing union between you and the ultimate, you and the divine. You have not to be united through an effort of the will, or through an effort of the body, but you have to be aware of the interrelationship, the organic relationship with reality. So when your *karmas*, your actions are rooted in that awareness, they are planted in the soil of that awareness.

One more requirement is mentioned: to plant your actions without attachment, in the awareness of Brahman. I would like to add one more shade to the meaning of attachment. Every word has many shades of meaning. For me the word attachment means: psychological involvement in what you are doing. Consciousness of what you are doing is one thing. But psychological involvement means: to be related to the feeling that I am doing it.

I get excited if that, which is to be done, is something that pleases me, or there is reluctance in me if that, which is to be done is not to my liking. If I am not sure whether I am going to succeed in a particular job, there is a tension, a worry, an anxiety. 'Will I succeed, will I not succeed?' 'Will it be accepted, recognized by society or by the family, or whoever is around? What will I get out of it?' All this is psychological involvement. That is not going through the relationships, the actions, the movements, as a part of Life, as a part of the game, as the content of the act of living.

After all, Life is for living and the content of living is your act. You bring the quality of your consciousness, the quality of your movement at the sensory level, the quality of your action into that movement.

First, there is psychological involvement: excitement, depression, worry, anxiety, impatience, hurry. All these are indications of psychological involvement. That involvement, when repeated, leads to what is called attachment, which implies that you depend upon the pleasure that is derived from that movement. If you do not get an opportunity to repeat that relationship, that action, that movement, then you become miserable. Beginning with involvement, it develops into attachment and culminates into obsession, which is loss of inner freedom.

Why does the *Gita* talk all the time about this non-involvement and non-attachment? Vasudeva has said: 'he who is free from attachment, detachment, and indifference, he is a *sannyasin,* a renunciate.' It is not an action on the psychophysical level, rather an attitude to Life, an approach to whatever you do.

With that as a background, let us look at what is to be renounced. Not action, not relationships, not the movement of Life. What is to be renounced? Psychological involvement and attachment is renounced, because of the awareness of Cosmic reality. What happens to that individual? His consciousness is not tainted by, polluted by sin, *papa*. We are coming to this very significant term, *papa*. The *Gita* is not a theoretical or religious book; it is a book about spirituality, about the science of Life. Spirituality and religion are to be distinguished and discriminated from one another.

The Vedic meaning or the Upanishadic meaning may be quite different from the meaning that is given or conferred on the words by religious books. For example, *papa*, the word 'sin', when it is used in the religious context, has a moral undertone and overtone. Spirituality does not talk about your morality and immorality. It deals with the ultimate, the supreme reality, the perception of it, understanding of it, being aware of it and living at the sensory, physical and psychological level in that awareness.

Here the word *papa* means that consciousness is not tainted, polluted by sin. What is this sin? Sin according to the Vedas and the Upanishads is: appropriating to the ego what really belongs to the divine. You appropriate something to your ego, to your I, which really belongs to Life. This attraction and interplay between the whole sensory system and the outer world is a part of Life, it is a movement of Life, you have not created it. You cannot take the credit of creating that relationship nor of building up the harmony, which was pre-existing. You may find this point a little difficult.

The Cosmic Life is a song of harmony between the earth, water, fire, the emptiness of space, etc. All these, which apparently seem to be incompatible with one another, cooperate with one another, whether the solidity of the earth, the gravity of the earth, the liquidity of water, the emptiness of space, sound and words exploding out of that emptiness of space. So the Cosmos is a huge song of harmony. Harmony is the nature of Life. When you disturb that harmony, you have committed a sin.

There is a built-in order in the Cosmos, there is a built-in order in your body, in the organs, how they cooperate with one another in your body, the kidneys, the liver, the pancreas, the digestive organs, your eyes, your ears. Without your volition they are functioning harmoniously. If you allow them to function harmoniously, there is the glow of health. Health is the eloquence of harmony. When you disturb the harmony, when you disturb the built-in order, then you are committing a sin.

'That individual who plants his actions in the awareness of the Cosmic energy, in the awareness of Cosmic Life, that person does not get psychologically involved in what he is doing, does not create tension, worries, excitement, anxieties, depressions, out of the movement. One who does not get attached, one who does not depend for inner peace upon the outer activities, that person never gets tainted (*papa*); his consciousness never gets tainted by anything. He is the ever virtuous person.'

Virtue and vice are metaphysical terms, they are scientific terms. Spirituality is a science of living. There is no make belief in this. It is not mere theory. The statements contained in the Vedas and the Upanishads are verified by investigation, exploration and experimentation. The Seers, the Rishis of this ancient land, have spent generation after generation converting their bodies, minds, brains, into laboratories, investigating the nature of ultimate truth.

Physics turns outward and investigates reality with the help of matter, of the smallest particles of matter. Spirituality is the physics of consciousness. Leaving aside the sensory organs and the movement of the brain, it explores the ultimate reality with the help of silence, with the help of that magnificent dimension of emptiness. The *Gita* gives the essence of the Vedas.

Consciousness is not tainted by any sin. And what is implied by sin, by disorder, disharmony, impurity? Even the words purity and impurity have no moral odour, they are scientific terms. Precision is purity, imprecision is impurity. Equanimity is purity and a disturbed state is impurity. A spontaneous poise, equipoise, is purity and a constant disturbed state, where the metabolic chemical neurological equilibrium is disturbed, is called sin. Please do see the implications of the words sin and virtue, because we'll come across them many times.

So, his consciousness is not tainted by the sin of stimulating, causing, provoking, any disharmony, any disorder by his behaviour. A *yogi* is one who is not only harmony in flesh and bones within, but his actions do not cause disorder or disharmony outside. That is the beauty of the science of *yoga*.

Let us proceed. How do you do such action, such *karma*? Krishna says: 'by the sense organs, by the whole body, by the mind, by the brain.' Krishna is now elaborating how the non-involvement is lived at the sensory level, at the mental level, at the cerebral intellectual level and at the level of your whole organism.

This non-involvement is not a wishful idea. You can't say: 'I am not involved!' while the state of your consciousness, the look in your eyes, the tone of your verbalization, the movements that you go through, all declare a very lively involvement. You may say: 'I have no tension', but a person will have to believe what the behaviour declares. Your behaviour is the mirror reflecting your inner tensions or conflicts.

Krishna is elaborating upon the study of non-involvement at the sensory level of the eyes, the ears, the nose, the skin, the speech, the intake through the eyes, the ears, the nose, the mouth, etc. He says: 'non-involvement is lived at all these levels, so there is no inattention.' A student of yoga is watchful about every sensation that is moving in his body, everything that gets expressed through his glances, words, intonation, pronunciation, accent, the movement of the body, how you touch space through your physical movements etc.

Whatever is done at all these levels is done for holistic purification. The science of yoga is the process of education in holistic purification. Not purification of some part of your life, not physical purification, then mental purification, then cerebral purification. If you just do *hatha yoga, asanas, pranayama*, etc., you do only the physical part of it, the mechanical discipline of it. Without the eightfold purification, it would be a partial purification.

You may have a symmetrical body, you may have a healthy body, but the inner purification through the eightfold discipline of the consciousness will not be there. *Yoga* is the science of holistic purification, that is simultaneous purification at all the levels of our life, the outer and the inner, the gross and the subtle, the visible and the invisible. So the student of *yoga*, engaged in holistic purification, does his *karmas* (actions), *Karma Yoga*, for purification. At whatever level he acts, looking is an action, bathing your body is an action, brushing the teeth is an action, sleeping the body is an action; all are related to the Cosmic wholeness. You are not separate from that. You either enrich the harmony, you get rooted in that harmony, or you disturb the harmony.

To nourish inner conflicts and tensions is called a crime against Life. Why is Krishna elaborating about this? Because in the second verse of the fifth chapter he had said that whether you follow the path of *Karma Sannyasa* or *Karma Yoga*, both lead you to the same reality. And yet there is something particular and unique about *Karma Yoga*, in that you get a chance of doing things for holistic purification.

If you just understand the truth theoretically and say: 'I understand the truth, therefore, I renounce everything. No responsibilities, no social life, I turn away, I become a recluse', in other words you withdraw, in that withdrawal you may have the awareness of the holistic Life, but there is not necessarily holistic purification. Because of the theoretical understanding of the truth, the holistic purification does not come about. Holistic purification requires self-education, *sadhana*.

Sadhana is not for obtaining anything. Divinity is not to be obtained, acquired; it is the nature of Life. Life is divinity, it is divine. *Sadhana* is not done for acquiring anything, but it is for eliminating the impurities, purifying the perceptions, purifying the cognitions, purifying the responses, etc. The karmas are gone through so that a holistic purification can take place.

When the word *karma* is used in the *Gita*, it is not a sheer action. It has a number of shades in it. *Karma*, according to the Vedas and the Upanishads, has different aspects. Some are called *nitya karma*, obligatory actions, to be done every day by each human being. For example getting up every morning is *nitya karma*.

Now, if you get up before sunrise, what will happen to you? The Vedas say that your waking up will be enriched by the energies of the pre-dawn hours. That is the enrichment. But the *nitya karma* is, that when you wake up, you get up. Cleaning your body is *dharma*, is your responsibility, is your *nitya karma*. Feeding the body, clothing it, this is all *nitya karma*. If you are a teacher you study, that becomes your *nitya karma*. If you are a farmer, you go to the field handling the plants, or as a teacher handling the text. There is no difference; there is no superiority, inferiority, higher or lower. *Nitya karma* is obligatory to every one.

Then there is occasional *karma*. If a child is born in your family and there is a little festivity, that is occasional. But it cannot be avoided. Suppose there is a death in the family; there is a kind of heavy mourning atmosphere and friends come to share your sorrow. The act of sharing sorrow, or sharing joy, is an occasional *karma*.

But the challenges of Life are ever new. The marvellous thing of Life is that it throws up new challenges at you every dawn. The challenges in the father's life are not repeated in the life of the son.

They are ever new. That is the infinity of Life. It throws up new challenges and keeps you alert, it keeps you awake.

Besides the daily necessary obligatory actions, there are occasional actions that are also obligatory, due to the community you are living in, the country you are living in, the race you belong to, the conditionings in which you are brought up, the socio-economic context of your life, etc.

I will refer to only one more kind of *karma*. One could in fact refer to ten, to twelve different kinds of *karma*, different nuances of *karma*.

The third kind of *karma* is that which is banned. Banned by whom? Not by some scriptures, not by some religious preachers or teachers. They are banned for the simple reason that, if you indulge in them, your own physical and psychological life gets disorderly, it becomes chaotic, it becomes anarchic.

A person, whose physical and psychological life contains disorder, disharmony, tensions etc., becomes an anti-social element. Thinking becomes imbalanced, words get imbalanced and the conduct also is imbalanced. Jealousy, impatience, annoyance, is a kind of imbalance. The desire to become aggressive, which is the beginning of violence, is anti-social.

Let me take an example. I function as a teacher for two weeks, while conducting the study course. It is prohibited on me to keep awake till midnight. Do you see how this prohibited *karma* comes about? If I am to be a teacher, I must go to bed early, wake up early and have sufficient sleep to energize the whole neuro-chemical system, so that I can give you my best. If I am to discharge this responsibility, certain things get banned or prohibited by the very nature of Life, by the very nature of your responsibilities.

If you take heavy meals in the evening, you will not have a sound sleep, because that food will lie heavily in your digestive organs and disturb the interrelation between the digestive organs and the pituitary gland and sleep will be disturbed. You will get dreams or you will not be able to sleep. So not to have heavy meals late at night becomes obligatory.

Supposing you want to meditate. Meditation requires an empty stomach. If the stomach is heavily burdened, then fermentation goes on. That fermentation going on in the digestive organs has repercussions on your blood pressure, on your blood circulation, etc. Then you may sit down in one posture for ten hours, closing your eyes or chanting *mantras*, silence will elude you, meditation will elude you. I have given you very simple examples why certain *karmas* are prohibited or banned for persons who are engaged in certain responsibilities.

Yukta is an adjective meaning being involved in *yoga*, and therefore *yukti* is a strategy of action, which has the perfume and grandeur, of propriety of time, of motivation, of style of breathing, because your action is an emanation of your inner being. As the Cosmos uncovers itself through the material objects, you uncover the essence of your being, the quality of your being in glances, in words, in relationships, in action. Your *karma* is you, the essence of your being.

As nature is the expression of divinity, your words, movements and actions are manifestations of the inner content of your being. That is the teaching which Krishna is trying to emphasize practically in each chapter. He says: 'Being aware of me (the Cosmic reality), go through the relationships on the battleground.' Life is relationship and to live is to go through these relationships, without causing any scratches or scars on the consciousness and without causing any mutilation to the wholeness of Life.

The *Bhagavad Gita*, for me, is very sacred because it deals with the organic wholeness of Life, it deals with the inbuilt complexity of Life, it deals with the interplay between the microcosm and the macrocosm and it persuades us to remain united with the ultimate reality, not only through intellectual understanding but through everything that we do at every moment.

In the next verse, which is beautifully expressed, a different aspect of action is emphasized. Planting your actions in the awareness of Cosmic reality is called dedication, devotion.

The word used is *nishtha* which ordinarily is translated as conviction. I submit to you, with all the humility at my command, that the English translations of the *Bhagavad Gita* and the Upanishads are, to my mind, to a very great extent, incorrect. The English can be misleading.

In simple parlance the word *nishtha* means conviction, but here, when you come to spiritual verbalization of the teachings of the Vedas and the Upanishads, the word *nishtha* cannot be translated as conviction. Every Sanskrit word has a minimum of twelve different interpretations, different nuances, according to the root from which it is derived, according to the phonetic nature of the word, the sound, the meaning, according to the science of *yoga*, according to customs and traditions and so on. Twelve different ways of looking at a word.

So, planting actions into the consciousness of the supreme reality, in the awareness of Brahman, is dedication. Why does this term dedication come in the verse? The actions are dedicated to the divine. You see how the synthesis of *bhakti yoga* and *jnana yoga* comes about. Krishna was a master synthesizer, he came to synthesize all the Six Systems of Indian Philosophy and showed the way to eliminate the contradictions and thus see the basic built-in principle of harmony in all of them.

After having talked of understanding, then of holistic purification through education, now we come to the term dedication. Krishna says: 'Though the *yogi* does *karmas* twenty four hours a day, at all levels, he may be in the midst of relationships doing *karmas*, yet he does not get bound by them because they are dedicated to the divine.'

The *yogi* does not want anything from that *karma*. He goes through it, because that is a part of Life. He goes through it, because otherwise the senses will suffer, will feel suffocated, strangled. So he allows the sensory system to live in harmony and go through the interplay with the energies outside the body. He is not the doer, because of the awareness of Cosmic reality and he is not involved or attached, because the actions are for holistic purification and he does not want any reward or fruit from them. Whatever is going to accrue from that action, he dedicates to the divine.

Out of the divine, the Cosmos has emerged. In the Cosmos I am born, organically related to the wholeness. There is no myth of separation between me and the divine, so how can I attribute anything to myself? As I am not the doer, I do not want the fruit for myself.

First came the renouncing of involvement. Now the fruit or result of the action is again dedicated to the divine, to the Cosmic reality. Do you see the beauty of it? The whole Cosmos becomes a temple, and all the expressions of Life become as sacred as any deity in any temple, mosque, church or synagogue. Whatever you do becomes the flowers that you offer to the divine. So, no involvement and no desire for appropriating, owning, possessing the fruit of the action that you are doing.

A piece of dry wood burns. The fire was contained in the piece of wood and it burns and there is the flame of Life. The wood does not try to hold on to the flame, the flame goes up in the sky and disappears. So the fire contained in the wood is dedicated to the emptiness of space. The seed is sown and there is the sapling, the plant, the tree, the flowers and the fruit. The tree does not own the fruit.

Coming to an example in people's lives: a daughter is born in a family and the parents raise her up. They do not say: 'Because she is born of us we will keep her.' She marries and she leaves the house and the parents feel happy: 'our daughter has got married'. The parents don't own their daughter.

In the same way your actions are your offspring, your offering to the divine and whatever is needed will naturally come towards you, because you are in the Cosmos. There is a constant interplay between the Cosmic and the individual energies. Whatever is required will flow to you. Indian people say: 'whatever is necessary God shall give us'. This is the language of the religious masses who cannot understand the *Gita* or the Upanishads, but the truth is the same. Those who have faith in God, towards them the provision of all their needs flows Cosmically. That is the language of Bhakti Yoga, the *yoga* of devotion.

The same truth is being mentioned here in a scholarly way. The actions that are gone through for holistic purification, without being involved or attached to them, are dedicated to the divine. So no action binds. The action does not become a bondage.

People are afraid that if you live in society, if you live in a family, there will be bondage. If you talk to people you will get attached, and if you do things for them there will be bondage. The *Gita* says no. Bondage is in the sense of involvement, of attachment, not in the action. Words never bind you, nor do your actions which are expressions of energies contained in you, given to you by nature.

Your actions, your words are consequences of the conditioning given to you by society, by education, knowledge, experience. You contain the history and evolution of the whole human race in you. Whether you act physically and biological energies get expressed, or whether you act psychologically, cerebrally and you express the conditionings harmoniously, you are not the doer. You are the field where the collective human aspect of civilization and culture gets expressed and the biological energies also get expressed. You are the field of the dance of energies.

The only thing one can do is to see to it that the spontaneous harmony and order is maintained, is sustained, is not violated. The violation of the spontaneous natural order and harmony is sin, and sustenance of it is virtue. One, who does not know the secret of doing action in this way, gets bound, even if he becomes a recluse. Because as such he only minimizes the occurrence of the activities, he only narrows the field of action, that is all.

You cannot live without action, even for a minute. You cannot live without the interplay; it is the nature of Life. The *Gita* says those who offer their actions to the divine, which is a process of purification, they are really sending back the energies to the Cosmos from which they came. They are getting united to the source of Life, the source of all energies.

And where is that divine, that ultimate reality? It is contained in the emptiness of space. In the emptiness of space there are innumerable energies. The energies, emanating from you, are dedicated to that. They go back there.

Those who do not understand the secret of this science of action, the law of *karma*, they are very worried about the fruit of their particular action. 'If I do this with this motivation, I'll get it, and then I will store it in my memory.' They either want to possess things materially, or psychologically. They want to own, possess, appropriate, keep in exclusive ownership. Therefore, the desire for exclusive possession and ownership is the bondage. But for a student of *yoga*, whatever action is gone through, nothing binds, nothing remains as bondage.

Let us proceed with one more verse. Vibhu, the ultimate reality, call it divine, Brahman, (all terms are man-made. The self-generated, self-created, all-permeating reality is name-free. All names are given by us for our satisfaction, so that we seem to be related to them. We verbalize for a sense of relationship), that ultimate reality neither appreciates your good action, nor does it punish you.

The language of reward and punishment, of heaven and hell, is frequently used in all religions. These terms are there. These ideas are there. They created a sense of fear as a motivation to make human beings aware. Reward and punishment have been used later by politicians for the state, for law, etc. Reward and punishment entered the field of education also. Here Krishna tells Arjuna that the ultimate reality, Brahman, neither appreciates, praises, nor punishes. Nothing is given by that ultimate reality, either as a reward or as a punishment.

If there is maladjustment with reality, if there is disharmony, then you suffer. That is the punishment. If there is no maladjustment, if the action is done scientifically, precisely, accurately, if the timing is correct, the way of doing things is correct, if non-involvement is there, the mind being kept very clean, then there is no bondage. Attachment pollutes the mind. You may be attached to two individuals or ten individuals, or fifty things, or to your ideas, or god knows what. But if you are not involved, not attached, then you are completely clean. That is the reward.

Have you ever watched trees and their leaves after a torrential rain? Have you ever looked at the hills, the rocks, the newly bathed earth? There is a sense of cleanliness about them. You breathe in that cleanliness, don't you? In the same way when the mind is cleansed, when there is no psychological involvement or attachment, then the state of non-anxiety, non-worry, non-tension is the reward. The quality of your consciousness, the non-tension, the non-involvement, the non-attachment, when acting, purifies. That purification is the result of your action.

You know, when water flows it is clean, but when you keep it in a small pit, then water begins to stink. So, if you have kept all your energies in abeyance, if you have not allowed them to flow, the energies either begin to rust or begin to stink. What is pride and vanity but the stinking of the ego, which is enclosed rigidly.

The last point is that there is no punishment and no reward by the supreme. People are made to believe that god punishes and god rewards. The fruit of the action is contained in the action itself. A tiny seed when sown becomes a huge tree. And again the tree gets the seeds. In the same way, the very quality of the action and the quality of the consciousness that was there when you were acting becomes the fruit, the reward, whatever you call it.

When Krishna says: 'they are dedicated to the divine', he immediately clarifies this by adding: 'do not personify the divinity.' By divine, Brahman, we are referring to the wholeness of Life, the non-individuated organic wholeness of Life. There is no punishment and no reward in it. First holistic purification through action, then dedication of the action and its fruit to the supreme reality. We have come to the point where Krishna explains that there is no creator apart from the creation, no creator sitting there in exclusive isolation to look at you, to punish you, to pat you on the back.

My friends, this is the field of non-duality, advaita, of not two. The *Bhagavad Gita* is called that which showers the nectar of non-duality. Every verse is showering upon you the nectar of non-duality, every word of the *Gita* brings you the perfume of the Vedas and the Upanishads. It is quite a responsibility to touch those words and communicate about them. As a person, who has studied the Upanishads, the *Gita* and the Indian Systems of Philosophy and who is still a student of those teachings, I am sharing with you, not as an authority, but as a friend.

The teachings of the *Gita* might help the teachers of *yoga* to communicate with their students, out of a clearer understanding of the secret of *yoga* and so to grow into a *yogic* way of Life. *Yoga* is an alternative way of Life and living. The ancient Indian culture has emphasized the precept of growing into the state of *yoga*, where there is a holistic equanimity, a spontaneous balance sustained by the biological organism, sustained in the psychological structure, in order to get manifested in daily relationships. *Yoga* is an alternative way of living.

Human beings are multi-dimensional creatures. There is the biological dimension, which they share with all the non-human species inhabiting the planet. Then there is the psychological dimension, which has been developed by the human race, through the process of civilization and culture. And there is the trans-psychological dimension of love, freedom, peace, which has never been conditioned and which defies conditioning.

These three dimensions have to be lived by human beings simultaneously, to harmonize the impulses incorporated in the biological structure, the physical body, to harmonize those instincts with the thought-structure, the patterns of thinking, the patterns of reacting and the value-structures built up by society. And this psycho-physical behaviour has to be in harmony, in an orderly fashion, with the Cosmic energies that are operating in the emptiness of space, regulating Life, not only of this universe, not only of this planet earth and the solar system that we know of, but with the Cosmos as a whole.

Harmony with the Cosmos, orderliness in the psychological structure and orderliness in sharing our needs with the non-human species, this holistic dynamics of living is an alternative way of living. Not only doing *asanas*, *pranayamas* or sitting down for concentration, doing *dharana* etc. These study classes will be quite boring unless one is interested in an alternative way of living, an alternative culture for human society, an alternative dynamics of human relationships.

Now, as students we are aware of this multi-dimensional nature of our life, we have the responsibility to consummate its growth. The state of *yoga* is the consummation of human growth; it is the consummation of all the potentials contained in the human being. *Yoga* is a state of consummation, simultaneous consummation of the biological, the psychological and the trans-psychological.

We have come to the second half of the fifth chapter. The sense organs have an energy, so that they reach towards their respective objects. You are awake and your eyes are open, the eyes have the energy of sight contained in them. There can be eyes that do not see. But eyes that see, they have the sight, the seeing energy. So you are awake and the eyes are open. You cannot prevent the sight from reaching towards the objects around you. It is not your volition. You do not have to make an effort, the seeing happens, because the energy contained in the eyes, the optical instrument, the nerves etc., reach out towards their respective objects, the form, the colour, the size.

Sight does not remain in the emptiness of space. It travels through space and reaches the object, and it brings back an impression of colour, sound, tone. That impression reaches the sense organ and it creates a sensation. This is our life. The energies contained in the sensory organs, the senses, reach out towards the objects, bring back an impression, which gets converted into a sensation. That creates an electric impulse in the body, which reaches the brain. It gets interpreted according to your upbringing, your education.

Krishna is explaining to Arjuna: 'that which is born of the contact with the outer, that sensation has a beginning and an end '. They are limited by space and time, they are limited by the physical condition of your body, they are limited by the state of your mind.

This reaching out towards the object, receiving the impression, feeling, the sensation, the conversion into a reaction, all this is a conditioned process. It is a very limited process, it depends upon your physical condition.

If you are ill, though you may be kept in a beautiful room, you may be awake, your eyes may be open and yet they shall not see, because the feeling is inward, feeling the sensation of the disease, of the pain, the agony. So, the contact with the outer is depended on the body, the mind, the brain, etc. That is one limitation.

Secondly, the interpretation of the sensation which is necessary for reacting or responding, is very much conditioned by the racial conditioning, the religious conditioning, by the country in which you live, by the national conditioning, the socio-economic conditioning, etc. Your interpretation of the sensation and your reaction to that sensation is heavily conditioned, first by the physical, then by the psychological.

Thirdly, the sensation does not last; it is a momentary fleeting event that takes place, which has a beginning and an end. Supposing everything is intact and you have reacted to the sensation, to the interpretation. That reaction or that interacting in turn leaves the feeling of like or dislike. So that which happens in a moment, gets continuity and remains in your memory as a pleasure or a pain, as a like or a dislike. They are the fertile soil for all the misery to grow.

Therefore, a student of *yoga*, an explorer of an alternative culture, an alternative way of living, does not attach undue importance to this drama of sensations, this drama of receiving impressions, converting them into sensations, interpretation, reacting. It has to go on, it shall go on in the limited orbit of the biological and the psychological, and the person will go through that drama without attaching very much importance to it, without feeling miserable, or feeling elated, or excited by it. The needful will be done. If the needful is done with a non-personal, non-subjective, non-attached, non-involved way, if it is done so, then the inner equanimity will be sustained.

But if every experience, every event of painful or pleasurable sensations and your reactions and the response of the other person, are going to give you a jolt every second minute of a like or a dislike, this is going to be stored in your consciousness as a preference or prejudice. Then there will be hundreds of inhibitions added every day.

Therefore, the student of *yoga* provides the needs on the biological level scientifically, does not get too much involved psychologically in the diet of food, clothing, surroundings. He provides the needs with the austerity of a scientific approach. That which is deserved is provided onto the body, without feeling very much pride or vanity for it, without denying it, because the biological needs are shared by it with all the non-human species. We cannot deny that we belong to the material world, to the biological world, to the creature world. We are creatures and there are creature needs of the body that have to be provided scientifically.

Yoga, the essence of spirituality, is a science of Life and living. And when it comes to the psychological, the conditioned parts, the student of *yoga* gets acquainted with them. Through *dharana*, through *dhyana*, through *pratyahara*, this acquaintance with the inner conditioning, inhibitions, distortions, imbalances, this acquaintance with them, will make him watchful, so that they do not interfere with the response to the situation.

The handling of the psychological realm is not allowed to create new wants every day. Biological needs are limited. But the psychological wants can be endless and can be innumerable, unlimited. So, the student of *yoga* is very watchful that the so-called mind does not go on creating wants, extending the sphere of wants. Please do see this.

I call it an alternative culture because the present civilization, which we are sharing with the rest of the world, says increase your wants. And when you increase your wants, you want more and more and more. Then you will start inventing things, so that your civilization will get enriched by that. Right from deficit budgeting to increasing the field of your psychological wants, is that the way to live?

Yoga says just the opposite. It says: 'understand the needs, provide for them scientifically, aesthetically, beautifully, healthily.' But in the psychological sphere, see that wants are not created, because wants complicate the realm of the needs. And people become incapable of discriminating the mind creating the wants from the needs of the body. They are interwoven together.

And as there are seven notes in music, there are notes in our body too, the biological needs are notes of music, and the psychological world has its notes. They should not be mixed up. Wants make you ambitious to acquire, to obtain. It stimulates what is called *kama*, desire. Please do not translate the word *kama* in an unscientific way, it does not refer only to the sex-instinct or sex-impulse.

'I am oneness, let me flower into the manyness.'(From the Upanishads - referring to creation)

The word *kama* means: the energy of desire. In the last verse of the fifth chapter we will come across this verse: 'a *yogi* sees the emergence of the impulse of *kama*, of desire, and the very perception of the emergence stops the emergence.' The impulse does not become operative, because he has seen it at the very beginning.

In this verse we are dealing with the important teaching of *yoga* that: if, on the biological and the psychological level, we give too much importance to the conditioned and limited sensations and their interpretation, letting them develop into preference, prejudice, likes and dislikes, etc., this will be the source of misery.

Although I would love to be brief, I must take you to the word *bhoga*. In a *yogic* way of living, according to the Vedic culture that has been verbalized in this part of the world thousands of years ago, *bhoga* implies experiencing. If you go through the drama of your body it demands according to its needs, and you are providing these, if you go through these demands in the same way as watering the garden, ploughing the field, washing the clothes, providing food, etc., if the needs of the body are provided for, without stimulating the sense of pleasure and pain, like and dislike, then such a person has gone beyond the drama of birth and death, beyond the pleasure of birth and the pain of death.

That is, to live through the biological events without allowing the mind to create an experience (*bhoga*) out of it. Without allowing the mind to create the experiencer and the movement of experiencing, and the end product which is storing the experience in memory people glorify themselves when they talk of their experiences.

Either events take place in life and the mind provokes an experience out of the event and carves pleasure or pain out of it, or it goes through the event without the sense of *bhoga*, without the sense of experiencing, without your self becoming the experiencer. This is the crux of Brahma-Vidya. That is the essential difference between a person who is a non-*yogi* and a person who is a *yogi*.

A *yogi* has food and clothes and a place to live in, and uses language, speech, etc. But when the inner movement in the person is involved, when one is attached or withdraws, one is inhibited, one is imbalanced. The *yogi* has spontaneous equanimity, which is sustained through the movement of relationship, through the events of birth and death, through the events of physical pain and agony. *Yoga* says: it is possible to live with this outer world of objects and their energies, inviting the sense energies and their interplay, without creating pleasure or pain. The sensation of pleasure or pain, preference or prejudice is called *klesha*, suffering, as one of the *sutras* in Patanjali Yoga tells us.

You know, spirituality is the ending of psychological suffering. If the psychological suffering does not end, whether you have done Mantra Yoga, Tantra Yoga, Hatha Yoga, whatever, it has no value. True spirituality is for the ending of psychological suffering. Physical pain cannot be ended, it is a part of the game, it is part of the biological life.

Understand that involvement, which has a beginning in time and space and that which ends in time and space, that which is born of limitations and moves through conditionings, is the source of misery and suffering. A student of *yoga* has a different perspective of the biological and psychological needs: 'This understanding shines, like the sun, in his whole being.'

What happens when the sun shines? There is no darkness. In the same way this understanding that has taken place in the consciousness of the student of *yoga*, shines like the sun. And then there is no darkness of ignorance, darkness of impurity or imbalance. It is a different life altogether.

'Those who, through holistic purification of the biological and the psychological, have established themselves firmly in the inner equanimity, they have an invincible peace of consciousness, though still in the physical body. They have transcended the drama of birth and death, pleasure and pain and therefore they are liberated.'

On this very planet, while being in the physical body, they have transcended the body, they have transcended through non-identification, through non-involvement, through non-attachment. That is transcendence.

Please let us not attach any mysterious meaning to the words liberation, enlightenment, transformation, transcendence. These are scientific terms. Spirituality is as precise as the science of physics or mathematics. So, there is no mystery about it, no mystic connotation in those words. It has a very simple meaning. You know, spirituality is so simple; there are no complications as in the social, economic, political structures. It is non-structural organic wholeness, very simply. We complicate the matter.

'They have already transcended the drama of birth and death, pain and pleasure, though they are still in the physical body, those whose consciousness is established very firmly in a spontaneous equanimity and holistic purification.'

Beautiful the way the *Gita* elaborates upon this issue. One more verse. Pain and pleasure are physical sensations. The agreeable sensation is called pleasure, and the disagreeable sensation is called pain. They are bound to happen on the physical level. When a thorn pricks the sole of the foot, whether you are a *yogi* or not, there will be pain.

What happens? A non-*yogi*, a person who has not studied *yoga*, creates an issue of that event: 'a thorn pricked me.' The thought gives it continuity. But instead of a thorn pricking the foot, I think the thorn pricked ME, I have pain. Do you see how the pain of the body, a physical event, is attributed to the person?

Even when agreeable or pleasant events take place, a *yogi* does not create a special sense of the pleasant experience out of it. He does not get excited when something very pleasing has happened and does not get depressed or sad, he does not enter inertia if something painful happens.

Because he is conscious of the unity between the biological, the psychological and the trans-psychological, he takes it as a part of the game and goes through the pain and pleasure without looking back upon the memory next moment. There is no continuity. A *yogi* does not suffer from chronic memory. He goes through the events without those events leaving behind the residue as memory. And unless there is a residue of memory, preferences or prejudices do not develop.

The understanding shines like the sun in the being of the yogi, because the pleasurable and the painful experiences do not leave any mark behind. The consciousness, though in the individual body, is rooted in Cosmic awareness. Living in the individuated particular expression of life, living in the individuated personified flesh-and-bone body, the *yogi* is rooted in the awareness of the Cosmic wholeness of Life.

The *Gita* has become nearly a perennial source of wisdom for human beings, who feel concerned about perceiving the nature of ultimate reality and understanding its relationship with one's life and living. It is an immensely rich piece of literature. Written as poetry, it is more powerful than prose. Though it has the format of a dialogue, it is many times more serious than a philosophical treatise or a thesis. Its treatment of the themes, taken up in each chapter, is not only logically flawless, but it would stand valid even after it would be verified by modern natural sciences. It is verifiable individually and also collectively.

As we have seen, the *Gita* explores an alternative human culture, a culture of orderliness and harmony which requires the psychology of cooperation instead of confrontation with one's body and brain, with the outer material world, with the conditioning stuffed into our brain, with the social structures which surrounds us. There cannot be a culture of harmony and austere orderliness, unless human beings are educated in the psychology of cooperation with themselves and others.

Peace is the perfume of an attitude of cooperation and the implementation of that attitude in human relationships. So the *Gita* explores an alternative culture of order and harmony and it educates us in the psychology of cooperation with the physical, the psychological and the trans-psychological. It educates us in holistic purification, which is the essence of Raja Yoga. And it leads us towards the avenue of self-generated self-sustained bliss, which is the by-product of communion.

Krishna has referred to the foundation of Hatha Yoga as well as Raja Yoga in verses twenty-seven and twenty-eight in particular. We have seen that the sensations of pleasure and the experiences of pain, carved out of the contact with outer objects, is the source of misery and suffering. Krishna says in verse twenty-seven:

'Minimize the contact with the outer world. First, restraining the contact with the outer world, secondly steadying the sight contained in the eyes and focussing it on the point between the two eyebrows. Thirdly, equalizing and harmonizing the movement of the in-going and out-going breath. Thus, a student of *yoga* enters meditation and grows into a state of *sannyasa* (renunciation).'

Verse twenty-eight indicates another important point. While verse twenty-seven is referring to the physical aspect of building up harmony, verse twenty-eight refers to the quality of consciousness.

The movement of the thought stream, the thought structure, is something to which we are addicted. We want the thoughts, the wishes, the desires, the ideas contained in us to act upon something outside of us, or we like the external to act upon our thoughts, ideas, etc. We wait for that contact and interaction. There is a wish, a desire for doing something to the outer, may be an object or an individual, or the outer doing something to us. The agreeable and disagreeable options we go on playing around with in our mind is something we are very much addicted to.

The bane of modern civilization is addiction to the movement of thought and to verbalization. One can't live without it. One feels that Life is empty, that there is something missing in Life unless this interaction between the outer and the inner, not only the physical, but on the psychological, takes place. That has to be renounced.

Verse twenty-eight says: 'you may fix your gaze on the point between the eyebrows, you may harmonize the ingoing and outgoing breath, you may minimize the contact with the outer world, but as long as you are addicted to the movement of the mind, you want the mind to move, you want the words and ideas in your consciousness to move towards something, or something to move towards you, that interaction has to be renounced, that addiction has to be renounced, if you want the path of *yoga* to be revealed to you.'

This addiction to favourable and unfavourable, agreeable and disagreeable options, this play of the mind, this constant restlessness of the thought structure, it may stop or it may not stop, but the addiction must discontinue. Your psychological involvement with it has to be renounced completely.

If it goes on and you are not psychologically involved with it, affected by it, if you do not want to suppress, repress, control, change, or improve it, if you don't keep busy dabbling with the thought stream, doing something to it, if you renounce all involvement, all attachment, all addiction, then only the path to *yoga* is revealed onto you. This is the brief meaning of verses twenty-seven and twenty-eight. Chapter six, which deals with Dhyana Yoga, is an elaborate commentary on these two verses.

We must be aware that we are multi-dimensional creatures and therefore the order and harmony at the physical and psychological level will be taken up simultaneously. In chapter six Krishna takes up the physical in the first verse, and in the next he takes up the psychological and in the third verse he leads us towards the trans-psychological. It is something very beautiful these chapters of the *Gita*.

CHAPTER VI

YOGA OF MEDITATION

Chapter six deals with a holistic restraint of your physical and psychological structure; the body and the psychic structure together, the body and the mind together. Educate yourself in *yoga*, through restraining the physical and the psychological simultaneously, putting the physical and the psychological in cooperation with each other, in harmony with each other. Don't pitch them against each other, don't think that there is a dichotomy, that there is an opposition, that there is a kind of constant clash between the two. So begins chapter six.

Krishna himself was a householder, Arjuna also, and most of us have homes, families to take care of, jobs and some kind of work to do. We live in society. Most human beings born and brought up in society live and die in society. They will not be going to mountain caves, or isolating themselves from social life or household responsibilities.

If you are a householder, (that is one who lives in a house, whether married or single, it does not make any difference), because you live in society, you have a job, some work to do, society expects certain things of you and you expect certain things from society, so there is a relationship between you and the surroundings, material or social surroundings.

For a householder, the actions, the *karma*, which are expected of the person's physical and psychological equipment, the social role that the person has taken upon himself, those actions (*karma*) become the means of *yoga*. *Karma* is not a bondage. The actions that you have to go through, because of your physical and psychological accomplishments, talents, the quality of the brain, the role that you have taken upon yourself, all these bring responsibilities. And to discharge them, you have to act.

So action or *karma* is in fact the expression of your relationship with society, according to your talents, your make-up, according to whatever you have chosen. You live in a city or a village, you work as a farmer or a teacher, you live as a married or single man or woman, your way of living enjoins upon you certain actions. They are called *vihita karma*, that *karma* which is unavoidable, inevitable.

For example, your friend Vimala was educated at college and university where she studied psychology, philosophy, metaphysics, logic, and ethics. Having been born in India and having lived with disciples of Mahatma Gandhi, gone round the whole of India and most of the world, what is her responsibility? To share whatever Life has passed on to her. This should not be blocked in this body, which is perishable, but it should be allowed to flow. When she travelled and gave talks, she was not obliging anyone. When she sits here and shares with you, she is not obliging anyone, she is just allowing that which has come to her, that which society has passed on to her, to pass on to others. That is *vihita karma*, an unavoidable, inevitable *karma*. If she says: 'I don't like to do this,' then she is blocking the movement of Cosmic understanding. Do you see how *vihita karma* comes about?

If you are married and you are raising a family, then functioning as a wife, a husband, a father, a mother, helping the children to grow, is your spiritual *sadhana*. Those actions (*vihita karma*) are not a bondage, those actions which are inevitable, are the means to your liberation. The actions, the *karmas* in the householder's life are the means to his liberation.

Krishna is pointing out something very beautiful. Once you get established in the state of *yoga*, of invincible equanimity, of self-generated peace and self-sustained bliss, then the abeyance of action happens by itself. You do not have to renounce actions, you do not have to give them up, you do not have to run away and escape from actions.

The abeyance, the slowing down of the speed of those actions, the necessity for their frequency, the necessity for their momentum, their velocity, all that subsides on its own. When his consciousness gets established in inner peace and bliss, in the clarity of understanding, then the extended field of action and relationship goes on shrinking by itself, goes on subsiding by itself. It is the law of Life.

Before you sit down and try and fix your gaze between the eyebrows or control the breathing system, or minimize the outer contacts, please see very clearly that *karma* is not an obstruction in your path. Every *karma* is a means. And the actions that come your way are somewhere your own creation. You are the cause in some way or other of those responsibilities coming your way. The only credit that you can take is that you do not run away from them, but discharge them

A householder has to purify his attitude towards his physical *karmas* and psychological relationships. Do you see how important is the suggestion given by Vasudeva to Arjuna?

Now, how can the outer *karma*, the physical *karma*, the action, become a means to liberation, a means to *yoga*, a means to *sannyasa*? By doing it because it has to be done, but not adding any subjective motivations to the action. You do it, as it has to be done, it is part of Life and living.

If you do something to please your husband or wife or children, in order to secure their concern or interest in you, then you have added your own motivation to the choice-less responsibility that has come your way. That action could have been a means to liberation, had you not added your motivation of pleasing, of securing the goodwill: 'I please you, so that you do not turn away from me.' You see, motivations are added to *karma*, and these motivations become the source of bondage, says the *Gita*.

No action by itself can bind you. It is a means to purify you, physically and psychologically, a means to eliminate imbalances, to provide an outlet for your energies. If you add the motivation of fear, of cowardice, then also you have spoiled the very nature of the action. Then it cannot be a means to *yoga* or *sannyasa*.

So, do not add any motivations to the inevitable work that has come your way, to the unavoidable responsibility that has come your way. Accept it. By the time you become twenty-one, and you know what is what and you accept a certain way of living, then there are many things involved in that way of living which you have indirectly accepted. No motivations are to be added.

Secondly, do not create a tension by expecting an exclusive fruit or result of that action for yourself. As you are the agency through which the work, the *karma* is getting done, as the Cosmic intelligence is getting it done through you, you are bound to get your share, as a physical agent, as a psychological agent, whatever the result of that action. You are going to get your share of the grandeur, the dignity, whether it is success or failure, you are going to get your share of it.

Do not anticipate, or wait for the fruit. Do not try to manoeuvre your behaviour in order to produce a particular kind of result out of the action. No worry, no anxiety, no manipulations for the results of the action, and no subjective motivations added to the inevitable unavoidable responsibility that comes your way, because you are living on the physical and psychological level in society.

One does whatever has to be done, without depending psychologically upon the result. If you are waiting for the result and you are trying to manoeuvre your actions and movements to make them produce a result, then again the interaction between the Cosmos and yourself has been polluted by expectation, by manoeuvring, manipulation, anxiety, worry. If you have done what you could, let that be the end of it.

We are talking about an alternative culture of harmony and order on the physical level and cooperation on the psychological level, so that there is love and compassion on the trans-psychological level. It is a way of living. It is a culture.

Today, is the culture of confrontation, disorder and chaos. Society is producing anti-social human beings through their educational institutions; temples, churches, synagogues and what have you. It is a culture of confrontation, assertion, aggression, violence.

Here, in this part of the world, the possibility of an alternative culture, an alternative way of living, an alternative psychology for the human race, has at least been perceived and verbalized. It has not been lived. The Indians have not done justice to their heritage. Individually there have been and there are demonstrations of the teachings of the Vedas, the Upanishads, the *Gita* etc. But collectively, as a society, Indians have failed their heritage, may I say, betrayed their heritage.

Firstly, *karma* is a means to liberation; through *yoga* and renunciation. You can do the karmas, which are necessary to be done at the physical and psychological level, and start educating yourself. What you do during the ten or twelve hours a day is as important as what you do in the *yoga* class. If there is no harmony in the attitude between the two, then they will be two separate co-existing dimensions. The one will not have an impact on the other, and the excellent *yoga* teacher may not be an excellent human being, may not have awakened the energies of love and compassion, the energies of peace and meditation in his or her life. When the householder has done this much, then he can proceed towards physical education.

Find a quiet place and clean it. While you clean the place, if you add your affection in that movement of cleaning, then it becomes pure. There is a difference between cleanliness and purity. Purity is something in your attitude and approach. Your state of consciousness, the quality of your consciousness confers purity upon cleanliness. Otherwise, it can be clinically clean and yet not pure. Cleanliness is on the physical level, and purity is the quality of consciousness you can bring to bear upon the physical act; the tenderness of affection, the tenderness of care. You know, you can go through physical work heartlessly, callously. You can be callously efficient. You have allowed your consciousness to be polluted by imbalances, impurities.

The *Gita* says: find a place, a room, some location, and clean it lovingly. After that it depends upon the climate and the place, whether in the mountains or on the plains, how you prepare for yourself a seat. The *Gita* talks of a seat made of dry grass. Crush the dry grass on that spot and spread upon it a cotton sheet if it is a hot climate, or a woollen sheet if the climate is cold. What could they talk about five thousand years ago?

Of course, clean your body internally and bathe it properly. Wear clothes that are not too tight on the body, that make the body feel comfortable. And then sit down in that clean and pure place, having prepared a nice soft seat. Not on a cement or concrete floor. This is Vimala's addition. In that case it is better to have a wooden plank and thereon prepare the seat. The seat should be level.

There should be no demand on your time and energy for at least some time. If there is work waiting to be done, then there will be tension on the nerves: 'I have to cook the meal, scrub the floor, send the children to school.' Find out a time when you will have at least one hour and a half. The *Gita* and the Upanishads talk about two hours and a half, but that is too long in the modern world. People can hardly afford two hours and a half at a stretch at their disposal, when they can be totally relaxed. So find out a timing, time your action for your self-education, when you can be totally relaxed.

Let the spine be erect, the body and the neck straight and steady. The posture should make you feel comfortable. Settle down in that. You help the body to sit in that posture by watching your breath for a couple of minutes. When the breath is rhythmical, not jerky, bumpy or shaky, then it means that the body has settled down in that posture.

It takes time to educate the body to remain steady, straight and at the same time relaxed. If it is not educated, the body becomes rigid instead of steady. And if you say: close the eyes, people close them so tightly, that the optical nerves are strained by the rigidity of the movement. The movement or the non-motion has to be undertaken in a relaxed way. No strain, no pressure, no tension, in any part of the body and no pressure on the breathing system.

When that is done, close the eyes in a relaxed way, so that the contact with the outer world is closed. When you close your eyes, you are snapping the contact with the outer space, the objects surrounding you. That snapping of the contact with the outer objects is a primary requirement.

Because, if the eyes are open and the sight runs towards an object, the perception of that object awakens the name.

It is extremely difficult to separate the perception from the cognition of the object. It is nearly impossible to separate the perception from the colour and your like or dislike about the colour. The neurological system reacts to the perception of colour agreeably or disagreeably. You do not say 'I like it' or 'I don't like it', but the cognition of the favourable or unfavourable-ness has already influenced the state of the nervous and chemical systems.

We have an extremely delicate organism, much more delicate than today's electro-magnetic apparatuses of high technology. When you perceive the colour, the like or dislike, in a non-verbalized state, it has already influenced the system. It happens. The memory becomes restless; it brings up associations of ideas, associations of events that have taken place.

Let keep them out, says the *Gita*, let the contact between the outer and the inner get snapped without violence. You don't have to leave your house and find some secluded place, some cave. When you close your eyes, you are in a cave, contact is snapped.

You have closed the eyes and you are abstaining from verbalization, from speech. That is the second step. Physical verbalization, and inner inaudible verbalization are the source of the movement of thought. It is to be restrained. And for that, watch the breathing, which is travelling in the body, the ingoing and outgoing movement through the nostrils, watch that. Abstaining from speech and closing the eyes is helped by this focussing your energy on the ingoing and outgoing movement.

If the attention has become steady now by focussing on the ingoing and outgoing breath, take that attention upward between the two

188

eyebrows. The cavity between the two eyebrows is a fantastically significant nerve centre. The optical, the auditory and the nerve centre connected with smelling, with speech, and perhaps all the important pleasure and pain points, balance points in the brain; (that grey matter contained in the head having innumerable cells), those nerves converge upon the cavity between the two eyebrows.

There is a cavity at the crown of the head, one between the two eyebrows, one at the back of the neck where the medulla oblongata (spinal marrow) reaches the small brain, one between the lungs and the heart, one at the navel point, one between the reproductive organs and one at the base of the spine. They are all important nerve centres. Those cavities, having space, emptiness, contain many energies which are not channelized, not moulded, not conditioned, in no way qualified or modified. It is not only the seven *chakras* that are important, but also these cavities where nerves and arteries converge and join one another, they are physically and psychologically important locations in our life.

If the attention, if the perception has become focussed and steady on the inhaling and exhaling, take it away from the activity of inhaling and exhaling, focus it on *kumbhaka* (retention of the breath between inhaling and exhaling), so that you inhale, you retain and then you exhale.

Now we are talking about equipping ourselves for *dhyana* (meditation). These are the requirements prior to the state of meditation. Take your attention and energy from inhaling and exhaling and try to focus it on the interval between the two, retaining the breath inside, and the same as it leaves on the outgoing breath. You have gone one step further.

First, you had focussed it on speech and you abstained, you closed your eyes and there you abstained from contact. Then you went to the invisible but audible breathing process and you focussed yourself there. Then taking it from the movement to the interval, the silence between the breathing. And that focussing on that interval between the in and out breath will help you to take the leap upwards towards the point between the two eyebrows. Rise up with the help of the *kumbhaka* and steady your attention, your energies, your focus on that cavity between the two eyebrows.

We are dealing with the physical. We have dealt with the psychological, how to look at action, *karma*, as a means of liberation and at the abeyance from *karma* after the state of *yoga*, as a natural consequence; not an act of the will. Now combine the two.

You do not act out of any subjective motivation when you are doing that which has to be done, that which is inevitable, unavoidable. And you do not anticipate or wait for a particular exclusive result for yourself, as you are free of psychological involvement in the result of action. Please, while you are focussing your energies while sitting down, do not create a tension of expectation such as: 'if I focus my attention and do the concentration, something will happen to me, powers will be awakened in me'.

If you create an inner world of expectation regarding to the occult and the transcendental, then you have missed the point. It cannot be education, it will be manipulation, it will be a kind of psychic gymnastics. *Yoga* is not physical or psychological gymnastics. It is something much more sacred. It is exploring a new dimension of consciousness, a new dimension of Life itself, a new dimension of energies that are unconditioned.

So, when one sits down in the posture, steadying the sight, focussing the energies, let there be no tension of expectation, let there be no desire, even unverbalized, for producing such result as: 'I'll become such and such a *yoga* teacher, l will excel others. This and that will happen to me.'

The mind plays tricks in everything that you do. You leave your house and you want to visit some holy place. While you are in the train, the mind starts playing. Whether you are going to a holy place, a temple or doing *yogasanas*, the mind wants to appropriate something to itself. You see the thought-stream; the movement of thought feels secure when something happens to it, or when it does something with others. But we have to be non-involved, non-attached, and non-addicted to this trap of the thought movement.

If you are doing all this and the thought movement goes on, wanting to manipulate in a very subtle way, it can even use violence against itself. The attitude of non-addiction towards the movement of thought is something that flows with you like an undercurrent. It has to accompany the student of *yoga* in everything that the student does. If that is de-linked, as it were, from what you are doing, then it will be only physical gymnastics. Everything has to be for holistic purification, that is education. Education is holistic purification.

Let me add now, slightly moving away from the verses, a friendly tip. We are used to constant restlessness, cerebral restlessness. The psychological restlessness is always reflected in your eyes. It is very difficult for people to keep their eyes steady. Watch the movement of your own eyes. The chemical movement, the chemical disturbance, due to feelings, sentiments, reactions, wishes, moving very fast inside you, that chemical disequilibrium gets reflected in your eyes.

The eyes keep on hopping from one place to another, even when one talks or when one listens. Very few people, one amongst thousands, whose sight is steady. The steadying of sight is arrived at when one learns concentration. Then the sight is steady. When people sleep, because their minds are not steady, their cerebral organ is not steady and relaxed; they see dreams. And for those who see dreams, the movement inside the eyelids is going on. Ask any doctor to analyse the dimension of sleep within him or her.

When you sleep, the restlessness of the cerebral organ results in the process of dreaming. Dream-consciousness is not a natural state. Remaining awake and remaining asleep, these are two very normal states in life, but dreaming is something which mankind has added. It is a grafted dimension, not a natural dimension. People who dream, their sight is not steady. Why am I mentioning this?

We are so much used to this cerebral restlessness and chemical disequilibrium, that when you try to focus your sight on this point between the eyebrows, you will feel the strain within a few seconds. Some people begin to feel giddy within minutes, because that steadiness immediately acts upon the chemical system. It acts upon the tone of your nervous system. That which is used to constant restlessness, constantly expecting feeding or expressing itself through an outside outlet, that steadiness feels stark.

So people who meditate on the point between the eyebrows, get many complications. Restlessness has become a natural way. So steadiness makes them feel abnormal; they feel giddy, they feel a strain, they feel heaviness in the head. I have seen some people vomit, they could not stand it. If a person is too talkative, if that person is asked to observe verbal silence, even for a couple of days, the person feels starved.

As a friend, because you are *yoga* teachers, I should point out that this does happen. That is why generally people do not prescribe this focussing the sight and holding it between the eyebrows, but this chapter mentions it, the end of the fifth chapter and the beginning of the sixth chapter mention this very vividly and it became my responsibility to explain to you all the aspects as well as their implications.

There is nothing to be afraid of, but if the restlessness is there, steadiness becomes a problem. Silence becomes a problem for people. If the mind moves, they are happy, they are comfortable. They play inwardly with thoughts, ideas, words. But if they sit down quietly and there is nothing to cling to, not even a word, not even a sound to cling to, then the mind feels orphaned and either it takes you to drowsiness, or it makes you restless and afraid.

If one is not a student of *yoga*, this complete renunciation of the thought movement is very painful. Not so for those who study the science of *yoga*. After all, renunciation is being in meditation. And meditation is renunciation of all psychological involvements and attachments in the movement of relationships, in the movement of *karma*.

In the third, fourth and fifth chapters, Krishna mentions that. When there is nothing to cling to, you feel as if you have moved away from the earth orbit. You are somewhere suddenly weightless. Freedom from thought-movement creates an illusion of weightlessness; you feel you have moved away from the earth.

People are sitting on their seats and they feel as if they have been raised up in the emptiness of space. So many things happen with this event of steadiness, if and when it is allowed to happen.

The *Gita* has been studied by different scholars, from different perspectives. You would be surprised that, till twenty-five or thirty years ago, women were not supposed to study or recite the *Gita*. It was only for the renunciates, *sannyasins*. The householders too were not encouraged to study the *Gita*, because it was feared that their interest in family life would disappear.

As with the Vedas and the Upanishads, there are different interpretations of the *Gita*: Shankara based his on advaita or non-duality, Ramanuja on qualified non-duality, and so on. For some, karma and karma yoga was the crux of the whole *Gita*. Mahatma Gandhi taught the *Gita* as teaching non-attachment; others found Bhakti Yoga, the *yoga* of devotion, in it.

A QUESTION ABOUT KARMA

You are asking me a question about *karma*, action. Life is living and living is interaction. In interaction, the interplay of action and response takes place. The *Isha Upanishad* says:

'Whatever exists and moves in the Cosmos is permeated by Isha, a principle of intelligence. The whole world is the abode of this intelligence.'

So too the *Gita*, in the second chapter on Sankhya Yoga, refers to the all-permeating intelligence. Again the *Isha Upanishad* enjoins on one, the responsibility to find out that you cannot live even for a second without *karma*. 'You have no choice. For you there is no other path. Action is the choiceless path for you, your consciousness does not get tainted by action.'

You want to know what the *Gita* has to say about *karma*, which is the movement of your daily living. Look friends, daily life is the only life which is available, either you meet Life in the present or you miss it. There is no life somewhere in tomorrow. Tomorrow is all an idea; it is all in the imagination. The eternity is here, before you, in the present moment, in the now and here is the wholeness of Life. You commune with it, you go through the interplay with it, or you miss the opportunity of living. Life is living and living is the interplay between the expressions of Cosmic Life, and that interplay involves action and response.

Now, what is our daily life? Are we awake? Are we acting? Do we see Life as it is, and do we do *karma*? That is the first question we should ask ourselves.

As there is the word *karma*, there is another word *kriya*. In English the word *kriya* would be translated as activity. Activity and action are two different things. They belong to two different dimensions of consciousness, and to two different dimensions of Life.

Activity is a compulsive movement. For example, in your body breathing goes on compulsively, whether you are awake or asleep. You are born with it. The movement of breathing in and out is an activity, incorporated in the biological structure. Blood flows in your body. You do not circulate the blood, the blood circulation goes on, that is an activity. Appetite is generated in the body and you take a meal. Taking a meal is a response to the needs of the body.

But if you sit down and get acquainted with the nature of your physical structure, you watch the needs of the body, the inclinations of the body and the reactions of the body to the various kinds of food that you put into it, you experiment, you explore, then taking a meal becomes an action, *karma*. Otherwise drinking water, going to bed, taking food, are all activities. You are reacting to the biological impulses. That is what we do.

But when you look at those impulses, what the movement of those impulses do to the heat, to the coolness in your body, to the blood pressure, to the tension in the nerves; just to watch. But who has time? We have no time. We are busy earning money, raising families, collecting things of sensual pleasure and social respectability. We have no time to live, to watch that body in which we live for sixty, eighty years and to respond to it.

Reaction is not a response. We are compelled to react. So taking a meal, feeding or bathing or clothing the body, are all activities in our life. They are not actions. The *Gita* wants us to be able to do *karma* and not waste Life, living in compulsive movements, which is *kriya*.

Come with me to the psychological structure. There are feelings, sentiments, patterns of reaction, value structures, orders of priorities, all fed into our brain, into our body, by society, by the community, the family, the parents, education etc.

You hear a word and you get annoyed. That annoyance is a reaction, a conditioned reaction. But you feel that it is very natural to get annoyed. You feel that you must give an outlet to the anger. But getting angry, getting annoyed, getting excited, getting worked up, all these are reactions.

Who has time to question the validity of these reactions? Why should a word stimulate the heat of anger, or the shrinking of fear in me? We have no time to question the validity, to question the worth of these reaction patterns, which have been fed into us and which go on repeating themselves.

Anger does not come to an end just by getting angry. Sixty, eighty years, people go on getting angry every day, scolding, abusing, getting annoyed, irritated, you know. They say it is human nature, it is the human condition. What you do out of anger is not an action, it is a reaction, it is an activity, it is *kriya* not *karma*. Do see the deep meaning of the word *karma*. Let us now look at the word *karma* from another angle.

A person has behaved with me in a stupid, clumsy way, in an unscientific way, in an incorrect way. And I, out of anger, annoyance, irritation, out of a feeling of humiliation or whatever, I react. What has happened? Something was thrown at me and I throw something back at that person. The relationship gets obstructed. The interplay gets arrested.

I may silence a person by getting angry or if I am in authority, I may make my children behave in a certain way, I may oblige them, but that is not an interaction. The authoritarian compulsion that we create out of our maladjusted reaction, obstruct the real natural interplay. The movement of Life is obstructed.

So *kriya*, activity, or compulsive movement, either out of biological impulses, or out of psychological conditioning, does not allow the natural Cosmic dance of Life, the interplay, the interaction to take place. There is no interaction between me and the other person with whom I get angry. Psychologically, there is a resistance that has come up. There can be a grudge against me. There can be an unverbalized friction between us, next time we meet. So, there is a gap between us.

If I am attached to a person, I create the same kind of gap through that attachment, through dependency. You know domination and dependency go together, it is the obverse and converse of the same thing. So, please do see that a compulsive movement, dictated by psychological conditioning and by biological impulses, is not *karma*. That is what the *Gita* wants to teach us.

And when there is no *karma* on my part or on the part of the other person, we may be under the same roof and co-exist and yet, there is no sharing of Life. Grudges, preferences, prejudices, attachment, dependency, fear, aggressiveness are operative all the time in our attitude and approaches.

Life is for living, and living is not only biological vegetation, living is not a mechanistic, repetitive movement of the mind and brain. Living is something beautiful, therefore, I wonder if we at all live, at all perceive Life as it is, and whether we have the fearlessness, the humility to respond instead of reacting? So, activity is reaction, and we want action and response. Karma Yoga is *yoga* through *karma*, through action, not through activity. Activity keeps you restless, physically, mentally.

The third angle, from which I would request you to look at the word *karma*, is as a movement of your whole being, not a partial movement of the biological impulses or psychological thought structure. It is a movement which has an effortless spontaneity.

Action is not manipulated behaviour, it is not out of calculation, it is not bargaining.

Relationships are counters for us at which we bargain for pleasure, for psychological security and so on. There is calculation, there is bargaining. I am talking of human relationships. You have to calculate, you have to organize, you have to plan, when you are working in different social responsibilities and roles. I am not talking about social or economic structures, I am not talking about the present commercialized life, where everything is to be bought and sold. We are dealing with a spiritual theme; we are dealing with the science of Life and living.

Another angle from which we can look at action or *karma* is spontaneity. Spontaneity involves, does it not, effortlessness? A small child, of six or eight months, smiles. That smile has spontaneity, like the blooming of a rose has spontaneity. When people meet each other, say politicians or in a shop a salesman and a client, when they smile at each other, it can be etiquette or courtesy. It has an effort or a conditioning behind it. For *karma*, to be the movement of your whole being, it has to have the dimension of effortless spontaneity. And how will that spontaneity, how will that effortlessness come about in our actions in daily living?

We saw, in the first fifteen verses of chapter five, how to be present with the moment, to see the challenge and meet it without adding our subjective motivations to it, without worrying about the fruit of the work. The first verse of chapter six says: 'a student of yoga acts, not depending upon the anticipated fruit or result of the work.'

When you are not worried, when you are not carrying the tension of expectation about the result and when you do not add your subjective motivation, then there can be a spontaneous effortlessness in your *karma*. Then you understand that challenge and you meet it as you are. You do not want to conceal anything, you do not want to pretend what you are not, nor hide what you are. So there is an elegance of simplicity and the majesty of spontaneity in the behaviour of such a person. Unless there is this attitude, there will not be real *karma*.

In the second chapter Krishna explained, that the magnificent simplicity of action in a human being, entitles him morally, spiritually, to act. He is not entitled to put a framework around the possible or probable results of his actions. The result of the action is governed by many factors: social surroundings, economic compulsions, the people with whom he is interacting, etc. Instead of tethering all your energies to the anticipatory fruit, focus your energies on doing.

The quality of your action and the quality of your consciousness, while doing that action, are the two important things on which you have to focus your attention. Then such *karma* does not create any bondage. You may go through the interplay of Life, interacting with people throughout the day and yet nothing binds you, because there are no manipulations for results. You did, because to live is to act and action is the expression of your relationship with Life.

Actions then can cleanse your consciousness. They reflect exactly the quality of your consciousness. Action exposes the factual content of your consciousness and shows you, like a mirror, what you are. Shankaracharya writes in his commentary on action, that *karma* liberates, it sets you free of images of yourself, of wrong judgements about yourself. Life is for living and living is the movement of relationships, and in relationships there is an interplay of action and response. Perhaps this helps us to understand in a deeper sense, what *karma* implies.

(End of question on *karma*)

Yesterday we were asked to sit down in a clean quiet place, holding the body erect, the neck and the head erect so that the breathing becomes rhythmical, not being disturbed by a wrong posture. Holding the body erect and steady but not stiff or rigid, you focus your sight to the tip of the nose, without looking in any direction.

Now, today we are taking one step further, by looking into this steadying of the gaze. The eyes are neither closed nor completely open. They are half-open/half-closed, not looking at anything outside. See the beauty of it, the outer world is not snapped away violently, as was done when closing the eyes. There is the possibility of looking and yet you are not looking. Chapter six is about the *yoga* of restraint, of moderation, in everything. By focussing on the tip of the nose, having the eyes half-open/half-closed, you are restraining the sight, which is an outgoing energy.

Whenever you are awake and the eyes are open, the sight contained in the eyes, the whole optical structure, rushes out. You can forcibly turn the sight inwards by contracting the outgoing activity. It has a little touch of violence in it. Now the *Gita* says: 'no, keep the eyes half-open/half-closed'. So restraint and moderation in the utilization of the energy of sight. What will happen if this is done?

This is education. After all *yoga* is education for holistic purification. Education takes place slowly, step by step. It is not that when you understand, you have a new awareness and are transformed instantaneously. That is not the claim of *yoga*.

Self-education for purification, that is for eliminating the imbalances and impurities, is necessary and it has to be done non-violently. You can't force education the way you train circus animals, by using a stick or a whip.

You are going to help your body and mind to transcend the limitations, to eliminate the impurities, imbalances, etc. If this is done every day, whenever you can afford to do it, then your mind will become steady.

It is not a static steadiness. *Prashanta* is the term used by the *Gita* in which there is a kind of joy along with peace. Your mind is relaxed, joyful and peaceful. Obviously you don't have to look at anything or think of anything, you don't have to respond to anything, you are relaxed: *prashanta atma*. There is a relaxation and a peace, which has a perfume of joy around it, within it, like the scent of a flower.

Fear disappears. There is nothing to acquire, nothing to change, nothing to suppress and therefore in that relaxation fear disappears. How can this happen and to whom?

Now comes the most controversial expression of the *Gita*: 'it can happen through Brahmacharya'. Brahmacharya is translated in English by celibacy, which is to my mind an insufficient and incorrect translation. It is not a negative concept, it is not abstaining from marriage or from a householder's life, it is not denying something.

Brahma, in the word *Brahmacharya*, stands for 'Cosmic reality', ultimate reality'. A Brahmachari is one, whose intelligence is dedicated to the Cosmic reality, one whose intelligence is all the time probing into the nature of reality. His intelligence is married to the Cosmic reality; there is a fusing between his intelligence and the Cosmic intelligence.

It is one, whose *hatha yoga* is not only for physical health, not only for some occult or transcendental powers, but whose primary concern is to perceive the reality, to feel it, to be soaked in it, to be bathed in it. He wants to get established in it, merged in it; one who has voluntarily determined to perceive the reality, to get grounded in it, to get established in it and to live in it, out of it; as you live out of thought now, living out of the perception of reality.

If that is done, if the study of *yoga* is gone through, if the *karma* is gone through, without polluting the action through subjective motivation or manipulation of the fruit, then the student of *yoga* grows into a creatively steady mind, into a fearlessness of consciousness. He grows into the fusion of the individual with the Cosmic consciousness. He does not attain it in one moment, he grows into it.

Last night the bud was not yet a flower, and this morning you went into the garden and you saw that what was a bud yesterday, has become a flower. It has not blossomed in one moment, but right from the birth of the bud, the tiny thing on the sapling was growing every moment, it was becoming a flower. But you saw it as one moment in time and space. Your perception is limited; but growth was taking place.

Growth is something holistic. You do not assemble the petals together and then make the flower blossom. It is a dynamic holistic process that is going on. That is Life, that is living.

When your creative energies are not utilized for outward activities, but focussed, along with the physical and psychological, on the Cosmic reality, on Brahman, then such a Brahmachari is fresh, vibrant and vigorous. Vasudeva is explaining this to Arjuna, in chapter six on Dhyana Yoga, from verses thirteen to seventeen. Now let us proceed further.

We have just seen that celibacy should not be taken in a narrow sense. We have seen why it is a help. It is after all related to the interplay of energies. Life is a dance of innumerable energies. Vasudeva talks about something marvellous. He says that an enquirer can be his own benefactor, well wisher and helper, or he can be his own enemy.

Man is his own saviour, his own redeemer. He does not need to wait for some saviour or redeemer to come and help him. Why don't you become your own saviour and redeemer, by utilizing the energies that are at your disposal in your body, in your mind? It is a question of channelling and utilizing energies. So human beings should look upon themselves, as their own saviour and redeemer. And in the second part of the verse he says:

'No one can obstruct your path of enquiry, or your liberation or transformation, except yourself. You are your own friend, or you are your own enemy.'

It is not a theory. Here you follow a daily schedule for one week or two, then you go home. You have understood the importance of this self-discipline, of getting up early, the significance of going through *asanas* or *pranayamas* daily, not as a repetition, because mechanistic lifeless repetition is not education. Self-education is, when everyday you are doing this discipline anew, with the same care and affection, the same concern.

You go home and you decide to do this, because you have felt the benefit in the camp. You go home, you do it for two or three days, then you stop getting up early. You have excuses; you have a busy home life etc.

We procrastinate doing the *yoga* exercises. Finding excuses and justifications is laziness. The result is that we don't do it. Nobody prevents me from doing it. I prevent myself. You are your own enemy. You may put the blame on others, or on circumstances. The *Gita* says: this is not true. Why do you deceive yourself? You are your own saviour and your own enemy.

'Arjuna you have to study this education because purification does not take place in one moment or in one hour.' Don't you bathe your body every day? Don't you clean the utensils, in which you cook the meal, every day? That is not a repetitive activity. Brushing your teeth, or bathing your body, is not a repetitive mechanistic activity. Don't you enjoy doing that? So punctuality, regularity, precision, accuracy, without anybody to compel me to be precise, please do see this. Do we need someone to dictate, to compel us to get it done? Small children have to go to school and have to be helped to study, but we grown-ups, we understand everything and yet we don't do it.

You can take a horse to the river, but you can't make him drink. In the same way, things can be explained theoretically, academically, verbally, the grasp of words and their meaning can be there, but if there is no urge, a deep dynamic urge to find out the nature of reality, to perceive reality, what it is to be with reality, if the urge is not there, then we may learn Hatha Yoga, Mantra Yoga or Tantra Yoga, if the incentive to live is not there, if we require stimulation, compulsion, we have become passive. Under our modern life, I must say, we have developed a style of living, where we have become passive consumers. It is a consumerist culture. And in the same way we need help to get things done.

Chapter six elaborates, in nearly forty-eight verses, the inevitability of self-education, the necessity of this education at the physical, verbal, and psychological level. To my mind, if the teachers of Hatha Yoga study only chapter six, it will help them in teaching Hatha Yoga in the European context. Because there things will have to be communicated in the context of science, of advanced technology, in the industrialized context of city life. So, chapter six is of utmost importance.

In the last part of chapter six, two issues are being brought up by Arjuna. The first question, formulated in a couple of verses, refers to the restless nature of the mind. Arjuna says to Krishna: 'your recommendation for study and the attitude of non-attachment towards sensual pleasures and sensory objects, is something I have understood very clearly. But it seems to me, that as one cannot control the movement of the wind, that powerful gush of air moving around in the sky, so we are not really capable or equipped to restrain or moderate the movement of the mind.'

He continues: 'Krishna, the mind is ever restless. To control the mind is as difficult, if not impossible, as it would be to control the wind flying in the skies. So, how can there be a steadiness and a continuity of study?'

One day, the mind resolves to study and within a short time it loses interest in the study. Its starts and it fails to continue. And the second question is:

'What will happen to the student of *yoga*, who has faith in the supreme reality, who wants to strive and begins and yet fails in keeping the study continuous. What happens to such a person and his efforts? Does everything that he has learned intellectually disappear, vanish? Does, whatever little effort he has made in educating himself in holistic organic purification, does all that get destroyed?'

Now, Arjuna was not a superficial intellectual academician. He had studied, as Vasudeva had, the scriptures. When he says that the mind is restless, please do note that he is referring to the energies of conditioning, contained in consciousness.

What you call matter, a particle of earth, has a quantum of energy contained in it, concealed in it and it is that quantum of energy which keeps matter ever changing. Life is a flux of change. We are living within nature that is ever changing, not only its form, colour, flavour, taste, etc., but even the ingredients, the constituent elements go on changing.

The students of yoga, who have studied the *Chandogya Upanishad* with me, will remember that it pointed out that thought is matter, emanating from your body. The body is a biological material structure, containing innumerable conditioned energies of impulses, of ideas, concepts, defence mechanisms, patterns of reactions, value structures, order of priorities, and so on. There is a vast ocean of conditioning contained in the human body. We are the product of the total human evolution that has taken place through untold centuries.

When a thought is provoked, when an idea, a feeling, a sentiment or an emotion is activated in the body, it is a neuro-chemical material activity. And when you think a thought, or a thought moves in your body, it has an inaudible sound, because thought is a word, the movement of thought cannot take place without the movement of a word. Word is a manipulated engineered sound energy.

So, when the thought moves, the inaudible sound contained in the word of that thought, moves in your body. If you articulate it, then it emanates audibly, visibly, from your body. And if you do not articulate it, do not verbalize it, even the non-verbalized thoughts, ideas, feelings, emotions, are material energies that emanate from your body and float around you in the ether. This has been verified at least fifty years ago and many scientists have written about it.

What you call mind or consciousness is full of conditioned energy operating in many ways in your body, through your body, as electricity operates through a microphone, a bulb, a heater, a fan; it operates in different ways through different channels of expression. This energy, of all the conditionings contained in you, be it education, knowledge, experience, etc., operates in your life throughout the waking or dreaming hours.

The mind is ever restless, because the nature of energy is not static. Energy is something that is moving. That is why in the *Gita* and in the Upanishads, the mind is called the eleventh instrument. There are five sense organs and five organs of intellection contained in the body and the eleventh instrument is the eleventh sensory organ, called mind, consciousness.

So, when Arjuna says the mind is restless, he is referring to that constant movement of energy going on. He seems to have forgotten what he was told in the first part of the sixth chapter, that when you are not involved in that movement yourself, when you do not identify with the movement, say of anger or jealousy, when you do not convert the movement of that energy into your personal experience and own it as your psychological possession, then that non-involvement, non-attachment makes the restless mind steady.

Krishna has shown a very magnificent way of handling the restlessness, and this is something worth experimenting with, for each one of us. If you do not get involved or worked up by the excitement or the depression, by the likes and dislikes, if you do not own them as your own, if you look at that, as the movement of conditioning, then there is a space between that movement and yourself. You can see it and your perception of the conditioned movement affects the movement itself. Perception has a tremendous dynamic power.

But let us do justice to Arjuna's question. He is talking about the material aspect of the thought movement, he is talking about the energy aspect. Energy can never be idle, as physics tells you. What is applicable to the physics of matter is also applicable to the physics of consciousness, as far as it is loaded with conditionings.

Arjuna says: 'you talk about moderation, about restraint, about steadiness, continuity, but how can you moderate the movement of the mind?' And Vasudeva answers, with his unique gentleness, love and compassion:

'Education, day after day, hour after hour, study, full of awareness of the purpose of studying, accompanied by the energy of non-attachment and non-involvement, will result, O Arjuna, in the restraint and moderation of the mind.'

'Vairagya' is a term generally translated as renunciation. It seems to me that *vairagya* has not only a negative content, but also a positive content. A particular positive dynamic interest in the supreme reality enables you to remain non-attached and

non-involved. Such is the study of yoga, accompanied by the love of the supreme reality.

Just as you would be concerned in finding a beloved person who is lost, looking for him or her; all your energies being pulled together in your perception, in your audition, in looking, in the same way one is looking for the nature of ultimate reality, with great love and tenderness. It is not a dry search for ideas of reality. But discovering, perceiving, so that one can remain related to it and one can correlate every breath to that awareness.

Krishna speaks about *abhyasa*, the process of education. Unfortunately, in English these verses have been translated in an incorrect unscientific way, *abhyasa* being translated as practice. Obviously, practising is repetition, therefore, it is mechanical. They derive conclusions, which really the *Gita* does not merit, neither do the Vedas or the Upanishads merit such superficial conclusions and theories.

Abhyasa is education. Not a mere mechanical physical ritual, not a mechanistic repetition. It is probing, discovering, going deeper so as to become more comprehensive. Education is alive. Training is sterile. Mechanistic repetition and ritualism are lifeless. The difference about these has to be appreciated very clearly; otherwise the study of *yoga* will become meaningless.

When you get up in the morning and do the *asanas*, you are not repeating. You are getting into a posture, not only to give exercise to the muscular, glandular, neurological systems, but to fit yourself to perceive the reality with the help of the posture and *pranayama*. You are making yourself so refined, so pure, that the organism gets equipped enough to feel the supreme reality. Putting yourself into that posture is a kind of worship to the divine. It is a sophistication, a refinement, it is sensitizing the body and the brain together.

Sensitivity is the only energy that will take us beyond the brain, beyond thought, beyond time and space. Sensitivity is a perceptive quality, sensitivity is a perceptive energy, it is the dynamic energy of the supreme reality. Sensitivity and creativity are two names for the same energy.

Let us proceed. These two: *abhyasa*, education and *vairagya*, non-attachment, non-involvement, will enable you to moderate and restrain the mental movement. The mental movement is the product of the past, it gets life because you give importance to it, because you become attached to it. It is your identification that provides the dynamism to past conditionings, contained in your body.

Supposing there is an upsurge of a powerful sentiment such as jealousy, fear, ambition or any other emotion. There is an upsurge and the whole body gets tense with it. You are awake enough to feel the effect of that upsurge, what it does to you. But instead of immediately rushing into action upon it, whether it is anger or jealousy or fear, you just look at it.

This looking at the movement taking place in the body, is a tremendously helpful aid which can be experimented upon, because *yoga* is an experimental science; it is not a mere theory, it is not a philosophy. Experimentation, investigation, exploration, verification, they are the essence of the science of *yoga*. In fact all spirituality that India talks of, is the science of Life and living.

The second question is: what happens to a person who has faith in the spiritual reality, who wants to educate himself or herself, who begins to do that, and fails to complete the study? What is implied? What happens if such a person dies before completing the education? What happens to all that he has learned, understood and whatever he had tried out, as an education, as *abhyasa*? What happens to that? Does it get destroyed? That is the second question.

Now, we come to a significant aspect of the Vedas and the Upanishads, who claim that there is nothing like destruction. Nothing gets created, nothing gets destroyed, there is the emergence and the manifestation of energy and there is the merging back of the energy. Emergence from the unmanifest into the manifest, emergence from the formless into that with form and the merging back into the formless, the unmanifest. Out of the invisible, the unmanifest, the non-individuated organic wholeness, out of it, emerge the particular expressions. They are limited by form, by conditioned energy and therefore there comes a time when the merging back takes place.

The emptiness of space does not have to merge back, it is formless, non-individuated. 'It is the first aspect of the manifestation of my nature.'

CHAPTER VII

YOGA OF KNOWLEDGE AND REALIZATION

'That supreme cause, or seed, or source, out of which the eightfold matter emerges, is my second aspect, my lower nature. The intelligence out of which all these eightfold expressions manifest, that intelligence is my highest nature.' (Verse four, chapter seven).

We have a description of the higher and lower nature: 'the whole Cosmos is composed of two aspects of my being; intelligence, which is my higher nature and the eightfold expression, which is my lower nature.'

Before we proceed, let us be very careful about the word ego, ego-ness. It is the principle of cohesion; it has a sense of entity-ness, a sense of identity-ness. All the elements, space, air, fire etc. could not have been together, if there had not been this sense of cohesion holding them together. The ego-ness, the ahamkara, is not the pride, the vanity, the egoistic nature which we understand in our daily parlance. It is a scientific term, which is being used in the *Gita* and also in the Upanishads and the Vedas. There is a sense of cohesion in the eightfold manifestation, which holds things together.

Look at what physicists tell us today. They say that the planet is a being, there is beingness in every expression, there is nothing like dead matter. It is all a dance of energies. Whether you read the *Tao of Physics*, or the *Dance of Shiva* of Capra, or the implicate and the explicate order in the universe by David Bohm, or other scientists, you will come across the expression that the ground of existence, beyond the nothingness of emptiness, seems to be intelligent. They call it supreme intelligence.

Supreme intelligence is contained in earth, water, fire, air, in the emptiness of space, in sound, in the thought energy, in reason. Even in the ego-sense, the sense of I-ness, intelligence is contained there too. This beingness of Life permeates the Cosmos.

Vasudeva is explaining the two-fold nature of Cosmic Life; the gross, that is the eightfold *prakriti* (the material out of which the universe is made up), and the subtle, called intelligence, present in every expression, and yet transcending them. Brahman is that transcending intelligence and the energies manifested in the so-called material expressions, are the individuation of that Brahman. Atman is individuated intelligence and Brahman is non-individuated supreme intelligence.

Sartre talks about the existential essence, that essence, which cannot be separated from existence. Descartes has talked about it too. He has gone as far as the thinking process: 'I think, therefore I am.' Emanuel Kant also talked about it, but Sartre did go a step farther, by referring to it as the existential essence. A new vertical line of thinking and analysing started with Sartre. It is a separate point from the philosophy of materialism.

I am trying to synthesize spirituality and science, because the twenty-first century is going to be the century of synthesis of these two. Gone are the days of mythologies and institutionalized religions. One global religion of human relationships, of human values, a religion of love and compassion towards all and the sharing of the earth and its resources as members of one family, is going to take its place.

We are proceeding very fast towards a Cosmic awareness, a global consciousness and a world family and maybe a world government, in the context that we have created for ourselves, with the help of science and technology, where time and space are ever shrinking. No human problems will ever get solved in any other way.

What does this explanation imply for you and me? It implies that there is no division between spiritual and material life, there is no separation. As reality is indivisible, Life also is indivisible, non-fragmented. The act of living has to be in the context of the awareness that Life cannot be divided, cannot be fragmented. But before we proceed to that final conclusion, which is implied in this, Vasudeva says:

'Arjuna, I am sharing with you this secret. Among thousands of human beings, hardly one turns his face from knowing towards learning.'

The word *siddhi*, used here, has been misused and abused. That which becomes part of your substance is *siddhi*, that which is assimilated and becomes the substance of your being, psycho-physically, that is *siddhi*. Not only occult or transcendental powers, as inferred in Tantra and Mantra Yoga. Here, only one among thousands strives for converting knowledge into understanding, means, that the rest strive, whether through *yoga*, whether through personal discoveries, or by other ways, but they stop halfway. Their learning and discoveries get blocked, obstructed. They begin to strive, but they do not arrive at their destination, their pilgrimage is arrested, either by their weaknesses, or by ambition.

We have seen that Arjuna was afraid of that obstruction. Therefore, he has asked Vasudeva: 'what will happen to a student of *yoga*, if he fails and his body perishes?' Vasudeva has in mind this question, when he says that among thousands, only one turns his face from acquisitive activity of knowing, gathering, memorizing, towards learning and discovering step by step.

You have to make an effort to observe, to coordinate the truth that you have observed, make an effort to live the truth in daily living, come what may, at any and every cost. Then only is jnana (knowledge) converted into vijnana (spiritual understanding and awareness of the highest truth). Unless it is verified by personal discovery, they cannot understand and grasp the essence of reality. The sixth chapter ends by warning Arjuna not to stop halfway. Do not give up, be one among thousands who arrives at the verified understanding of the essence of existence, of the nature of supreme reality.

Krishna is a dear friend, not only a teacher. He is pointing out: 'I am the nectar in water, look, the supreme reality, this intelligence, has expressed itself in water, in the vitality of water. I am the light and lustre in the moon and the sun.'

Where did the sun and the moon get their light and lustre from, if they were only heat? Because Life is light. The supreme reality, the supreme intelligence, is light and sound, both. That is the point where physics stands today. The primordial two elements of creation are sound and light, they are convertible energies.

Vasudeva says: 'the sound energy contained in the emptiness of space is the evidence that my intelligence exists in that emptiness of space, my vitality exists there. Many flavours, scents, juices are contained in the earth. Where did they come from, Arjuna? I am the supreme reality in all those things: in flavours, juices, nectar in cereals, in vegetables, fruit, in a drop of water, all that is the evidence of my existence.

It is the evidence of the existence of the supreme intelligence, of Brahman, existing in the earth, in water, shining through the sun and the moon, Brahman, speaking through the sound energy of the skies, of the emptiness of space.' He proceeds: 'the emergence of the syllable OM, the potential dynamic energies contained in that self-generated whole sound, is not born out of any friction. It is the spontaneous content of Cosmic Life.'

Krishna says that in the syllable OM you will find the energy of wholeness. In water you will find the vitality of Brahman, of eternal Life. He goes on explaining in various ways, in a number of verses, the existence that is the immanence of the transcendental energy, the immanence of intelligence in the so-called material objects, to prove that matter and Brahman cannot be separated. After all, the *Gita* is the essence of Vedanta, the philosophy of non-duality, the philosophy of *advaita* (not two). Krishna is showing how the source of creation permeates creation. He uses a very interesting phrase:

'The reality is the causeless cause, the seed and the source of creation, out of which millions of universes have emerged and merge back. And yet the seed-ness, the cause-ness of that supreme cause, the source-ness of that supreme eternal source does not get affected at all.'

The seed remains the seed, in spite of it becoming a tree, says Vasudeva. The seed of a banyan tree grows into a tree and gives back hundreds of seeds. So the seed became the tree, without damaging, mutilating its nature of seed-ness. So nothing is decreased or damaged, though universes merge out of Brahman. There is this *mantra*:

'Purnam adah purnam idam
purnat purnam udacyate
purnasya purnam adaya
purnam evavasisyate.'

'The whole (Brahman) is all that is invisible; the whole (Brahman) is all that is visible. The whole was born out of the whole. When the whole (the universes) is absorbed into the whole (Brahman), the whole alone remains.'

The supreme reality is not deprived of any of its essence and quality, though millions of universes have emerged out of it and may emerge even in future. You cannot divide reality into creation and creator. The cause becomes the effect, without loosing its cause-ness. This is the secret of the philosophy of *advaita*, of not two, of non-duality.

Krishna begins with Sankhya, the philosophy that postulates two realities, as spirit and matter. He describes *yoga*, he describes *karma*, action, then he speaks of self-education, of discovery, of observation etc., and he leads Arjuna towards *advaita*, non-duality, that reality as the imperishable causeless cause, which becomes creation. This point we have to understand.

We have to understand the difference between the self-generated divine supreme reality, that the *Gita* talks about, and the god and goddesses, that are current and prevalent in India. In the one the secret of creation is that creator and creation are the same. It is the source that has become the Cosmos.

The all-pervading, all-permeating, formless, reality is something that ordinary people, like you and me, cannot be aware of. It is difficult to be aware and correlate every breath of ours, every act of ours, to that energy. It becomes very difficult. So the invisible, intangible, unnameable, immeasurable, unknowable reality becomes a concept for most people. The Indian genius found a way, in the physics of consciousness, of helping the masses, by clothing that concept of male and female energy, contained in the Cosmos, into human forms of gods and goddesses.

There is a science for preparing these images and statues for worship. Excuse me for a personal reference. In my young days, when I was still studying at high school, I had been to Calcutta and other places and there I had the occasion to study the science of making faultless images of gods and goddesses out of clay, metal, marble, etc. A very interesting science. People in Kerala, in East Bengal, and in some parts of Nepal and Tibet, had specialized in this art and science. It is not only an emotional sentimental play to make a metal or stone idol and then to take it home. You also project, with the help of *mantras*, *pranas*, into that idol that you have made. Unless the idol is bathed with those *mantras*, it does not become worshipable. It is quite a science.

That is why, I am saying that the Indian genius found a way of helping the people, right from childhood to old age, by giving them a symbol. As you have the science of symbology in western psychology, we have a science of symbology in India. If you cannot correlate to the invisible, the intangible, the all-permeating omniscient, omnipresent, omnipotent divinity, have an idol in your house. Bathe it as you bathe yourself, clothe it as you clothe your body. Put ointment on it as you put ointment on your body. You don't like to live in darkness, so put a light there, have some incense. So the divine became a companion for the common person living here. Gods and goddesses were not only mythological; they were a strategy of love and compassion.

Not everyone can understand the Vedas and the Upanishads. The Vedic Sanskrit is very difficult, not everyone can study that. To enable the common person to remain united to that reality, the worlds of gods and goddesses, with magnificent temples as their dwelling places, were dedicated to that reality. And householders going there, at least once a day, contributed to maintaining this, through Bhakti Yoga, the *yoga* of devotion. Now everything has deteriorated, everything is distorted, misused. Religion also has become commercialized.

In Bhakti Yoga, to which the twelfth chapter is attributed, Vasudeva is not referring to gods and goddesses, he is not referring to the world of symbology, he is not referring to the world of concepts and ideation, not even verbalization. He is referring to that transcending supreme all-permeating intelligence. In one verse Vasudeva says:

'In all that exists and moves in the world, that which lives and moves in every expression, I dwell both as the source and as the manifestation. I am there as the source, in the form of intelligence. There is no expression in the Cosmos, which does not have intelligence. So, I permeate all my creation, both as the source, the seed of intelligence and as the manifestation.'

Please correlate this to another expression of Vasudeva: 'in the heart of every human being dwells the Lord supreme.' Not in the sense of an idol or image, but as the divine. So here, in the seventh chapter, let us learn to discriminate Bhakti Yoga (the *yoga* of devotion) which is the mental abode, the dimension of symbology, and Jnana Yoga, which is the orbit of ideation and conceptualisation, discriminate both these two, from Vijnana Yoga, the *yoga* of supreme knowledge, which gives the secret of creation both transcendental and immanent, the intelligence both immanent and transcendental. The supreme intelligence, dwelling in each human being, as Atman, Paramatman or Brahman, is the same in essence, the same in quality.

'That Mahatma, that enlightened being, who can see with his sensitivity that Vasudeva, the supreme, dwells in everything, is really rare. Whether in a dog or a scholar, the same supreme reality dwells there.'

What is referred to, is the divinity, please do see this. The self-generated Cosmos is not a man-made world. Societies are man-made, science and technology are man-made, wars are man-made, but the Cosmos is a self-generated, self-sustained, self-regulated, self-harmonized reality.

The Brahma-Vidya and *yoga shastra* (knowledge of transcendental reality and *yoga* practice) help the enquirers to harmonize their energies with the Cosmic energies. Harmonization of the energies is the secret of *yoga*. And Ayurveda, which is the science of harmonizing psychophysical energies, is the secret of health. Spirituality is the science of harmonizing individual and Cosmic energies, discovering the harmony and living in such a way, that the harmony is not violated, that the orderliness of Cosmic Life is not violated.

So first *jnana*, knowledge, then *vijnana*, insight into supreme reality, then Purusha and Prakriti, the cause of creation and creation, as inseparable. We are looking briefly at the essential points. This language of immanence and transcendence of reality, the inseparableness of matter and spirit, the interwoven nature of the manifest and the unmanifest, the everything-ness contained in the nothingness of space, is something indescribable. That they could verbalize and describe it, even in such terms, shows a marvellous human genius. Every time I study the *Gita*, which I have been studying for at least the last fifty years of my life, every time you touch it, you find a new nuance, a new ray of light coming out of the words.

Let us look at the eleventh verse, chapter seven. Every verse reveals the majesty of the Vedic perception of Life and every word, in the seven hundred verses of the *Bhagavad Gita*, are like gems that shine with the glow of pristine purity and ultimate reality.

Here, the word *bala* has to be noted specially. It cannot be translated into English by the word power or strength. For power and strength there is another term in Sanskrit: *shakti*. *Bala* refers to the energy aspect of the physical body and the psychological structure combined together. So, the energy vibrating in a living person or creature is a manifestation of the presence of Brahman in that creature. But what kind of energy?

The qualifications come in the second part of the verse, namely, the energy that is neither attached to any object or individual, external to the person, nor attached to its own cognition inside the person. If a person is conscious all the time that there is energy in him or her, then the desire to utilize that energy, for satisfying attraction or repulsion, ambition or comparison, comes about.

Here, *bala* is the pure energy unfocussed, unattached to any external object or individual and free of obsessive consciousness of its own presence. Vasudeva says that divinity is reflected in that energy. *Bala* is a very dangerous expression, which has been misused and abused by practically all the modern schools of spiritual teachings in India and perhaps elsewhere.

Let us now look at the word *dharma*. Here the word *dharma* does not indicate any institutionalized code of conduct. It is the principle of cohesiveness, that helps the Cosmic intelligence to sustain the built-in orderliness and harmony in the Cosmos, sustaining harmony and orderliness in the community or society, where human beings live together. Living together or sharing Life becomes nearly impossible, unless a principle of cohesiveness or a feeling of togetherness exists among the members psychologically; in their perspectives, in their approaches, in their attitudes.

Here, the divinity is the principle of cohesiveness, expressed through desire. The first line refers to energy, *bala*. It is specified and defined by calling it the energy of desire, *kama*. *Kama* is the pure energy of desire. Generally, it is understood to imply the sexual impulse, but it seems to me, that we narrow down the content of that word by applying it exclusively to sexual relationships. The whole sacredness, sanctity, of the energy of desire, *kama*, gets polluted, damaged by narrowing it down to sexual instincts, impulses or sexual interaction.

We will look at that energy, *kama*, devoting a few minutes to it, because it is an important aspect of the teachings of the *Gita*. The *Gita* does not prescribe that you extinguish the energy of desire in you. If there were no energy of desire, then there would be no warmth in life. It is like having blood without warmth, having all the organic vitality without the warmth of desire.

Now, that energy of desire is called the companion of the divine. You might have come across the words Shiva Shakti. Shiva is always accompanied by Shakti, which is the dynamic aspect of godhead which creates, preserves and dissolves the universes, (Shiva here represents Brahman, the transcendent absolute aspect).

This energy of desire is a constant companion of Life. Whenever there is Life, there is this energy. One has to discover its nature. Look at the flame of desire kindled in your heart, without directing it towards any object outside of you, or without directing it towards any of the organs of your body. To look at that flame of desire, its heat spreading through the body, to watch its upsurge, is great fun.

People cannot sustain that pure perception of the fact of this energy or *kama*. They cannot perceive the fact of desire, without accepting or rejecting it, without condemning it, criticizing it, or getting victimized by it. Whenever this energy of desire stirs in the body, it gets activated: in the period of puberty, by the time the child crosses the age of twelve or thirteen. Then there is a metabolical turmoil in the body, and various energies begin to get activated, among them this energy of desire. And the person does not know where to direct it.

Education is supposed to provide the direction. Civilization and culture are supposed to help the growing human being, to direct it towards the principle of cohesiveness, towards the principle of harmony and orderliness in human relationships, in relationship with nature, in relationship with one's own body and all the organs in the body, looking at them, watching them healthily, cleanly, without attaching any moral overtone or undertone to the perception. That is not done.

Here Krishna is telling Arjuna about that energy, especially because, at the end of the first chapter, Arjuna had dropped his bow and arrow and said he would not fight. He wanted to retire to the forest, he wanted to relinquish his right to the throne, he wanted to give up everything. He was obsessed with negativity towards Life, as if he had lost all desire to live.

He said: 'it does not matter if they kill me, if the Kauravas kill all of us, it does not matter.' A kind of death-wish, that Freud had rightly pointed out in analysing the human psychology, the concealed death-wish leading towards depressions, indulgence in depression, intentional provocation to depression, wish for suicide and all sorts of negativities, had got hold of Arjuna.

Imbalance and a neurotic mind is the sickness of modern society. I am pointing this out, because the two lines in this verse are very significant, exposing the yogic psychology. The energy of desire by itself is holy. Do not look upon that energy, *kama*, as sinful. It is neither unholy nor sinful. If it is oriented towards sex, then let the sex impulse be looked at in the light of your whole life, in the life of society and enjoy that without violating the harmony, the health and orderliness of society, that which is not contradictory to the principle of cohesiveness. In fact Krishna uses the words:

'Desire, that is conducive to the principle of cohesion, expressed in social life, in relationship to nature and in relationship to your own body and mind, that desire is *dharma*, it is a necessary part of Life.'

The whole Cosmic manifestation is an interplay of male and female energy and to discover the secret of harmonizing these, in our own lives and keeping them harmonized in the lives of the members of society, is a great challenge we are facing.

Suppression or repression of *kama*, denial, rejection of it, either in the name of celibacy or renunciation, has led to hypocrisy, to sinfulness. Encouraging this impulse or instinct, creating a god out of it, developing a cult of sensual pleasure, utilizing the basic energy of desire and also the energy contained in the sex organ, for the limited purpose of fleeting pleasure, for escaping boredom, for compensating frustration, for forgetting failures etc., is a violation of *dharma*.

Neither the cult of suppression, nor the cult of indulgence, but the cult of harmony and orderliness, a healthy cohesiveness for sharing Life, is mentioned in the *Gita*. That current runs through all the chapters. We have looked at the sixth chapter, the *yoga* of restraint and moderation. Then we proceeded to see *yoga* through knowledge verified by experimentation. And now we have come to the seventh chapter. The Vedas, the Upanishads, the *Gita*, are not against the display of desire, provided it does not violate harmony.

Let us proceed. How this energy of desire violates *dharma* and lead people astray, or misleads them, is pointed out in the next verse. In this verse there is a reference to *sattva, rajas* and *tamas*. Now *sattva, rajas* and *tamas* are called *gunas*, attributes. There is a difference between an attribute and a quality, though in common language they are used as synonymous. But, philosophically speaking, there is a world of difference between attribute and quality.

When out of Brahman, the unmanifest, the organic wholeness of Brahman, emerged *akasha* (space) and then *vayu* (air), *agni* (fire), water and earth, when the contents of Brahman, the vitality of Brahman, the intelligence of Brahman, was manifesting itself progressively through the emergence of these, the movement of manifestation generated these three attributes, *sattva, rajas* and *tamas*. It is the motion from nothingness. Now everything was becoming visible, tangible. The unindividuated was manifesting itself in individuation.

There is a beautiful word in Sanskrit: *bhava*. There is the word *bhavana*, feeling, sentiment, which is a momentary flash. *Bhava* is the attribute which has durability. It can have a life-long durability. *Sattva, rajas, tamas*, these three *bhavas* or attributes, come into existence, generated by the friction contained in motion.

Sattva has a radiance of transparent cleanliness, a radiance of brilliance, of intelligence. Intelligence is reflected, as it were, in the shine of *sattva guna*. *Raja guna* is activity, motion at its best. And the best of steadiness is in *tamo guna*. When *tamo guna* deteriorates, it becomes inertia. But if it is not distorted, if it is not obsessive *tamo guna*, if it is there without any distortion, then it is the principle of steadiness. *Rajo guna* is the principle of motion. And *sattva guna* is the principle of radiance or, let me say, brilliance of intellect.

When out of the unmanifest, the individuated life emerges, limiting ourselves to human life, then *sattva*, *rajas* and *tamas* shine in the personality and behaviour of human beings. Vasudeva is explaining to Arjuna why people go astray. Instead of focussing their energy on the ultimate reality, even after having known that out of this supreme reality comes the whole Cosmos, they go astray, they run around and their energies are scattered in many directions. *Sattva*, *rajas* and *tamas*, these three attributes, are reflected in their behaviour. People start reacting to them.

If you see *sattva guna*, you get attracted by its healthy shine, by its brilliance, by its coolness of peacefulness. You are attracted by the vitality, the motion expressed through *rajas*. The same with *tamas*. When they are reflected in behaviour, you react to them. Vasudeva says that these three gunas create delusion, *maya*. *Maya* is not something false or untrue, it is not unreal. It is a delusion, a kind of screen that comes between you and the real, between you and the truth.

People are busy getting attracted or repulsed, getting involved in these expressions. You will find these expressions not only in human behaviour, but also in mountains, rivers, fire, fruit, vegetables. There are *sattva guna* vegetables and *tamo guna* vegetables, there are *raja guna* fruit and cereals, and so on. Whatever has come into existence, into the framework of space and time, that which has a form and substance, has attributes. All are expressions.

Having known the distinction between the wholeness and the individuated particularized expressions, having known the limitedness and the un-limitedness of both, human beings get entangled by this inevitable emergence of the three *gunas* in the very act of manifestation. It creates the delusion, the *maya*, which keeps people moving from one birth to another. All their lives they are busy with *sattva*, *rajas*, *tamas*, victimized by one, obsessed by the other, infatuated with the third one, they run hither and thither. They forget that behind these three gunas, behind the whole so-called material world, there is a supreme reality. It is however their responsibility to remain united with that reality, with the help of awareness.

A few verses are spent in describing the emergence of the three *gunas*, their glamour and the world getting deluded by them. That is why, after having acquired knowledge about the nature of reality, people still grope and struggle in the world of relationships, attracted or repulsed by the *gunas*. This is reflected in people's behaviour. Because their perception does not remain focussed and steady on the reality, they do not grow into the dimension of awareness.

The journey from knowledge to understanding, from consciousness to awareness, seems to be a long journey. They travel through many words, before the verbal knowledge gets mature and blossoms into verified understanding. Unless there is verified understanding, understanding verified by interaction, (through observation there is interaction, and through interaction there is understanding) unless there is understanding, there is no energy of awareness. Like the energy of desire, there is an energy of awareness.

This long journey through birth and death, through one life or many lives, becomes necessary. Verbal knowledge satisfies people in the beginning. They feel it will give them the attainment of reality, thinking that gross words would cause transformation. Getting emotionally carried away by the *sattva guna*, they feel as if transformation is round the corner. It does not come, because the interaction has not taken place, interaction of consciousness through the act of observation of truth as it is.

The next verse says that there are four categories of people who aspire to know the reality, to perceive it and to dwell in it.

Firstly, there are those who are distressed by the shocks of pleasure and pain, by the jolts of honour and humiliation, by the jerks of joy and sorrow, failure and success. Persons get so shattered by these frequent shocks, that they feel distressed and they want to turn away from the material and psychological life. Their motivation for turning towards divinity is a negative motivation; they are distressed. They want some security, some place where they can relax.

They require a place where they would be accepted as they are and would not be judged, compared or evaluated. Such a distressed person wanders around, trying to find a path, a technique, a formula, to get united with the divinity. This is an ego-centred, self-centred motivation, a negative motivation. It is not based on the desire to understand what truth is.

Then there are those who want to find out about reality through verbal knowledge, who want to know about reality. They read books about truth, reality, divinity, religion, spirituality, wandering about the globe hearing talks, discourses. They discuss, meet so-called religious holy persons. They make changes in food, diet, in this and that. They are obsessed with knowing and experiencing that accompanies knowing.

First the distressed person, then the seeker of knowledge. And then the seeker of wealth. The word *artha* (wealth) is significant. It does not refer only to money or currency, it refers also, in the Upanishads, to economic life. It is difficult to translate. If you have land, cattle, clothes, food, children, all that is wealth. That which makes your life meaningful is *artha*. So when you are married, you have a child, which is the consummation of your marriage. Life has become meaningful. You have provisions to satisfy the basic needs decently, without exploiting anyone, all that is called *dhanam artham*. As there are seekers of knowledge, verbal knowledge, so there are seekers of wealth, *artha*. Wealth is their goal.

And last, comes the wise one. A wise one is a person, who has come across the transcendence of verbal knowledge, instinctively, intuitively. He has seen the futility of the gross word, its meaning does not satisfy him anymore. He is seeking that which is transcendental, that which transcends the gross, the verbal, transcends words and their dictionary meaning. He is interested only in liberation and nothing else.

These are the four categories who turn towards the investigation and the exploration of divinity, or in Krishna's language: 'those who turn to me'. Symbolically these are the four categories of devotees, those who are dedicated.

'When a distressed person turns to me with devotion, though he may be self-centred, ego-centred, having a very exclusive and narrow investigation, still I do not reject or condemn him.'

In fact, the Cosmic intelligence helps that individual to sustain that focus, so that once the feeling of distress and depression, the feeling of negativity subsides, there is the potential of intelligence, residing in all human beings. So, he is not discouraged or rejected by the supreme intelligence, but helped to feel secure, to feel accepted, with the hope that negativity will be transcended.

A seeker of knowledge is the benediction of the grace of the divine. Helped by the supreme intelligence, the Cosmic intelligence, who generates a sense of emptiness in spite of all the knowledge acquired, the person feels empty and shallow. It is a very strange way, in which the *Gita* looks at this beautiful fact. Unless the seeker feels empty, feels, that even with the acquisition of knowledge, Life is shallow, there will not be an urge to penetrate that shallowness, cross that shallowness and go beyond.

A compassionate tenderness was felt by the Cosmic intelligence, in the case of the first seeker, the second one is being treated rather harshly, by allowing the person to be tormented by emptiness and shallowness.

Before I proceed, let me tell you, that the Vedas, the Upanishads and the *Gita* explain that human beings have a fourfold responsibility. A human life is fulfilled when these four: *dharma, artha, kama* and *moksha* (the principle of order and harmony of Life, economic security, fulfilment of legitimate desires and ultimate enlightenment, *moksha*), are realized. Liberation from all identification, dispelling of all ignorance including the ego-consciousness, that is the ultimate *moksha*, the ultimate liberation.

So *kama* (desire) precedes *moksha* (liberation). If there is a desire
for wealth, if the person feels that the fulfilment of his life would
come by wealth, his energies will be focussed on the divine by
chanting *mantras*, worshipping, visiting holy places, giving
charities, etc. Unless all this is done with the urge for liberation,
the seeker of wealth will get entangled in his own wealth and will
suffer. The Cosmic intelligence helps the seeker of wealth, by
inflicting upon that seeker the pain and agony of attachment, the
fear of losing the wealth, until the glamour of wealth disappears
from the heart and he turns to *moksha*, ultimate liberation.

We are trying to cover two verses in one. There remains the last
category, that of the wise one, who has seen the duality of life, the
pain and pleasure, the glamour of honour and the agony of
humiliation, the tears of pain and smiles of pleasure. He has seen
all that and has seen the repetition. So, the wise one does not feel
at all attached to the whole drama of duality. He walks through the
corridors of duality, in the majesty of inner renunciation and his
goal is focussed only on the ultimate reality of Life, on the ground
of existence.

Among the four, the *jnani*, the wise one, who is united with the
Cosmic reality, united with Brahman through awareness, is nearest
to the divine, to divinity, says Vasudeva. This person lives in the
awareness of divinity; they are inseparable. Wherever the person
moves, whatever the person does, the holiness of Brahman, of the
reality of Life, is reflected in everything that the person does.
Because the awareness is the energy that keeps him united with
the divine, even though he is visibly, tangibly the particular,
however the content of his consciousness is universal, it is Cosmic,
therefore he represents the Cosmic, he represents the divine.

'There are four categories of my *bhaktas* (my worshippers), but
the *jnani*, the wise one, is the one who represents the divine in
daily living.'

What we have to learn and understand very clearly, is the definition
of *bala* as energy, the definition of *kama* as the energy of desire
and that the energy of desire is itself *dharma*, the principle of
cohesiveness, order and harmony.

The second point that we have to remember is how the unmanifest cannot become manifest, without generating the three *gunas*. The three *gunas* do not exist separately by themselves, but they get generated in the movement of manifestation. Something beautiful has been pointed out.

Then we have to remember the delusion that these three *gunas* or attributes cause to the human brain. The human brain gets entangled in *sattva, rajas, tamas*, through infatuation, obsession, repulsion, hatred, etc.

Then, how the four categories of worshippers are defined. The first two have relative motivations, the third creates a network of entanglement for himself, through amassing wealth. And the fourth is free of all these entanglements, being united with the divine through awareness. That was the point.

I am trying to correlate your study of the *Gita* with daily living. If the study does not help us and does not cause a qualitative change in the texture of our behaviour, the texture of our relationships with others, then, whether we study the *Gita* or Patanjali Yoga, or the Upanishads, it is of no use.

The human race is on the brink of collective self-destruction, in so many ways destroying itself physically and psychologically. In such studies of the *Gita*, I pour my being, my flesh and blood, in the words, in the hope that the human race shall see that it is possible to have an alternative human culture, an alternative way of living, not for the privileged few, not for those living far away from society and the travail of life. Spirituality is for you and me, who are in the midst of the din of human life and relationships. It is the quality of our relationships that has to go through a transformation. A new dynamics of our relationships has to come about.

People get entangled in activities through utilizing the three *gunas* - *sattva, rajas, tamas* - for self-centred purposes. Or their lives are spent in reacting to them, in human relationships.

Sattva guna has a steadiness, giving the intellect the capacity to discriminate the true from the false. So many persons, attracted by *sattva*, spend their lives acquiring knowledge, ruminating, thinking, contemplating that knowledge, turning away from the movement of relationships. They mistake the isolation brought about by verbal knowledge, isolation from Life and living, they mistake that isolation for renunciation (*sannyasa*) and are therefore deprived of the interaction with Life in its various aspects.

Those who are fascinated by motion, the movement that *rajas* has, utilize that for acquiring material goods, wealth, power. They feel gratified through domination over others, through their mobility and smartness, through the competence that *raja guna* gives, the easiness with which they can move physically and psychologically. They can engage themselves for eighteen hours a day, in various activities. So, they get entangled there. Then they begin to compare themselves with others. Ambition is the sickness that people, dominated by *rajas*, generally suffer from. They remain restless throughout their lives.

And those who are inclined towards *tamas*, utilize *tamo guna* through negativity; the capacity to suspend movement, suspend thinking, suspend reacting. They very cleverly try to avoid shouldering responsibility, they avoid every crisis that may come their way. So negativity becomes a weapon. *Tamo guna*, inactivity, passivity becomes a weapon to avoid responsibility, avoid meeting challenges. And like the people who are attracted by verbal knowledge and bask in the isolation that knowledge brings, the people attracted by *tamo guna* enjoy passivity, and many a time mistake it for the spiritual quality of renunciation.

There is no renunciation in *tamo guna*. Passivity and negativity have not the dynamism of renunciation, nor has isolation. The dynamism of austere renunciation can breathe only in the movement of relationships.

We have seen how the world is deluded, how most of us are deluded by *maya*, these three *gunas*, which are generated in the process of manifestation of the unmanifest. They really do not have a separate existence, except in the manifest limited aspect of life, that which is in space and time, that which is solidified energy. In that aspect of life these three gunas are generated and they function. They have no roots of their own.

You may have come across the verse where Vasudeva says: 'Arjuna, go beyond the three *gunas*, *sattva*, *rajas* and *tamas*, transcend them, while living in your physical body, while witnessing their operation. Never get involved or attached to anyone of these *gunas*.'

Why are people fascinated by the three *gunas*? We come to the last portion of the seventh chapter. Because their desires are oriented externally. Their desires run towards that which is outside their body, towards objects, towards the world, that is fleeting and changing every moment. And they want to gain those material fleeting objects, they want to derive pleasure from the contact with those objects. They want either possession, or at least an interaction that will give them pleasure, repeatedly.

This desire for sensual psychological pleasure, this desire for acquisition and possession, damages their knowledge. Their verbal knowledge gets damaged and mutilated by their desire for pleasure for objects, which are changing all the time, for circumstances that are changing all the time. They are seeking pleasure, which is a fleeting sensation. After all, pleasure is a sensation which has a very short durability.

It is not like joy, that once generated, lasts with you as a perfume which lingers. The perfume lingers for hours. Joy lingers with you perhaps till the last breath.

Attracted by the energy of the three *gunas*, wanting to manipulate them for gratifying desires, most people do not penetrate beyond the shell of the *gunas*. The *gunas* are the outer shell. Whatever is in a form, be it an animal, a bird, a tree or a human being, there will be *sattva*, *rajas*, *tamas*, in varying degrees in each. But that is only the outer crust of the being. It is not the essence. It is like the skin of a fruit, not its substance. The three *gunas* are useful for gratifying the sensation of pleasure. People do not see beyond the glamour of *sattva*, *rajas*, *tamas*.

But all the glamour is from the source, Brahman. They forget the original source, the seed, the causeless cause, which itself has become the effect. The seed that has become the gigantic Cosmos. They forget that and they get entangled.

As they use *sattva, rajas* and *tamas* to gratify their desire for pleasure, they also worship the man-made forms, the idols called god and goddesses. They worship them with all the prescribed rituals, with great faith, in order to fulfil their desire for money, for a job, a child, success, power. *Mantras* that use sound energy, and *tantras*, in which various *chakras* are used, become a great source of help to these people. They are busy worshipping the forms, the idols, begging them to give them this, give them that, protect them, and so on.

Instead of penetrating through the *gunas*, they get stuck with the outer, the external, the form, the attributes. And their lives are spent in such worship. They do it with great faith. They trust that the way they are doing their worship, as prescribed by the scriptures, will get them what they want.

Vasudeva says that it is their quality of faith, their integrity of purpose, the steadfastness with which they do the worship, it is this faith that gives them their reward. But they feel that the gods or goddesses are giving them this.

'That is not the truth, Arjuna. It is faith that produces the result. And the Cosmic intelligence helps them get those rewards.' It is not the idol that is doing it. It is the interaction between their faith, the way in which they turn to it and the response of that quality of faith from the Cosmic intelligence. 'I respond to their invincible faith.' Come what may, they stick to their *mantras*, their worship, the pilgrimages, etc.

In about three verses, the attitude of steadfastness, of one-pointedness, of integrity and its interaction with the Cosmic energy, is described. You have heard it said: 'faith moves mountains'. In the Vedas and the Upanishads there is a mantra which says: 'the quality, the texture of your being is according to the depth, the intensity of your faith.' Faith is an alchemy, which can bring about unimaginable results. It can produce marvels. So why are they not liberated by this faith?

Because they are asking for short-lived gains, they are asking for something, which is finite. They may get all the wealth, all the power, they may have children, they may get what they ask for, but what they ask is finite.

Within every human being there is infinity, divinity, Atman, the eternity that has made the human body its abode. So, there is an unverbalized aspiration for the infinite. While worshipping the finite, seeking pleasure from the finite, there is simultaneously a dissatisfaction about the finite and an aspiration for merging with the infinite, for being blessed by the eternal, the infinite.

Being conscious of one's imperfections, while justifying those imperfections, those distortions, there is the concealed aspiration for purity, for perfection. Knowing fully well that the body is mortal and is going to die, there is simultaneously an aspiration for immortality. There is a feeling somewhere, that I am immortal, eternal, I am the infinite.

They get what they asked for, the Cosmic intelligence responded to them favourably, but the gains are short-lived. And they get dissatisfied with the finiteness, the non-durability, the fleetingness of those pleasures and gains. Even when receiving the results of that worship, that ritualism, having followed the patterns prescribed by their religion, still the aspiration for the infinite does not leave them.

So, there comes a time, when they see the futility of all this and they turn towards that, which is not momentary. They begin questioning what they have been doing and their divine discontent, their dissatisfaction, gives them the energy to push themselves towards that, which is beyond the body, beyond the material, beyond thought, mind and brain.

Vasudeva says that divinity is patient, divinity is love. The Cosmic intelligence, that has responded to their faith, is aware, as it were, that seeing the futility of all this, their intelligence will guide them towards the divine. When they thus turn their faces, even after having gained what they wanted in the physical material world, the first realization that dawns upon these people, is the superficial nature of the division of reality between subject and object.

They see that Life is a wholeness and the ego is only a principle of cohesiveness, to keep the body, the brain, the mind together. It has no role to play, it has no utility in one's life, more than that. Formerly, they had imagined that there was really a subject, an ego and the rest of the world was the object for it. Now, they see that the ego is a shell, in which there is the divinity of Life, Brahman residing in the Atman. The ego was mistaken for the Atman. Ego is the shell.

As they see the futility of pleasure, the repetitiveness of gains and losses, humiliations and honours, pleasures and pain, they wake up to the reality, that this division is superficial. In fact, the 'me', the ego, could never be totally satisfied. The more you give it, the more it demands. It is only a shell. That which is demanding the infinity, the eternity, the immortality, is the very principle of divinity, Brahman, residing in the human body, within the shell of the ego. Inside the ego is the Atman, which is a ray of Brahman.

One had looked upon the ego as the essence, the thought-movement as the action of living. All that drops, in the sense that all identification with it, drops away. There is no more psychological involvement. The ego is just an instrument to be used. It is the shell and within the shell is the Atman, the divinity of Life.

Now what is divinity? That which is self-generated, which is self-sustained, that which is not constructed by human hand or manipulated by human thought. So Life is divine. Life is divinity. Within us is the divinity. Therefore, there is a yearning within us for Brahman, which is the Cosmic divinity. It never seems totally satisfied, unless it is united through awareness, living in the limited, united with the unlimited. When you become aware of its presence, that awareness unites you.

The temptation, the attraction for the division subject/object, the game of possessions, ownership, the temptation for widening,

broadening the field of me-and-mine, all that subsides. It does not
have to be denied. The understanding of reality causes the subsiding
of identification, subsiding of all attachment and involvement with
that which is false, which is untrue. Gone is the tension of duality.

We have to take care of two terms: *dvaita*, duality, and *dvandva*,
which is a subjective tension one has imagined, between the two
points of duality. There is no denying the fact that the person sitting
there is Rosanna, who has a physical body and the person sitting
here is Vimala, who has a physical body. There is a duality, duality
between or among the objects, among the expressions of Life, the
manyness. The blossoming of oneness into manyness is a fact that
cannot be denied. And as a self-conscious being you feel the duality,
you perceive the duality, that is a fact.

But then one imagines a tension, that is when *dvaita* becomes
dvandva, the illusion of dichotomy, of opposition between the two.
Then relationships become battlegrounds, because of this fear of
the other, this illusory opposition.

'They are free from all the tension of duality, when they perceive,
that within the shell of the ego, in each human being, is that
Brahman itself.'

This is individualized, and that is non-individuated. Please do see
with me that individuation does not mean fragmentation. We are
not pieces of Brahman. You can cut pieces of a cake, you can cut
pieces of a cloth. The divinity of Life, the Parabrahman, the
Paramatman, cannot be fragmented, Life cannot be fragmented.
So we are not a fragment cut from Brahman, separated or isolated
from it. We are organically related to it.

There is a constant inter-play going on between that and us, until
the screen of our own desires, our attachment to objects, gets
removed. *Sadhana*, self-education, does not do anything else but
remove this screen; the illusions that one had harboured.

Those who have transcended the tension of duality, while living in
the midst of people, interacting with nature, with people and with
the demands of their bodies and minds, right there they are completely

free, liberated, emancipated from the clutches of tension, from suffering. Their suffering has ended. They are emancipated, whose psychological suffering is ended completely, unconditionally.

What happens to such an emancipated person? What happens to his perception and to his responses? Everything is divine. It is the consummation of psychic growth, the consummation of maturity.

Because there is no consummation of psychic maturity, our interaction with the Cosmic intelligence does not take place properly. It is clouded, it is arrested. But one who perceives the divinity of Life, perceives that everything that is, or every being that is, is divinity, is divine. The characteristic that accompanies the event of emancipation is this transformation in perception and transformation in responses. That transformation in the responses is clarified in the last two or three verses of chapter seven. First we refer to perception.

There are stories, not mythological stories, but historical ones, of the lives of saints and *yogis* and emancipated ones. There used to be a tradition and perhaps it still exists, that pilgrims who went on a holy pilgrimage, went on foot. They would walk, carrying water of the Ganges to the southern tip, to Rameshvaram, and perform the water ablutions in a temple of Shiva. Then they would take the water from Rameshvaram and go back to Kashi and perform the water ablution there.

There was a sage called Ekanas. This sage was carrying water. Such pilgrims always walk in groups, singing *bhajans*, cooking their meal somewhere under a tree. That is their way of living. So, he had crossed half of India and by the side of the road he found a donkey, who was very thirsty. The other pilgrims just looked at the donkey and walked on. But Ekanas stopped and gave the water to the donkey, and the donkey was so happy drinking that water. But his companions got wild, they said: 'you have brought that holy water for the holy purpose and now you have given it to the donkey.'

Ekanas answered: 'The Lord has come here, I do not have to walk any further. The Lord from Rameshvara has come here and he has asked for water.' That was his perception. It was not a belief. He

was a great scholar, he had written many commentaries on holy
classics. He did not do it on impulse. He said 'the Lord came from
Rameshvara and asked for water.' What does that mean?

He perceived, that a donkey is a creation of Brahman, as much as
he was. Why should he take the water to that temple and the idol
there? If he had not seen the donkey, it would be a different matter.
But he saw it there, by the roadside. The worship of the Lord was
fulfilled by satisfying the need of the donkey. You see, this is the
perception of the emancipated. Perception gets transformed and
that transformation is reflected in your movements and relationships
from morning till night.

Now, let us proceed. What happens to the responses? One, who
has transcended the tension of duality, has transcended the glamour
of the world and the three *gunas*. Then what happens? The point is
clarified in a very interesting way in this chapter. Do you remember
that the *Gita* was referring to energy? The Cosmos is a field of
energy and our body, as a microcosm, is also a field of energy.
There is a constant interplay going on between the Cosmic energy
and the particularized individual energy. That is what we have been
talking about, since the fifth chapter.

Now here, the whole perspective of *karma* changes, says Vasudeva.
One, who perceives the highest truth, for him the perspective of
karma and therefore the style of *karma*, the culture of action,
changes. It is an alternative culture of Life. To observe and help
the interplay between the individualized and the non-individuated,
between the particularized and the whole, to let the interplay take
place, that becomes the definition of *karma*.

Your action implies creating an opportunity for the invisible, the
unmanifest interplay of energies, to become manifest. Your *karma*
is not your *karma*, it is not the expression of the petty little self, the
ego. It is a Cosmic event; whether you take a meal, whether you
bathe the body or brush the teeth, scrub the floor, talk to a person,
do whatever you do on the physical, psychological or the non-
psychological level. You become an instrument in creating an
opportunity for the manifestation of the unmanifest interplay

between the individual and the total, the individual and the whole, the particular and the total. That is your *karma*.

You are no longer driven or pushed by desires for fleeting pleasures or momentary gains, that has disappeared. As the quality of perception changes, the attitude towards action changes. It goes through a transformation, respecting the interplay of energies. Taking a meal is an expression of *samadhi*, it is the interaction between the compassion of the earth and the divine appetite in the human body. So when you take a meal, it is a *yajna*, a sacrifice. Your actions, your responses, while living in society, the manifestation of the interplay, your *karma*, is a sacrifice on the physical level.

Suddenly, Vimala sees a flash of what she had seen at the age of five, far back in the past. When her mother or grandmother would go to the kitchen, they would touch the piece of wood on the stove and I would ask why they did that? They would say: 'the wood is god, it cooks the meal for us'. Fire, too, was something holy. There was a feeling of sacredness and holiness about everything. Watering the plants, plucking the flowers, cooking the meal, even bathing the body, they would chant a *mantra*. This transformation in perception and transformation in the quality of your action, gives the flavour of sacredness, holiness to your whole life.

Wherever you move, your presence has the perfume of sacredness, your glances, your words, they have a kind of holiness. Without that touch of sanctity, sacredness, there is no charm in living. Mechanical repetitive activity, being driven, pushed, pulled, in many directions by impulses, desires, etc., that is not living. The *Gita* says that the physical action becomes a sacrifice on the invisible, the occult and the transcendental level. Now what is that action on the invisible, the occult and transcendental level? Let us spend a moment or two on this.

Supposing you are living with a great sense of responsibility, being very alert, sensitive and, as to your understanding, you are doing things correctly, your motivations are correct; no distortions, no imbalances, no impurities and yet the action, the relationships bring a completely contradictory result, unimagined by you, inconceivable for you. There was no distortion in the motivation for action, nothing and yet there is an absolutely contradictory inconceivable result.

Generally, we blame the other person who causes all that; the suffering, the insult, the humiliation, the condemnation, etc. The *Gita* says that the motivation to hurt, to cause a scandal, the motivation to insult or humiliate, all this has some background somewhere in the past. You must have been born a hundred times in your journey and the other person also. Somewhere this enmity or ill will, this gap in communication, must have existed, it is a continuity.

If this occult aspect of relationships and their inexplicable distortions and imbalances is appreciated, if this occult aspect is understood, then you do not react to violence by violence, you do not repay hatred by hatred, you put a stop there, because you do not want to give it anymore continuity. The only way to stop it, to finish with it, is not to react. 'Resist not evil with evil. If somebody hits you on the cheek, give the other cheek, if somebody asks for a shirt, give it to him.' Jesus of Nazareth was not a stupid person; he had a dynamic approach to peace.

The simplicity of Life that he talked about, or his new dynamics of human relationships, we, his children, have not understood, nor have we understood the teachings of Buddha about non-violence. They talk about an alternative culture, not a particular activity, but a way of living.

Respecting the interplay of energies, respecting also what must have happened in the occult, that which we don't know, one does not react in the same way. You don't hit back, you don't shout back, you don't insult, not because of cowardice, but because of understanding that somewhere the vicious circle has to be broken. The whole Life becomes a sacrifice, a wheel of sacrifice.

As Buddha talks about the wheel of *dharma*, the *Gita* talks of the whole Life being the wheel of sacrifice, not in the sense of negativity or giving up something, or being deprived of something. There is no scope for giving up, when you understand something and you do not do it. It is not giving up, there is no deprivation. The transformation in the quality of relationships, in the quality of *karma* or action, is manifested on the physical and the psychological level. The whole Life becomes a wheel of sacrifice.

We have talked about *yoga* as the science of holistic purification. The study of *yoga* is education in holistic purification; purification in perception, in response, purification in action. This is Vijnana Yoga. Vijnana Yoga along with Raja Yoga, along with Hatha Yoga, becomes really the sacred avenue for total emancipation, for unconditional emancipation.

In the last part of this chapter, one verse speaks of divinity as timeless. The reality of Life is timeless and being timeless, there is simultaneity of all the events that are occurring. Vasudeva, an expression of divinity, is talking in the first person: 'for me there is no past, present and future.' In the divinity, in the Cosmic reality there is no division as past, present and future. It is all simultaneity, it is all an is-ness, there is no past tense in it.

Human beings cannot perceive this phenomenon of simultaneity. As they have created various measures to measure the reality-they measure infinity with kilometres, they measure eternity with time, psychological time - in the same way they have created the concept of past, present and future. In reality there is nothing like past, present or future.

That which is, is the intangible becoming manifest. This Cosmic dance of the unmanifest becoming manifest and in that becoming, the oneness flowers into manyness. And again the manyness goes back into oneness. 'It has ever been like this; there is neither birth nor death, O Arjuna.' Because you cannot see the phenomenon of the wholeness, you cut it into pieces, and you call one event birth and another event death. Now, this nature is characteristic of the reality as the unmanifest, and reality as the manifest, and the interplay between the two. It has ever been so and it ever shall be so.

Now, he takes one step further and says: 'For a *yogi* who has transcended the myth of the ego, who has perceived the ego as a shell containing the gem of Atman, of reality, that *yogi* gets the sight and is capable of perceiving the drama of simultaneity.'

This is the metaphysical aspect of the teachings of the *Gita*. And we had to look at this verse because I think this will be the introduction to the next chapter, chapter eight, on Akshara Brahma Yoga, the Yoga of the Imperishable Brahman.

CHAPTER VIII

YOGA OF IMPERISHABLE BRAHMAN

The *Gita* is a dialogue between Sri Krishna and Arjuna. Dialogue is the style of the ancient Indians for presenting the subtle and deep truths, as given by the Vedas. Dialogues are neither propagation, nor mere narration. The interaction between the teacher and the student, in the dialogue, results in a transmission of the truth contained in the words.

So the *Gita* is a dialogue about *yoga shastra*, the science of *yoga*, which shows the way to live the truth revealed by the Vedas. This truth is called *Brahma-vidya*. It is the revealed truth about Brahman, the imperishable supreme reality, the eternal infinity of Life, which contains inexhaustible potential of manifesting its being. So, *yoga shastra* is based on *Brahma-vidya*. The dialogue between Krishna and Arjuna is an exposition of *yoga shastra*, based on *Brahma-vidya*. This is what we have seen so far in the chapters that we have studied together.

Now, before we proceed, may I say a few words about the revealed truth? It is not a truth that is propagated or systematized as a philosophy. When a person is capable of putting aside the movement of mind, the movement of brain, when a student of *yoga* enables herself or himself to transcend the mental movement, then there is receptivity, uncontaminated by thought. A receptivity that can receive, without converting that receptivity into an idea or a thought or a philosophy.

The ultimate truth reveals its nature, you may call it the grace of the supreme reality, when a person has transcended the mental movement. Revealed truth is not born of thought, not born of a theory, not born of a system. It is a spontaneous expression.

Some of you might have heard how the truth was revealed to Jesus of Nazareth, when he spent forty days on the mountain top. When he came down, those who had been with him could not recognize him, could not understand his language. The elegance of simplicity was baffling. The words were felt to be born out of something they had never known before. Such was the case for Gautama Buddha: the truth was revealed to him while seated under the bodhi tree. I am giving you examples from the historical period. The Vedas are pre-historical. Even in historical times there are examples, instances of individuals to whom the supreme reality, Brahman, the divinity, revealed its nature.

If that is clear let us proceed. When the truth reveals itself, the unmanifest reveals its own nature. It has been found that invariably some things have been communicated to such individuals, both in the Vedas and outside the Vedas.

The first is that the unmanifest and the manifest are one: the unmanifest, the indivisible holistic reality, which is Brahman and the perishable manifested reality, the plurality, are one. The one contains the many and the many contains the one. The unmanifest contains the manifest and the manifest contains the unmanifest. Every expression contains the wholeness of Life. So, the one and the many are one, the manifest and the unmanifest are one. This unity of Life, this organic homogeneous indivisibility of Life, has been a common point, whether you turn to the Patriarchs in China, to Confucius, to Laotsu, to Indian Teachers, or in the west to Plato, Socrates, Aristotle, Plotinus and others.

When there is agreement, that the whole manifested reality; the plurality, the perishable variety of expressions of Life, are born out of the imperishable oneness, that supreme reality, the question arose in the minds of those who read the revealed truths: 'how do we live with the perishable, while being aware of the imperishable?'

We have to live with the perishable reality. That which is there now, may not be there tomorrow. How do I deal with the moment, being aware of the moment-free eternity, time-free eternity? The manyness is not an illusion, it is not *maya*, it is very much there. It has a physical form. Matter, the source of manyness, the matrix of manyness, has energies, so many energies. How do I deal with the energies in the perishable manifested reality and yet be united with the unmanifest, indivisible wholeness of reality? That question must have come to every person who was in quest of reality.

Let us come back to the Indian Vedic Darshanas (the Six Systems of Indian Philosophy), how these Six Systems (Sankhya, Yoga, Nyaya, Vaisheshika, Mimamsa, Vedanta) dealt with this issue. This is the crux of the issue, call it a sense of spirituality, call it the quest of religiosity, call it by any name, use any term. Among the Six Schools or Systems of Philosophy, Sankhya found a way.

It said: 'Look, the source of creation, the Brahman, the Purusha, does not move, does not do anything, he is not the doer, he is not the creator. Purusha just exists.' The supreme Purusha, the Paramatman of the *Bhagavad Gita*, the Purusha of the Sankhyas just exists.

Then how does this creation come about? They said: 'There is *prakriti*, matter, the twenty-four ingredients of *prakriti* they call *mula prakriti*. It is *prakriti* which is the source of creation. It moves. Purusha does not operate, does not function. It just exists.'

This was interpreted by some ancient Indians that this manifested world, this *prakriti*, this source of all actions, has to be ignored. Concentrate on Purusha if you want to be emancipated, liberated. Withdraw from *prakriti* and focus your energies on Purusha, identify yourself with Purusha, so that you are out of the whole paraphernalia of this manifested world, this Cosmos and you are united with the Purusha.

This union was on the intellectual level, on the emotional level. It could be on the ideational level, the idea of being united with Brahman, '*Aham Brahmasmi*' '(I am Brahman).'

But you are living in the body, and your physical body, your material existence, is organically related to Cosmic matter. The energies contained in it cannot be wished away. You may withdraw from the outer, but what about the inner? The *prakriti* is very much there in your material physical existence. This idea of isolating yourself from *prakriti* and intellectually and emotionally identifying yourself with Purusha, remained only an intellectual conviction, an abstraction. It had no dynamism.

Those who isolated themselves from the stream of Life, from interaction with nature, with fellow human beings, with non-human fellow beings, they went into isolation for sustaining the intellectual identification, sustaining the emotional unity. Their isolation did not lead to any dynamic living. They were starved of the interaction with Life.

Yoga comes to supplement the incompleteness of Sankhya, comes to correct certain distortions. To Sankhya, the science of *yoga* says: matter and all the innumerable energies contained in matter, do not exist by themselves. They are not entirely free of Purusha. Purusha is the source of creation. Brahman or Purusha, is the source of even *prakriti*. How can you ignore, neglect *prakriti* and try to be one with Purusha?

The science of *yoga* says: you cannot reduce the supreme reality, the divinity, to a non-doer, denying it the freedom of movement and action. The science of *yoga* brings back divinity. That which permeates everything is Brahman, it is the source of creation and it is contained in every expression of manifestation. Obviously, there is movement. So, the dynamism of Brahman, the dynamism of Purusha, converts it into an Ishvara of the *yoga shastra*. It is beautiful how the science of *yoga* supplements and complements the teachings of the *sankhya shastra*, takes away the distortions and harmonizes prakriti and Purusha. The beauty of the science of *yoga* lies in harmonizing the Purusha and *prakriti* of the Sankhyas into one indivisible whole.

Prakriti, matter and all the energies contained in it, are the manifestations of Purusha, or Brahman, the supreme reality, the source of all these energies, the source even of matter. *Yoga* harmonizes the unmanifest and the manifest. *Yoga* is radically different in this from the approach of Sankhya.

I wanted to introduce you to this crucial approach of the *yoga shastra.* On the one hand *yoga shastra* has converted the in-operative is-ness of the Purusha of the Sankhyas into the operative Ishvara. That is one beauty of it. And secondly, the science of *yoga* says: if matter is a manifestation of Brahman or the supreme reality and the energies in matter contain the supreme reality, matter is surely not negligible. You cannot neglect your physical existence. You have a physical body, which is matter, with a beautiful physical form. You cannot ignore it, calling it *maya*, calling it dead matter.

You have to get acquainted with your physical existence, with your mental existence. You have to get acquainted with the energies operating in the physical existence, because you share those physical energies with the rest of the Cosmos; with the mineral, vegetable and animal kingdoms. You share with them those energies. *Yama*, *niyama*, *asana*, etc. are ways of getting acquainted with the various autonomous systems operating in the body and getting acquainted with the energies and interactions in those systems. Unless you get acquainted with those energies, with the way they operate and interact, how will you be able to discipline them, purify them through education, harmonize them?

Every detail on the physical level is taken care of by the science of *yoga*: how you sit, how you stand, what you eat and how much, how you sleep and how you breathe. Do you know the beauty of getting acquainted with the minute details of physical life? Getting acquainted with the impulses of appetite, of thirst, sex, sleep and so on? The science of *yoga* says: you cannot afford to ignore or neglect or dishonour, disrespect, the physical existence. The physical body, the physical existence, is the foundation on which you are going to build your spiritual quest, your explorations, your experimentations. They are going to be here in the physical existence.

Then get acquainted with the mental existence, your mental body. There are five bodies in all, or five sheaths. The *annamaya kosha* is the gross physical sheath, which is nourished by food. The *pranamaya kosha*, the subtle or vital sheath, vitalizes and holds together the body and mind. The *manomaya kosha* is the sheath of the mind, which receives the sense impressions. The *vijnanamaya kosha* is the sheath of intellect, referring to the faculty of discrimination. And the *anandamaya kosha* is the sheath of bliss, the causal body, nearest to the blissful Atman.

You begin with the *annamaya kosha*, the physical body, the gross body as it is called, which lives by interaction with the gross world outside. You have to eat food grown in the earth, nourished by water, by the sun, the moon, the stars. It is an interaction between your gross body and the gross body of the Cosmos, gross body of the Purusha, the Brahman, or whatever you call it. The physical body, the gross body, is a part of the biological world. Constant interaction is going on between the two.

Then we come to the mental body. But the mental existence is something built-up by the human race. It consists of knowledge, of patterns of reaction, of codes of conduct; it consists of so many things. Your mental existence is built-up by the human race and you live in it. As you live in the gross body, which is the foundation of your existence, you live in your mind, which is the mental body. It has an infinite field of energy; the energy of thought, of imagination, of memory, of calculation, so many energies contained in this mental body, built up systematically by the human race, through civilization, culture, development of science and technology, etc.

This mental body, this mental existence, is as important as the physical. The physical, the gross body, is said to be real because of its interaction with the gross Cosmic body. And now, there is an invisible interaction between thought, knowledge, value structures and patterns of reaction among other people and yourself. This interaction is invisible. On the physical level the interaction is visible, you can change it, you can mould it. How do you mould the mental energies, how do you discipline them?

You can cultivate discipline about food, about diet, exercises, *asanas*, *pranayama*, you can purify those physical energies. You can even convert the gross physical energies, transform them into something subtle. What do you do with these mental energies; the mind, which consists of thought and knowledge, words and sound energies? The physical body is constituted of gross things and so it is easier to discipline them, educate them, purify them. How do you purify and educate the invisible, the intangible mental existence?

The science of *yoga* has found out ways of disciplining the invisible mental body, which is constituted of vibrations, through *pratyahara* (withdrawal of the mind from sense objects), *dharana*, (concentration) *dhyana* (meditation), and *samadhi*. It is a beautiful way of purifying the thought energy, by learning to plunge into silence and the energy of silence watching all the clods and toxins of the thought realm.

So, thought-energy is transformed by silence-energy. The uncontrollable, unrestrained momentum of an idea, of an emotion, of a sentiment, can be controlled by learning the art of self-restraint. Not denial, not using any force, but by learning restraint. So, the art of restraint for controlling the uncontrollable invisible momentum and the energy of silence to purify the contamination, that takes place in the orbit of thought. This transformation of intellect into intelligence, thought-energy into silence energy, the energy of knowledge into the energy of understanding and awareness, takes place through *dharana* (concentration), through *dhyana* (meditation), and so on.

The science of *yoga* says: when so-called matter (mind is a part of matter, or matter is solidification of mind, whichever way you put it), when *prakriti* (matter) is purified, it is brought on par with Purusha (spirit). When the energies of the perishable are converted and transformed into higher energies, those higher energies become the vehicle for Brahman, the supreme reality, to manifest itself.

The physical body remains the same, the mental existence, the articulation, the speech remain the same and yet the body, the mind, the speech become resplendent. They become gloriously shining, because the supreme intelligence, the Paramatman, the energy of the supreme Chaitanya (spiritual or awakened consciousness), Brahman, uses the purified matter for its expression. The supreme intelligence, the Paramatman, Brahman, is concealed in matter, it is concealed in us. Because we are involved and entangled, attached to the physical and the mental to a certain extent, the supreme gets covered up by our attachment. I have dwelt upon this because the eighth chapter begins with the question:

'What is Brahman? What is *svabhava* (the intrinsic property of a thing)? What is *adhyatma*? What is *adhibhuta, adhidaiva*? What is *adhiyajna*?'

In the eighth chapter the very first verse contains seven questions. The whole chapter deals with those seven questions, one by one. I wanted to deal not only with the dialogue, with *yoga shastra* and Brahma-Vidya, but deal with the approach of *yoga shastra* and how it supplements and complements Sankhya, how it synthesizes the rest of the Schools of Indian Philosophy, just so as to give you the background. Once, you have the background, then we can plunge.

It is the purification of matter; the harmonization of energies and the transformation of the gross energies or material energies, that enables one to become the instrument of expression of the supreme reality. The unmanifest becomes manifest in the individual. We have become acquainted with the word *Brahman*. The questioner (Arjuna) asks Krishna: 'what is that Brahman you talk about?' And Krishna says:

'It is the imperishable source of creation.'

It is that, out of which the inexhaustible potential of Life bubbles up and emerges and takes on so many forms. The unmanifest voluntarily limits itself into a form; the imperishable accepts the role of appearance in the perishable and so on. We have looked at the term *'Brahman'*, the source of creation, the matrix of creation, the supreme reality, also called Paramatman, the supreme Cosmic energy in terms of physics and ethics. The second question is:

'What is *svabhava*?'

Sva means ego, *bhava* means the feel of ego-ness. Arjuna was a very intelligent person. He says: 'if creation is the manifestation of the supreme, where does god come from?' And Krishna answers:

'Look, when it is unmanifest, it is not individualized, it is not individuated, it is not divided, it is not specified, it is just a void. But when it takes the form of an individual human animal, then that process of individualization generates the feeling of I-ness, generates the feeling of I-am an entity, I have an identity separate from the rest of Life.'

Svabhava is the feel of being an entity, having an identity, independent of, separate from the others. When the unlimited becomes limited, the very process of becoming limited, when it becomes individualized, that process itself generates this limitation. The supreme reality in your body gets covered up by the cloud of this feel of identity, the feel of I-ness. And what happens then? As soon as there is the feel of I-ness, this feel of I-ness looks upon the rest of life as the object: I as the subject and the rest as the object.

The individualization generates a sense of identity and entity and that sense of entity and identi ty leads to the division of Life. It is not a split. It is not degeneration. Look at the beauty of it: it just results in a division of non-dual Life into a dual life. And Krishna says:

'Look Arjuna, if there was not this *svabhava*, if there was not this sense of I-ness and me-ness, which enables the interaction with the rest of life, how would there be plurality? The interaction of duality leads to plurality.'

The essence of the science of spirituality is to understand the limitedness of the I and the me, to understand how it came about, and transcend it. Use it where warranted, where it is relevant, where it is needed, on the physical level, on the mental level. Use this beautiful division that has come about by the individualization of Cosmic Life. Use that division beautifully, constructively, creatively, handle it properly, enjoy the plurality that it generates, as you enjoy the energy of sex in your body and create other human beings out of your body. In the same way enjoy the division. Otherwise, how can you have relationships?

It is the sense of plurality generated by the division, which itself is the result of the process of individualization, which enables you to enjoy the various colours, the forms, the shapes, the manyness of the expressions of Cosmic Life. The plurality can be enjoyed, because there is this ideational division of me and not me.

If you did not have the sense of me, if you did not have the sense of being the subject and the rest being object, leading to interaction, whether on the mental level or on the physical level, you would not be able to live in relationships. And spirituality says: live in it, enjoy it, but do not get entangled in it, because that is only a part of your existence, which has a beginning and which has an end.

The event of death will put an end to all the relationships. Your essence is not in the perishable, your essence is not in mortality, the existential essence of your being is in the immortal. The perishable is only a part; enjoy it without getting entangled in it, without getting attached to it. If you get attached, you are sowing seeds of misery, because some day, sometime, it will be snapped away from you, or you will be snapped away from all that.

So, retaining the immense freedom, enjoy. And the science of *yoga* teaches the secret of concentration, meditation and the dimension of *samadhi*, the super-sensuous and super-conscious, super-mental dimension of Life.

I hope that you are aware that you have come to the ancient land of Shiva and Shakti, where the Vedas and the Upanishads have been written, where the great epic of the *Mahabharata* has also been written. Our energies should be focussed on the ancient land and the snow-capped Himalayas beyond the hills and on the song of wisdom, the *Bhagavad Gita*, expounded by Sri Krishna.

Shiva is figuratively imagined to be the unchanging imperishable principle of Life and Shakti is the executive power of that imperishable non-changing eternity. Shakti is the cause of creation, the executive power of Shiva, who brings out the content of his being. The earth, water, fire, *pranas*, space, are all the substance of the being of Shiva. They are his blood, they are his flesh and bones. And Shakti is the executive power contained in the unchanging imperishable principle of Life, called Shiva. Both dwell together.

Shakti is what the Sankhyas would call *mula prakriti* (Cosmic matter). This mula prakriti, this Shakti, is the field of innumerable energies, which constantly move and it is their interaction that causes the changes in the perishable world. The perishable plurality of expressions of Life are caused by the interaction of energies. You could call *prakriti*, matter, the matrix of existence, and Purusha, the unchanging, eternal imperishable principle of Life. So, the unchanging principle remains unchanged, though the manifestations go on changing forever.

The manifestations into perishable plurality express themselves through birth, growth, decay and death. This dance of birth, growth, decay and death goes on, on the universal scale. Through this *lila* or dance, the manifestations are becoming more and more refined, sophisticated and mature, as it were.

For example, the energy of consciousness existing in the mineral world is mute; it does not express itself by itself. In the vegetable kingdom the sub-conscious mind retains its individual existence. It has a survival instinct, it is not as mute as the mineral world. So, the consciousness is there, less mute, more expressive and it expresses itself through resistance to destruction. The plant world, the vegetable kingdom maintains its existence. Every tree, every creeper, every sapling, struggles to retain its survival against the forces of nature.

The *svabhava*, the sense of identity, the sense of entity-ness, of separate existence, is already manifest in the vegetable kingdom, in the crops, in the plants, in the trees. The mountains stand erect but mute. The vegetable kingdom has become expressive.

In the animal and bird kingdom, the birds and the animals not only resist, not only fight back the forces that want to demolish them, but the expression of consciousness or the expression of mind is more eloquent in them. They have sound, they can sing, they can scream. Through their eyes they not only look at you, but they can even respond. So, they are more refined expressions of the unchanging principle in the changing manifestations.

And then you come to *Homo Sapiens*, the human species, which up till now is the epitome of refined and sophisticated consciousness that nature is expressing progressively. Please do see this. So, *mula prakriti*, universal matter is itself imperishable, though its individual expressions in forms, shapes, objects, etc., are perishable.

A tree perishes, a bird, an animal, perishes, the individual expression perishes. But again animals, birds, get born. There is no end to it. The event of individual perishing or dissolution of that conscious matter contained in the body of the animal, in the body of the tree, in the body of the bird, though that perishes, the *mula prakriti*, the universal *prakriti* does not perish. It is a flux of change, but change is not destruction.

We have seen that the Indian philosophy does not recognize destruction as a principle of Life. It does not recognize death as a symbol of destruction; it is only the drastic way of changing the form, the cohesion of various principles. That cohesion is dismantled, so that it can get recreated. Creation and dissolution, emergence and merging back, that is how the dance between the unchanging imperishable principle, Purusha and this whole manifestation goes on by *prakriti*, through proliferation, through plurality, as described in the *Gita*. It is poetry, it's a poem. The dialogue between Krishna and Arjuna is a poetic way of putting the serious most things to us. So we have to distinguish between the *mula prakriti*, Cosmic matter, and *prakriti*, matter in us.

We are coming to the word *adhibhuta*, universal matter. The expressions of universal matter perish, but it does not. They perish and the *prakriti* in us, this body constituted of the five elements of nature, does perish. And yet, the unchanging principle of Life, Brahman, Shiva, the intelligence, the subtle most energy of intelligence, Chaitanya, *samvit*, does not perish.

As the dance of Shiva and Shakti goes on at the Cosmic level, the dance of Shiva and Shakti goes on in this human body. As that *prakriti* creates the proliferation of material expressions, this *prakriti* is capable of giving birth to another individual, like itself. It has the same creative energy that the Cosmic *prakriti* has, that the *mula prakriti* has.

This is the *manushi prakriti*, that is to say the *prakriti* in human form. And that is *mula prakriti*, the original, the causeless, rootless, beginningless essence of existence. This body also can create other human beings, if it so desires. It can also move, it can look, listen, share, interact. So, a human being is called condensed Cosmos.

If Shiva, Brahman, the unchanging principle in the Cosmos is there, here in the human body, Atman, the energy of intelligence is there also: Atman/Paramatman, Atman/Brahman. We have to get used to these terms. What is Brahman in the Cosmos, is Atman in the human body. What is *mula prakriti* in the Cosmos, is *prakriti* in the human body. And they dwell together, they always dwell together, supplementing, complementing and enriching each other.

Where there is individuation, there is birth, growth, decay and death. That cannot be avoided. This body is a perishable material existence and the consciousness attached to the senses, as the consciousness attached in nature, goes on progressively refining itself. Here, the consciousness in the human body is yearning for getting more and more refined. The science of *yoga* gives an expression to that aspiration of progressive refinement, progressive purification, progressive transformation.

We have to get acquainted with another word, along with *adhibhuta*, because both are associated and connected with each other. That other word is *karma*. The capacity to sacrifice the content of your being, for creating something new, is called *karma*.

Karma is essentially a sacrifice of your being. You give something out of your being, which will never return to you. You bring forth a child out of your body, the male and the female together, but that child of yours never comes back into this body. That which is created, irreversibly does not come back to you. Creation is a sacrifice; it is a movement of creative energy, which results in creation. Nothing to do with impulses, desires, sentiment, wishes, etc. It is a sacrifice of the total being.

I wonder if you remember that this whole universal Life was called a cycle of constant *yajna*, sacrifice. The being, the Brahman, Purushottama, is giving out all the time the contents of his being.

The eternal Life is a *yajna*. A variety of *yajnas* are going on in the universe. The burning of the sun, giving out heat and light, warmth, the healing energies, the creative energies in the universe, all are *yajnas*, sacrifices. *Soma*, the moon, gives out creative energies, the nectar of energies. *Soma* is *amritam*, nectar. The sun creates and the moon pours nectar for the subsistence of that which has been created.

A Cosmic *yajna* is going on in the whole universe. In our life, at the perishable level, at the level of that which is born and which is going to die, the sacrificial outpouring of the being, whether you give birth to a child, whether you pour out your being through speech, whether you pour out your being through love and sharing, it is all a sacrifice, a *yajna*. Human Life itself is divinity and to live is to manifest that divinity, the purity of that divinity in relationships.

Note the exceptional brilliance of Sri Krishna, when he associates action or *karma* with the contents of the being of *atman* and the executive power of *shakti* or *prakriti*. I may say I have given birth to a child, the *Gita* says no, the *prakriti*, the *mula prakriti* which has that executive power, resides in you, we are only given an opportunity to that executive power of Cosmic Life to manifest itself.

By calling *karma* a sacrificial movement of creative energy, the *Gita* nips in the bud all attachment, all psychological involvement. Enjoyment yes, involvement none.

Adhidaiva, adhibhuta, these two words are used in this chapter. *Adhidaiva*, the divine that has made its abode in your body, the divine that is existing in you, operating in you. *Adhibhuta*, the perishable form through which it expresses itself.

Let us go back to the point of how one retains the awareness of that absolute principle of Life, the unchanging eternity, the Brahman, the supreme reality, while living in the perishable, utilizing all the energies contained in the perishable manifestation, going through pleasure and pain of the movement, that is the question, which the *Gita* is dealing with. And the discourse says: by doing *abhyasa* it is possible to dwell in the perishable, enjoy the movement of the energies, contained in the perishable material existence, interact with the help of your mental existence and yet not become a prisoner of it, not get stuck in it.

Let us look at the word *abhyasa*. *Abhyasa* is not repetition; it is re-doing but not repeating. What is the difference between repetition and re-doing? When you do something for learning, when you are learning there is no repetition. Re-doing is for learning, deepening what you have learnt, intensifying what you have learnt, taking the root of your understanding deeper into your flesh and bones. So, while re-doing you are quite attentive.

You love that re-doing, because learning is taking place and your understanding is becoming clearer by the re-doing. In repetition there is passivity, not attention. And when you are not attentive, learning does not take place. When you are passive, when you are inattentive, then the movement of creativity that takes place in learning, cannot take place. The movement of creativity requires the light of your attentiveness, your alertness, your receptivity. When you repeat, there is no receptivity, when you repeat, there is no learning. You repeat because it has to be done.

Abhyasa is not compulsion, it is not repetition, it cannot be mechanical. It is a stroke of genius that, by re-doing the thing that you have accepted doing, for the sake of learning, for the sake of education, for the sake of purification, you do it attentively, lovingly, with all the sensitivity at your command. So, repetition is passivity; re-doing is active alert attentiveness.

In repetition you are looking for experience: 'what did I get out of it by doing this? I did *japa* for three months, what did I get out of it? I was spending time in silence, what did I get out of it?' Repetition is result oriented, acquisition oriented, experience oriented. But learning is not experience oriented.

Look, when we take a meal, every day we take a meal, or perhaps, in a day we take twice food, is it repetition? You are re-doing it every day and you enjoy doing it. You do not eat for the experience of eating, but you take a meal, because that nourishment becomes the substance of your body. In the same way when you re-do things and learn, that becomes the substance of your consciousness. It does not remain knowledge, a foreign element in consciousness. Knowledge is a foreign element, because it has words, but understanding has no words.

In the process of learning, the energy contained in the words, that is the meaning, are converted, they are transformed into understanding. But knowledge is a collection of words, of ideas, theories, which are transferred to memory for use when necessary, like a bank balance. But as your health is not a bank balance, it is something that manifests itself every day, it is used through your movement and the more you use it the healthier you become. The energy consumed gets replenished by the interaction, by the expenditure.

So *abhyasa* is re-doing lovingly for learning, for education. And education does purify, it sophisticates, it refines. You know, refinement is purity. When the darkness of ignorance is eliminated, when a chaotic collection is converted into an orderly understanding, obviously purification takes place. Purity is orderliness, purity is intelligence, purity is cleanliness, no toxins of vanity, pride, no toxins of doubt generated by ignorance; ignorance about one's own nature, ignorance about the sense of discrimination between the imperishable and the perishable, the unchanging principle manifesting through changes.

So *yoga* says that through *abhyasa* it is possible to dwell in the perishable, doing the *karmas*, that is to say use the creative energies contained in the perishable material body, as a sacrificial act. You cannot exist without *karma*, because the energies contained in your *prakriti*, in your material body, cannot remain idle. If you use them in the sacrificial spirit, then refinement takes place.

You know what a sacrificial spirit is? Not act exclusively for your own benefit. When you do a *yajna*, it does benefit you indirectly. When you put in the best that you have in a *yajna*, when you do use the creative energies in your eyes, ears, speech, sex, in every part of your being, not exclusively for yourself, when you share it with others, when you pour it out for others, the benefit is sure to come back to you, without making you conscious of it. Because the spirit of sacrifice poured into the act, or saturating or permeating the act, brings back the benefits to you indirectly.

Abhyasa is for educating the senses, the body, the physical existence, educating them, purifying them, so that they are capable of a spontaneous sacrificial act, capable of *karma*. They do not get stuck up in *kriya*, activity, which consist of being pushed around, being pulled around by the impulses in the body or the ideas in the mind. When you are pushed around, there is an inner compulsion. Then it is *kriya* or activity, and when it is the movement of your whole being, in an unselfish way, with the sense of a *yajna*, then it is *karma*.

The *Gita* distinguishes between *karma* and *kriya*, action and activity, repetition and re-doing. It is a very subtle way, because the *Gita* gives you the essence of the Vedas and the Upanishads. The Vedas and the Upanishads are the cows and Sri Krishna is the milkman. He is milking the cows of the Vedas and the Upanishads for Arjuna. The ancient Indians were essentially poets; they would put everything in a figurative language.

So *abhyasa* is necessary. The re-doing of things, which you have intellectually understood, is necessary. First, you have to understand it with the help of the intellect, which can discriminate between things, which discriminates between the false and the real. After all, the faculty of discrimination is contained in the intellect, in the brain. Once, the brain has done its function of discriminating, pointing out to you what is proper to be done, what is proper to be avoided, etc., then it is your responsibility to go on re-doing the way the brain has pointed out, until it becomes a spontaneous movement, until it becomes your nature.

If this point is clear, let us proceed. This is a class; this study is not a mere intellectual abstraction, not a theory. We are studying together and when I study with you, my learning becomes more pronounced and more joyous. Though I sit here and talk with you, I am studying.

How does the *abhyasa* take place, so that one is aware that the whole manifest world comes out of the unmanifest reality, so that one remains aware that Life is full of two contradictory principles, harmonized together in one wholeness: the unchanging principle of eternity, the Purusha, the Brahman, and the changing principle of *prakriti*, matter? So that one remains aware that this body, which is a condensed Cosmos, contains both: Purusha and *prakriti*? The Purusha in the human body is called Atman, and of course *prakriti* is called *prakriti*.

You are aware that matter and spirit do not exist separately, they do not have an existence independent of each other, exclusive of each other, they are mutually inclusive. They include each other. Shakti includes Shiva, and Shiva includes Shakti. It is beautiful in Sanskrit, they are called *sanprukta*, that is: they dwell in each other. Shiva and Shakti are inseparable, the changing and the unchanging principle, dwelling in each other, enriching each other, the stability of that divinity, that unchanging Brahman, enriches the perishable changing material world.

Now, how and where does this apply within? Let us take the sixth or seventh verse of the eighth chapter. The senses are the windows or the door, through which the consciousness, the mind, runs towards the outer objects. The listening capacity, the audition in the ears, runs towards sound, to catch it, to get a sensation of what the sound is like, or what the words are like. The sight in the eyes runs towards the outer objects, to get a sensation of contact and pleasure out of that contact. After all, you seek contact for pleasure. The same with the tongue, the same with the skin. The sense organs, the windows, are to be educated. The consciousness is simultaneously to be educated.

What do we do, so that the sense organs do not get mutilated, do not get damaged in any way? How do they get damaged? If you indulge too much in sensual pleasures, then your sense organs and the senses get damaged, because they become loose by too much indulgence.

We are living in an era of the cult of sensual pleasures; it is very much honoured. We do not use the senses and the sense organs to receive what is necessary for physical survival, a decent, a healthy, a reasonable survival. That is not our purpose. We go on grabbing at pleasures, whether necessary or not, just to satisfy the idea, just to satisfy the imagination. We plunder the outer objects of sensual pleasure. They may be objects, they may be individuals. Too much indulgence, too much usage makes the senses very loose, they do not have the tone, the tension which is required in a healthy state.

The science of *yoga* emphasizes restraint. A voluntary curtailment of your freedom is restraint. Voluntary limitation of the capacity for experiences is restraint. The unmanifest accepts voluntarily the limitation of the solidification of its energy. That is why this material world comes into existence. If the unmanifest does not pour its being into matter and voluntarily curtails freedom, then the Cosmos would not be there.

In the same way the science of *yoga* emphasises the cultivation of this faculty of voluntarily accepting control, accepting regulations. The eyes look at only that which is necessary. The seeing may go on involuntarily, because the sight is there in your eyes, you are awake, your eyes are open, they see, but you do not look at an object or an individual, unless that glance is warranted. You don't look at persons out of jealousy, out of suspicion, out of anger, for getting some pleasure out of that. You do not eat just for the sake of pleasure. The contact with food is health oriented.

So, the senses have to be educated in voluntary restraint. That is the pre-requisite of *abhyasa*. You cannot do *abhyasa*, you cannot educate yourself, if you allow the mind to wander through the senses, at every other moment, just going around collecting some sensation and getting pleasure out of that sensation, feeling that you are living. That is how worldly people live. Then you get more and more entangled in the perishable world. Then you want to keep that object or individual under your control, you want to own it, you want to possess it and you give birth to attachment. Attachment comes into existence by indiscriminate indulgence in pleasure.

If you do not indulge excessively, unwarrantedly, unscientifically, in pleasures of the body or the mind, there will not be any attachment at all. There will be a beautiful relationship of perception, contact, enjoyment and the thing gets finished. No residue of the desire for its repetition and no desire for pleasure is left behind in memory. Enjoyment gives you a sense of fulfilment, so the mind does not want to look back upon it.

Once you have a good meal, for four or five or six hours there is no desire to look back. In the same way you go through your relationships, sensual and psychological, in a magnificent restrained way. The science of *yoga* does not propagate any denial, any negation, any rejection, any suppression, nor does it prescribe any indulgence. It goes mid-way; it is the path of the golden means, the golden path of restraint.

When you do the *asanas* day after day, you are keeping the muscular, the glandular and the other systems in your body at the required tension and tone, so when bodily movements are required, the body can move in a supple way, in a rhythmic elasticity, till old age. When you do the *yama* and *niyama*, the purity of the inner organs is retained. When you do *pranayama*, the whole blood system gets oxidized, right from the crown of the head to the big toe. Then the purity of the inner organs, the de-toxication of the blood system and the faculty of restraint help together in your education of *dharana* and *dhyana*.

If this is done, if the *abhyasa*, at the material existence level through *yama*, *niyama*, *asana* and *pranayama*, are done, then *pratyahara* (restraint of the mind towards sense objects) stands as a bridge between the physical and the mental level. The first four are done on the physical level. *Pratyahara* is the bridge to *dharana*, *dhyana* and *samadhi*, the last three at the consciousness level.

Pratyahara is also a purifier, a purifier of the atmosphere around you. The first four purify the inner autonomous systems and *pratyahara* purifies the atmosphere in the house, atmosphere wherever you move. The way you move, the way you look, talk, the way you interact, aren't they expressions of *pratyahara*? Not forcing upon yourself 'must' and 'must not', 'should' and 'should not', 'ought' and 'ought not', no compulsion. *Pratyahara* is spontaneous restraint. It is not withdrawal, it is not rejection. Look at the beauty of it. Withdrawal and rejection stink of violence. Restraint or spontaneity has none of it. So, one is educating the senses through the faculty of restraint.

What do you do with the mind? You have educated the senses. You persuade the mind, through the self-conscious energy, to retreat, to go into abeyance in the dimension of silence. The sense organs are educated towards restraint, and the mind is educated to retreat into silence. The heart is called the abode of silence by the *Gita*. So you persuade, you plead with the mind. It is a self-conscious energy, you can't force it.

Your handling of the body is at one level. But the handling of the mind, of the self-aware self-conscious energy full of so many *samskaras* and conditionings, you can't force that, you can't use violence. You have to plead with it, you have to persuade it to retreat into silence in the heart. Now that you have learned *abhyasa*, you have to learn to persuade the mind to retreat into silence. It does not go by itself. So, you sit with your mind.

When you sit down, you abstain from activity, abstain from speech, abstain from looking around. Close your eyes. You are preparing for the encounter with the mind and when you thus close your eyes and mind brings up, exposes before your intelligence all its contents, now the persuasion begins. You don't judge it, you don't evaluate it, you don't blame it. It brings up its contents and you look at it.

You don't get caught up in it. If you accept it, you are caught, if you reject it, you are caught again, because you build up a relationship with it. Just looking at it, call it observation, call it watching, looking, any term, but a new relationship has come up. Up till now it used to dictate your behaviour. Now, the mind knows that, though it brings up its wishes, desires, passions, etc., it has lost the power to create an inner compulsion that forces you into a movement. Please do see this. A new relationship happens just through your patience of looking at it, your patience of observation.

And you re-do this. The mind brings up and you just look, without getting tired, without getting bored. Because, if you get bored, its a negative energy. If you feel tired, if you hate what is exposed, again it's a negative energy. If you get angry by perceiving what is exposed, it is a negative energy. If you feel elated when you come across something good, your excellence, again you get stuck up. So, with *abhyasa*, this re-doing of pure perception, of bare cognition, day after day, renders the mind powerless to create an inner compulsion, which pushes and pulls you around as it wants.

And the moment comes, when the exposure subsides completely. Sooner in the lives of those who are very intense, than for those who have not got the depth or the intensity. For them it may take a little time, but the time by calendar, time by your watches has no relevance here. One person may require a week, another a month, a third a year, it cannot be compared. If you compare then you will become depressed, because in your life it has not happened, and then you loose the intensity to persist in the *abhyasa*, in the re-doing of it. So, a moment comes when the exposure subsides completely.

The contents get exhausted, the conscious, the subconscious, the unconscious are exposed, and you sit there like a mountain, not getting affected at all. No, not like a mountain, like space through which the rains come, the sunrays come and even the snow flakes come, and yet the state of the sky remains unaffected. In the same way your perception remains unaffected by the tantrums of the subconscious or the unconscious. No comparison, no judgement, no evaluation.

A moment comes, when there is no more exposure and you are in the dimension of silence. The ending of the exposure, the ending of the mental movement, because it has nothing more to expose, it has exhausted its potential of exposure. That is the beginning of silence. You are in a new dimension, you are in the womb now of the Cosmic space, space containing both you and the Cosmos. They are undivided by your flesh and bones, undivided by your physical existence.

If you are a student of *yoga*, you know how to harmonize the five major *pranas*: *prana*, *apana*, *vyana*, *udana*, *samana*. If that energy of *pranas* can be directed upwards, harmonizing the five *pranas*, if you direct the energy of *pranas* upwards, it leaves the orbit of your body and enters your head, the uppermost point in your head, the crown of your head. As a spacecraft leaves behind the orbit of the earth and the gravity contained in it, in the same way when the *pranas* are directed upwards, then the identification with body consciousness and the identification with the ego-consciousness is left behind. This is what is called meditation.

Through the science of Hatha Yoga you educate the energy of *pranas*, making, day after day, the study of directing it in an upward movement. Not through force. It has to be gradual. *Abhyasa* is gradual, progressive. It is not a cognition of a theory, which the intellect catches in a moment. This is a Life process, the unmanifest becoming the manifest, the manifest merging back into the unmanifest. So, the identification with the material existence and mental existence goes into abeyance or non-action, becomes non-operative, and the identification with the supreme reality takes place.

The *Bhagavad Gita* is an exposition of the science of Life and also a poetical presentation of a scientific way of living. It is our daily experience that understanding the truth intellectually, academically, does not result in lifting up the consciousness to a higher level or enable the consciousness to manifest the truth that has been understood at the mental as well as physical level. This science of Life explains the nature of ultimate reality. The brain understands this, with the help of words. And then one has to educate and equip the sensual, the physical and mental structures, to assimilate the truth and manifest it or express it in every movement in daily living.

Plotinus used to say that, for the quest of truth, for the understanding of truth, you have either to be a lover or a philosopher. Love releases the energy of devotion, without the self or the ego asserting or interfering. And the philosopher has a dispassionate vitality for discovering the truth and an irresistible urge to live the truth. So, the philosopher has the energy of dedication and the lover has the energy of devotion.

A student of *yoga* requires either of these, so that through *abhyasa yoga* he educates the senses, disciplines the mind, and is capable of transcending the mad drives of the body and the restless wanderings of the mind, in order to be grounded in the reality that is perceived by him, that is academically, theoretically understood by him. In this upward path, the ascending path of understanding and assimilating the truth with your mental and physical body, one has to study first to restrain the drives of the body and merge them in the mental body.

The mental body, the body of consciousness, has two layers. One is the layer of memory, which provokes the inherited trends, tendencies, pulls and pushes, without your volition, which cannot be controlled by your volition. It is a higher level of *buddhi*, reason, rationality, that can perceive the truth, discriminate the true from the false and carve out voluntary disciplines for regulating and moulding the inherited *samskaras* (tendencies etc.).

So, the senses and their drives are helped to merge into the mind. The lower level of the mind, the past, is helped to merge into the higher, the present, to sink the emotional, the sentimental dimension into the dimension of reasoning and rationality. All this can be done through *abhyasa*, learning and re-doing what is learned and understood.

At this moment, let us be aware very clearly that Life is a multi-dimensional phenomenon and what we call our existence and our being is also a multi-dimensional phenomenon. We have the physical body joined together, invisibly, with the whole biological and material world. We have the mental or the psychological body, invisibly connected with the total human knowledge and experience, with civilization and culture, which is the past. And we seem to have a still higher level or dimension of consciousness which is not connected with the past, which is not a content of the past.

The inklings, the flashes of the contents of this higher dimension, are exposed to us in the precious moments of love, of innocence, of profound sleep, and so on. The first two, the physical and the psychological, have been blended together and the human being today is the physical and the mental animal blended together. There seems to be a missing link between the rational and that which transcends reason and rationality, between the mental and the super-mental, the individual and the Cosmic.

Humanity has tried to discover the missing link between the mental and the super-mental through theology, through philosophy, they have given ideologies, theories, practices, for connecting the two. But it seems that that third dimension of our being, of our existence, defies all such efforts. The pathetic history of human evolution and the bloodiest century, in which we are living, is not only contaminated but permeated by violence, hatred, jealousy, lust, and greed. We are living in a century, which is permeated by all sorts of negative energies. Dark energies have clouded the horizon of human perception, human consciousness.

The intellectual effort of stretching rationality beyond its periphery or circumference has not yielded this third dimension. We may have the finest ideas about divinity or the highest dimension of Life through the Vedas, the Upanishads, the Bible, the scriptures of Judaism and Islam, we have had all that for many centuries and yet we do not know how to live on the earth in peace and friendship with one another.

So, the science of *yoga* has relevance at this point. The science of yoga points out that consciousness cannot be raised to higher levels through academic steps, through abstract intellectual theories. You have to exert and educate your senses and your mind. That is the real value of *astanga yoga shastra*, that is: education and purification of the sensual through the disciplines of *yama, niyama, asana, pranayama,* and education and purification of the mental body through *pratyahara, dharana* and *dhyana*. And all this education, culminating in the dimension of *samadhi*, enables you to take a quantum leap, as it were, into the higher non-rational supra-mental dimension of divinity. This is the teaching of *adhyatma yoga*.

There are two more points. One point is: uncovering the mystery of death and dying. It is the brilliance of Sri Krishna, or Vyasa, who put the *Gita* into words, into a poem, to refer to birth as the emanation of Cosmic energy and death as the dissolution of the same energy back into its source. The eighth chapter uses the phraseology of creation and dissolution many times, in order that lay persons like you and me, could understand this mystery of dissolution and creation.

In the second half of the chapter Krishna says: 'look, Arjuna, in the day time, when you are awake, you manifest the content of the unmanifest consciousness contained in your being.' In the unmanifest consciousness, in the so-called mind and brain, there are so many thoughts, ideas, wishes, ambitions, desires, pushes, pulls, all that is unmanifest, unverbalized. You yourself may not even be conscious of the contents of your unmanifest consciousness. From dawn to dusk, from morn to night, your every movement manifests the contents of consciousness. Consciousness is unmanifest. It becomes manifest through your movements.

The moment you wake up and stir your body, whatever you do intentionally, unintentionally, consciously, absent-mindedly, your movements are the manifestation of your consciousness. The manifestation is through your perception; it is through your speech, your gesticulations, your interaction with nature, it is through your interaction with fellow human and non-human beings, all that is a manifestation.

You build up your own world around you through your actions and reactions. Even your reactions are the manifestations of the unmanifest consciousness. And when the day ends and the night descends and nature dissolves its activities into darkness, what happens to your manifestation of consciousness, what happens to your physical, verbal, psychological movements?

Then the senses sink into the mind, and the mind sinks into, merges into the *buddhi*, the intellect, and the *buddhi* merges back into the *Atman*. Doesn't it happen in profound sleep? The manifested world is dissolved back into the unmanifest, every night. That which is

beyond the *buddhi*, into that merges back all the manifest world of
yours.

Then your senses are not aware of the room in which you are
sleeping. You are in your own home, but your senses have
withdrawn into the mind, and there is no consciousness. And the
mind, with all its thoughts and ambitions etc., has gone back into
reason and rationality and the reason returns to its own Lord, the
Atman, the Chaitanya.

So, what happens in your body is the emergence and the merging
back, every day. Every day you die and every dawn you are reborn,
as it were. Birth-and-death is the emergence and the dissolution.

Now, an additional aspect of this phenomenon is also narrated,
beautifully. Every seed has a potential of creativity. When the
unlimited limits itself into a form, when the nebulous fluid energies
accept solidification voluntarily and get clothed into a form, the
form has a limited potential of creative energy. And then that
potentiality manifests and with every manifestation the potential
creativity is consumed

A seed, for example, becomes a sapling, the sapling becomes a
plant. Some plants live for a few weeks, others for a few months,
some grow into gigantic trees and they survive four or five centuries.
And yet, at the end of the centuries, the potential of creative energy,
energy of sustenance and survival, is exhausted and even a five
hundred year old tree dries up and goes back to the earth, the matrix
from which it has sprung up.

In the same way, the seed of human life, created by the male and
the female out of the creative energies contained in their bodies,
has some potential. It may last ten years, it may last hundred years,
it may last fifty, sixty years. So, as the tree dries up, old age begins
to dry up the energies, if you allow the human body to beautifully
die a natural death. When the moment comes, that the survival
potential is exhausted completely, the body stretches itself in death,
movement stops, all the indications of life disappear.

The tree, the leaves, or the bark of the tree, or whatever, goes back to the earth, gets converted into dust, to be reborn again. It is passing from life to life, it is passing from one form into the other. That is why dissolution is not destruction, death is not the end of Life. You just pass from one dimension of Life to another.

When you burn a piece of dry wood, the wood dissolves and produces the flame, the flame dissolves and produces light, light consumes itself and gives you heat, and heat gets converted into your body in healing energy, sustenance energy, etc. It is a dance of energies. The energies get transformed, they interact. That is not destruction, but dissolution of one form, to get converted into another form, whether you bury the body or you cremate the body, it gets converted into another form containing another energy.

Dust has energy, water has energy, fire has energy and the emptiness of space also contains energies. Life is a dance of innumerable energies. Capra calls it beautifully the dance of Shiva. He talks of the Tao of Physics. This is an aspect of *abhyasa yoga*, to be aware that death is not the end of Life. It is the end of living of a particular form, that is all. It is passing from life to life, from one form to the other, one variety of energy to the other. So, the fear of death disappears from the mind of a student of *yoga*. All the anxiety, worry and tension, associated with the idea of death as destruction, disappears and the consciousness is cleansed completely.

If this is sufficiently clear, let us proceed to another important point. The eighth chapter, in the last part of the second half, uses two terms: the northern path, and the southern path. Even on the planet earth, if you go to the arctic zone, as your friend Vimala has done, you will see the clarity of northern light. In Norway, Finland, Sweden, the North Pole, you will see qualitatively different light in the north. The sky is clear, no clouds, the sun pours its splendour, the days are indescribably bright.

The sages and rishis of the Vedas have used the term northern path and northern light figuratively. The *Gita* is a poem, even though it is a dialogue. So, figurative language is used to indicate very deep fundamental truths or indications of reality.

In the human body, the crown of the head is called the northern pole. Figuratively, it is said that there is a lotus with a thousand petals at the crown of the head. There is a lotus at the navel point with fifty-two petals and there is a lotus with only two petals between the eyebrows and so on. The ancient Indians were poets par excellence. They would look at nature, at the human body, at the anatomy, etc., through their transcendental perception that a poet has.

We see the same things as the poet and yet we do not see what he sees. This is also the case with an artist, a sculptor. There is a qualitative difference in perception. So, the yogic anatomy, given by the science of *yoga*, *tantra*, *mantra*, is quite different from the ordinary anatomy of the human body that we talk about, when we mention medical aspects.

The northern path refers figuratively to two phenomena. One is the period of six months, from December to June, when the skies are clear of clouds, the days are bright, bathed in shiny sunlight and there is no humidity. This is one aspect of the northern path, physically, materially speaking. And the *Gita* says it is desirable that one gives up one's body during these six months, when days and nights are bright and everything is clear and clean.

From June to December the days are cloudy, humid, rainy. The atmosphere can cause depression, pathologically and also psychologically. So it is not desirable, says the *Gita*, to depart from the planet in that depressing atmosphere, during the smoky, cloudy, humid days. That is the physical external meaning of the words northern and southern paths.

But what does Sri Krishna want to say, by using those terms? Perception of truth, resulting in clarity of understanding, is the northern path. As the sun shines and makes everything bright, understanding makes everything bright and clear. When the understanding takes place with the help of intelligence, that is the sun in the human body. Intellect is the moon and intelligence is the sun, according to the *Gita*. I am here to tell you what the *Gita* says, not what Vimala wants to say.

It is the *Gita* that we are studying and the knowledge or understanding of the ancient Indians, their perception, that has taken place five thousand years ago, that is the beauty of it. So the path of intellectually understanding, then discovering the truth through perception and getting grounded in that understanding, is the northern path, the path of ascendance.

The *Katha Upanishad* deals very elaborately with this and in modern days Sri Aurobindo of Pondichery has used the *Katha Upanishad*, as well as the eighth chapter of the *Gita*, when he builds up his integral *yoga* and talks about the ascendance of matter and the descent of the divine.

When you purify matter in your body, transforming the energies contained in matter of your physical body, through *yoga sadhana*, you are ascending. It is the ascent of matter. When you create orderliness in the chaotic emotions and anarchic desires and ambitions in your mind, you create order, a cohesiveness, then you are following the path of ascendance.

From chaos to order, from ignorance to knowledge, from knowledge to understanding, from shabbiness and dirty-ness to beautiful cleanliness and purity. This is the path of ascendance, figuratively called the northern path. Then there is light and clarity. Abhyasa Yoga says a student of *yoga* chooses the path of light, the path of ascendance of matter, through purification.

If you surrender to the impulsive drives in your physical body, allow the impulses in your physical body to create a compulsive demand, if you allow the appetite to degenerate into creating compulsive eating, if speech is misused for flattering and praising oneself, or flattering others out of fear, etc., concealing the truth, then you have given into the drives of speech, that is called the southern path.

The southern path is the path of darkness, where a human being gives in to the pulls and pushes of the biological nature, instead of educating, refining, purifying it. You just surrender and you allow yourself to be pushed around by the impulses of the body. You do not create a cohesive wholeness out of the existing variety of drives.

The physical needs are limited, so may be you regulate and create an order, a cohesive being in them. But when it comes to the mind, the mind has silly demands. They are not needs, but they are self-created, self-provoked wants, and human beings give in to the wants of the mind. The demands of the mind are unending, it is a bottomless pit, and the desires, the wishes, the ambitions go on changing as the body grows. The mind is constantly restless. It makes you wander around chaotically, consuming and burning out all your vital energies unnecessarily. That is called the southern path.

Whether day-dreaming, whether stretching your day into the night and dreaming at night, whether brooding, worrying, creating tensions out of challenges of Life, then you are following the southern path of darkness. It keeps you to the orbit of matter in you, both the physical structure and the mind, which is subtle matter, thought as subtle matter. You get involved and entangled in the orbit of matter, entangled in the human past in you, the *samskaras* in you. You give into them, instead of regulating, educating, restraining, building up a cohesive, blended, homogeneous person out of yourself.

You have a choice, either to follow the southern path or to follow the northern path. Krishna says: 'O Arjuna, I plead with you not to succumb to the easy path, the southern path. All your life follow the northern light. Hard work it may be, straining your energies may be and yet every step that you take brings you nearer and upwards to the Purusha, the Brahman, the supreme reality.'

The study of *yoga* becomes the bridge; it becomes the link between the rational and the super rational. Because a man is what he thinks, not only what he eats, but what he thinks. If you keep in yourself the awareness of the Cosmic dance of Life, where creation and dissolution follow rhythmically and when you see around yourself the flux of changes, the dance of energies ever changing, then you have no inclination to get attached to the perishable aspect of your life.

The physical body is the perishable aspect of the manifestation and the idea of a separate identity and entity and addiction to that, attachment to that, is also a perishable fact. Look, falsehood is perishable, truth is indestructible. When you understand the truth, the false perishes. In the same way, when one discovers the source of intelligence contained in silence, then the addiction to reason, to intellect, to logic, to argumentation, disappears.

On the one hand you allow your *sadhana* to consummate into the dimension of *samadhi* and on the other hand, in daily living, in the movement of relationships, you keep away from the southern path of darkness and restlessness and follow the northern path. Then the awareness that is released through *samadhi* blends the individual consciousness into the Cosmic supreme consciousness and there is no returning back to the mental orbit, the orbit of the ego-consciousness.

The *Gita* has used a very significant phrase: 'living tethered to the mind, living addicted to the body and its drives, creates misery.' If you remain tethered to the physical and the mental, then there is no ending of misery, there is no ending of suffering. You may progress with science and technology, you may evolve new theologies and organize new religions, you may read all the philosophies of the east and the west, but suffering and misery remains a psychological fact in your daily living. Ignorance darkens your life, wrong identification creates attachment or detachment. So, 'Arjuna, follow the path of light, not of darkness.'

People in India have emphasized the external path, that is: in which month to die and in which month not to die, how to keep alive, how not to die. These external factors do not give you the essence of the teachings of the *Gita*. Surely the *Gita* was not expounded by Krishna to describe in which month to die and in which month not to die.

There are many verses in the *Gita*, which are figurative language used by a poet and the stupid brains, addicted to tradition, take the dictionary, see the literal meaning and create a ritualism out of it. Please, you who come from Europe, the land of science, rationality, please save yourself from such interpretations. And if I happen to give such interpretations, just discard them.

The *Gita* is an exposition of the essence of the Vedas and the Upanishads. It is a scripture, that explains to you, that systematically, progressively, scientifically, it is possible to transcend every obstacle of distortion and perversion and come upon the path of harmony and synthesis of the individual and the collective, where matter and spirit are not looked upon as separate entities.

Matter is not ignored and neglected because of the spirit and the spiritual is not ignored or neglected for the pleasures of matter. Spirituality simplifies this apparent contradiction. It inspires us to discover the concealed harmony in different dimensions of our being.

In the last verse of the eighth chapter, Sri Krishna says to Arjuna: 'they may read the Vedas (he is referring here to Vedanta, the Six Systems of Indian Philosophy), doing *yajnas*, Mantra Yoga, Tantra Yoga, Hatha Yoga, taking upon themselves numberless austerities, (you know, those who follow the path of *tapas*, will stand on one leg, raise one hand, do *japa*, chant *mantras* for hours on end, etc.), those who extol and admire the austerities and hardships of the body, for attaining certain powers, or those who study and specialize in the teachings of the Veda and Vedanta, none of them has raised the physical and the mental to a higher level, to a higher dimension. They still remain in the physical and mental dimension, they still are victims of greed for money, lust for sensual pleasure, jealousy of one another. So, Arjuna, instead of getting entangled in all these, why not understand the dance of Shiva and Shakti, of *prakriti* and Purusha, not theoretically out there in the Cosmos, but here in your own body.

Why don't you understand the dance of Shiva and Shakti going on, as the emergence of activity, of action, and merging back of all the activities and movements, as in the state of awakening and the state of sleeping, the dimension of creation and the dimension of dissolution?

Why don't you understand and discriminate between the perishable and the imperishable? Dedicate your energies towards the imperishable and live with the perishable, doing justice to the energies, but not succumbing to them. If you do this, if you live this way, then you will find yourself in the abode of divinity, the eternal abode of

Paramatman and you will not be born again as a suffering miserable human mind.'

The emphasis in the *Gita* is not on the physical birth. It is on the birth of the sense of identity, not being a separate entity independent of the rest of Life. Krishna says, "you are part and parcel of the Cosmic Life; you are in it like the fish in the ocean. If you understand this, then even at the moment of physical death, of dying, you will be passing into the ocean of eternity, the dwelling of Paramatman."

It is a joy to me, no, an ecstasy to me, when friends of European countries, teachers of *yoga*, come here and create an opportunity for me to share the best with you. One feels inspired to share, because you are in the midst of that. And with the study of every chapter I hope, there will be improvement in the Hatha Yoga aspect and a transformation in the quality of your consciousness. Hopefully, there will be an ending of psychological suffering and misery in your life. Religiosity or spirituality is the ending of psychological suffering. Thank you.

CHAPTER IX

THE YOGA OF SOVEREIGN SCIENCE AND SOVEREIGN SECRET

We have come to the ninth chapter. It is a crucial chapter, as it deals with a secret path, leading to secret revelations. Before we plunge into this chapter, let us make a brief summing up of the previous chapters.

I hope every one of us is aware that the science of *yoga* aims at establishing a contact between the individuated consciousness and the non-individuated transcendental consciousness, which is called Brahman. The science of *yoga*, every branch of it, presumes an omniscient trinity, of which we have to be conscious when we try to study the *Gita*.

The transcendental principle of Life, Brahman, is an indivisible organic wholeness. It is called Brahman by the Vedantins, Ishvara or Lord by Hatha Yoga, and Purusha by the Sankhyas, and so on. So, there is that transcendental Brahman, or Lord or Ishvara. Then there is un-individuated universal matter, which is called *mula prakriti* by Hatha Yoga and perhaps, by other branches of *yoga*, and called *maya* by Vedantins. And the third is the individuated consciousness which is called *jiva* by Hatha Yoga and by Raja Yoga, and which is called reflected Brahman, reflected Ishvara by Vedanta.

I am putting before you different terms, which are used for the same thing. The omniscient trinity, for the sake of our study of the ninth chapter, is Brahman, *prakriti* and *jiva*. These terms will be used in this chapter, so let them be very clear; the individuated consciousness in the human, universal consciousness in the universal matter or *mula prakriti* and that which transcends the individuated and the non-individuated consciousness. *Yoga* aims at establishing the contact between the individuated consciousness and the non-individuated transcendental wholeness or holistic consciousness. That is the purpose of the science of *yoga*.

The *Gita* begins with the frustration and despondency of Arjuna. It sets out Sankhya Yoga. It proceeds, in turn, with Karma Yoga, Jnana Yoga, Vijnana Yoga and Sannyasa Yoga. Then it comes to Abhyasa Yoga in the eighth chapter. And today it is going to deal with Raja Yoga.

In between Sankhya Yoga and Raja Yoga stands Hatha Yoga, which all of you have studied for years and practised for years. Hatha Yoga tries to establish the contact between the individual and the transcendental consciousness, by working upon the physical body. The physical body has all the energies that universal matter or *mula prakriti* has. It has all the energies, that Cosmic matter has.

But the unified Cosmic energy, contained in that universal matter, is diversified in the human body. You have the eyes and there is the sight. So you feel that the energy of sight is an independent autonomous energy. You have ears and the whole structure of audition and you feel that the energy of audition is separate from the energy of perception. There is the energy of your vocal cords and you feel that it is a separate autonomous energy of speech. You look upon them as separate energies.

You have the pro-creative organs and the sex energy. You feel it is also an independent autonomous energy. You have the digestive organs, the food sheath, a variety of energies. In the *mula prakriti*, all these energies are unified and work in a unitary holistic way. But, in the human body, they are distributed to different organs, they are given independent functions. So this diversification and distribution of energy into separate organs, creates an illusion that they are all independent energies and the person identifies with one, or with some of them, or with many of them.

The science of *yoga* shows us the way of gathering the distributed energies together, uniting the diversified energies and then educates them to function holistically instead of fragmentarily. Hatha Yoga uses the body, the *asanas* and *pranayama* especially for this purpose, disciplining the body, disciplining the energies. It uses the *prana*, the dynamic vital energy, for disciplining and educating. *Asanas* and *pranayama* are the essence of Hatha Yogic discipline.

If you turn to Bhakti Yoga (the *yoga* of devotion), there you use the emotional aspect of consciousness for uniting the energies, harmonizing them through dedication and devotion to one point. The whole emotional energy is focussed on Ishvara (the highest reading of the absolute by the human mind). And through the concentration of emotional energy, Bhakti Yoga tries to purify the physical and the mental body.

Jnana Yoga uses the cerebral organ, the faculty of will and the faculty of ideation and through that knowledge it experiments in purifying and uniting the diversified energies, thus establishing contact. We need not go on elaborating each branch and how each branch has a way of establishing the contact, through taking some part of our physical and mental being as an instrument.

Hatha Yoga uses the body as the instrument and through the help of the *pranas*, it awakens the *kundalini*, the coiled up energy of *prana* at the base of the spine. And the awakening of that coiled up *prana* energy, energizes your whole being, energizes your consciousness. But the path is long, it is laborious, it consumes much time and energy.

So, Sri Krishna says: 'Look Arjuna, instead of taking these long and circuitous paths of Bhakti Yoga, Jnana Yoga, Karma Yoga, and even the hard laborious path of Hatha Yoga, I will show you a secret path, which will not consume so much of your time and energy.'

These words, at the beginning of the ninth chapter, give us in a nutshell the essence of the whole chapter. Sri Krishna says: 'I will share with you the supreme revelation of truth and a secret path to that revelation, because I have known it and I have experienced it'.

It is for anyone and everyone who wants to be blessed by the revelation of that truth and who is willing to tread the secret path to this secret revelation. You will get there, it is not the privilege of the few. You do not have to accept it on the authority of any scripture. It is within the reach of every human being, provided that it becomes the top priority and there is a willingness to walk alone, on that secret path, for the revelation of the secret truth.

You may be acquainted with Mme Blavatsky's volume *Secret Doctrines*. I am sorry for Mme Blavatsky, but they are not doctrines. They are truths, they are not theories. But the brave lady used that terminology a century ago. Her mother tongue was not English, it was Russian. But we have to correct the incorrect expression. It is not a secret doctrine, it is a secret truth.

When you get obsessed with the truth you have discovered and you begin to assert it, instead of communicating it, it becomes a doctrine, a dogma. But truth defies such imprisonment, it defies any cage of a theory or a doctrine or a dogma, it eludes you the moment you try to imprison it.

Sri Krishna says that it is experimental. *Yoga* is an experimental science, spirituality is an experimental science, within the reach of everyone. Investigate, explore, experiment, verify, and truth will be yours. You see this emphasis on the inner freedom of every individual, the psychic freedom of every individual. It is an important part of the teachings of the *Gita*.

It is within the reach of everyone. It is easy to pursue. Once you have perceived it, once the contact has been established, it can never be snapped away, it can never be severed. The understanding never lapses into forgetfulness. Knowledge can be forgotten, understanding becomes the substance of your being. The light of truth is imperishable, indestructible.

All these words are very important. This sovereign supreme truth and the secret sovereign path, which purifies your being, is not going to use the emotional part of your mind, nor the willpower of your cerebral organ, but *chitta*, the depository of all the psychological energies. So, neither *karma* nor *bhakti* nor *jnana*, nor *dhyana*, but it is going to focus its energies on *chitta*, the repository of all conditionings. It will not neglect the body, the physical body. The *asanas* and the *pranayamas* will accompany you on this path, but it is not necessary for you to do the eighty-four *asanas* and all the different kinds of *pranayamas*.

Whether it is Hatha Yoga or Raja Yoga, how are we going to establish the contact? Look, universal matter, *mula prakriti*, has individuated into a human body with a certain equilibrium. In the physical body there is a natural equilibrium and a natural harmony of energies, though dispersed, distributed for diversified functions. There is an equilibrium, which is sufficient for our normal existence and relationship with people, living in society etc.

But if you want to establish a contact with the highest, the transcendental, it will be an upward voyage, it will be an ascent. These energies and the equilibrium are useful for horizontal functioning, relating to the orbit of the earth, relating to matter, relating to human structures. So, for horizontal functioning of all your energies of eyes, nose, ears, skin, sex, speech, that equilibrium is sufficient.

But if you want to take an ascending path, upward from matter and the energies contained in matter, towards the super-sensuous, super-mental and super-Cosmic, which is transcendental, then you have to create a new equilibrium in the physical body. You have to create a new equilibrium in your so-called mind or ordinary consciousness.

Hatha Yoga helps you to create that new equilibrium, through *asanas*, *pranayama* etc. and *kundalini* and Raja Yoga helps you to build up that new equilibrium, through a mastery over your *chitta*, the repository in the consciousness, the ground of your consciousness. For it is a question of creating a new equilibrium in the body and in the consciousness. It is not only certain practices and certain *siddhis* that are important, or the awakening of the *kundalini* for the sake of enjoying the *siddhis* or powers. That is not the purpose of *yoga*. That is a by-path. The essence and the fundamental object are quite different.

It is called the supreme and sovereign path, because it gives you the capacity of self-rule. Generally in life, the impulses of the body rule the mind. In a mentally evolved knowledgeable person, the mind controls the physical impulses and yet rules the reason or rationality. The inheritance rules the conscious mind, the subconscious rules the conscious mind, emotions overwhelm reason and rationality, so there is no self-rule. For some time you are governed and ruled by the impulses in the body, sometimes you are ruled and governed by even incompatible desires, contradictory wishes and aspirations and you are torn within.

Raja Yoga is called the Prince of Yoga, King of Knowledge, because it enables you towards self-rule. The body, the energies contained in the biological impulses, the mind with all the faculties and energies contained in that mind, they voluntarily follow your inclinations, your intuitions, your perceptions. You don't have to force them, they become voluntarily companions, they become your elegant assistant, to fulfil. It is called Raja Yoga, the Prince of Yoga, because it teaches you self-rule.

It is called the 'royal secret', because what you do is not visible to others. When you do *asanas*, *pranayamas* etc., you do them collectively and people know and you are also conscious of what you are doing. You measure the consequences; how far you have progressed or failed, etc. This secret path will not be visible to anyone else except you, the individual consciousness and your invisible master, the transcendental consciousness. It is an affair between the two. If I have been able to some extent in conveying the meaning of the first three verses of the ninth chapter, let us proceed to the fourth verse.

What is the secret truth that was revealed to Krishna by Brahman, by the transcendental principle of Life, the indivisible non-individuated holistic consciousness? What is this truth? Krishna puts it in very simple terms. For understanding what he has explained to Arjuna, I would prefer to give you an example, before taking up the verse itself.

You may have come across someone who writes plays, dramas, or novels. In his brain, in his mind, all the characters of the play are there. Every character is developed and the relationship between the characters, the hero, the villain, or the sequence of events, you know, the whole play and all the characters, are there. Nobody sees them, but he is aware of them. They are all still unmanifest. So, he takes pen and paper and writes the play. The unmanifest characters, the story, their interaction, now becomes manifest on the paper, with the help of words.

There can be a very noble character, there can be a very ignoble one, there can be some love-incarnate character and some very cruel one. But once they have come on the paper, they are set there as characters, playing their roles. Now, the writer is not one of those characters in the story. He is the cause or the creator of the story and the characters, independent of those characters. Please do see. Because after a few weeks or days, he can write another play with some other characters. Although he has created the characters and the play, he transcends them.

Brahman, the Lord of creation, the transcendental supreme principle of intelligence, causes the explosion of universes; causes the manifestation of all the energies contained in matter and yet, it is not there. It is transcendental, as the writer is not in the characters of his play, he is independent. He has his own existence and he lives that existence. In the same way, Krishna says:

'Look Arjuna, the truth revealed to me is that the Lord, Brahman, is transcendental. It is not limited by creation, by the innumerable universes that have come out of him, that are born out of him. The existence of the transcendental intelligence is sustained.'

Now, here is another aspect of the same example. If the playwright is the author, but if he has not experienced those sentiments, emotions, if he has not identified himself to some extent with the characters, he will not be able to write about them. He has seen, somewhere, the permutations and combinations. In some way the writer has expressed his character into the characters of his play.

In the same way the intelligence, the supreme holistic transcendental intelligence, is reflected in the individual consciousness. This is the immanence and transcendence of Life.

Krishna explains to Arjuna the play of the unmanifest and the manifest. The unmanifest sustains the manifest, the unmanifest is the source of the manifest and yet remains transcendental. It is not contaminated by the behaviour of the manifested expressions. As the play of the characters does not contaminate the author, in the same way, what human beings do, human individuals who are emanations of that Brahman, that Paramatman, that Ishvara, what they do, does not contaminate the transcendental principle.

Well, if their behaviour does not contaminate the transcendental consciousness, does it contaminate the Atman in them? Krishna says 'No. Atman is not contaminated, not polluted by the behaviour of the body and the mind.'

The contaminations, the distortions, the perversions, are all in the two-dimensions, the two orbits, the physical body and the mental body. The language of bondage and liberation is relevant only to these two dimensions of your life, physical and mental. Beyond that, the language of bondage and emancipation loses its relevance.

I am sorry if it becomes hard, but Krishna is going to explain and clarify the dance of the unmanifest and the manifest. The supreme transcendental Brahman, Paramatman, intelligence, Chaitanya, samvit, whatever you call it, travels through universal matter, *mula prakriti*, and gets individuated. So you become a human individual being, you have your individuated matter, you have your individuated mental energy and yet you retain, within the physical and mental, that transcendental element, the Atman.

So, remember the trinity, Ishvara, *prakriti* and *jiva*. In the individual body, in the individual human life, there is this 'I'-consciousness, which we have seen in the eighth chapter, the I-ness, the me-ness, the consciousness of a separate existence.

Now, that separate consciousness, which we call the ego-consciousness, has to purify itself through silence, energize itself through silence, through meditation, through *dhyana* and ascend to the realization that it was never born, that it shall never die, nothing can kill it, nothing can destroy it. It is like the air, like space.

So, the secret path is the purification of the centre of consciousness and the I-ness, the me-ness. The ego-consciousness is the centre. You know, tackle the centre, the *chitta*, in which the ego-consciousness dwells. That is the point which we are going to deal with. Raja Yoga deals directly with the *ahamkara*, with the ego-consciousness, leaving aside the periphery.

The intelligence, contained in our individual body, has clothed itself into a separate I-consciousness, ego-consciousness, because of wrong identification. It has identified itself with this limited physical structure; it has identified itself with the mind; the knowledge and experience of the human race. Therefore it becomes a separate divisive destructive thing.

If the identification moves from body and mind, from the physical and mental and surrenders its existence to that super-mental or transcendental intelligence, it no more remains the separate ego; it no more remains a destructive I-consciousness, the source of all misery, conflict, etc.

Purification will come through two processes. One, in allowing all the mental movements to go into abeyance, which is silence, which leads you to meditation. And another, through educating the *chitta* to set itself free from *avidya* (ignorance of the truth), *raga* (attachment), *dvesha* (detachment) etc. Correct the identification, that is all.

It is the nature of *chitta* to remain identified somewhere. If it remains identified with the physical body, then it will succumb to the impulses of the body, its drives, its pushes and pulls. If it remains identified with mind, with knowledge and experience, it will be overwhelmed by the whole human past. So, identification is to be corrected.

Who is going to correct the identification? If the ego enjoys the identification with the body and the mind, surely, it is not going to correct it. It has not got the vitality to do it. Where will be the source of vitality of that additional energy?

There are two ways of having that energy and vitality. One was already given to us by Hatha Yoga, through *asanas* and *pranayama*, *asanas* that relates to the respiratory parts of our body, that exercises the respiratory organs through *pranayama*, and *asanas* that strengthen the chest, the lungs, the heart, that keeps the back straight. Very few *asanas* are required for that. So, energizing through *asanas* and *pranayama* is one thing.

And secondly, allowing the mental movement to discontinue itself completely. Neither exercising the brain for new knowledge, nor exercising the mind for new experiences, is the path of total relaxation. Not for one hour or two hours a day, no, throughout the day inner relaxation.

I wonder if you have observed in your study of Hatha Yoga that, when you relax in certain *asanas* it is not creating passivity, it does not stimulate any inertia or heaviness. If you really relax and breathe rhythmically, even for ten minutes in that *asana*, it re-energizes you. I am trying to share with you how relaxation energizes. Relaxation of the whole body and abeyance of mental movement, they should be combined together.

If you just relax on an *asana* and if you don't combine it with the relaxation of mind, (non-action of the mind is relaxation of the mind), you may relax the body, but if during the *asana* you go on thinking, if you go on having your tension, you may be stretched in *asana* for half an hour, nothing will happen except the physical relaxation. As you sit in silence, in an *asana*, there should be total abeyance of mental movement. They have to be blended together. For the secret path, pointed out by Krishna, you should combine the two.

The blending of Raja Yoga and Hatha Yoga together is a brilliant stroke. The physical body is completely relaxed; there is not the slightest tension in the nervous, the muscular and the glandular system. And because thoughts do not move, nothing moves on the mental level, there is also relaxation there. And it is that which intensifies the vitality, energizes body and consciousness together, the physical and the mental together. The simultaneity of these two works miracles.

For this total relaxation, Sri Krishna uses the word surrender. Not through effort, but through effortlessness, not through your movement, but the abeyance of all movement, through the surrender of the physical and the mental exertion. Then there is a transportation into a higher level of Life.

The diversified functions of all the organs, the distributed energies, have been gathered together through relaxation, they have been united. They were dispersed, they were distributed, but through relaxation, through silence they are unified, they are gathered together, they become a unitary force. Please do see with me, they become a unitary force now and therefore the quantum jump or the transportation occurs.

Through the individualization, through the distribution of energies into different organs, through the diversification of their function, we get separated from the *mula prakriti* or universal matter. In this hour of relaxation, in this hour of surrender, the separation comes to an end. Because the diversification, the distribution etc. has been eliminated, you are already united with the *mula prakriti*, the matrix of Life, the universal matter. This is called *samadhi*, beyond *dhyana* or meditation.

Dharana corrects the identification. *Dhyana*, through the emptiness of consciousness and the relaxation of the physical body, energizes and intensifies vitality. And through the elimination of the separation with universal matter, *mula prakriti*, there is what you call the dimension of *samadhi*. 'Arjuna, *samadhi* is the cave in which the revolution can take place.' It is only now a question of *mula prakriti* and Brahman, it is only a question of *maya* and Ishvara. You have already crossed from *jiva* to *mula prakriti* or *maya* and now the last stage.

I am trying to do justice to Raja Yoga, *raja vidya*. We are working hard to understand Raja Yoga, without taking shelter in any of the interpretations of Shankaracharya or Ramakrishna or Aurobindo.

You know, I am trying to put into words a non-sectarian, non-dogmatic, simple way, as I have perceived it, understood it. I have never done it before; in fact I have never taken classes in *Gita* or the Upanishads. But for you, this would not have happened in this birth of mine. So, if I can't make it very lucid, it is because I am groping for words.

The total relaxation of the physical and the mental results in the by-product of *samadhi*; a new dimension of consciousness. The transcendence of the physical and the mental has already taken place. *Samadhi* is a supra-mental dimension, *samadhi* is a supra-cerebral dimension, it is beyond thought, it is beyond time. Call it the dimension of utter unconditional surrender of the ego and its activities, call it the dimension of utter unconditional uninhibited relaxation, non-action.

At this level of consciousness, free of all the wrong identifications, free of all the consequences of impurities of wrong identifications, it is a purified consciousness. It is like the rarefied air on the mountaintop, the purer the air, the more rarefied it becomes. The higher you go, the purer you become. It is a dimension of which I have to talk in negative terms: as non-physical, non-mental, non-rational. You know, there are no positive terms to describe that dimension of *samadhi*. And Krishna says to Arjuna:

'There I live, that is my dwelling place. And so can it become yours, if you want it, Arjuna. You are a dear friend of mine and you deserve this revelation of the mystery of the unmanifest and the manifest. You deserve the revelation of the mystery of the organic wholeness getting individuated and becoming a human being; and the mystery and the secret path, how the individual goes back to the non-individuated wholeness of consciousness. This is the imperishable truth, easy to perceive and experience, indestructible, when the light of truth is perceived.'

It is directly experiencable, within the reach of every human being and yet it remains secret. It cannot be codified, like the *asanas* or the techniques of *pranayama*. It cannot be organized, it cannot be standardized. It is unique to each individual. Therefore, it is called the secret path, the royal path of *Brahma-vidya*. With your cooperation, we have looked at the first seven verses of the ninth chapter.

Among all the branches of *yoga*, Raja Yoga is called the King of Yogas and the secret path, indicated by Raja Yoga, is called the sovereign path. It is thus called, because it synthesizes practically all the other branches of *yoga*, harmonizes them, blends them together and creates a fascinating majestic path for self-education, self-refinement, for the evolution of a new equilibrium in the body, a new equanimity in consciousness, and thus striving to perfect the physical body and the mental body, given to a human being.

Those of you who are acquainted with Sankhya Yoga and Dhyana Yoga, on which Vedanta is based, must be aware, that Sankhya and Dhyana Yoga focus all their attention and energies on the Purusha, spirit, Paramatman, Brahman. *Prakriti*, matter, is ignored, is neglected. The refinement or purification of *prakriti* is not taken care of. Intellectual identification with the supreme Lord, Brahman, Paramatman, is the essence of Sankhya Yoga, Dhyana Yoga, Vedanta, etc.

Bhakti Yoga utilizes the emotional part and expounds the path of uniting with the supreme Brahman, through emotional identification. There the supreme Lord is called father, some call him lover, beloved, some call him the child Krishna. So, father, mother, child, friend, all these relationships are imagined and imposed upon Paramatman, Brahman and again *prakriti* is neglected.

The intoxication, the ecstasy of *bhakti* in the life of Ramakrishna Paramahansa or other such Indian saints, created an imbalance on the physical level. Intellectual identification with the Paramatman, Brahman, emotional identification with Ishvara, imposing, imagining relationships, psychological relationships with that, is one aspect of some branches of *yoga*.

Hatha Yoga, Tantra Yoga and Mantra Yoga, focus their attention on *mula prakriti*, Cosmic matter, or on the individuated *prakriti* in their body. They emphasize matter and its energies. Then Hatha

Yoga manipulates matter and its energies contained in the body, with the help of *prana* energy. Mantra Yoga manipulates the inner organs, their relationships and energies with the help of sound energy. Tantra Yoga manipulates the seven *chakras* in the body, the crucial significant points in the body, where various nerves and arteries converge upon one another.

So Mantra Yoga, Tantra Yoga, Hatha Yoga, focus their attention on *prakriti*. The sound energy can provoke latent or dormant powers in your body. Manipulation of *chakras*, also with *mantras*, with the help of very subtle sound, can provoke the latent energies concealed in the human organs. And of course, Hatha Yoga, with the help of *pranayama*, *prana* energy, awakens the *kundalini* and other psychophysical powers. So, the focus and emphasis is on *prakriti*.

The other three had emphasized the Purusha. And these three emphasize *prakriti*. Karma Yoga, the path of action, uses *prakriti*, the mental body and the physical body, through beneficial or good *karmas*, towards the society in which a person lives. It wants to eliminate the separative ego-consciousness. It uses thought power as well as physical power. So, intellectual identification, emotional union and physical striving, emphasize either Purusha or *prakriti*.

Raja Yoga is the only path, where equal attention is paid to Ishvara, *prakriti* and the individual ego. It is not purifying or refining one, at the cost of the other. It is not deifying one, at the cost of the other. It takes into its purview and compass all the three, simultaneously. And that is the beauty and the uniqueness of Raja Yoga.

Surrendering all actions to the awareness that the unmanifest and the manifest are the dance of one and the same Brahman, the same principle of sovereign intelligence. Matter cannot be separated from spirit or the supreme intelligence, and the supreme intelligence, the Lord, Ishvara, Brahman, can never be isolated from *prakriti*. That it is the basis of Raja Yoga,

We have seen how, in the state of *samadhi*, the energies contained in the physical body are surrendered through unconditional total relaxation and the mental energies of knowledge, thought, experience, *samskaras*, are surrendered through silence. It is the total silence of the conditioned mind and the total relaxation of the physical body, that constitutes the essence of samadhi, the dimension of *samadhi*.

Now, if this background and the holistic perspective of Raja Yoga are sufficiently clear, let us proceed. We cannot proceed unless the background, the foundation, the compass, in which the *Gita* places Raja Yoga, is understood clearly, at least theoretically. We have come up to the seventh verse and we are beginning with the eighth today. And I hope to take you along with me up to the twenty-first verse of the ninth chapter.

Krishna is pleading the case of Brahman. It is a dialogue and he communicates in the first person, as if Brahman. He is pleading the case of Brahman, Paramatman, the Lord, Ishvara, whatever you like to call that transcendental principle of intelligence, Paramatman, the sovereign intelligence. That intelligence, through Sri Krishna, is revealing its secret.

Please do note that Brahman, the Lord Ishvara, is *sat*, indestructible *sat*, and *prakriti* is *chit*. You might have heard that they call the Lord *sat-chit-ananda*. If somebody asks what is Brahman, they say: Brahman is indestructible truth, *sat*, self-generated awareness, *chit*, and spontaneous bliss, *ananda*. Now, the intelligence, Purushottama, Brahman, says:

'Though *prakriti*, *chit*, matter, with all the innumerable energies contained in it, emanates out of my being and carries on the dance of manifestation, individualizing objects, flavours, shapes, sizes etc., I never look upon myself as the doer of it; it is not my doing.

Though it emanates from me, emerges out of me, I never appropriate the dance of manifestations, the material world, the dance of energies because, whenever matter gets individualized, it not only takes the form of an object, it also has a specific energy, which that object contains and expresses.'

Purusha, Brahman, the Lord, says: 'I am not the doer, I do not appropriate that as mine, as belonging to me. I am absolutely unconcerned about what the *prakriti* does, the Cosmic matter does, when it progressively goes on individuating and expressing itself, in the form of mountains, rivers, oceans, trees, animals or human beings, and what happens in their interactions. I am neither the doer, nor do I appropriate those movements to me. I am unconcerned, uninvolved and unattached.'

Very significant terms are used here. 'The movements of matter do not affect me (Brahman) at all. They have their own autonomy, the energies have their own way and their interactions again generate novel energies. And the drama of the manifest world goes on. I may be the presiding principle of the intelligence.' And he proceeds to clarify the issue, by giving an example. 'The sparks from a blazing fire rise up in the sky. Though they emanate from the piece of wood, the wood is not the doer of the fire or of the sparks. The rays of the sun emanate from the sun and they bring with them, to the earth, light, warmth, healing energy, etc. But the sun is not creating the rays and sending them to the earth. There is no volition, there is no action on the part of the sun.'

The sun is light, the being of the sun contains light, it contains heat, it contains numerous healing energies. The rays of the sun issue forth from the sun, like the sparks issue forth from the fire. The fire does not send out the sparks, they issue forth, they emanate. The unmanifest potential manifests itself without volition, without an effort. The being of the sun is light and therefore the rays of the sun bring the light with them to the earth.

In the same way the supreme intelligence says: 'The content of my being is sat, the indestructible reality, the content of my being is intelligence. So when matter plays around with the dance of manifestation, the timeless manifestation of matter, may be a blade of grass, it carries to the earth a ray of my intelligence, because matter emanates from me.

So, the blade of grass contains organic intelligence. It is limited by its shape, by its size. It may last only a few days or hours. Every flower, every petal of a flower, every electron, proton, neutron of matter, contains the quantum of energy and the organic intelligence, because it emanates from me. I do not give it, I am neither the producer nor the giver and yet it emanates from me.

Arjuna, please observe this dance of the unmanifest and the manifest, this magnificent majestic aloofness of Brahman, Purusha, out of whose being the Cosmos emerges, the infinite dance of matter and its energies. I do not produce it and yet it happens. If you understand this, then let that understanding happen in your daily living.'

You have the physical body, matter, with various energies of specific organs. You have the energy of time and space, you have the energy of earth in your bone structure, you have the energy of water in your blood, the energy of the sun in your sight, the energy of wind in your audition. You have all those energies of matter; the Cosmic matter individuated in your form, in human individuals.

The interaction of these energies in your body, with the same energies outside of your body, takes place because the energies in your body are attracted towards the same energies, their counterpart in nature. Attraction, perception, contact, interaction and you call it your action. It is not your action. It is the appetite in your body that demands food and receives the appetite. You are not eating.

Look at this beautiful secret that Sri Krishna is revealing. The body demands complete rest and the faculty of sleep, the ever virgin sleep descends upon your body, it creates an inner compulsion, you only lie down. 'As matter in nature contains my creativity, your body also contains this creativity.'

I hope you have observed, that there is nothing in matter that does not have healing powers, creative powers. Clay can heal you, water can heal any impurities, any imbalances. Chemical imbalances, neurological imbalances are corrected by the sun, the moon, water, earth, the sea. The same creative and healing energies are contained in your body.

In outer matter mind is subconscious, it is mute. But in your body, the mind is eloquent; it has created words, languages. So, in the mental body is the energy of thought, ideation, of imagination, calculation, energy of memory. There is a constant interaction between the energies in the consciousness, the *samskaras*, and the energies in your body. You may conduct them and manifest the concealed harmony in them. You are not the creator of harmony, but by conducting the mental and the physical in an orderly way, you may allow the inner harmony to express itself. You are not the doer.

The law of *karma* goes on, because energy cannot be idle. The interaction of energy and the result of the interaction are called *karma*, whether taking place in Cosmic matter, the universal *karma*, or in individual *karma*, through the interaction between the mental body, the physical body and outer nature. It is a beautiful triangle in which you are caught and which is the frame of your existence in which you have to live.

I wonder if you are aware that Tantra Yoga has the triangle as a symbol, showing the human body in various triangles. As the Mantra Yoga speaks through a circle and indicates the wholeness of life through a circle and the cyclical movement in nature, *tantra* talks about this triangle, through individual matter, Cosmic matter and Brahman, also called Purusha, Ishvara, or the Lord.

Realize that the interaction of energies is bound to go on. The past in you, the *samskaras* in you, the conditioning in you and the energies in your body, are going to interact, act upon each other. Their interaction sometimes may result in something beneficial to others, sometimes in something harmful to others. If you find that out of the interaction of your mind, body and nature something beneficial has come about, do not appropriate it and say: it is my good action. Don't feel that it is your good action. It has happened through you; you are the opportunity, you are the individuated life, maybe the springboard for it to happen. It is a law of Life, a principle of Life.

Maybe, something harmful, something evil takes place through this interaction, then you have to be alert and find out, where things have gone wrong. The goodness of your action indicates that somehow you have arrived at a point of harmony with the universal Life, with the Cosmic energies. And the harmful result indicates that somewhere you have missed that; some disorder, some disharmony, some impurity has come up, some imbalance has caused it. This alternated expression of good and evil, through you, is for your learning.

If evil takes place through you, don't go on creating self-pity and lapse into melancholia, into depressive psychosis: 'so much evil has happened, I am a cruel person, I am this, I am that.' Don't do that. This is an opportunity for you to discover why the imbalance has taken place. It is an opportunity for learning.

If the evil gets expressed, something is wrong somewhere. Find that out, correct it. And if something good happens, the point of rhythm, of harmony, has somehow been reached through you. Rejoice. But there is nothing to get attached to, neither to the good nor to the bad actions that happen through you.

Krishna is showing the path of unattachment, of renunciation, the inner *sannyasa*. As Brahman remains unconcerned, uninvolved, unattached on the Cosmic level, the individual intelligence should remain uninvolved and unattached.

The responsibility is to keep the physical frame pure, clean, wash out the toxins, the imbalances, the impurities, through *yama*, *niyama*, *asana*, *pranayama* etc. And keep the mental frame pure through *dharana*, *dhyana*, *samadhi*. If at all there is anything that one can do, one can correct the imbalances, wash out the impurities.

Then Life universal, in you, expresses itself, which is pristine splendour. Your body and mind become resplendent with that. Hatha Yoga gives you longevity of life, proportionate body and the glow of health. Raja Yoga gives you the glow of peace, the glow of *samadhi*, the surrender of matter to Purusha.

If it has been possible for me to put this point clearly across, then let us proceed. We have reached verses twelve and thirteen. The union with Purusha, that is Brahman in Sankhya Yoga and Dhyana Yoga.

Vedanta remains abstract, because it is based on such ideas as: 'I am Brahman', 'The whole world is Brahman'. They remain ideas or theories for the intellect. The brain catches that, gets intoxicated with those ideas: 'I am not the limited body, I am the unlimited Brahman'. It is an abstraction. And because that intellectual identification with an abstract idea makes you not only ignore *prakriti*, that is your body and matter outside in nature, or ignore society, not only that, but you reject matter, your treatment and handling of the physical frame is not one of reverence.

The same with the mind. You try to give it clutches. You give it some pattern to follow; you give it a code of conduct etc. Matter is not only ignored, but it is nearly rejected. No reverence for it, no acceptance of it, no love for it. And you withdraw because if you are Brahman, you are not responsible to society, you have no responsibility towards the family. As if the imaginary union, through intellectual identification with an idea, gives you moral authority to do all this. It is an abstract union; it is an abstraction generating withdrawal, irreverence etc.

In Bhakti Yoga it becomes union through emotion, imposing relationships of father/mother, child/husband, lover/beloved, whatever. There are so many varieties of Bhakti Yoga in India. It is obsession of the emotions, with an idea of relationship. There it was an abstract idea, here it is a relationship which is imagined, imposed and you get obsessed. Again the balance of Life, through the treatment of the physical and mental frame, is not there.

Through Raja Yoga there is no suffering of any kind, be it from ignorance, attachment, aversion, etc. Living without mental suffering is the essence of Raja Yoga. Physical pain and sicknesses will be there, but psychological suffering of attachment, infatuation, obsession, irreverence, hatred, all that is not there.

Raja Yoga says that, when neither the *prakriti* nor the Purusha are neglected, neither is rejected and you create a new equilibrium in your body and mind, (a new equilibrium in your body through Hatha Yoga and a new equilibrium in the mental frame through meditation etc.), then the consciousness is lifted up.

It is no more a game of abstract ideas, it is no more emotional imposition. It is a concrete life. A new equilibrium, a new balance through purification, through refinement of the physical and mental frame has been generated.

Consciousness gets lifted up, not academically, not theoretically. It is not a game that you play with yourself, it is not self-hypnosis. The union takes place between the individual consciousness and the supra-mental consciousness or transcendental consciousness. The union that takes place in individuated consciousness, between *jiva* and Ishvara, the transcendental principle, becomes a fact. It does not remain an idea, or an emotional obsession. The uplift can be noticed in the life of a Raja Yogi.

The refinement of the physical and the mental frame, the uplifted consciousness getting united with the supra-mental or transcendental consciousness, that union generates what we call *ananda* or bliss. In the life of an individual there is the manifestation of *sat-chit-ananda*. The awareness of the transcendental principle of intelligence is *sat*. The handling of the past conditionings is *chit*. The handling of the physical frame or conditionings is also *chit*, because it is matter. *Sat-chit-ananda*, the resplendent characteristics of sovereign intelligence, manifest in the human body.

Sri Krishna says: 'This is what has happened in my life. People call me an incarnation, they call me divine. But you are also capable of divine action. Matter, purified and refined, expresses the divine quality concealed in it, the immanence of that supreme intelligence in you. And divine action, action, which is free from attachment, free of involvement, action which is spontaneous and effortless, allows that interaction to happen. You allow that *karma* to happen in the field of your body and mind. That becomes a divine *karma*. Arjuna, you are also capable of this divine *karma*; every individual is.'

Raja Yoga gives an assurance to all human beings, like you and me, that this ascending path of light, this upward path towards the supreme intelligence, is within the reach of everyone. It is not just for the privileged or the chosen few.

The urge to learn and discover and the awareness of the indestructible Life around you, when you see this, that the cycle of Life goes on, then you become aware that Life is a cycle of emergence and merging back. Then you do not pay undue importance to birth and death. Like the ripples on water are generated and merge back into the water, as the rays of the sun merge back into the sun, so also species emerge out of matter and merge back when their potential is exhausted.

Then you do not pay undue importance to what happens through you, claiming it to be yours, not getting despondent because something goes wrong with you, through you. If you follow the upward path of refinement, purification, harmonization of energies, the rest follows.

Verses nineteen and twenty explain that, if the awareness of Ishvara, Brahman, the sovereign transcendental principle of intelligence, if the awareness is there like an undercurrent in everything that you do, you do not have to pronounce it verbally, you do not have to create any ritual out of it. If the awareness is there, (you are aware of your name, of the country, the place to which you belong, you do not have to be conscious of it, you do not have to talk about it, inwardly the awareness is an undercurrent in your consciousness of who you are, what you are, where your home is, who are the members of your family, all that is there unmanifest but as an undercurrent in consciousness), in the same way, if there is an undercurrent of awareness that you emanate from the Purusha, from that sovereign intelligence, the matter in your body and the matter in nature originate from that source, if you are aware of that, then that awareness is the bridge between matter and spirit.

The awareness is the bridge between the manifest and the unmanifest. That awareness functions like a link. Then you are never lonely, you are never afraid.

If the awareness is not there, then you go through the downward path of darkness, indicating the path of mental suffering. One is the path of light, where there is no psychological suffering, and the other is the path of darkness, the path of attachment and identification with matter, with mind. 'You have to choose Arjuna, between the path of light and the path of darkness.'

One more point. In Raja Yoga there is one danger. As the excellences have been pointed out, now Sri Krishna wants to warn Arjuna. There is the temptation in Hatha Yoga, through *kundalini* (awakening of psycho-physical powers, and using those powers for occult experiences), the temptation to indulge in those powers. The pleasure of those powers is there.

In Karma Yoga there is the temptation to be admired by others, nearly to be worshipped or looked upon as a hero or a leader, or the temptation to indulge in the feeling of respectability in society, among the people. That temptation is there.

And in Bhakti Yoga there is the temptation of indulging in the intoxication of music, dance, rituals. When you chant *mantras*, it creates a kind of intoxication for the nervous system, for the chemical system and you love that intoxication, you indulge in it. And there are pitfalls in other *yogas*.

In the same way, when the physical activities are surrendered through total relaxation and mental activities are surrendered through silence or meditation, and when the consciousness is lifted up to the dimension of *samadhi*, which is beyond the waking, dream and sleep consciousness, a different dimension altogether, when the consciousness gets transported into that dimension, in the beginning, when you have touched that point of *samadhi*, it has also an intoxicating effect, because it results in trance.

You know what trance is? It is not your normal consciousness. It is a kind of unusual consciousness, because the mental orbit, the known, the conditioned mind, the thought structure, has become inoperative. You have been lifted up into a different dimension.

But the energies in that dimension have not yet released themselves. They have not been activated, they have not been mobilized, they have not percolated right down to the sentient level. The dynamic energies are there. And when the dimension of *samadhi* is touched, obviously the whole body, the physical frame and the neuro-chemical system get dazed. Trance is a kind of daze for the neuro-chemical system and it has pleasure also.

So, there is a temptation of becoming very fond of being in that no-man's land. As salt or sugar melts into water, the individual consciousness has disappeared. It has not yet melted, but it has disappeared, it is no more operative.

And in that trance, when the movement of unconditioned energies takes place and unknown powers become operative in your body, you see the history of a human being in his face, you see the so-called future. You see the thought movement in another person, without he or she opening their mouth. You can see from a distance, from one hundred, two hundred miles. You have clairvoyance, clairaudience. You may touch a sick person and he may get cured.

The manifestation of unconditioned energies, when they begin to operate in the state of trance, that phase is a dangerous phase. People begin to notice the extraordinary nature of energies in your body, the glow, the magnetic attraction towards you. 'Arjuna, that is the danger, the phase of trance; the whole human unconscious gets exposed to you, and you can talk about it to people. So that phase of trance has to be assimilated quietly.'

It is not to be expressed, used, utilized. Otherwise, a person gets stuck up in trance, the by-product of *samadhi*, and misses the real bliss of *samadhi*. The by-product becomes very attractive. That is why you will appreciate the importance of the *sutra*: 'humility is very necessary when the consciousness is surrendered to the mighty power concealed in Brahman or Purusha.'

You remember, we began the chapter by saying that the whole universe is a sacrificial act, it is a movement of sacrifice. If all the actions are done in the attitude of sacrifice and if this upliftment is looked upon as the result of the grace of the divine and not your own attainment, not your own achievement, if that humility of surrender is there, if either the sharpness of awareness or the humility of surrender, either the clarity of awareness, the light of awareness or the humility of surrender is there, then one passes through this last obstacle of the phase of trance.

If you want to indulge in the pleasure of the trance, then you will come back downwards, to the path of darkness. You will come back to the frame of mortality. Then the identification with the physical brain, with the thought structure, will come back, will become operative. It is the source of misery, of death. Here, the word 'death' is used figuratively. It represents the realm of mortality, where you suffer and the agony, the pain, goes on sucking your vital energies. It is like a gradual suicide.

The upward path is the ascent, the awareness of the all-pervading Brahman, the reverence for matter and the energies contained in it and the humility to allow those energies and the sovereign intelligence to express themselves through you.

When you have entered that dwelling place, you live where your mind is. You are what the quality of your consciousness is, not only the physical frame. That is the outer sheath, but you are what the quality of your consciousness is. You are what your mind is, where your mind is. If your mind has found out the dwelling place, the awareness of the supreme Brahman or Purusha, then there is an end to mortality, there is an end to death.

Krishna says to Arjuna: 'you have reached the supreme abode; it is my abode, that is where I live. I live in that realm of immortality, the realm of awareness. There the sun of awareness is shining bright. I live there. And if you come there, Arjuna, there is no going back to the path of darkness anymore.'

We are aware that the dialogue between Sri Krishna and Arjuna has taken place on the battleground of Kurukshetra. Arjuna had wanted to escape from the responsibility and commitment of fighting against the Kauravas. Not only had he mentally prepared himself to fight the Kauravas, he had also collected a huge army for the purpose and had requested Sri Krishna to help him in fighting back. But when he arrives at the battleground, he is overcome by depression and frustration and he wants to escape.

The first chapter of the *Gita* is full of meaningless talk by Arjuna, where he tries to explain, to Krishna, how wars and violence and bloodshed are very disastrous to the human species and the world.

It is not only that it happens to Arjuna; everyone one of us wants to escape sometime or other, in our life, from the commitments that we have made with ourselves and others, on the physical, mental and intellectual level. We want to escape from the responsibility of fulfilling the commitments. And, therefore, Sri Krishna starts expounding *Brahma-vidya* and *yoga shastra* to his very dear friend and student Arjuna.

He describes, how the whole of Life is a *yoga*, is an effort to recognize the union of spirit and matter. And after intellectually recognizing it, to realize it. Recognition is abstract, realization is concrete. The realization takes place in the gross and subtle matter, recognition is only a cerebral acceptance of the fact. Sri Krishna wants Arjuna to be reborn as a *yogi*. 'Arjuna, grow into the state of *yoga*, get reborn out of yourself.' For getting reborn or growing into the state of *yoga*, it seems to me, that three factors are inevitable, not only necessary, but they are inevitable.

First, the intellectual knowledge and recognition of the infinity and eternity of Life and the dynamism of Life as a fact, which can be touched by the senses, grasped by the brain and experienced by the heart. So, intellectual knowledge, with the help of words and recognition of the dynamism of that infinity and eternity, at the sensual and mental level. The absoluteness of the infinity and eternity of Life is a must for the study of *yoga*.

The second factor is the intellectual understanding and recognition of the power of this truth, the absolute truth of Life, the absolute truth of the eternity and infinity of Life. How does that infinity and eternity operate, how does that dynamic principle of Chaitanya, of Purusha, of Brahman operate?

The infinity and eternity of Purusha, in operation, generates what you call Cosmic matter. In order to manifest that Life eternal is omniscient, omnipotent and omnipresent, to manifest its characteristics, it blows out space. For unless there is an emptiness of space, how do you prove that you are omnipotent and omnipresent? Omnipresent means simultaneously present everywhere. But that everywhere has to be manifested first. Space is the first proof of the operation of the infinity and eternity of Purusha, Brahman or Chaitanya.

Into the space is blown the *prana shakti* (the energy of *prana*). While dynamism, omniscience and omnipotence are proved by the emptiness of space, the dynamism of that eternity, that principle of intelligence is indicated and proved by the movement of *prana*, *vayu* (wind).

The movement of *vayu* in the emptiness of space generates *agni*, fire. From the movement of *prana*, in the emptiness of space, issues forth what you call *agni*, the principle of fire. *Prana* is *agni*. But *agni* is concealed in *prana*, and that is manifested.

The movement of *agni* and *vayu*, the principle of fire and dynamism of *prana*, generates water, *apa*. And the interaction between water, fire and *prana*, in the emptiness of space, generates *prithvi*, the solidification of the energies contained in space. *Akasha, vayu, prana, agni* and water, are solidified and you call it *prithvi* or earth.

The operation of the absolute truth, of the dynamism, infinity and eternity of Purusha, the Lord, Ishvara, Brahman, whatever term you use, from that, in operation, has issued forth Cosmic matter. It is still un-individuated, but now you have seen the omniscience, the omnipotence and omnipresence of that Chaitanya, of that Purusha, of that eternal Life. This is the second factor that has to be understood, recognized and realized, through perception, personal perception, personal encounter at the sensual and cerebral level. This can be recognized and realized.

And the third factor is the individuated matter, which is called objects, which is called species. You and I are the third factor, the individuated Cosmic matter, individuated Purusha, Chaitanya or Brahman.

Krishna explains this to Arjuna, in the second chapter on Sankhya Yoga, which is on intellectual knowledge. But this intellectual knowledge, intellectual recognition and even limited realization, partial realization at the sensual and mental level, does not result in a new birth. That knowledge, that recognition, that partial limited realization, the flashes of reality through perception, through experiences, does not transform or transmute the physical frame. It does not transform the energies contained in the mental frame. That is why Hatha Yoga and Raja Yoga become necessary.

There, re-organization of energies contained in the physical body, re-arrangement and re-conditioning of energies contained in consciousness, become necessary. The re-arrangement and re-organization of the energies contained in the physical frame can be done through Hatha Yoga. But the re-arranging, re-organizing of the mental energies, so that those energies are transformed into new energies, so that those mental energies shed all the limitations and conditionings imposed upon them, is not attained through Hatha Yoga alone, even if you do *dharana*, the study of concentration, and contemplation. That is why, one has to proceed with Raja Yoga.

Now, the mental energies have a monitor, called the ego, the I, the sense of me, that assumes the role of a cohesive principle, keeping the energies of gross matter, the physical frame and the subtle matter, the mind, under its control.

The I-consciousness, the ego-consciousness, wants to assume the role of omniscient, omnipresent, omnipotent Brahman, Purusha, Chaitanya. So, it tries its level best to control, to regulate, to mould. But the physical frame and the mental frame have an arrangement of energies, which do not begin with your birth.

You are the product of thousands of years of evolution. Evolution in nature and evolution in the human species. You are the product of all that. So, the energies and the momentum are very ancient and the ego, with the help of consciousness, finds, though it tries again and again, that the energies defy its governance. It rebels. The physical frame and the mental frame rebel and revolt against the control, the regulation, the direction of the I-consciousness, the me.

Something drastic has to be resorted to, in order that these energies get oriented towards a new life, get released from the hold of the past on them, because we are a bundle of physical and mental patterned habits, structures of habits. That is what we are, physically and mentally. And some habits are very rigid, they don't like to change. Those energies like to flow in the direction that they have been trained into, hammered into, forced into.

So, not intellectual effort, not emotional struggle, not cruelty with the physical frame of repression, suppression, denial, rejection, negation. All that is unscientific. Spirituality is a science of Life. Everything has to be gone through scientifically, with a scientific attitude, with a scientific temperament, a scientific way of functioning. Some drastic way has become necessary, has become inevitable. And what can that be?

That is the theme of the last part of the ninth chapter. Sri Krishna was not only a friend of Arjuna, not only a person with a transmuted and transformed physical and mental frame. He was also a teacher par excellence, who knew the psychology of human beings. After all, *yoga* is practical psychology. We are dealing with verses twenty-two to thirty-one.

Look at the beauty of his teachings. Sri Krishna says to Arjuna: 'the physical and the mental frame have been trained to grasp things, to grasp them for sensation, for experiences. This acquisitiveness is rooted very deep into the physical and the mental frame. Why not begin by educating the physical and the mental frame, to reverse the process from grasping to giving?' Before the whole Life can be a sacrifice consecrated to the divine, before it can become a holistic sacrifice, let us begin at the very beginning, educate the body and the mind to give instead of grasp. If it grasps, at least let it part with a part of what it grasps.

And a beautiful verse comes: 'Arjuna, if a person offers a leaf, a fruit, even a little water, to the Lord, it is a beginning; you are giving something which you consider your own, you are parting with it. Start giving, and if you cannot give it in the name of the Lord, the divine, which is invisible, you can offer it to your teacher, you can offer it to the needy in society, learn to offer, learn to give.'

Your physical frame is trained to exert itself only for acquiring, obtaining, achieving. Why not educate your physical frame to serve others? Give and offer and then serve through your action. Why should all actions be self-centred? Why should they not be offered as an offering to the divine?

Do service to the needy, as if offering it to the Lord. Not that you are obliging a sick person by serving him or her, a hungry person, by giving food. You are not giving something, you are not obliging, you are serving the Lord, the invisible, who is omniscient and omnipresent in everything, in every being, in everyone.

Service through Karma Yoga, offering your actions, your money, your knowledge to others. But start with giving and parting, rather than acquiring, absorbing, holding on, all the time. Four or five verses are spent in describing, how this sharing, this offering, this sacrifice, can take place, gradually, step by step, because you have to educate.

Unless the physical and the mental frame are educated on the periphery to give and to share, to sacrifice and to offer, the last offering, that of the ego-consciousness, will not come. Because the ego is the centre, the monitor, much deeper than the other habits, the last offering, the consciousness that you have a separate entity and identity and you are somebody, something of great importance in the universe, that idea of separateness, that idea of being an entity, that will be your last offering. To let the individual consciousness merge into the universal consciousness, through meditation, is the last offering.

Before that, there is a long way that you have to go. Otherwise your intellectual recognition of the permeation of Purusha in *prakriti*, or Chaitanya in matter, will not be lived. Your frame will not accept that the divine is in everyone and in everything. The physical frame will not accept this, because it is trained to work for its own preservation, its own procreation, the survival instinct, the instinct for sustaining and preserving the physical body, the mental body. That is the conditioning, that is the culture. It is a self-culture, not a spiritual culture.

'So Arjuna, start educating by offering, giving, serving, parting with your acquisitions.' That has to be gone through, otherwise the physical frame may not cooperate with you. Then you start studying Raja Yoga. The mental frame may not cooperate with you, it can put up obstacles and hurdles in the path of the ascent, the upward voyage, following the path of light.

Secondly, the physical and the mental frame does not want to exert itself, unless it is assured of some benefit to itself which can be measured, which can be shown to others, which can be compared. So, after acquisition and ownership comes the instinct of comparing, measuring, evaluating, saying: 'I have this'; not only money, a house, family and children, but 'I have knowledge, experience, extra-sensory experiences, occult powers', if not material powers. How do you counteract this tendency of sustaining the separateness? Through acquisition of knowledge and experience? No.

Through conscious surrender, educating the mental frame in humility. Humility will come through a recognition, that the whole matter out of which you have the individuated body, has emanated from the invisible, the infinite, the eternal Life. You cannot exist outside that Purusha, Brahman, Chaitanya. You cannot be isolated, you cannot be separated.

So, before you utter a word, remember that speech is possible due to the *prana*, which has emanated out of space, which has originated in Purusha. When you take your meal, you are partaking of the compassion of Brahman, the compassion of the Lord supreme, the divine. Because food, the crops, the vegetables, the fruit, are grown in the earth and the being of earth has come out of water, fire, *prana*, space, out of the ultimate source of Purusha. All your existence is due to that, all your activities and movements are due to that. Why not dedicate consciously every activity, every movement of yours, to the Lord? And how do you dedicate?

Be aware of it. Awareness is the expression of that inner psychological dedication to the divine. Otherwise, the mental frame will be dedicated, devoted, to its own habit patterns. It will be devoted and dedicated to the physical frame and the physical frame to its past, its conditioning, and the mental frame to its conditioning. Somewhere it will be dedicated.

In order that the I-consciousness can be a steady centre, it needs to gravitate around something. Either it will be dedicated to that horizontal gravitation around the past, around the habits, it will be devoted there. Or its dedication can be upward, ascending, vertical.

Raja Yoga is the secret of vertical dedication and devotion, because you are offering to that which is all permeating. Your senses cannot see it, your mind cannot reach it, words cannot reach it. Mind tries its level best but has to turn back, without touching it. Words cannot touch it. It is only the emptiness of space that can be the ground for the revelation of Chaitanya. Silence, the emptiness of consciousness, is the only field where the revelation can take place.

The mind, the word and the physical senses, cannot reach that. It is not an individuated specific object, or an individual, whom you can claim to be your own. Horizontally, it is not perceptible. Vertically, through the feel of it. Understanding can be with the help of words, but the feel has got to be with your sensitivity. It is the sensitivity that rises upward, vertically, where words cannot reach and mind cannot reach. The sensitivity, the perceptive sensitivity, which is intelligence, can reach, because intelligence is subtle. Intellect is the faculty of the brain, but intelligence is sensitivity, it is the energy of emptiness, the energy of silence.

You have to begin with the gross. Take the physical frame to part with, to share, to give, to serve. Then come to the mental frame. Educate the mental frame to change the point of devotion and dedication. Instead of being devoted to your own thoughts, your reactions, your likes, your dislikes, change the point of devotion and dedication, from the I and the me to the it, the he, the she, whatever you call the Lord, whatever you call the source of creation, intelligence.

Change the point of dedication, that is the drastic thing Krishna talks about. This conscious dedication, this determination that one's life should be a consecration, so that all the physical and mental movements are now an offering to the divine, a consecration to the divine, an offering to the Cosmic Life, an offering to the omnipotent, omnipresent omniscient god. This point of changed dedication releases an energy of awareness, which is a very rarefied energy.

Thought is matter, the physical body is gross matter, mind and thought are subtle matter. The energy, the velocity, the colour of thought, all this has been measured, discriminated. Books have been written about it by psychologists and scientists. But silence cannot be measured, love cannot be measured. This rarefied energy, which was concealed in the wholeness of silence, this energy of intelligence is immeasurable.

The *prana shakti* that is permeating the whole Cosmos is immeasurable. When you breathe in, in the inhaling process, you are not only breathing in wind, *vayu*, you are inhaling the Cosmic *prana*. Otherwise *pranayama* would just be gymnastics. So *prana shakti* is immeasurable. In the same way the rarefied energy of intelligence, which is perceptive sensitivity, which is called *prajna* in the Vedas, the Upanishads, the *Gita* and the Brahma Sutras, is capable of ascent, of vertical movement.

It can dissociate itself from the physical frame, from the water element, that is the blood circulation in your body, from the *prana shakti* in your body. It can dissociate itself from all these and get united with the unlimited, the immeasurable, the all-pervading. This is the last sacrifice or consecration, doing everything for the sake of the divine, as an offering to the divine. Every movement of your life, the act of living itself becomes an offering to the divine.

If this happens, then moving from the horizontal to the vertical, not sacrificing the one for the other, but coordinating the two; the horizontal at the sensual level and the vertical at the mental level. Then this upward ascending movement of the energy of intelligence in you, permeates your whole body. Please do see this.

The body, like the earth, has organic intelligence. It tells you when to eat, how much to eat, when to sleep, how much to sleep. Listen to that intelligence and do not get victimized by the past, the habits, the traditions, the conventions, the beliefs, the superstitions. If you are not ruled by that (the past) and you listen to the body, it tells you what it needs, what are the deficiencies in your body, when to give it proteins, minerals, provide the vitamins, etc.

The human body is a manifestation of the Cosmic reality. The more you understand the complexity of your physical body and the miracle of its movement inside, its power of analysing, converting energies, transmuting energies, when you watch that, the more you are stunned, because the human body is such a miracle, as far as I can see it.

So, the physical movement, consecrated to the divine, requires that you keep the body free of all impurities, because it is an offering to the Lord. How can you overload it with food or underfeed it, how can you over-sleep it or not allow the proper sleep to it, how can you misuse speech, which is a divine gift, by abusing it, how can you use the faculty of thinking, imagining, remembering unwarrantedly?

There is a *sutra* that says that purification is the only energizing principle in our life. Survival instinct and sustenance instinct, which were imprisoned in exclusive acquisition, are set free of it, so that survival and sustenance are for purification of the body, which becomes a proper offering to the Lord. The same with the mental frame, the mental body; the I-consciousness, the ego-consciousness, it becomes concerned about the purity of its movement.

I am not using the term purification in any ethical or moral sense. I am using it for a scientific orderliness, a re-arranging, a re-organization of energies. Harmonization of energies is the purpose of science. Order is nothing but harmonized energies functioning smoothly.

The physical and the mental body of ours become an instrument in the hands of the Lord and the mundane actions have the flavour of divinity. *Yoga* is a science of divinizing what is material, divinization of human life. Not running away from the human to so-called abstract spirituality, but here and now allowing the divine to express itself, as it expresses itself in Cosmic matter, in the *mula prakriti*, allow that to express itself in this *prakriti* also (the human body and mind). This Raja Yoga is so fascinating, this secret sovereign path of ascendance to the path of light, from where there is no lapsing back into the path of misery and darkness.

In Life, in the Cosmic Life, the dance of the imperishable and perishable, the eternal, the infinite and the finite and limited, the timeless and the time-bound, that dance is going on. The dance of emergence and dissolution goes on. In the same way, in the life of an individual who has learned the secret of purifying gross matter, of refining the mental frame and nearly divinizing them or transforming them as a proper instrument for the divine supreme to express itself, the same dance goes on between the perishable and the imperishable.

One has to learn the last point in chapter nine, that once you have transcended the intellectual understanding or intellectual recognition, through the awakening of intelligence, which is an invisible bridge that fits the gap between the unmanifest and the manifest in your body, once that bridge is built, it is never dismantled, it cannot get destroyed. Though you dwell in the manifest body of yours, you dwell also in the unmanifest source of creation.

Krishna's teacher was a sage called Aghora, and his teacher was a sage called Angirasa. Krishna points out to Arjuna: 'I have learned this secret of being in the imperishable, the eternal, the infinite, the divine and being in the perishable, the limited, the mortal, simultaneously, from my teachers. Not only when I sleep, during profound sleep, do I get transported by consciousness into the infinity. No, no, even while living in the waking hours, whatever I do, there is the simultaneity of my dwelling. I dwell in the infinite and function in the finite. My consciousness, my awareness is in the divine, the eternity, the Brahman. I am in the source, with the source of creation, with the Purusha, the Brahman, and I am with the *prakriti*. Arjuna, you too can learn this art of being simultaneously in the unmanifest and the manifest.'

If any of you has studied the Buddhist philosophy, there too is this living at the source of intelligence. And here, in the *Gita*, the Vedas and the Upanishads, you have also the individual permeated by *prajna*, intelligence. The physical energies are limited by our form, mental energies are limited by our habit structure. But this energy of *prajna*, intelligence, born of the silence of meditation, is limitless, is immeasurable, is infinite.

Our physical and mental frame becomes the abode of the dwelling place of *prajna* or intelligence. That is called transformation. What people call emancipation, transformation, liberation, *moksha* is nothing but a person being filled with that intelligence, which is not attached, dedicated or devoted to the physical biological body, which is not attached, devoted, identified, dedicated to the mental body, which is constituted of the past, of conditionings, of samskaras, but which is dedicated and devoted only to Brahman.

'Arjuna, then you have arrived at the home in which I dwell, from which there is no going back, no lapsing back.'

This is the most secret Raja Yoga, the path of the imperishable light. And thus ends the ninth chapter, the sovereign path of creating the balance between the awareness of the imperishable and the equilibrium in the perishable *prakriti*. You neither ignore matter nor get obsessed with spirit, nor do you get obsessed by matter and ignore spirit, but you create a new equilibrium between the relationship of the two, the functioning of the two. This new equanimity, this new equilibrium is called the essence of *yoga* which we have seen in the second chapter: 'equanimity inner and outer is the essence of *yoga*.'

CHAPTER X

YOGA OF DIVINE MANIFESTATION

There is this *mantra*: 'From the absolute transcendental divinity originate millions of universes and yet nothing is detracted from the wholeness, the perception, the completeness of that divinity. The universes issuing forth or emanating of that divinity are also complete. They are manifestations of organic wholeness, so they are also *purna* (whole).' If this *mantra* is understood and one is aware of it, then we can begin our study of the tenth chapter.

This chapter is the source of Vaishnavism, they who follow the path of devotion to God as Vishnu. This includes the Hare Krishna movement, or the Vaishnava cult of studying *yoga*. This cult still exists, with all its various branches. The personification of the transcendental reality is called incarnation or *avatar* in India. But the idea of reality or divinity getting personified or embodied in a human form is not the exclusive privilege of the Hindu society and their philosophy.

There are Christians who look upon Jesus as the personification of the transcendental reality and they take the words of Jesus as the sanction for their fate, their redemption. 'I and my father are one', 'it is only through me that you can approach the father', and so on. There are so many simple elegant sentences of that Prince of love and forgiveness. He was looked upon as the embodiment of reality, of divinity, as God on earth.

Gautama is looked upon as the personification of *nirvana* by Buddhists. The exponent of the Jain philosophy is looked upon as such an embodiment and the Ten Gurus of the Sikh community, starting from Nanaka, are looked upon as such personification. I am just giving you instances.

In the tenth chapter, Sri Krishna, in the dialogue with Arjuna, represents the transcendental divinity and he talks about himself in the first person. He uses the term I: 'I am the source of everything manifest and unmanifest, I am immanent and yet I am transcendent.' All the devotees in India have built temples of Krishna, worship Krishna as the Lord, the incarnation, the embodiment, the personification of that Lord. It does not remain an all-embracing, all-inclusive perception, but it becomes an exclusive sect. As soon as you accept the theory of the personification of reality, you proceed towards an exclusive path.

One can look upon Sri Krishna and what he says in chapter ten, eleven and twelve, to a great extent as a representative of the divinity, the exponent of that non-personal absolute wholeness. Or one can look upon him as the personification. It is up to the person who studies the *Gita*, because in India, for attaining perfection, for studying *yoga*, not only one rigid path is recommended.

There are as many paths as there are individuals. Every individual can carve a path for himself or herself, as for one's inclinations, aesthetical taste, cultural upbringing. One can worship *prakriti*. One can worship Purusha and renounce the world. One can harness all the energies towards selfless action in the service of mankind, call it Karma Yoga and make it an instrument of perfecting your physical and mental frame. Or one can enter the path of meditation and let the whole mind and its movements come to an end. There are so many paths.

This can be confusing to non-Indians. For how can there be people in India, where there has been Vedanta, the Vedas, the Upanishads, who worship deities, trees, animals like cows? Why do they do so? Because they are looking for a path for perfection. And here the ancient Indians say that there cannot be one rigid path. The direction would be one, the object of aspiration would be one, but the paths would be various.

The chapter begins with Sri Krishna saying to Arjuna: 'look, Arjuna, you are a very dear friend of mine, I am going to share with you the secret of my being.' Either you can take these words referring to the son of Vasudeva, Sri Krishna in that human body, or you can interpret these words as an exposition of an approach to Life. He says: 'I am going to reveal to you the secret of my being.' What is that secret?

Second verse: 'I am the source of all that is in the Cosmos, I am the source of manyness in the Cosmos.' Just look at the words: 'I, the one, the unique, the incomparable, the absolute, I am the source of manyness. The manyness of matter, the manyness of manifested matter, is contained in me. The manyness, the manifestations are born of me.' So the one is the source of the many. The oneness of Life, the organic wholeness of Life, which is unmanifest, is the source of the manyness, the manifest-ness of Cosmos. 'This is the secret of my being.' says Krishna.

And then he says: 'look at the splendour, the richness of the state of *yoga* in which I, the Cosmic Life exist.' The whole Life is in a state of natural *yoga*, the harmony, the order, the intelligence, the cohesion of Cosmic existence. So, all Life is in a state of natural *yoga* but it is not conscious of itself. That state of *yoga* is not self-aware. It is given to the human race to manifest the self-awareness of the state of *yoga*, which exists already in matter, in the Cosmos, in all the universes. Have we understood the meaning?

'I am the source, I, the unmanifest wholeness, I, the unmanifest organic perfection, homogeneity, indivisibility, out of me issues forth the manyness, millions of universes and they don't detract anything of me, Arjuna.

Because in the manifest nature of my being I retain the inexhaustible potential of creativity. I am divine because there is the inexhaustible potential of creativity. Universes come and go, species inhabit the Cosmos and disappear, and yet the creative energy, the virginity of that energy, has the capacity to express itself in still fresh forms, fresh permutations and combinations of matter. It is retained in me because of the state of *yoga*.'

The unmanifest and the manifest join together in a majestic equilibrium, the one appears to be many, it takes the appearance of the many and yet retains its oneness. How does it do that? We come to the third verse. Krishna says:

'Look, my creative energy gets reflected in every expression of matter.'

You must have observed the reflection of the sun in water, in a river or pond. If you sit by the side of a lake or a small pond and you watch the reflection of the sun in the water, it is not only the circular form of the sun that is reflected, but the water gets heated, it becomes warm. If the moon (*soma* or the principle of coolness) is reflected in the water at night, the water imbibes that coolness along with the reflection. If you take a piece of glass and hold it under a ray of the sun, the sun will be reflected in it, the glass will absorb the energy of heat and it can also transmit the energy of the sun, transmit it through a prism, which can set a piece of paper or wood on fire.

I am not going into the immaculate scientific expressions of this poetic dialogue that is the *Gita*. Sri Krishna says: 'my energy of wholeness, my energy of creativity, my energy of indivisibility, my energy of dynamism, all that gets reflected in every material expression.' What does that mean?

That implies, does it not, that 'I permeate the Cosmos. They are not only issuing forth, they are not only my manifestations, they are not separate from me. Though they originate in me, of me, and become multifarious expressions in matter, I permeate them, I am there, I am immanent in every material expression, in rocks, in atoms, protons, electrons, neutrons, in the form of energy. I am there in the quantum of energy contained in an atom, in an electron. I am there in clay. That is why there is fertility in the earth. I am there in water, that is why it not only cleanses your body, but it re-vitalizes and re-energizes you. I am there in the emptiness of space. That is why, when you breathe in empty space, standing under the skies, you feel refreshed.'

So he says: 'they are originated of me, they partake of my substance, my energies are reflected in them, therefore, I am immanent in the Cosmos though I am transcendental, though I retain my inexhaustible potential, though I retain my absoluteness, my indivisibility. Yet, I appear as many. The material expressions are not fragments of me, please look at that.'

Now, we are proceeding to the fourth and fifth verse. He says: 'they are not fragments of me, parts of me.' There is a difference between a part of a totality and an emanation of the wholeness. You can assemble parts of a bicycle and build up the structure of a bicycle, you can collect parts for an aeroplane, a computer and assemble them together, assembling parts and building up a totality. The Cosmic Life is not a totality, it is not constituted of parts, it is a wholeness. And everything is organically related to the wholeness.

So: 'please, Arjuna, do not look upon the material expressions around you in nature, as fragments of me. Because of your sensual limitations you can only take in one object at the time and you feel it is separate from the other. It is your sensual approach. Or, even if your approach is cerebral, through an idea, it becomes a particular, because of your idea. But in each is all and the all is in each. That is the secret of my Being.'

The wholeness in each, contained in the unmanifest imperishable reality, has to be recognized. This faculty of permeating every expression is called *vibhut*. The name of the tenth chapter is Vibhuti Yoga. *Vibhuti* is the capacity, the faculty, the energy to permeate something which emanates out of you, though you retain your uniqueness and individuality at the same time. To be immanent and transcendent at the same time is called *vibhuti* in this chapter. It is a beautiful word.

So *vibhuti* is the rare yogic faculty of permeating and yet remaining transcendental. 'This is my Vibhuti Yoga, this is the resplendent state of *yoga* in nature, in which the smallest particle contains the wholeness and the wholeness contains the manyness and minuteness.' Why has this exposition become necessary? Why does Sri Krishna deal with this aspect of the *yogic* mystery of his being, the secret of his being?

Let us come to that point now, before we proceed to what Arjuna

asks, in response to this exposition. Look, as students of *yoga*, we
study *dharana* (concentration), *dhyana* (meditation) and *samadhi*,
the last three of the Ashtanga Yoga. And in that *dharana, dhyana,
samadhi*, we begin with the study of concentration, turning inwards.
Not going outwards. We may choose some object of concentration;
it may be the flame of a candle, a sound, a *mantra*, whatever one
likes to take up. But it is an inward movement.

When you move exclusively inward, the outer is left aside, you do
not reject it, but for the sake of study, the outer, the material, the
collective nature around you, has to be brushed aside temporarily.
So, for the study of concentration, you take an exclusively inward
movement.

After studying concentration and steadying the body and quietening
the mind through that, you may proceed to *dhyana*, meditation,
where there is an all-inclusive concentration. You are trying to
embrace all the energies in the body, gather them together and with
the help of *prana*, take them upwards towards the crown of your
head. It is now in meditation, according to Hatha Yoga. It has
gathered all the energies, helped by *prana*.

Like an antenna of a television set, here, near the pituitary gland,
like an antenna of a television set, there is an opening through which
the Cosmic energies of sovereign intelligence, supreme intelligence,
operating in the emptiness of space outside your body, can be
received. When all the energies are gathered together, helped by
prana and move upward and are concentrated here (near the pituary
gland), then the receptivity is intensified, it is strengthened. The
velocity of the receptivity is heightened and, therefore, the individual
consciousness and the supreme sovereign Cosmic consciousness
are helped to mingle together.

This happens through meditation. And you grow into, you are lifted
up into a dimension of *samadhi*, an absolutely different dimension
of consciousness. This is an inward exclusive movement of
sadhana, education. But this is not the end of *sadhana*, this is only
a part of *sadhana*.

Raja Yoga says there should now be an all-embracing concentration. Look at the apparent contradiction in terms: now the concentration would not be exclusive. It would be all-inclusive. It would not be an inner or outer, it would be holistic. A holistic all-embracing concentration, leading to an awareness that the wholeness, the oneness permeates the all-ness, and the all-ness is contained in the oneness. For growing into that state of awareness, this all-embracing, all-inclusive holistic concentration and dedication and devotion is necessary. Then the study of *yoga* is complete.

Till then it was incomplete, because you have realized it only inside the body. But what about nature around you, *prakriti* around you? Even if you have realized Purusha, concealed in your own *prakriti*, the Atman, the reflection of Paramatman in your body, what about this nature out of which you are born? Unless you realize the Purusha, the Lord supreme contained in the *prakriti*, in the Cosmos, your study is incomplete. It is not yet perfect. Perfecting the study of *yoga* is necessary.

'Now, how does one', Arjuna asks, 'do this all-embracing, all-including dedication and devotion?'

And Sri Krishna replies in a very characteristic unique way, as if a teacher is teaching a small child. After all Arjuna was not only a friend of Krishna, not only a relative of Krishna, he was also a student of Krishna. The dialogue in the *Gita*, in the Upanishads, between the teacher and the student are models of pedagogical psychology. So Krishna says:

'Look, I am there in the plant called *tulsi*, I am there in the cow, I am there in the earth, I am not only a theory. The fertility, the creativity, the so many colours, flavours concealed in the earth, are due to me. It is that energy. So I am in the pituitary, I am in the earth, I am in the water, in a tree.'

When you see the Hindus worshipping certain plants, like a banyan tree, or worshipping a cow, or a small *tulsi* plant, and so on, the Hindu society did not enter into the metaphysical meaning of that worship. It was not explained to them, it became a ritual, it became a tradition. The consciousness got loaded with the external and physical part of it, without any appreciation and grasp of the significance behind the worship.

Krishna is trying to help Arjuna, he is trying to explain: 'every expression in birds, animals, in other non-human species, the splendour of my nature, the nature of Life, the nature of wholeness, the splendour of indivisibility or dynamism, is reflected in every object, not its wholeness but some aspect of it.

A tree manifests one aspect of my being, the mountain manifests the aspect of steadiness in me, the ocean manifests the depth of my being, the cow or the deer manifest the innocence, the elegance of innocence in me.'

The tenth chapter is devoted to the elaboration of how the oneness, the wholeness, the dynamism of indivisibility, permeates all the different material expressions. Out of forty-two verses, twenty-seven are devoted to this elaboration.

After having elaborated upon all this and having pointed out the path of Raja Yoga in which, when dealing with an object, be aware that the energy contained in it comes from Brahman, he points out that this is not only the path of dedication, of devotion, the path of concentration, sitting down in some posture, closing your eyes and turning inward. Here, the all-embracing, all-inclusive concentration has to happen in the movement of your waking hours, in every relationship, in every movement.

So, whether you drink a glass of water or partake of a meal or you see objects in nature, be it flowers, fruit, the beauty in nature or in human beings, if you are aware that the source of that beauty, that elegance, that flavour is that Cosmic energy, then multifarious-ness or manyness of the expressions will not bring about the energy of desire. If you are aware that it is the one that permeates all, then you will not be allured, infatuated, with the manyness.

Otherwise, the energy of desire in you says: 'I want this object, I want that object, I want that kind of food today and I want that kind of jewellery tomorrow.' You will be attracted by beauty in the human form and you will get attached. You will get attracted and infatuated by the beauty in nature and your energy of desire, which should be harnessed towards the all-embracing concentration on the source of energy, will be dissipated. Then you will run after different objects, different individuals and you try to collect them, because you are attracted by them, you try to acquire them, obtain them, grab them, hoard them. Your energy will be dissipated.

All your inner energies have one source and the outer energies also have one source. This study of concentration, in an all-embracing all-inclusive way, will save you from the pitfalls of dissipating your vital energy in running after the illusion of manyness, running after appearances. Your relationship with the many will be a scientific relationship of providing what the bodily energies require. There will be a scientifically elegant interaction.

This scientific relationship is called austere because it does not enter into any excesses. If it is not a scientific attitude then you lapse into excesses. You can lapse into withdrawal or you can indulge into excesses. In the scientific attitude there is no rejection, there is no indulgence, there is no withdrawal, there is no aggression. Your relationship with matter, its manyness in manifestation, will not dissipate any of your energies. There will be a contact, there will be an interaction of energies, there will be an enjoyment and yet the physical, the mental, the vital energies will not be dissipated, scattered. They will remain whole.

It is because of the cohesiveness of energies, the non-dissipated-ness of energies, that they will not be scattered. Otherwise, you would get attracted through the eyes, when you see something beautiful. Immediately, you get attracted, you will want to run after it. You lose the balance. You do not wait to see if this contact or this interaction is consistent or harmonious with the perception of your whole life, of what you want to do in your whole life.

If a sudden imbalance comes out of that contact, whether attraction, infatuation, then there is a tension in the nerves. Then the natural path of the stream of energies gets clogged in your body. If you like some music, if you have imbibed it, there is an interaction between the beauty of the music and your receptivity. It has given you some fulfilment. But the thought comes: 'I want to repeat it.' That is not enjoyment. You want pleasure and your energy becomes exclusive, it goes exclusively in that direction, again an imbalance.

Unless, there is a holistic approach and an all-inclusiveness of attention to the source of Life, to the source of energy, there are bound to be temptations, imbalances and impurities. You cannot cure them by imposing upon yourself abstract codes of conduct, forcing disciplines on yourself. They have to be cured at the very base.

So, exclusive concentration or study within your body and all-inclusive concentration, leading to the awareness of one source of Life, both these will create a new equilibrium, that we were talking about in the ninth chapter. A new equilibrium in your physical and mental frame. That equilibrium itself will lift up the consciousness to a different dimension.

I will take up one more point. Sri Krishna refers to the energies of the psychological mental frame: 'truth, *satya*, that you perceive, is my energy, the energy of my dimension. If there is the faculty of restraint in you, because you have discriminated the truth from the false, that power of discrimination contained in your reason is due to my wholeness, due to my absoluteness of transcendence.' He refers to various psychological energies, such as forgiveness, truth, love, compassion, restraint, all these so-called noble characteristics, are all reflections of the energy of transcendent reality.

Inside you there is nothing yours, it belongs to the divine nature. You are only an instrument of expressing that divinity. And the outer matter is an instrument of manifesting the divinity. 'The procreating energy is the reflected energy of my creativity.' He sanctifies sex, he says it is the pure reflection of my creativity, do not misuse it, do not abuse it. You have a responsibility to use the sex impulse, the sex instinct and the procreative energies in harmony with the rhythm of Life.

Referring to all the energies, right from truth and love and compassion, to the sex energy, sight, audition, he asks: 'where do all these energies come from?' In the matter of your body. Physical matter is capable of receiving and reflecting that energy in a human form. 'Therefore, Arjuna, those who are born in a human form, aren't they very lucky, they are evolved expressions of consciousness. So, be dedicated to me, be dedicated to the source of all-ness, be dedicated to that transcendental divinity.

They who are not only aware of this secret of my being, but those who share it with others, who sing about it, those who teach it, those who talk about it, they have no fear left in Life, because they have joined together with the wholeness. Living in a particular body, encased in a particularity, inwardly the consciousness is merged into the totality, the wholeness. So, they have no fear. They are called *yogis*, Arjuna, they are Raja Yogis.'

Not Hatha Yogis, Karma Yogis, Bhakti Yogis, not emphasizing only one aspect of *yoga*, but they have taken the royal path, the sovereign wisdom, the path of light, the path of ascent. So, their suffering comes to an end.

We have looked briefly at the first thirty verses of chapter ten. There are twelve verses left in the chapter. In the next chapter Krishna shows, in his body, the whole Cosmos to Arjuna. As students of *yoga*, we have to focus our attention at the concealed meaning of these verses. We have seen how the oneness, retaining its oneness, permeates the all-ness. How the transcendental energy sustains its absolute transcendental-ness, yet is reflected in all matter. We have looked at the exclusive inward concentration and at the all-inclusive outward. I don't know if it has been possible for me to convey to you, through words, the mystical exposition of the secret of Cosmic Life. One would like to finish the remaining part of the tenth chapter and begin the study of the eleventh chapter.

'I am the seed of all existence. Whatever has existed, whatever is existing and shall ever exist, is originated and shall originate from me' says Krishna, as the representative of Ishvara, the Lord, or Brahman, Paramatman. These terms are used to indicate the sovereign principle of dynamic intelligence, the supreme principle of dynamic creativity.

In this dialogue with Arjuna, Krishna is speaking on behalf of that principle of intelligence or creativity. Silence is the voice of divinity and divinity can communicate through words or deeds only when it accepts the limitations of being born in a human body and going to the travail of that limited life. Otherwise, silence is the sound of creation, silence is the voice of the divinity.

So, Krishna says 'the divinity, the creativity, the intelligence is the seed.' To understand the principle of the unmanifest seed, let us come back to our daily life. If you have ever sown the seed of an apple tree, a mango tree, an avocado tree, a tiny seed, that tiny seed contains the sapling, the plant, the tree, the thick bark of the trunk of the tree. That tiny seed contains all the branches, the twigs, the fruit, the flowers. You may take the most powerful magnifying glass and look at the seed, those manifestations of its dynamic energy or creativity will not be perceived by you. The seed contains the whole tree, but for your senses, your brain, your perception, that manifestation is invisible, imperceptible, yet it is contained there.

In the same way, this innumerable variety of separated and individuated forms, with the sheath of matter around it, that manyness, incalculable, immeasurable manyness of manifestations, is contained in the unmanifest principle of creativity. In the void of space, according to the Buddhists, in the fullness contained in the emptiness of space according to the Vedantins, in the unmanifest *mula prakriti* or Cosmic matter according to the Hatha, Raja, Tantra and Mantra Yogis.

'I am the seed of all existence.' The divinity is the seed of all existence. It is unmanifest, it is un-individuated and yet out of that wholeness, out of that un-individuated-ness, the separate existences and manifestations on the material level issue forth. They originate out of that.

Krishna proceeds: 'I am not only the seed or the source of creation, I am the existential essence in that creation.'

This is a very significant statement. The principle of intelligence, Chaitanya, the sovereign principle of dynamic creativity, that

Brahman, that Chaitanya, that energy, is the content of material existence. The essence of existence is divinity. Please do see this.

It is quite a different note from the existential essence pointed out by Sartre, Eckhart, Emanuel Kant, and other western philosophers. Because of that, different ways of living and different cultures arise. It is the perception of the nature of reality and the character of reality, that results in differences in human culture and civilizations.

Here, Sri Krishna tells his friend and student Arjuna that divinity is the existential essence of matter. Matter and spirit have never been separated and they shall ever remain inseparable. They are together. 'So, Arjuna, the manifest and the unmanifest, the movable and the immovable, contain the dynamic creativity of intelligence, as their basis.'

'How do I recognize and realize this?' asks Arjuna. And as an arrow comes the reply from Krishna: 'I give you a clue, Arjuna, to recognize me, to identify me, to identify the principle of intelligence, to identify that dynamic energy of creativity.

In every material expression, in every human form, included in the material existence, wherever you come across the stability and sustenance of truthfulness, of truth, wherever you come across the awareness that truth is indestructible, Life is indestructible and wherever you come across the benevolence of love, which is a recognition of that truth, of that unity of Life, of that principle of Chaitanya pervading, permeating everything, wherever you come across these, you can recognize me being there, you can recognize the eloquence of divinity through that splendour.

All the three may not be existing in one and the same place, they may, but even if you find one of the three expressing or manifesting in the movement of that matter, in the movement of that form, you can be sure that I have expressed or manifested my being.'

All beings have their life in the divine being. The being of earth, of sun, of stars and planets, the being of all the species, human and non-human, they are living because they have their being in the divine beingness.

'I am the seed of existence, I am the content of existence. My splendour gets manifested. In some manifestations, one aspect is more pronounced, in other manifestations, more than one aspect becomes pronounced. And there are exceptional human beings or material beings, where perhaps all the aspects, *sat*, *chit*, *ananda*, indestructible truth, self awareness of that indestructibility and the bliss of love and joy, all these are manifested simultaneously. That manifestation is resplendent with my splendour.'

Krishna has given a clue to Arjuna, for identifying, recognizing and coming into first hand personal, intimate touch and encounter with the divine in the material existence.

It seems to me that these three verses (thirty-nine, forty and forty one): 'wherever my glories of manifestations exist, there find me', these three verses give us the crux of the whole tenth chapter of the Vibhuti Yoga, the *Yoga* of divine manifestations.

In the last verse of the tenth chapter, Krishna says to Arjuna: 'what is the use to you or relevance to your life, if I go on enumerating my *vibhutis*, or how I make the material manifestations my own abode and express the splendour of my being through them, they are all incalculable, they are immeasurable, they are unknowable. Why don't you understand that the manifest contains the unmanifest, each individuated form contains the all. Though the forms are separated, they are not fragments of the wholeness, they are expressions of the wholeness'.

The difference between fragment and expression is to be appreciated very deeply. When there is individuation, there are separate forms. The mountains appear to be separate from the ocean, the trees are separated by their form. But that does not mean that reality is divided, that does not mean that they are fragmented or part of a totality. They are emanation of the wholeness.

As a ray of light from the sun contains the principle of light and enlightens the planet earth, in the same way every manifestation is like a ray from the divinity. It originates and it contains. Unless one appreciates the significance of the teachings contained in the last three or four verses, it will be nearly impossible to grasp, even intellectually, the communications that we are going to look at in the eleventh chapter, called Visvarupa Darshana Yoga (the *yoga* of the vision of the Cosmic form). This was the science of *yoga* for reaching the divine, through the material manifestations.

CHAPTER XI

YOGA OF VISION OF THE COSMIC FORM

And now comes the perception, the comprehension and realization, simultaneously, of the manifest and the unmanifest. The Cosmic *yoga* as it is called. Before we take up the verses of the eleventh chapter, it would be helpful, if we understand the trends that have existed since antiquity in the universe, and are noticeable even today in the consciousness of the human species. It is to give more attention, more emphasis, on the separateness of the form, looking upon the separateness of the form as the essence of Life, as the essence of existence.

When you look upon the separateness of the form, say your human body or the bodies of those who are near and dear to you, or your friends or whatever, then you feel that this form and its movement, its preservation, is the goal of life. The preservation of the continuity of that form becomes the aim, the goal, the ideal of our life.

When one is too much concerned about the preservation of a particular form or a procreation of a similar form, then in that desire of sustaining the separateness of the form, the survival of that particular form, the preservation of the form, and the craving to procreate a similar form, creates an assertiveness in human consciousness which is called the ego. The ego-consciousness, the I-consciousness, is born out of this ignorance of looking at the separateness as the essence of existence and of getting concerned about its preservation, its survival and its continuity through similar forms generated through pro-created energy.

Krishna is giving the genesis of ego, the genesis of I-consciousness. You see, we are still with Raja Yoga, the secret path, the sovereign path of union with the transcendental consciousness. So, the human consciousness assumed assertiveness, due to this ignorance about the real utility of form, the individuation, the separateness of form in the dance of Life.

The oneness manifested in manyness and the manyness getting again dissolved into oneness, that is the dance of Life. This is the nature of Life. Energy cannot be idle. So, from oneness into manyness, from manyness into oneness, to form the vehicle of expression of Life. By its very biological nature, it cannot have duration of longevity beyond a point.

But human beings get concerned, terribly concerned, about the preservation of the form on the physical level and on the mental level also. The separateness is emphasized through assertiveness, then aggressiveness, then comparison, competition, the idea of security, fear of being insecure and preparation for violence in the name of defence, mental or physical. So, a whole culture evolved out of this primal ignorance about the nature of Life.

If there is an awareness that the separateness of form is only a vehicle or a medium for expressing the wholeness, is only an instrument of expression, a vehicle of expression, then a culture will not be based, a way of living will not be based on the preservation and continuity of that separateness.

We are coming to the very basic fundamental point in the Vedic *darshanas*, the teachings of the Vedas, and Upanishads, this awareness of the unity of Life manifested in the diversity, unity running through the undercurrent of diversity. Diversity being inter-related with unity, not connected artificially with the thread and needle of your philosophies of dualism and non-dualism, but by the very nature of Life. In fact diversity is a stream of unity.

So, those who emphasize the form, look upon it as the essence of existence, they evolve a kind of culture represented by the Kauravas in the *Mahabharata*, the whole family of the Kauravas, called *rakshsasas* by Krishna.

A *rakshasa* is a very interesting Sanskrit term, derived from the root *raksha* to keep secure, to defend. One, who is terribly obsessed with the idea of preserving or securing, becomes a *rakshasa*. They are not devils. They are not a separate species. Evil does not have a separate existence; evil is the consequence of primal ignorance about the nature of Life. In Indian philosophy, you will not come across evil having a parallel separate existence from the good. The eleventh chapter is going to deal elaborately with the genesis of good and evil.

Some are not obsessed with the preservation and procreation of a separate form, but they are concerned, involved and obsessed with preserving a particular kind of energy, expressed through that form. We have looked at the word *rakshasa*, those who are obsessed with the idea of security and preservation of the gross physical form, so their whole psychology, based on that, comes about by being obsessed with the gross physical form.

Asubhava: *asu* means *prana*, the dynamic energy contained in the form, related to the potential durability of the form. This *prana* energy, this vital energy expresses itself. Some are concerned with the continuity of that energy, longevity of the expression of that energy, through a particular form. So, these are the two: the one is concerned and obsessed with a particular form and the other is concerned and obsessed with a particular expression of energy.

You know, the organized religions are very much concerned with the preservation and continuity of a particular kind of energy, manifested through their way of living. It is not so much a concern for the preservation of houses, machines, money. The first variety is concerned obviously with that, with the gross. But the second variety is concerned with the subtle, the energy aspect of matter.

Krishna is pointing out that, if there is ignorance about the following three points. One, that divinity is the seed of all creation. Two, that divinity is the existential essence of all creation. And three, that every separate form in this creation contains some aspect of that energy. If these three things are not understood, then, what you call evil comes about. Evil can be out of fear, out of aggression, out of too much obsession with self-defence, out of jealousy, competition, urge to dominate and convert others to your way of living. All this comes about. Evil originates from primal ignorance.

There is another trend, noticeable in the human species since antiquity and this trend would be there, as long as the human species inhabits the planet. They are not so much concerned or obsessed with the form, with matter, or a particular expression of energy manifested through that separate material form. They are aware that there is one in all and the all is contained in the one. They are aware of that. So, their handling of the form and their handling of the energies in their body and outside of them is not for the preservation of the form, but for the preservation of the awareness of the unity of Life.

They want to preserve the truth, the unity, through their awareness. They are concerned more about the awareness of the nature of reality. The ignorance is dispelled in them. They look upon the material and the mental separate forms only as an instrument of expression and not as something to be preserved, worshipped. So, they are not allured by, attracted by, or obsessed with the separateness.

They are aware of the interrelatedness and they want to handle and utilize the separateness to express the inter-relatedness. They want to express the wholeness of Life, the unity of Life. So, matter and mind, the physical frame and the mental frame, become instruments for manifesting the unity, the wholeness, the indivisibility of Life. This trend is a homecoming trend, through their awareness they want always to be united with the source of creation.

The others are going out from that source of unity, enchanted by the manyness, the manifestations, preserving them, holding them. You know, it is an out-going way. The evil is in moving away from the source in awareness, and the good is homecoming, being aware of the unity, the wholeness.

Good emphasizes harmony, oneness, and evil emphasizes separateness. That is the only difference between the good and evil according to the *Gita*. Not something to be hated, to be fought against. Remove the ignorance and the wrong identifications will get eliminated, and the fermentation of *raga* and *dvesha* (attachment and repulsion), originating from wrong identification, will get dispelled by themselves, without moving a finger.

The fundamental *avidya* (ignorance) has to be dispelled. So the genesis of ego or I-consciousness, obsessed with the idea of security and fear of being eliminated, has been pointed out to us. *Yoga* is practical psychology for you and me. It helps us to understand our mind, the source of ignorance existing in us, and attachment and repulsion, jealousy and hatred. It explains to us, if we observe, our concerns and our obsessions.

The form, that has come into existence, is going to be dissolved into the unmanifest, one day. That which is born, is bound to die some day. Once the fear of death disappears, then there is a release of creative energy. It is fear that blocks the flow of healing or creative energies in body and mind. It is the idea of security and preservation which creates a non-verbalized inhibition in your being.

Do you see the blockages in the path of creativity, flowing like a blood stream in the body? The blockages do not originate outside of you; there is no bondage outside of you, no blockages originating anywhere else but in the mind. It is the emphasis on separateness and obsession with the preservation of the separateness, that obliges you to bring an enclosure around you, an enclosure of 'me and mine' and 'you and yours'. It is not only assertion, aggression, etc. It creates a pronounced division between the me and the not-me, the enclosure resulting in a kind of isolation. And suffering arises out of that non-verbalized sense of isolation, loneliness etc.

The genesis of good and evil, the obsession with separateness of forms and characters, has to be appreciated rather deep. If this point has been made sufficiently clear, let us proceed. Now, we begin the eleventh chapter, whether it is part of the original *Gita*, or whether it has been added on later.

There are portions in the *Gita* which one feels as incongruous, sometimes superfluous with the main teachings of the *Gita*. But they have been there for hundreds of years and no commentator has ever talked about this possibility, which I talk about, so we will go through the chapter. But I do feel, about the whole of the eleventh chapter, that it feels like an addition. It has a different quality and texture of its contents than the other chapters. It could be that people living in a tropical country like India, had and have a different psychological make-up, temperament and they need elaboration, they need materialization of truth in gross form. They want instances, they want everything to be perceived through their senses, to be named, identified. This may have made the author elaborate, also upon elemental factors, which feel to be unnecessary for the celestial music of the *Gita*.

Now, after hearing in the tenth chapter that divinity is the seed of all creation, is the existential essence of creation, etc., Arjuna is saying: 'can I see that splendour of your Cosmic existence in your Cosmic Body, containing all the manifestations in the oneness of your being, containing the manyness? Can I see that, Krishna, in your physical body? I would love to see that, if it is possible.'

You see, the question itself drags you down from the level which you had reached in the previous chapter. He wants to see it on the physical level, in the physical frame of Krishna. That is how the worship of the form of Krishna has come about in India, and has been exported to Europe and America through Hare Krishna and the Krishna Consciousness Movement. And temples have come about. Wherever you go, in any country, you will find the worship of the form.

Here, Arjuna wants to see the manyness, the dance of good and evil, everything in the physical frame of Krishna. He says: 'my doubts have been cleared, whatever you have explained, there are no doubts in my mind. But there is still this desire of seeing your Cosmic Form at the sensory level, at the sensual level.' Well love knows no logic or reason, so Krishna, out of love for his friend Arjuna, for his brother Arjuna, says: 'yes, it is possible, why not.'

Let the *siddhis* (*siddhi* is the capacity to express, on the material physical level, the invisible. Krishna must have had occult powers for all we know). So, Krishna says: 'it is possible. Why not. But it will not be possible for you to see it with these eyes. I'll give you another sight. You want to see something which this optical instrument and the frequency of the movement of that energy cannot see. So, I have to give you a different sight, divine sight, sight, which will enable you to see the splendour of my *yogic* powers.'

And then the small frame of Krishna's body gets enlarged, his feet are on the earth and his head touches the sky, it is an enlarged magnified body now. And Arjuna sees the Pandavas and the Kauravas, he and his brothers, and his army, and the Kauravas and their army, all in the body of Krishna, fighting with each other.

He sees a number of suns and solar systems moving in Krishna's head. Many verses have been devoted to the description of what Arjuna sees in Krishna's body. He sees mountains, rivers, people getting killed and blood flowing, everything in that body. If you do not take the meaning literally, it can be a poetical way of expressing how every form contains the divine and how the divine contains all manifestations.

Krishna had expressed in chapter ten, in Vibhuti Yoga: 'I am the flavour in the earth, I am the magnificence in the lion, I am the handsomeness in a horse, I am the light in the sun, the nectar in the moon, the depth in the ocean, the steadiness in the mountains', and so on. He had described and enumerated his powers, expressed through various species. So, figuratively speaking, it seems to me that Arjuna became aware, that the earth beneath his feet contains Krishna, contains the divine; the skies under which he and the army were standing, contains the emptiness of space, which is filled with divinity.

He got terrified by the awareness of the so-called wickedness of the Kauravas, grabbing the share of the Pandavas, grabbing their part of the kingdom and all that, as a Cosmic movement. He became aware of it and he became frightened. Till then he had the tension of energy, because he thought he was to fight against the wickedness, he was preserving *dharma* (righteousness) and he was going to regain the kingdom, which had been grabbed, appropriated by the Kauravas.

But now he sees that the difference between good and evil, the bad and the good, is due to ignorance, ignorance by the Kauravas of the real purpose of Life. The goodness of the Pandavas is only the recognition of the purpose of Life.

No human being is one hundred percent evil. There are circumstantial causes and reasons, weaknesses of the good people, provoking the latent or dormant crookedness among others, sinfulness in a group, provoking the aggressiveness in the other, and so on.

I am not here, to elaborate upon the whole psychology and philosophy of how evil comes about in a collective form, in social order. But it seems to me, that Arjuna must have seen the essence of Krishna's teaching. He got frightened when he got sight of the omnipresence, omniscience and omnipotence of the divine.

As an idea, the intellect appreciates it. But when you really become aware of it, with your whole being, when you get consumed by the perception and the realization of that truth, then you get swept off your feet. So, when Arjuna sees all the Cosmos in the physical frame of Krishna, he begins to tremble. His being cannot contain the perception of Cosmic reality, the Cosmic truth.

When the realization comes, you fight the evil, not because of hatred, not because of anger, but just as part of the game in the Cosmic dance. You play your part, killing without hatred. That is what Krishna has been telling Arjuna, since the second chapter. You have to fight in this battle, without attachment to your family or relatives and hatred of the others. If you can fight without hatred, without attachment, then you have lived the *dharma*, you have fulfilled the spiritual purpose for which you are born.

But if you do it out of attachment or hatred, then you have added to the stream of the ego in an indirect way. Whenever you cherish an attachment or a repulsion, a hatred or an obsession, then you give in to the separate tendencies, you are following the stream of the ego in an indirect way. Your evil is on the subconscious level, and those whom you call evil persons, violent, aggressive persons, their evil is on the conscious level. Yours is on the subconscious level. Krishna says, there is a difference of conscious and subconscious, that is all.

It may be that Arjuna became aware of the truth of what Krishna was telling, not only as an intellectual academic understanding, but perhaps, in the last few verses of the eleventh chapter, he became really aware, his whole being was vibrating with that awareness, and that terrified him. So, he says to Krishna: 'I cannot bear the perception of the Cosmic reality, it is too much for me, I am trembling.' He was trembling in the first chapter, when he did not want to fight. Now, he wanted to see the truth and when he was helped to realize the truth, he again begins to tremble. Arjuna represents us, you know.

He says to Krishna: 'please, gather all this manifestation of your *siddhis*, please, do appear to me again as you were, my illumined friend, in your physical frame of Sri Krishna. Not this Krishna, I can't stand it. I have now understood what you mean by saying that you are the seed and you are the essence of everything, that nothing exists without you.' And Krishna smiled and gathered all his *siddhis* unto himself and became the physical frame that Arjuna was accustomed to.

Take this literally or figuratively. Literally, there is personification of divinity and worship of divinity, in a human form, be it of Krishna, Buddha, Ramakrishna, Ramana, or whatever; looking upon that form exclusively as a manifestation of divinity. Or figuratively, to indicate that every form is an incarnation of the divine. One can choose the impersonal, the non-personal content of truth and reality, or one can accept the manifestation, localized in one human being, and worship it. It is up to the individual.

I am concerned with understanding the truth and sharing it with you. For me the wholeness of Life is worshipped through the quality of your own act of living. That is the only worship I know: the quality of your living, the texture of your actions, the state of your consciousness in the movement of your relationships. That is worship for me. The whole Cosmos is a temple, and whatever exists is flesh and blood of the divinity. But I do not say that you should take the interpretation this way or that way. Who am I? I am only opening for you the different ways of understanding the eleventh chapter.

The perfume of that freedom, the vigour, the vitality, the resplendence, it has to be lived. You just can't go on saying: 'I am unattached now, there is renunciation now that I have taken *sannyasa*.' Those intellectual claims are meaningless.

Amongst a thousand, one perhaps has the patience and perseverance to live that freedom. I thought I should clarify why Arjuna was frightened. It is not only Arjuna who was frightened, you and I also get frightened. The understanding of truth frightens you, because you are afraid that the dimension of truth will compel you to change your way of living. It will destroy your status quo, it might turn everything topsy-turvy. You would like the understanding of truth to allow you to continue the old physical and mental ways of living, the culture that you have built-up for yourself. And you are afraid that if the truth is understood, it will create an inner compulsion and dismantle, demolish, your previous ways of living.

Like Arjuna, we are sore afraid, when the *Gita* points out to us, or Patanjali through the Yoga Sutras points out to us, that liberation is possible for every human being, that suffering can be ended. The claim of Patanjali is that the ending of psychological suffering is within the reach of every human being. That is the beauty of Raja Yoga. You can call it the *yoga* of meditation, of awareness, of understanding; any name can be given to that. It is comprehensive, it is holistic. No more a question of changing ideas, no more a question of filling your brain with a new way of living intellectually. It is a holistic transmutation of the physical and the mental, together, that is required or demanded of the enquirer.

So, Arjuna says to Krishna: 'I have seen in your body the whole dance of creation and dissolution. You are beginningless and endless, you filled the Cosmos. I had not realized it before, I looked upon you as a limited human being and thought of you as my friend, my brother, and I was laughing with you, cutting jokes with you, taking liberties with you. Now, I realize that you represent the ultimate principle of sovereignty, you are Ishvara. I bow down to you and as the Rishis, the Sages of ancient days surrendered themselves to you, O Krishna, O you the Lord of creation, you the Lord of death and dissolution, I bow to you from all directions.' There follows a number of hymns in which Arjuna praises Sri Krishna's divine nature.

After listening to that, very patiently, Krishna turns to Arjuna and says: 'if I have filled the Cosmos, have I not filled your body too, am I not there in you, within you? Why don't you wake up to your divine nature? Do not think that I am the only divinity, but the divinity is also within you. So, from the material and mental being, why don't you also become a divine being, like me, so that all your actions have the flavour, the perfume of divinity, of clarity, of equipoise, of harmony, of orderliness. If you have seen that in me, it is there in you, why don't you allow that to get manifest?'

That is the beauty of this dialogue in the *Gita*. Even in the eighteenth chapter, after having explained everything, Krishna says to Arjuna: 'be as you want to be.' He shows the path, but he says 'walk on it as far as you want to walk.' Arjuna says 'I will do as you ask me to do.' Krishna answers: 'No. Do as you have understood. After understanding, do what you want to do.' That is how the eighteenth chapter ends. Beautiful three or four verses between Krishna and Arjuna. 'Now my doubts are dispelled, I have regained my awareness of divine nature. I'll do as you ask me to do.' And Krishna says: 'I don't ask anything of you. I have explained. If you have understood, have you re-collected the essence of your nature?' And Arjuna says 'Yes.' 'Then do as from your understanding.'

This sense of freedom, which is the breath of the *Gita* and the Upanishads, is something that has generated a tremendously deep love in my heart for these teachings of the Vedas and the Upanishads. Not because I am born in India, not because they were verbalized here in India, but because of this emphasis on the inner freedom, this emphasis of contributing to the natural harmony in the universe through your action and behaviour. This emphasis on equipoise, equanimity, equi-balance, is something marvellous, very rare to come across in the scriptures of the world.

So, Sri Krishna says: 'let the arrogance of your intellect and ego, which constantly wants to move away from its centre towards aggression, assertion, domination etc., let that arrogance of acquisitive and assertive activity of the ego be subdued by humility generated by this new awareness. Then your life will become a *yajna* (sacrifice) dedicated to the divine. Then whatever you do, is done for me.'

Now, let us understand what is meant by this doing for the divine, dedicating to the divine, and how does that arrogance of the ego, which wants to assert through acquisition, how does that get subdued. What does this attitude of humility or surrender, of devotional dedication, do to it? That is the point we should try to see very clearly.

Otherwise, these words: surrender, devotion, dedication, are apt to be misunderstood, misinterpreted. They might stink to the ego of slavery, of subordination, etc. You know, words are liable to be misunderstood, especially words that come from the Sanskrit and which we are trying to understand in English. Languages born in different cultures are the product of different ways of living and we are trying to understand the scientific implication of those words.

Look, once that awareness that Life is divine, that the Cosmos is filled with divine energy, unlimited beginningless and endless divine energy, having inexhaustible potential in spite of millions of years of manifestation, once that awareness comes, dawns upon you, what will it do to you?

Then, when you feed the body, clothe the body, bathe the body, sleep the body, because you are aware of that divine energy contained in matter, you have a respect and a reverence, reverence for Life, for every expression of Life in your body as well as outside of you. If that reverence for the body is there, then your attitude towards your physical behaviour is bound to be changed.

Your body is no longer to be used the way you like, that is impulsively, instinctively, aggressively, indifferently. It is the body of the divine, it is an expression of the divine energy. The Lord, the divine, resides in that body. Without creating a fuss, the whole attitude, approach and tackling of the physical behaviour goes through a transmutation. It is a new approach, a new attitude and a new way of handling the physical behaviour, which purifies. The behaviour is re-oriented, and the energy potential is enhanced. That is why the study of yoga can lead to longevity of the physical existence.

I have come across *yogis*, met them and talked with them, who had lived for more than two hundred years physically. I took the trouble to go to the government offices and getting myself satisfied by seeing the date of their birth registered, because I would not take it on the word of their disciples. So, this longevity of the body is the result of the transmutation of those energies and transformation of the natural equilibrium.

The surrender to the divine, dedicating the physical to the divine, means being aware of the divine presence in every minute particle of matter, in animals, in birds, in trees, in water, in everything. It is reverence for Life that generates a sense of sacredness or holiness.

You know, life has become very cheap now in the commercialised civilization, bargaining, calculating, acquiring, hoarding. We are a pleasure-mongering race. The bodies are used, even the sex energy is used just as an instrument for pleasure, speech is used as an instrument for pleasure. Not reverence for the faculties, the energies, the sacredness of the sex energy, the sacredness of the speech energy, the sacredness of the energy of appetite, the sacredness of the energies contained in the digestive organs, in the lungs, in the heart.

If you have reverence, then that attitude of reverence generates what you call holiness or sacredness. You don't handle your body cheaply, in vulgar ways, in an impulsive manner. To live this way is fantastic, it is great fun. You are born anew. We have seen it in the ninth chapter that you get re-born. With the study of *yoga*, if you are honest and there is integrity and genuineness behind the study, you get reborn. Energies get restructured, reorganized, rearranged. The ego is subdued and it is the promptings of the intelligence, which the ego-consciousness has to obey. It is the intelligence which functions through knowledge and thought that the I-consciousness had collected.

The words surrender, dedication and devotion, indicate a qualitative radically new attitude of reverence towards total Life, inside you and outside you. 'Bowing down, showing reverence, let every action of yours, Arjuna, be a symbol of your awareness and dedication to the truth, that the awareness has conferred upon you.' When you bow down like that, you are symbolizing your attitude. It is not physical gymnastics, it is not verbal gymnastics, it is a symbol, and after all, Life is expressing itself through symbols, whether you shake hands and say good morning, or make a *namaskar*. It is a symbol of your affection and reverence for one another.

Now Krishna says: 'Arjuna, see it very clearly that your every action, every movement, should be a symbol of that new awareness and a dedication to that new awareness. Dedicate everything to me.' Krishna is speaking there on behalf of the Lord, Ishvara. He is using his body as a symbol for that. That is how you will arrive at the supreme abode of consciousness.

The intelligence, concealed in that consciousness, is not meant to live on the material level with inertia, neither governed by it, nor subdued by it. The energy of intelligence, divinity, Chaitanya, is not doomed to be a prisoner of the thought structure. Its abode is somewhere else, in the transcendental divinity, the sovereign supreme intelligence. So: 'Arjuna, when your actions become dedicated onto me, the Lord of creation and destruction, that is to say, when they are filled with the awareness of my omnipotence, omniscience and omnipresence, then your actions will become as divine as my actions are and your consciousness will have reached its final abode, the ultimate abode of consciousness.'

We have seen in the eleventh chapter the physical demonstration of the *yogic* powers of Krishna for his darling friend and student

Arjuna. The recognition and realization by Arjuna of that omniscience, omnipotent presence, and the very brief description of the transmutation caused by the realization of the divinity as Cosmos.

We have seen the existence of divinity, through meditation, within our body. We have seen the body of silence in which the divine was concealing itself, in the tenth chapter, and in the eleventh chapter we see the whole Cosmos as the flesh and blood of the divine. It is called the Cosmic *yoga*. It is the *yoga* of seeing God in the manifest Cosmos, as you have seen it in the unmanifest, un-individuated silence.

We have worked hard from the ninth chapter to the tenth, and now we conclude the eleventh chapter. Raja yoga, the ninth chapter, was itself a very complex one, Vibhuti Yoga, the tenth chapter, was comparatively easy, but difficult to grasp because of the metaphysical aspect of Indian philosophy. And the eleventh chapter, Visvarupa Darshana Yoga, every word of it was very complex.

CHAPTER XII

YOGA OF DEVOTION

Arjuna was frightened when he witnessed in the physical frame of Sri Krishna's body, the dance of existence; people getting born, getting killed, fighting each other, the interaction between good and evil. He was frightened and he was eager to see Sri Krishna again as an individual, in the so-called normal human form.

This whole episode signifies the terror, the fright, stimulated in the mind of the enquirer when suddenly, in a flash of awareness, the physical frame of his body, matter in his body, the mind operating in that matter, have no independence of their own. There is a higher power than the physical and the mental which does not have a visible tangible knowable form.

The physical body has a form, it can be touched, it can be seen, it can be moulded, it can be handled. And also the mental body, constituted of conditionings, can be perceived, because the mind is constantly moving and the movement of the mind as thought, as feeling, as sentiments, can be observed. The way to handle the mental body, to mould it, to control it, to regulate it, is qualitatively different from the mode of handling the physical body.

But when the enquirer, through his alertness and sensitive receptivity, becomes aware of the energy of intelligence (which has the body of silence, of emptiness, which is unknowable, untouchable, unperceivable and yet it is there), when he sees the light of that intelligence permeating and pervading every part of his body, every organ of the body, every drop of blood, even the marrow in the bones, then he becomes frightened. Because then he realizes that he cannot plead any excuses in the name of the physical body or the mind, for living in an impure, imbalanced, disorderly, unscientific way. That creates a fear.

We, the human beings, share the earth-nature, inertia, called *tamas*. The earth is dominated by *tamas guna*. *Raja guna* is the energy for movement and activity, and *sattva guna* is the energy for understanding and clarity, they are both there in the earth, in matter, but they are subdued. *Tamas* is the dimension which dominates in our life.

We have in us that inertia which causes laziness, sluggishness, postponement of action, postponement of decision, clumsiness. When we give into that laziness, sluggishness, postponement, procrastination, irregularities, unpunctuality, etc. in our daily living, we plead in the name of the body: 'my body requires this' and 'my body requires that.'

The awakening of intelligence and the perception that the energy of intelligence permeates your body, makes you feel uncomfortable, because the whole defensive mechanism built-up in the name of 'poor body' crumbles, collapses like a house of cards that children build in play.

Our life is full of defensive mechanisms that we build up in the name of our mind. Mind is subtle matter. Body is gross matter and it contains the subtle matter called mind. Mind is dominated by *raja guna*, the energy of movement, motion and activity. The subtle body, called mind, is ever restless because of *raja guna*, and it finds excuses for that incessant constant movement in the name of likes, dislikes, preferences, prejudices, value structures, ideals, ideologies. We build up defences for the unscientific, even the disorderly movement of the mind, its peculiarities, its idiosyncrasies. They are all defended by us, at least in our own minds, to ourselves.

When it is realized that mind is not the ultimate energy for living harmoniously, for sharing the harmony of the Cosmos around one, that it is not the source of intelligence or clarity of understanding, then the possibility of living in an imbalanced, impure, disharmonious, disorderly way is gone, and that terrifies a human being.

Human beings share the *raja guna* with animals. It is the dominant nature of animals. Animals are governed by instincts and biological inclinations. The pressure provoked by those instincts, traits, inclinations, are ruled by hunger, thirst, the pressurized compulsion for procreation, and they give in to that. Human beings like to do that also, to be governed by hunger, thirst, sex.

Now, the impulses in the animal body have their own velocity, their own momentum. It is a universal momentum of the human animal. We are animals. As we have the earth-nature as *tamoguna*, we also share the *raja guna* of the animal kingdom and we like the animal in us. Animals kill, not for hurting, but to survive. But we like to hurt with words, with glances. We may not kill, but we kill with words and glances, through indifference and domination.

This *raja guna*-dominated-behaviour also has no scope after the dawn of that clarity of intelligence. Justification for imbalances, impurities, waywardness, disorder, disharmony, everything collapses. And the perception of that power of intelligence, energy of intelligence, releases the *sattva guna* in you.

Some people like to discontinue their ascend towards the divine at this point of the liberation of *sattva guna*. It has relative clarity, which has relative unattachment, which has a limited capacity for freedom, because it has still the capacity of choice in it. With the liberation of the *sattva guna* in our life, we feel that we can control raja and *tama guna*, we can control the mind through discipline, codes of conduct, surrendering to some ideology, conforming to certain patterns, by creating parallel mechanistic movements of tamas and rajas in our being, by creating mechanistic movements of matter, tamas, in our body, because matter is governed by certain laws and moves in the framework of birth growth decay and death.

And there is also a mechanical movement of *raja guna*, which is constantly moving, provoking, imagining, building up aims, objectives and goals for that mental movement. So to those two parallel movements, a third parallel, relatively mechanistic movement, is created by the liberated *sattva*, that is relative limited clarity and freedom of choice. It is convenient to create such a parallel mechanistic repetitive movement in the name of Bhakti Yoga, in the name of Hatha Yoga.

Raja Yoga does not leave you free to do that. That is why few people like to study Raja Yoga. They are satisfied with the various disciplines (*yama, niyama, asana, pranayama,* etc.) and they like to stop there. Raja Yoga leaves you uncomfortable, because you are not building up any parallel repetitive or mechanistic automated movement on the intellectual plane, with the help of thoughts and ideas. It transcends even the *sattva guna.* Raja Yoga is transcending not only *tamas* and *rajas* but also transcending *sattva.*

That was the challenge before Arjuna, when he perceived the whole existence in the body of Krishna, realizing that in his own body the same principle was at work, and that he had to surrender to that Ishvara, that higher intelligence, residing in his own body.

The realization that the physical and the mental and the intellectual has to be dedicated to that which transcends these three, that is uncomfortable. Because there you see that you are not controlling matter, you are not controlling the mind. You realize that Purusha, the Ishvara, the supreme divine, is doing it. You have only to be alert, awake and receptive for that light, to control your life. Not that you are in charge of your life, but that the supreme, the sovereign divinity, or the primal creativity, is going to take charge of your whole life.

This message of dedicating and devoting the physical, the mental and the intellectual, to the transcendental supreme principle of Ishvara, principle of divinity, that is not very much relished by the mind. As Krishna says: 'Ishvara, the Lord of creation, resides in every human heart. I am the seed of all creation. Without me, movable and immovable matter does not exist. I am the content of creation. I am time, the principle of disintegration, culminating in what we call death. Creation is my breath, and also disintegration, culminating into the event of death, is my breath.' When Krishna says that, Arjuna begins to tremble.

Sri Krishna explains to Arjuna that birth is the beginning of death. In the seed of birth is concealed the event of death. The movement of creation becoming manifest out of the womb of the unmanifest, is what you call time. There is no other time but the unmanifest becoming manifest. That movement creates an idea of time. The unmanifest becomes the manifest, the seed becomes a sprout, a sprout becomes a sapling, a sapling growth into a tree. Growth is taking place. And when you watch the movement of growth, you impose the idea of time upon it, the idea of continuity upon it.

Because human beings do not see with their senses that every growth is an autonomous event. They have an idea about time, as if there is a continuity in time. The physicists have realized however, that what you call the continuity of time is not a continuity; what you call every moment is an emanation of the timeless. The moment is the timeless emanation of timelessness.

In the same way, what you call the seed, disintegrates in order to become a sprout, the sprout disintegrates to take the form of a sapling. This disintegration accompanies the movement of growth. And when the growth culminates into a full tree, there is a stabilization. The seed has established itself in the form of a tree.

The seed of a human being has established itself in a full-grown adult body. It has crystallized the growth, it has stabilized. You know, in order to get established, you need to get stabilized. In the adult human being the growth has stabilized, it has also crystallized and in that crystallization, in that stabilization is the seed of disintegration. Because after middle age, the process of disintegration, disorder, disharmony, begins to manifest in the body.

Then you require meditation, medicine, treatment, to help order, harmony and equilibrium in the body. But the process of decline and disintegration has already begun. In the very moment of stabilization and crystallization or the full blossoming of the growth, you can see the seed of disintegration, a new disorder, a new disharmony culminating in what you call death.

Then, in order to preserve the equilibrium and harmony in the body, you take medicine. But then the body grows old and even the support of meditation fails to maintain the equilibrium, the order, the harmony, and irreversible departure follows. Birth is the beginning of death. The movement of matter from unmanifest to manifest is the beginning of dissolution. In the movement of manifestation is concealed the movement of dissolution, in the movement of emergence is concealed and contained the movement of merging back into its source. The movement which Capra calls the 'Dance of Shiva.'

The method to surrender the movement of the physical and mental body, including the intellectual thought body, to surrender that to the ultimate divine supreme sovereign intelligence, is very uncomfortable. What does that surrender mean? Surrender means: directing those energies towards freedom, not allowing those energies to follow passively a pattern, a mechanistic repetitive pattern. Through *dharma*, *dhyanam pranayam*, etc, you are trying to persuade those energies of the physical body to slip out of the pattern, the natural pattern of matter. You are trying to liberate those energies, which are mechanized, patterned, repetitive, structured, from mechanistic behaviour.

The body of a *yoga* student; every pore is intelligent, it wants to break through with a freshness, with a vitality, which has nothing to do with the age of the body. Matter has been liberated from inertia, the physical body. It may not happen in Karma Yoga, Bhakti Yoga, shear limited Hatha Yoga, Mantra Yoga, Tantra Yoga. If you want proof, you can visit the *ashrams* and see the so-called *bhakta* and Mantra Yogis and Tantra Yogis. Look at their bodies, look at the relationship with diet and sleep, walking, sitting, moving the body, and you will see that matter has not been purified, it has not been liberated from inertia, it has not been energized in a new way.

You know what *yoga* is; it is creating a new equilibrium in the material body, the physical frame, and a new harmony in the mental or the thought structure, and transcending them. That is *yoga*. It describes mutation of the physical and the mental, so that the physical and the mental are equipped to relate to the outer nature in a different way altogether, finding new ways of directing the mechanistic, patterned, structured energies towards liberation, towards freedom.

Emancipation is not only grasping some idea about transformation and intellectually identifying with that idea, a cerebral identification with an abstract idea. It has no meaning for Life. It is an inner, intellectual luxury, indulging in that self-hypnotic abstraction and identification.

The purpose of Life is transmutation of matter and mind contained in you, because you also contain the Purusha, the Ishvara, in you. It is not only out there in the Cosmos that the Lord has his abode, his abode is here too, within you. So dedicating, devoting, surrendering is not a poetic idea.

Bhakti Yoga is called 'the nectar of the whole *Gita*.' The word *bhakti* is mostly misunderstood and misinterpreted. It is mistaken for a reckless abandonment of emotionalism, for excessive indulgence in the abandonment of emotions. And every imbalance, physical, verbal, mental is justified in the name of *bhakti*. The excitement and nervous intoxication are not only justified and defended, but claimed in the name of *bhakti* and spirituality. It is a dangerous word unless one probes into the fundamental or original meaning of the term in the Sanskrit language.

Before we proceed with this chapter, a little clarification is necessary about the dialogue between Sri Krishna and Arjuna: Sri Krishna and Arjuna, as two mortal human beings, relations, friends. One is the teacher of the other, that is Krishna.

But when, in his communications, he uses the first person, I and Me, he refers to the eternal Krishna, equated with *sat-chit-ananda*, the indestructible truth, intelligence which is a characteristic of Life. *Chit* is self-awareness contained in that truth, which releases a cohesive principle of orderliness in all its movements, and *ananda* is bliss, generated by the harmony built-in in the cohesive orderliness of life.

Sat-chit-ananda, indestructible truth, self-awareness in the truth, cohesive orderliness because of self-awareness, and harmony because of the orderliness resulting in bliss or *ananda*. This is the eternal law of Life. Sri Krishna as the eternal law of Life, eternal principle of Life, and Sri Krishna as a mortal human being; Arjuna's friend, relation and teacher.

I wonder if any of you have heard about a fantastic person who came to India in 1924 from Great Britain, Mr. Nixon, who got initiated into the Vedas, the Upanishads, the *Gita*, etc, renounced life and was given the name Krishna Prema by his *guru*. Krishna Prema was a brilliant person, who wrote a number of very significant books on Indian philosophy. He had mastered Sanskrit, Bengali, Pali, and he was also a great scholar of Buddhist philosophy, etc. Once he was travelling through India and someone asked him, because he had some beads round his neck: 'whom are you devoted to?' And he said: 'to the eternal Krishna.' 'And where does your eternal Krishna live?' He said: 'in my heart.'

You see these two characteristics of the personality of Krishna, the son of Vasudeva, who has identified his whole being, dedicating his whole being to the eternal Krishna in him, the eternal law of Life in him. He is called a perfect incarnation of the absolute reality, because all his actions, from childhood to the last breath, manifest the clarity of intelligence, the orderliness due to self-awareness and a causeless ever bubbling bliss or *ananda*.

In this chapter, this discrimination of the two will have to be remembered. Those of you, who have studied all the eleven chapters with me, will remember that Arjuna had heard about Sankhya Yoga, Karma Yoga, Sannyasa Yoga, Akshara Brahma Yoga, Vibhuti Yoga. And in the eleventh chapter, he had a vision of the Cosmic manifestation by seeing the whole Cosmos in the physical frame of Krishna.

He understood that *prakriti*, Cosmic matter, is the abode of Purusha, spirit. The Purusha does not dwell outside of, isolated from the *mula prakriti*, but permeates the whole Cosmic matter, and makes every material expression resplendent with his splendour, with the wealth of his being. So Arjuna has that vision, that matter and spirit, *prakriti* and Purusha, are blended together. Now he asks a question of Sri Krishna:

'Look, Krishna, there seems to be two paths of *yoga*. One is through *prakriti*, the Cosmic manifestations, using those manifestations as opportunities for discovering the built-in intelligence, harmony and bliss in them, thereby liberating the *rajas* from the clutches of the *tamas*, and the *sattva* from the clutches of *rajas* and then transcending even *sattva*. That is one progressive gradual path of ascent, it is an ascendance.

The other path seems to be to renounce inwardly the manyness of the manifestations, merely to turn your back on the allurement of Cosmic matter and allow your mind to be grounded and rooted in the absolute reality, with one stroke of perception, observation, one stroke of understanding the truth contained in the perception. One withdraws emotionally from Cosmic matter and remains rooted in the absolute reality.'

There is no progressive or gradual ascendance, not a god-ward ascent. But it is something that you allow to occur radically, holistically, at the moment of understanding. It is an instantaneous transmutation of your whole being.

These two paths seem to be there. One deals with manifest matter and the other deals with the unmanifest being. We have now got acquainted with the terms that Krishna uses to indicate the absolute unmanifest un-individuated Life. Whether with one leap of understanding you get rooted into that, using the unmanifest to unite your consciousness with it, or using the Cosmic matter in your body and the Cosmic matter around you for a progressive gradual ascent.

'Which path is better Krishna? Which is superior? Who is closer and dearer to you? The one who relies on the unmanifest or the one who takes help of the manifest?' That is the question.

The vision that Arjuna had seen in the eleventh chapter of the whole Cosmos contained in the physical frame of Krishna, must have created a temptation in Arjuna's mind to take one leap, a short-cut, to holistic emancipation. But Krishna is a past master per excellence in human psychology, in handling the questions. Yet, my poor English cannot render the elegance and majesty of the original Sanskrit text. This is a poetic dialogue, the lucidity, the beauty of the diction defies translation into any other language, even any other Indian language.

Krishna gives the answer in the second or third verse in chapter twelve. He says: 'those whose actions and movements are filled with the awareness of the divine presence within and around themselves, whose actions are dedicated to me, the eternal truth of Life, they are the best *yogis*. Their mind rooted in me, grounded in me, and even their intellect, reason, rationality, filled with my awareness, wherever these two criteria prevail, they are doing my *upasana*.'

Upasana is a very interesting word; literally it means: to be established in the proximity of the divine. 'They are always in intimate proximity to me, because their consciousness is united with the transcendental principle of life.' Their consciousness is united with Purusha, with Brahman, the Lord, Ishvara. Whatever they may be doing on the physical plane, whatever their actions, there is an invisible inner proximity between the individual and the absolute. 'If it is there, Arjuna, they know the secret of *yoga* and they are living in union with me.'

Seeing that Arjuna was puzzled by this cryptic answer, Krishna, the eternal principle eloquent through Krishna, says: 'my proximity is through consciousness.'

But then the teacher, the friend, in a very gentle and affectionate manner, begins an elaboration of what he had said. There are only twenty verses in the twelfth chapter, one of the short chapters in the *Gita*. He says: 'look Arjuna, those whose minds and hearts get rooted or grounded in the awareness of absolute reality, the unmanifest wholeness of Life, they find that their living on the physical and mental level becomes rather strenuous and painful.'

Those who get dedicated to the unmanifest, the invisible, the immeasurable, the unknowable, the unnameable, without taking the quantum leap, this dedication having happened through the flash of understanding and the flash of a vision of that Cosmic reality, what about their body, what about the cerebral organ loaded with conditionings and the biological structure limited by habit patterns? What about them?

The awareness and the union through awareness have not got enough vitality and dynamism to lift the physical and mental frame out of their conditionings. That is why living on the physical and mental level, surrounded by manifested Cosmic and individuated matter, becomes a painful thing for them.

They do not know how to handle the mind, the knowledge, the experience, the conditionings. So, the physical and mental frames tend to follow the mechanized and patterned behaviour and the sting of that awareness goes on pricking them, every time. The physical and the mental are in disharmony and disorder with the content of that awareness. Look at the pain! So, there is more pain and suffering in their lives, for those who happen to understand the unmanifest, the absolute, the transcendental reality and cannot live it.

It is easier for human beings, who are embodied matter, who are condensed Cosmos, who share with Cosmic matter all the energies, it is easier for mortal human beings who have a limited span of time, the potential in their biological structure has a limited duration by its very nature, for them it is easier to transmute, refine, purify and lift the physical frame through that purification, or transmute, purify and refine the mental frame through new conditionings, unlearning the old and learning the new. That is what you call education.

'Those who would like to reach me, to get merged into me, the transcendental reality, do so through education.' Education is a process of purification, of eliminating the impurities in the body and the mind.

In one of the previous chapters, Krishna had said that the reality of

Life can be assimilated through renunciation of the false and education of the physical frame of getting in tune with the understanding of truth. The physical frame has to get tuned in to the new energy of truth, the new energy of understanding, of clarity, of orderliness, intelligence. It is just a tuning in.

The physical and mental frames have been tuned into something else. Now, they have to get tuned in. Education is for tuning in the glandular, the muscular, the nervous system, the cerebral organ, the receptivity, the capacity of retaining all these faculties, having tuned in to a certain natural order in matter. Now, consciously you want to tune the biological and psychological organism to something new. It is a vertical movement that you want those structures to take.

'So, Arjuna, it is easier through education to understand and refine and tune again the physical and the mental. Just don't grasp greedily the truth, with the help of the brain, of reason and rationality, and say: 'I have it here.' Grasping the truth is not the living of it, recognition does not mean realization. Knowledge does not imply necessarily understanding. So it is easier to follow the path of manifest matter, by which you are surrounded and which is in your body: individuated and un-individuated matter surrounding you and the embodiment of individuated matter as your frame, as your instrument for living, as a field for your operation.'

Do you see with me that Sri Krishna is explaining a way to not only combining *dhyana* and Karma Yoga with Bhakti Yoga. It is not a combination, it is a blending of them into something else, as you mix two colours and you get a new colour. In the same way, the *dhyana* part that is the understanding of Jnana Yoga and the motion of Karma Yoga are blended together; motionlessness and motion.

Dhyana, understanding, makes you steady. Combining the motionlessness of *dhyana* and the motion or movement of *karma*, these two elements are brought together by Sri Krishna under the name of Bhakti Yoga, so as to be eternally proximate to reality, never to be separated from the transcendental. Never to be separated from the seed, though you have become the tree. *Bhakti* is non-separation, a science and art of non-separation. Individuated: yes, separated: no.

We will go into the details of Bhakti Yoga slowly, step by step, very carefully, because it is nectar. We have come to the essence of the *Gita*. From the thirteenth chapter onwards will begin the metaphysical part, the theoretical philosophical part. But from the second to the twelfth chapter, we have the scope to understand, learn, study and get transmuted or transformed.

Krishna talks again about *abhyasa*, education, learning. Learning for discovery not for acquisition. Learning for transmutation and not for exhibition of scholarship or erudition. Learning is fantastic. You learn while you live and you live while you learn, it is a holistic movement of Life.

When it comes to the choice between the path of renunciation and the path of restraint, Sri Krishna recommends the path of restraint. We have talked at the end of the eleventh chapter how all matter contains the three *gunas*, *sattva*, *rajas* and *tamas*, the steadiness of *sattva*, the motion of *rajas* and the inertia or passivity of tamas. Subduing *tamas*, restraining *rajas* and utilizing the steadiness of *sattva* is called *abhyasa*, according to the *Gita*.

For subduing the sensual structure, the earth or principle of inertia in our body, for subduing that, restraining *rajas* in the mind or the mental structure, Krishna introduces a new dimension, the energy of love. He says the godward voyage, the vertical ascendance becomes pleasurable, enjoyable, not painful, if you realize that the purpose of human life is divinization of matter. They are fantastic terms used by the *Gita*, divinization of matter and humanization of the divine.

The eternal law, the Lord, Purusha, Brahman, whatever it is called, and *sat-chit-ananda* have to be manifested in the human body holistically, in the whole being of the human animal. It is the humanization of the divine principle or the eternal Krishna, and divinization of matter. As long as matter and spirit remain isolated from each other, due to ignorance, an illusory separation being imposed upon *prakriti* and Purusha, matter and spirit, there is bound to be suffering, says Sri Krishna.

Do you know, what divinity is? It is that which is not created by human thought, it is self-generated. We call that divine or divinity because it is self-existent, self-generated, self-controlled, it is a causeless cause which is cause and creation together, which is a rootless root or source of creation. We call that divine or divinity. It has not been brought about by human thought, it has not been shaped by human hand.

When the three *gunas* in matter, in *prakriti*, are oriented towards order: (*sat-chit-ananda* are oriented towards truth, self-awareness and the bliss of harmony), then matter gets divinized, chaos is replaced by order, anarchy is replaced by cohesiveness, stress and strain of effort are replaced by spontaneity. And a dry implementation of knowledge is replaced by a tender and gentle flow of understanding through the sense organs.

This is what is implied by the terms divinization of matter: to allow the clarity of intelligence, the order of self-awareness and the bliss of harmony to manifest in your body, in your brain, in your glances, in your speech and in your sensual behaviour. Unless the divinity is manifested right down to the sensual level, yoga is not complete.

'The humanly possible perfection of matter or prakriti, and the spontaneous manifestation, the uncovering of the being of Purusha, *sat-chit-ananda*, into everything that you do, these two, (one with the help of consciousness united with reality, and the other, *abhyasa* helping matter to come out of anarchy and chaos), Arjuna, if you realize that the purpose of human life is this dual divinization and humanization, like inhaling and exhaling of breath, then there will be an inner urge. Your whole being will respond to this realization. And that inner urge is called love.'

It is a non-rational element; it is the energy of desire focussed on the transcendental reality. When the energy of desire moves outward from your body, towards perishable objects and wants to derive momentary short-lived pleasure from them, then it keeps you stuck to the horizontal level, the earth orbit or the orbit of matter.

But when the energy of desire is directed towards the one and only Brahman, the whole Life is divine. When the energy of desire is directed towards that unique oneness, towards that homogeneity, that indivisibility of Life, towards that Paramatman, the supreme Atman, then that energy gets transmuted into what we call love.

When it is directed towards perishable objects or towards mortal human beings around you and you want to derive pleasure from that contact and interaction, and you want to cling to those objects or individuals because they are the source of your pleasure, then the energy of desire can very well degenerate into lust for pleasure, greed for money, lust for power. It is the same energy, whether you allow it to get transmuted and manifested as the energy of love, vitality of love on the path of light, focussed on the divinity or Lord or whatever you call it, focussed on Life, or you allow it to get dissipated by directing it towards the many objects around you for the sake of pleasure.

'Arjuna, why not use the energy of desire which is the bud out of which love can flower. If you use that while you are doing *abhyasa*, then that *abhyasa* is called *bhakti*. Let not the union with me, let not the identification with me be cold and harsh, only on the level of an idea or a cerebral perception. Let it be mellowed down. Because absoluteness is very austere.' The sharpness and penetration of intelligence or truth is very sharp. Let it become mellowed down, let it become gentle through focussing your energy of desire, wanting only the *yoga* (union) with the divine, wanting only to live the reunion of individuated matter with the non-individuated divinity.

If that energy of desire is oriented godwards and focussed on that eternal law or principle of Life, then there will be a new vitality, a new passion. And the *abhyasa* of purifying, refining and tuning in matter, tuning in your thought structure to the unknown energy, the Cosmic energy, will become an enjoyable voyage from the known to the unknowable, from the measurable to the immeasurable, from the manifest to the unmanifest and that which is beyond both manifest and unmanifest.

'How do I do this education, this *abhyasa*, this refinement, this tuning to new frequencies of energies?' asks Arjuna. We have now come to the eighth verse of the twelfth chapter. And the teacher says: 'you have seen that the good and the evil reside in my being. The source of Life is contained in what you call the good and the evil.'

The source of what you call evil is the drive for self-assertion as a separate entity. It is the I-ness, the ego-ness and its aggressive acquisitive movement, the obsession with the idea of separateness and the yearning to preserve and propagate that separate identity. It is the source of what you call evil or maladjustment with the wholeness of Life. After all, evil is maladjustment or lack of adjustment and good is harmony with the indivisible wholeness, non-fragmented wholeness of Life.

So, Krishna says to Arjuna: 'the good and evil are contained in me. The senses, which are the source of pleasure, pain and sensation, are contained in me, in matter. You have seen how what we call pain, pleasure, hot, cold, birth, death, growth, decay, everything is contained in the seed of Life. I am the seed, nothing exists without me, I am the content of all Life and I am the seed of all creation. If you have seen that Arjuna and you have realized it, then begin the *abhyasa*, by maintaining equanimity when your body and mind are visited by pleasure or pain. Don't get excited by one or shaken by the other.'

Begin the study of *abhyasa yoga*, a new orientation to your life. Become aware that they have the same source, one is a harmonious trend, the other is a disharmonious trend. You have to educate your mind and body not to get excited, tense, frustrated or worked up. If you learn to maintain equanimity in the face of pleasure and pain, success and failure, honour and humiliation, if you learn that, then by sustaining this equanimity, it will become a very vital force in you.

You have to live in the world, you have to live surrounded by your co-human beings and other species. Why not begin the study, the *abhyasa*, this duality of life is bound to be there, wherever you move. You are embodied matter, you have a considerable long span of life in this body, though it is perishable. You are going to be interacting, as embodied matter, with matter around you, individuated and non-individuated. Why not begin the study.

Awareness of the wholeness and non-fragmentability of Life will enable you to sustain an equi-balance at the sensual level, and equanimity at the level of your mind, inner and outer. Equanimity, or equi-balance or equipoise, give a steadiness, a stability to the being.

When you get excited every few seconds, jolted, shaken, disturbed or upset, it is not only your mind that gets disturbed, it is your whole being. It affects the nerves, the chemical system, the muscles. They shrink, they become tense, the flow of blood, the rhythm of breathing, everything gets disturbed. If you give in to the excitement of pleasure or the frustration or disturbance of pain, and that happens many times every day, then there will be no vitality, you will be drained of all vital energy. The system has to fight against these jolts. Creativity is used for resisting these jolts and there is no creativity left for the *abhyasa*.

'So Arjuna, it is a pragmatic thing that I am telling you. In the face of honour or humiliation, when someone behaves as if you are a friend or treats you as a foe, if you learn not to allow the equi-balance at the sensual level to be shaken rudely or crudely and equanimity or peacefulness or steadiness begins, then proximity to me will be sustained in your life. That is *upasana*, worship of the divine. Your living will become a worship of the divine, if you educate yourself in maintaining the truth.'

In Sanskrit two very interesting phrases are used. One is: '*yoga* is skill in action.' Equi-balance at the sensual level, is called skill. Not to be shaken, upset, disturbed, frustrated, depressed. You know, new imbalances are generated out of those moods and one imbalance leads to another. It is a very chaotic and anarchical daily life. The anarchy and chaos may be inward, non-verbalized.

And the other term is 'inner equanimity'. These two terms are masterpieces for the students of yoga. To be still in action is called *yoga*, because you skilfully dodge the tensions of duality. You have found out the art of a warrior or a fighter, to dodge them, not to allow them. When you have an onslaught on your physical being, your matter is disturbed by that onslaught. You are saved from that onslaught through inner equanimity. The quietening of the thought process arises while you are dealing with the manifest or unmanifest world. Yoga is practical psychology, the science of Life and living. It is not a make-belief. It is not emotional or intellectual.

The joy that the Vedic philosophy has given to the whole of humanity does not belong to the Indians only, it does not belong to the Hindus. It is the science of Life and living, it is the physics of consciousness. The physics of matter are studied in the west, and the physics of consciousness are studied in the east. When they will be blended together, there will be a new human race. I have no doubt about it. By the turn of this unhappy, sad, unfortunate twentieth century, by the end of this century, a new human being will get born and manifested; a new dynamics of human relationship will evolve out of their interaction. And serious people, like you, are the verification of this. Otherwise why have you come to this small far off village in India? It is the Cosmic plan which seems to be pushing you in that direction.

Equanimity is the real *tapas* (discipline). Somebody talks to you in an insulting way, somebody wants to humiliate you. But the equanimity of your heart does not get disturbed by it, you do not get hurt by it. You recognize what is what and you respond to the challenge of the relationship without giving in. You refuse to get hurt. It is a dual learning: the one on the mental level with the help of the Yoga Sutras of Patanjali; the other, the equi-balance and skill in action, with the help of Hatha Yoga. You can blend it together.

Why complete withdrawal from the material world, from this manifested world? Through this learning of equanimity and equi-balance, that does not become necessary. Krishna points out that because you are embodied matter and matter is energy, your body is a seat of many energies, they are there. Life cannot be idle and energies contained in matter cannot be idle. They are going to be active. How can you withdraw from Life? How can you turn your back on all *karma*? *Karma* is your destiny.

There is both this law of *sat-chit-ananda*, of the supreme reality, but there is also this law of *karma*. Even moving through the span of hundred years of human life, doing *karma*, *karma* is not a source of bondage and there is no other path for you. *Karma* is the best thing for individuated embodied matter. In the non-human species, in animals and birds, if their intelligence is at the subconscious level, *karma* is at the instinctive level.

It is the privilege of human beings to get liberated from the clutches of mere instinct and impulses. Complete withdrawal from *karma* is not possible. If the *karmas* or the movements are centred round the I or the ego, if they become thus self-centred, then the enclosure that they create around them or build around them, in the name of security, results in isolation, psychological isolation.

Self-centredness generates fear, it puts you on the defensive, and the person who is constantly tortured by fear and is constantly on the defensive, is bound to be isolated from others. The otherness of the other generates fear, tension, duality, defensiveness and a defence mechanism is put up psychologically, also physically. See the isolation, as if Life is a constant battle.

The psychology of fear leading to the psychology of aberration will never come to an end, unless the *karma* is looked upon, not as a prerogative of the I or ego, always acquisitive or defensive, but is understood as energies contained in my body, as the Lord of nature.

Because the energy of appetite is there, nutrition in cereals or fruit or vegetables has a meaning. These two energies meet together and yet transmute in a new energy. So the *prakriti* in me, matter in me, the energies contained in my embodied personality are moving, and yet I am not the doer. It is my privilege and honour, my destiny to think. It is a privilege of the human species to think, to discriminate the true from the false.

So, Sri Krishna says: 'Arjuna, you cannot turn your back on *karma*. Karma Yoga is your destiny, Jnana Yoga is your prerogative. And you manifest truth with the tenderness of love, utilizing the fire of the energy of desire, when you have blended the Karma Yoga and the Jnana Yoga and generated Bhakti Yoga.'

When a person has done the *abhyasa* and merely perfected the physical and the mental structure as much as it is possible in human form, what are the characteristics of such a person? How do you recognize such a person? And what is the quality of his behaviour in the world and with nature? That is the subject of the next ten verses.

There are three important aspects in the last part of the twelfth chapter. One aspect is the differentiation between *yajna* and *sannyasa*. Another aspect would be the step, suggested by Bhakti Yoga, for a progressive ascent or divinization of matter. And the third aspect is the logical and natural consequences of either, looking upon the whole Life as a wheel of sacrifice or *yajna*, or looking upon the whole Life as a consecration to the sovereign divinity. Before we take up these three aspects, may I remind the students of *yoga* of some important teachings of not only the *Bhagavad Gita*, but of the Upanishads and the Yoga Sutras by Patanjali.

According to the Upanishads and Yoga Sutras, Cosmic Life can be analysed into three organic dimensions that are blended together. One is the individuated specified manifested world, in which matter is individuated, particularized and therefore consist of various material objects; the mineral and vegetable kingdoms, the kingdom of birds and animals and the human species, and so on.

In this manifested world we have to dwell, we have to interact and we have to organize our relationships, so that our behaviour does not disturb the natural *yoga* or harmony and order in the universe. Life is a natural *yoga*; it is a state of intelligent order and harmony.

If you proceed from this manifest world towards the unmanifest, then you find yourself in the dimension of non-manifested non-individuated non-particularized Cosmic matter, *mula prakriti*.

In the manifested world, every object, even the minutest particle of matter, has its own quantum of energy which is an indication of mind contained in matter. That quantum of energy does not operate on the conscious level, it has not got its initiative. The mind, through that quantum of energy contained in particles of matter, is subdued, it is at the sub-conscious level. If someone tries to activate that energy, the mind contained in matter, then it functions, it operates.

At the unmanifest level, that is at the non-individuated and non-particularized level of *mula prakriti*, there are no particular objects in Cosmic matter. There is a Cosmic mind, the mind of Cosmic matter, which also does not function on the conscious level, but which can be activated through Hatha Yoga, Tantra Yoga, Mantra Yoga, Nada Yoga, Laya Yoga, etc.

There are so many scientific ways of activating and mobilizing the Cosmic mind, which sages like Ramakrishna Paramahansa or Aurobindo called the Cosmic mother. Shankaracharya used to call *maya* the mother of the universe. So, individuated mind and non-individuated Cosmic mind. Therefore, where there is matter, there is energy and wherever there is energy there is consciousness. It may not have sound and speech, after all silence is the sound of existence. But it can get activated.

Now, if these two points are sufficiently clear, let us proceed to the third dimension, that which is beyond the manifest and the unmanifest, beyond the visible and the invisible, beyond the sensory and the occult, that which is transcendental, beyond the Cosmos, beyond the *mula prakriti*. The terms manifest and unmanifest become irrelevant to the existence of the transcendental energy of truth awareness and bliss, *sat-chit-ananda*, the Purusha of the Sankhyas, the Ishvara of Raja Yoga, the Brahman of the Vedantins. There is no mind there; there is truth, awareness and bliss, *sat-chit-ananda*.

These are three dimensions of Life and the understanding or clarification of these three dimensions, blended into what you call Life, is necessary for the study of *yoga* in general and study of this twelfth chapter on Bhakti Yoga in particular. Let us proceed, if these points are clear. We are taking a very important verse from the twelfth chapter.

'Renouncing all the *karmas* unto me, the divinity, the transcendental law or principle of truth and bliss.'

Now, this word renunciation is very interesting. Mostly an abused, misused, misinterpreted word. 'Renouncing all the *karmas* unto me' does it not imply that all your energies are holistically, (not separately as emotion, as thought, as a theory, a physical activity), all your energies are holistically gathered together into their homogeneous wholeness.

When these energies are focussed upon the essence of existence, truth, awareness and harmony, that act of focussing the energies, is the content of renunciation. Please do see with me, it is not withdrawal. Renunciation, *sannyasa*, is not something negative, it is the most positive and creative movement that human beings are capable of.

When all the energies are focussed upon the ultimate reality, the sovereign supreme Chaitanya, Paramatman, Brahman, then that very act of holistic focussing on truth, on awareness, on harmony, that very act contains the seed of redemption. When all the actions are renounced unto the divinity, the essence of existence, the sovereign transcendental principle of truth, this redeems the *bhakta*, the devotee.

You see, we feel secure in the idea that there is some saviour, some redeemer, who will wash away all our sins, who will purify us. Now the *Gita* is telling us, in this verse, that your act of dedicating all your energies to truth, to the ultimate intelligence, not dedicating them to your ego, not dedicating them to the motivations of your ego, but dedicating them to Life, that activates the redeeming energy. It becomes a source of your redemption. It is a tremendously important and very fundamental point of the teachings of the Vedas and of the *Gita*.

So there is no worry about the consequences of the actions. Life is divinity and the act of living becomes its own fulfilment. The act of living becomes the act of worshipping the divine. You are worshipping Life through every movement of yours. Because you are the physical and psychological embodiment in which you live. Your dwelling place has all the energies given unto you by the supreme Life.

You cannot afford to allow them to waste away, they are not going to remain idle. So channeling them, utilizing the energies in order to manifest the concealed truth, awareness and bliss in you, this is renunciation. The *karma* is released from the clutches of the ego. It is no longer done for the sake of the ego. Because there is a conscious mind conferred upon the human animal, it is the responsibility to handle and channel all the energies harmoniously towards the truth. Do you see the beauty of the implication of *sannyasa*, renunciation? And how roughly, how crudely, how mercilessly the word has been used?

'Well, Arjuna, if you are not capable of such a holistic dedication or renunciation, if the reverence for Life does not inspire you to dedicate all your energies and movements towards the truth, if you are not capable of doing that, there is another alternative.'

The alternative of handling and using the physical and mental energies as an offering to the divine, consist not of renouncing, but as an offering. When there is renunciation, there is no expectation of any reciprocation from anywhere, because the very act is its own fulfilment. The very act liberates, it is instantaneous emancipation or liberation, abandoning all claims on the result of action. If that is not possible, then coming down a little from the dimension of this renunciation, Sri Krishna suggests:

'Is it possible for you, Arjuna, to look upon Life as a sacrifice, as an offering, not as *sannyasa*, renunciation, but as a *yajna*, a sacrifice.'

Look, the tree sacrifices. It gives the fruit and the flowers to us. The river sacrifices its water for us and fertilizes the earth. The earth sacrifices its fertility and gives us so much. The sun sacrifices its light and warmth and healing energies for us. Can you look upon Life and the movement of living as a wheel of *yajna*, sacrifice? The *Gita* talks of the wheel of sacrifice.

Now, what is the difference between *sannyasa,* renunciation, and *yajna*, sacrifice? In renunciation you have abandoned the claim on the result of the action. You do not expect any reciprocation. But in sacrifice, you are offering, with the hope that you will receive your offering and energy back in purer form.

Because doing *karma*, moving into relationships, you are consuming your energies, you are consuming the impulses, the momentum, the velocity contained in your body, physically or psychologically. And when you do that, you are offering, so that you get back the energy in a purer form, in a more refined way, at a higher level.

Offering expects enrichment of your being, through that act of offering. Not in terms of money, wealth, power etc., because we are talking about the *bhakta*, the devotee, and we are talking about Bhakti Yoga. Can you look upon your actions and your movements as an offering, as you do in a sacrifice? You offer pieces of sandalwood, the best clarified butter that you have, rice, sesame seeds and so many other things. The best that you have is offered. In the same way, offer the best of your being in every act of yours. It does not matter if you hope or expect reciprocation.

Where will the reciprocation come from? And here is the interesting point. The reciprocation will come from the Cosmic mind, the energies contained in that *mula prakriti*. That Cosmic matter will respond, because your actions are oriented towards the divine, though not dedicated towards it. They are oriented, they have taken the direction of a higher level of life. You are not claiming the results only onto yourself, but your horizons are widened, the enclosure of the ego is becoming wider, through every sacrifice, through every relationship.

If you are not capable of *sannyasa*, the proximity to truth, awareness and bliss, through your consciousness, if that is too austere for you, if *sannyasa* is too sharp and too austere, too direct and penetrating for you, why not learn to do every action, to move in every movement, as an offering to the divinity?

When you do that, your *abhyasa*, your education of matter and mind for progressive refinement and purification, will go on and the actions offered as an offering will purify matter. 'Arjuna, if you are not capable of *sannyasa*, can you do *abhyasa* and *yajna* together, so that the reciprocation from the Cosmic mind, the Cosmic energy of *mula prakriti*, will be there?'

In the first option there was redemption. In the second there is reciprocation, progressive purification etc., and the gratification to the ego that it is doing something. In the first, the ego-consciousness and its motivations have nothing to do with that dedication. In the second there is a gratification to the separate consciousness of the ego, that it is doing the offering.

'If that also is too much for you Arjuna, if you can't look upon the whole of your life as a wheel of sacrifice, offering everything to the divinity, can you do one thing?' This is the third option offered by Sri Krishna to Arjuna.

'Do your *karma* as you wish to do it, want to do it, but don't worry about the consequences or the result of that action.'

Follow the motivations. In the first two, it was a transmutation of the motivation. In the third option there is full freedom to the motivations of the I-consciousness, but no control or manipulation of the result. That is renunciation of the fruit of action. Here we might have to go slowly, because the points are very critical for a student or teacher of *yoga*, it is a very essential aspect.

What is the difference between *karma phala tyaga*, offering the fruit of action, and *yajna karma*, action as an offering?

In the first case, in which you offer the fruit of action, Sri Krishna is not questioning your motivations at all. Whether you dedicate it to the divine and are conscious of offering the action, just go ahead, enjoy that satisfaction and do it thoroughly, fully. But while doing it, be aware that you do not manipulate the results. *Yoga* is practical psychology.

When you do certain things which the situation expects of you, which your commitment and responsibility expects of you, when you do that, it is not a simple doing. But while doing it, we try to manipulate and control the result by the doing of it. Please do see this. It is a simple straightforward action, being alert and attentive. That is one thing, without adding this subjective craving for certain results.

We have not only a motivation, we have a craving for a particular result from that action. It is not the doing of it that satisfies us. Look at the human mind. We have a particular result in our mind and by doing it, there is not only rationality, equi-balance, no, no, not only that. We try to speak in such a way that our concealed craving for the result is secured, manipulated. We manoeuvre while doing the action or the movement of relationship, we try to manoeuvre, manipulate and engineer the result. We don't allow the action to produce the result. Don't we do that?

Narrating a fact, describing a fact, we describe it in such a way, not impartially, not objectively, but we describe it in such a way that we get the concealed result in our mind, imprinted upon the mind of the other person. The manner of doing this is not simple or innocent, it is not clean. It is contaminated with these concealed manipulations and manoeuvrings, because we are worried about the result of the action.

We have no faith in the Law of Karma, that, if the *karma* is done cleanly and rationally, it will produce its own result. We do not allow the *karma* to produce its natural result, we interfere with that *karma*, and try to secure the craving and yearning that we have in our mind. 'Arjuna, can you sacrifice that?'

You act out of ambition, you act out of assertiveness, you act out of your desire for acquisition, etc. Go ahead and do it, but do it in such a way, that the movement of action is not polluted by any manipulations for the result, *Karma phala tyaga*. People think that you do the *karma* and then you give up the fruits of the *karma*. It is not that. It is while doing the *karma* that you are not to be worried or bothered about the possible or probable result of it.

This does not relate to your life in society, where you handle your economic, social, political matters, where you deal with science and technology etc. This is about human relationships, relationship with nature, with fellow human beings and with fellow non-human beings. To manipulate the fruit (*phala*) while you are doing the *karma*, that is the evil. Have you got the courage to give up this temptation of manipulating, manoeuvring the results of your actions? Can you do that?

We do our *karma*, we go through the actions in the day-time, and at night we go on worrying about them: 'I have done so and so, but I don't know what will happen?' Let it happen, whatever happens. You have done your best. Why not leave the rest to Life? But we don't.

It is a very subtle point of human psychology: no manipulations in the movement of *karma*. Energies contained in the body, in reason and rationality, envelop your mind. If there is an awakening of the tenderness of love in you, then let love, rationality and the energies contained in your body flow freely.

These are the three options Sri Krishna talks about. If this is clear let us proceed. He describes the steps of progressive purification, progressive ascent on the path of light, bliss, and awareness, on the path of *sat-chit-ananda*.

'Arjuna, *dhyana*, meditation, is superior to *abhyasa*. Even verbal knowledge, is superior to mere physical practice.'

Now, why does he say that *dhyana* is superior to *abhyasa*? In *abhyasa* you have to use your psychophysical body. For that, you have to follow certain systems given by science. You have a physical body, an anatomy, physiology, hygiene, etc. etc. Now, if you have to handle the body, for example if you study Hatha Yoga, there is a system. You can't say: 'I will do *asanas* as I want to.'

For the *abhyasa* (practice) of *yoga*, you have to refer to the science of Hatha Yoga.

If you want to do the study of Mantra Yoga, utilizing the sound energy for the purification of your being, then you have to follow the science of sound metaphysics, you have to follow the science of Mantra Yoga. So in *abhyasa* certain systems are involved.

Now supposing a person follows the system without understanding it, then it becomes a repetitive mechanistic thing. There is a possibility and a danger in Abhyasa Yoga, to go through the physical activities systematically, without the understanding of why it is to be done so. They just study the how of it, but they don't see the why of it.

Why should a particular *asana* be done, why should *pranayama* be gone through, etc. etc.? Without understanding the why of it, there is a possibility of just merely following the system, which becomes mechanistic, repetitive, which looses its charm, its vitality if you just practice it for the sake of practising it. Because there is the possibility of this repetitive mechanistic practice, *abhyasa* should be accompanied by *dhyana*. Understand why you are practising.

Let the *abhyasa* be accompanied by *dhyana*, which is a higher energy. You acquire knowledge with the help of the cerebral organ, which is a very subtle organ in your body. It contains millions of cells, interrelated in a very complex way and the interrelationship of the cells in the brain control and manage your whole body. For *dhyana* you have to exercise and utilize your cerebral energy, a subtler energy.

When Krishna says that *dhyana* is superior, higher than *abhyasa*, please do see even the beauty of it literally. But supposing you acquire *dhyana*. *Dhyana* is to be acquired with the help of words. Can there be knowledge without words? Obviously it can't be. So you have to use the words, also the sound contained in the words, the meaning contained in the words.

Supposing you understand only the dictionary meaning of the

words, the traditional or conventional meaning associated with the words, and you don't bother to come face to face with the meaning that the words have given unto you. If you allow the knowledge to remain only at the verbal level, at the theoretical academic level, you will not discover the meaning through a personal encounter. Words indicate truth, don't they?

The word 'horse' indicates the existence of an animal called horse. The word 'horse' is not the horse. You may read all the descriptions about a horse, but unless you go out to the stable and look at the horse, touch him, ride him, only then will you get acquainted with the handsome display of energies in the body called horse. That personal encounter, that personal interaction at the sensual level, at the psychological level, is necessary.

Supposing you read the words god, divinity, sovereign intelligence, truth, *sat-chit-ananda*. The word 'god' indicates the existence of divinity. But only the word 'god', or chanting the word 'god', does not enable you to have that encounter with reality. The cerebral energy, exercised for acquiring certain words and their conventional meaning, is not sufficient.

You have to transcend the word, as you have to transcend the physical energies and rise to the cerebral subtle matter and subtle energies. From there you have to transcend the word and its conventional meaning. How can you transcend that knowledge, how can you transcend words? Through meditation (*dhyana*).

As for the acquisition of knowledge through cerebral energies, you allow physical movements to go into abeyance. You sit down in your place and then acquire knowledge. In the same way it is possible to allow all the cerebral movements to go into abeyance, the movement of words in your consciousness to discontinue, to go into abeyance. That is meditation.

There is an inner encounter with the meaning of the word. The movement of the mind, the movement of thought, the movement of all *samskaras* (past knowledge and experience) comes to a standstill. It is not destroyed, nothing is dismantled. Everything is intact within you, but only its movement comes to a standstill. Non-action, non-movement, you know zero point, it comes to that.

Then only meditation, the ending of all this movement, activates the latent and dormant energies in the emptiness of your consciousness, in the emptiness of space within you. You have gone to the emptiness of space, through meditation. You are rising higher and higher.

The energies contained in the inner space get released in the dimension of meditation. Therefore, it is called higher, figuratively and also literally. What then? Supposing the energies, the unconditioned energies, the unknown energies, the Cosmic energies, are released, are activated, and you are transported into an ecstasy, into a bliss, into a new energy of awareness. What then? Is that the final point?

Sri Krishna says no. You have realized that within. Now you have to have an encounter with the same energy outside your body. As you have an encounter with those unknown energies, unconditioned energies, within you, you have to have an encounter, an interaction, a release, a mobilization of those energies outside of your body. And how can that happen?

That can only happen through the renunciation of the fruits of action, the offering up of the fruits of action in daily living.

Now, for doing *karma*, you are in society. There is either interaction with nature or interaction with human beings. If in that interaction, which is called a relationship, with human beings or non-human beings, in nature, if the energies in your body, the physical and the psychological, the energies of love, compassion, all those energies are allowed to flow into expression, they are allowed to manifest themselves in their pristine purity, without manipulation for a particular result, when there is the offering up of the fruits of action, then there is an everlasting peace.

A holistic all-embracing peace does not result only from the inner, inward encounter. That encounter has to be complemented, supplemented and enriched by the movement, in relationship with the world. Because you cannot live without *karma*, it is impossible. In isolation, there is no living; there is only existence, vegetation. Living is interaction; living is exchanging of energies, and generating new energies through that exchange and interaction.

So, this inner peace is not complete, not perfect, not everlasting, unless you have an encounter with the same energies outside of you, while you are doing your *karma*. And once you remain unconcerned and unbothered about the *karma* of others, about the result of the actions, you pour your being in a responsible way with the energy of attentiveness, alertness, if you do that, then peace reigns within such a person. And peace is there in the movement of relationship. There is no fear, no worry or anxiety; one is not bothered about the reactions, the ripples and the waves generated by interaction.

We have seen Jnana Yoga and Karma Yoga blended together into Bhakti Yoga. So *abhyasa*, jnana, dhyana, the renunciation of the fruit of action, and peace, these are the steps for progressive dissolution of the authority of the I-consciousness into the transcendental supreme sovereign intelligence of Purusha or Brahman or Paramatman.

I will ask you to accompany me to the last portion, the third aspect. If this is done, if the steps are taken from gross to subtle, from individuated subtle to non-individuated subtle, then from the non-individuated subtle to the transcendental principle, the law of Life, the eternal law of truth awareness and bliss, then what happens?

Then, Sri Krishna says, the person grows into quiet a radical fresh dimension of consciousness. Here, at the consummation of Bhakti Yoga, at the consummation of Jnana Yoga and Karma Yoga, you are transported into a state of consciousness where there is no hatred for anyone at all in your heart.

Hatred can begin from jealousy, you are jealous and therefore you hate. Or you expected something from the person and you did not get it, so the frustration of expectation leads to hatred. You dislike a person and the dislike crystallizes into contempt and contempt aggravates into hatred. If you are attached exclusively to certain things, then you begin to hate that which is not consistent with your object of attachment.

When there is no attachment or the opposite, revulsion, it generates friendship. Not only that one is not afraid of others, not only that there is no dislike or prejudice against others, but you begin to trust. In friendship there is trust. Mutual trust, mutual respect is the foundation of friendship, and trust and respect generate compassion. *Karma* is compassion.

We become excited when we get something we want, something we had hoped for. But because the person had not hoped for anything, not expected anything from his actions, but had gone through the action as the law of Life, lovingly and yet dispassionately, then there is no excitement. Nor is there depression or frustration if the action does not lead to a desired effect.

What does one do, if the action does not lead to a desired effect? One finds out if there had been an incorrect way that has resulted in that. One turns inwards. Was there any impurity, was there any incorrect or unscientific way in which one did the action, was there any maladjustment?

When the action does not lead to the result that it would naturally have, then the *bhakta* (the devotee) starts introspection, not blaming others. We generally blame others, hold others responsible for the failure. We like to put the blame on someone else, but a devotee turns inwards and that inward looking cleanses the consciousness.

Excitement, frustration or fear, victimizing the *bhakta*. The devotee lives in a dimension where there is no fear, no hatred. There is trust and compassion, and therefore there is no inner compulsive violent momentum. Like compulsive eating, compulsive sex instinct, compulsive sleeping, there are certain compulsive desires and their violent momentum which victimizes us in our daily living. We may watch and we will find out.

Then the *Gita* goes on describing how equanimity in the heart and equi-balance at the sensual level is sustained effortlessly. There is equanimity, when people look at one as a friend or a foe, this does not disturb him or her at all, for there is an attitude of trust and affection. Cold, heat, rain, disagreeable weather or climate does not disturb the devotee. He finds an inner resource to adjust with the unpredictability of Life. He goes through the corridor of duality with equanimity at heart and equi-balance or equi-poise at the sensual level.

We have come to the last verse of the Bhakti Yoga chapter. Those who have listened carefully and understood, striving to live with their whole being what they have understood, whose movements of relationships become an ascending path towards immortality, the path of indestructible truth, spontaneous bliss and majestic self-awareness, not only imagining mentally or emotionally, not only intellectually or theoretically, as this secret of immortality, of suffering-free living has been shared scientifically, they become entitled for immortality.

You know what is mortality? Suffering caused by the idea of death. We have seen there is no death, there is no destruction, there is no dissolution, there is only passing from one form into another.

You remember what Arjuna had asked, in the first verse of the twelfth chapter? 'Who are dearer to you, those who worship you through the Cosmic matter or those who worship your absolute nature?' Those who worship the visible or those who worship the invisible? Now in the last verse, Sri Krishna gives the answer, that those who live this way and holistically follow the secret path, the sovereign path of immortality and religiosity, they are exceedingly dear to him. Here Sri Krishna, the son of Vasudeva, is speaking on behalf of the eternal Krishna, the eternal law of Life and thus ends the twelfth chapter of Bhakti Yoga of the *Bhagavad Gita*.

Throughout my life I had never conducted study courses. In a study course you share the deepest, the most fundamental, you do not have to dilute. You can share on the verbal level, the purest and clearest possible message of the Vedas, the Upanishads, the *Gita* etc.

You have no idea how grateful I feel towards you. But for you, I would not have spoken about these things. I have studied Indian philosophy at the university, but these communications would have been concealed in my heart, if you had not dared to take the journey, year after year, to India, creating an opportunity for these sacred study courses. This is my supreme *yajna* (offering).

None of you should feel at all obliged to me. I have not given anything to you that belongs to me. You see the Vedas, the Upanishads, the *Gita*, belong to you, they belong to the whole humanity. It is a human heritage, as your science and technology is a human heritage, just as Plato, Plotinus and Aristotle, Diogenes and Socrates are. Something that belongs to you is conveyed to you. Thanking you all, not as a formality, but for sharing my joy for the interaction you have allowed to take place.

Listening is as creative an activity as speaking is. Receiving is as much a generosity as giving is. If there is no mutuality, if there is no reception, the sharing does not become a giving at all. There has been a give-and-take between you and me. You gave through silence, I gave through words, thus sharing something very beautiful.